READINGS IN THE PHILOSOPHY OF EDUCATION

edited by
JOHN MARTIN RICH
UNIVERSITY OF KENTUCKY

WADSWORTH PUBLISHING COMPANY, INC.
BELMONT, CALIFORNIA

L. C. Cat. Card No.: 66–23451
Printed in the United States of America

PREFACE

This book differs from previous anthologies devoted to philosophy of education in a number of significant ways. First of all, its organization is based on the conviction that philosophy of education is a branch of social philosophy. As a social philosophy, it examines educational aims, develops theories of human nature and their meaning for education and social life, philosophically formulates the place and function of education within the social order, and interprets educational values and their role in shaping the development of youth. With these tasks in mind, the book is arranged in three major parts. The first part deals with the major areas surrounding the conception of philosophy of education as a social philosophy. The second part focuses on the problems of knowledge and philosophical analysis. The third part presents the nature and function of philosophy of education.

Particular care has been taken to choose readings appropriate—as well as comprehensible—for those studying philosophy of education for the first time. The readings are quoted in their entirety, or at considerable length, in order that each position will be as understandable as possible. Selections are not limited to contemporary writers, but also draw on a number of great works of the past which are relevant to present educational concerns. The selections are taken from social and political thought as well as education and philosophy.

Whenever feasible, an attempt has been made to choose selections that represent the ideas of a leading figure on each of the major positions on each topic, so that students can confront the major positions and their leading proponents. The task of understanding and contrasting each position stimulates the student to think philosophically, to sustain and reorganize his thought, and develop and defend a philosophical position of his own.

Introductions are provided for each of the seven sections to assist the reader in gaining an overview and perspective on the readings; questions for discussion, designed to stimulate further thought and analysis, follow each section.

CONTENTS

PART TWO/ PHILOSOPHICAL ANALYSIS AND EDUCATION

PART THREE/ THE PHILOSOPHIC QUEST

PART ONE /

EDUCATION, SOCIAL PHILOSOPHY, AND ETHICS

CHAPTER ONE /

AIMS OF EDUCATION

COUNTLESS expressions of educational aims can be found in a study of the educational history of Western civilizations. Some of these aims actively guided the educational system and the ideals of their time; others merely received lip service.

We are not altogether clear in the United States whether our primary aim is liberal education or vocational preparation, whether essentially we wish to create the capacities of appreciating humane culture or to prepare students for the duties of citizenship. Lately, citizens have become increasingly conscious of the education of the gifted and the necessity of preserving the talent of the country for national preparedness and defense while, at the same time, operating our school system on the basis of the principle of educational equality.

Recently we have concentrated on the improvement of techniques, devices, and means in education and have given less attention to the goals to be achieved in education. Furthermore, in a pluralistic culture (which, in theory at least, is hospitable to a wide range of beliefs) differences of opinion will naturally lead to disagreement as to what education should do. It may be possible to secure agreement at the local level, but not on a national level. Some would welcome a national consensus. Others, however, believe that it would lead to excessive control and dictation of local policies.

Through the years educators have struggled with problems in attempting to set educational aims. One approach to resolving the general confusion would be (as some educators have done) to derive aims from the essential nature of man by determining man's distinguishing characteristics.

With such determinations as the guiding criteria, the aims of education would be everywhere the same. Others, however, have thought that the aims of education should be based on man's fundamental need to adjust to his environment and live successfully in his society. Since societal demands may differ, aims would not necessarily be everywhere the same. Finally, according to John Dewey, education is all one with growing. Therefore, he believes that educational aims should be an outgrowth of existing conditions, must represent a freeing of conditions, and be sufficiently flexible to meet changing situations.

The aims of education have always been considered within the province of the philosophy of education, except in those cases where some educators have believed that a "scientific" assessment of aims could be ascertained quantitatively by surveys and questionnaires. Aims are expressions of values of greatest worth, and the philosophy of education has always concerned itself with an analysis and justification of educational values. Consequently, before educational aims can be established, a theoretical framework is needed to analyze the values underlying the proposed aims. In the selections that follow, four different approaches on educational aims are presented; each position has had considerable influence on educational thought.

A nineteenth-century English social philosopher, early sociologist, and social Darwinist, Herbert Spencer, has indirectly exerted a significant influence on American education. It is generally held that his essay (Selection 1) affected the formulation of seven *Cardinal Principles of Education* (1918), which, in turn, shaped the direction of subsequent educational-commission reports. Spencer's main argument is that education should be useful, and of all the useful pursuits science heads the list. Rather than beginning with the needs and interests of youth, he is more concerned with what knowledge is most necessary for youth to learn. In sharp contrast with Robert Hutchins' position, he claims that a scientific education is most necessary and, thus, opens the door for a specialized curriculum.

Robert M. Hutchins is widely known for his educational leadership, his concept of liberal education, and his championing the cause of academic freedom in the scholarly community. His position of classical humanism represents a major outlook in the history of Western thought—one that strongly disagrees with several popular contemporary views. Selection 2, by Hutchins, closely relates educational aims to his concept of a liberal education.

Thorndike and Gates (Selection 3), two influential educational psychologists, take a behavioristic or "connectionistic" approach to educational aims. Their position is premised on the observability (and hence, accurate appraisal) of human wants, which, in turn, ought to be universalized. It is through education, they hold, that these wants can be satisfied.

John Dewey is generally recognized as the leading figure in the philosophy of education during the first half of this century. His essay (Selection 4) envisions aims as outgrowths of existing conditions, giving direction to activity and making a choice of alternative possible. He attacks the separation of means and ends, and shows that an end arising out of an activity as a plan for its direction is both ends and means, and every means is a temporary end until attained. Finally, he criticizes the way educators look upon aims as some sort of fixed and final terminus for educational activity.

1 / HERBERT SPENCER

What Knowledge Is of Most Worth?

It has been truly remarked that, in order of time, decoration precedes dress. Among people who submit to great physical suffering that they may have themselves handsomely tattooed, extremes of temperature are borne with but little attempt at mitigation. Humboldt tells us that an Orinoco Indian, though quite regardless of bodily comfort, will yet labor for a fortnight to purchase pigment wherewith to make himself admired; and that the same woman who would not hesitate to leave her hut without a fragment of clothing on, would not dare to commit such a breach of decorum as to go out unpainted. Voyagers uniformly find that colored beads and trinkets are much more prized by wild tribes than are calicoes or broadcloths. And the anecdotes we have of the ways in which, when shirts and coats are given, they turn them to some ludicrous display, show how completely the idea of ornament predominates over that of use. Nay, there are still more extreme illustrations: witness the fact narrated by Captain Speke of his African attendants, who strutted about in their goat skin mantles when the weather was fine, but when it was wet, took them off, folded them up, and went about naked, shivering in the rain! Indeed, the facts of aboriginal life seem to indicate that dress

Herbert Spencer, "What Knowledge Is of Most Worth?" in *Education: Intellectual, Moral and Physical* (New York: James B. Millar and Co., 1884), Chap. I.

is developed out of decorations. And when we remember that even among ourselves most think more about the fineness of the fabric than its warmth, and more about the cut than the convenience—when we see that the function is still in great measure subordinated to the appearance—we have further reason for inferring such an origin.

It is not a little curious that the like relations hold with the mind. Among mental as among bodily acquisitions, the ornamental comes before the useful. Not only in times past, but almost as much in our own era, that knowledge which conduces to personal well-being has been postponed to that which brings applause. In the Greek schools, music, poetry, rhetoric, and a philosophy which, until Socrates taught, had but little bearing upon action, were the dominant subjects; while knowledge aiding the arts of life had a very subordinate place. And in our own universities and schools at the present moment the like antithesis holds. We are guilty of something like a platitude when we say that throughout his after-career a boy, in nine cases out of ten, applies his Latin and Greek to no practical purposes. The remark is trite that in his shop, or his office, in managing his estate or his family, in playing his part as director of a bank or a railway, he is very little aided by this knowledge he took so many years to acquire—so little, that generally the greater part of it drops out of his memory; and if he occasionally vents a Latin quotation or alludes to some Greek myth, it is less to throw light on the topic in hand than for the sake of effect. If we inquire what is the real motive for giving boys a classical education, we find it to be simply conformity to public opinion. Men dress their children's minds as they do their bodies, in the prevailing fashion. As the Orinoco Indian puts on his paint before leaving his hut, not with a view to any direct benefit, but because he would be ashamed to be seen without it; so a boy's drilling in Latin and Greek is insisted on, not because of their intrinsic value, but that he may not be disgraced by being found ignorant of them—that he may have "the education of a gentleman"—the badge marking a certain social position, and bringing a consequent respect.

This parallel is still more clearly displayed in the case of the other sex. In the treatment of both mind and body, the decorative element has continued to predominate in a greater degree among women than among men. Originally personal adornment occupied the attention of both sexes equally. In these latter days of civilization, however, we see that in the dress of men the regard for appearance has, in a considerable degree, yielded to the regard for comfort; while in their education the useful has of late been trenching on the ornamental. In neither direction has this change gone so far with women. The wearing of ear-rings, finger-rings, bracelets; the elaborate dressings of the hair; the still occasional use of paint; the immense labor bestowed in making habiliments sufficiently attractive; and the great discomfort that will be submitted to for the sake of conformity, show how greatly, in the attiring of women, the desire of approbation overrides the desire for warmth and convenience. And similarly in their education, the immense preponderance of "accomplishments" proves how here, too, use is subordinated to display. Dancing, deportment, the piano, singing, drawing—what a large space do these occupy! If you ask why Italian and German are learned, you will find that, under all the sham reasons given, the real reason is, that a knowledge of those tongues is thought ladylike. It is not that the books written in them may be utilized, which they scarcely ever are; but that Italian and German songs may be sung, and that the extent of attainment may bring whispered admiration. The births, deaths, and marriages of kings, and other like historic trivialities, are committed to memory, not because of any direct benefits that can possibly result from knowing them, but because society considers them parts of a good education— because the absence of such knowledge may bring the contempt of others. When we have named reading, writing, spelling, grammar, arithmetic, and sewing, we have named about all the things a girl is taught with a view to their direct uses in life; and even some of these have more reference to the good opinion of others than to immediate personal welfare.

Thoroughly to realize the truth that with the mind as with the body the ornamental precedes the useful, it is needful to glance at its rationale. This lies in the fact that, from the far past down even to the present, social needs have subordinated individual needs, and that the chief social need has been the control of individuals. It is not, as we commonly suppose, that there are no governments but those of monarchs, and parliaments, and constituted authorities. These acknowledged governments are supplemented by other unacknowledged ones, that grow up in all circles, in which every man or woman strives to be king or queen or lesser dignitary. To get above some and be reverenced by them, and to propitiate those who are above us, is the universal struggle in which the chief energies of life are expended. By the accumulation of wealth, by style of living, by beauty of dress, by display of knowledge or intellect, each tries to subjugate others, and so aids in weaving that ramified network of restraints by which society is kept in order. It is not the savage chief only who, in formidable warpaint, with scalps at his belt, aims to strike awe into his inferiors; it is not only the belle who, by elaborate toilet, polished manners, and numerous accomplishments, strives to "make conquests," but the scholar, the historian, the philosopher, use their acquirements to the same end. We are none of us content with quietly unfolding our own individualities to the full in all directions, but have a restless craving to impress our individualities upon others, and in some way subordinate them. And this it is which determines the character of our education. Not what knowledge is of most real worth is the consideration, but what will bring most applause, honor, respect—what will most conduce to social position and influence —what will be most imposing. As throughout life not what we are, but what we shall be thought, is the question; so in education, the question is, not the intrinsic value of knowledge, so much as its extrinsic effects on others. And this being one dominant idea, direct utility is scarcely more regarded than by the barbarian when filing his teeth and staining his nails.

If there needs any further evidence of the rude, undeveloped character of our education, we have it in the fact that the comparative worths of different kinds of knowledge have been as yet scarcely even discussed— much less discussed in a methodic way with definite results. Not only is it that no standard of relative values has yet been agreed upon, but the existence of any such standard has not been conceived in any clear manner. And not only is it that the existence of any such standard has not been clearly conceived, but the need for it seems to have been scarcely even felt. Men read books on this topic, and attend lectures on that; decide that their children shall be instructed in these branches of knowledge, and shall not be instructed in those; and all under the guidance of mere custom, or liking, or prejudice, without ever consider- ing the enormous importance of determining in some rational way what things are really most worth learning. It is true that in all circles we have occasional remarks on the importance of this or the other order of information. But whether the degree of its importance justifies the expenditure of the time needed to acquire it, and whether there are not things of more importance to which the time might be better devoted, are queries which, if raised at all, are disposed of quite summarily, according to personal predilections. It is true, also, that from time to time we hear revived the standing controversy respecting the comparative merits of classics and mathematics. Not only, however, is this controversy carried on in an empirical manner, with no reference to an ascertained criterion, but the question at issue is totally insignificant when compared with the general question of which it is part. To suppose that deciding whether a mathematical or a classical education is the best, is deciding what is the proper *curriculum*, is much the same thing as to suppose that the whole of dietetics lies in determining whether or not bread is more nutritive than potatoes.

The question which we contend is of such transcendent moment, is, not whether such or such knowledge is of worth, but what is its *relative* worth? When they have named certain advantages which a given course of study has secured them, persons are apt to assume that they have

justified themselves; quite forgetting that the adequateness of the
advantages is the point to be judged. There is, perhaps, not a subject to
which men devote attention that has not *some* value. A year diligently
spent in getting up heraldry would very possibly give a little further
insight into ancient manners and morals, and into the orgin of names.
Any one who should learn the distances between all the towns in
England might, in the course of his life, find one or two of the thousand
facts he had acquired of some slight service when arranging a journey.
Gathering together all the small gossip of a county, profitless occupation
as it would be, might yet occasionally help to establish some useful fact—
say, a good example of hereditary transmission. But in these cases every
one would admit that there was no proportion between the required
labor and the probable benefits. No one would tolerate the proposal to
devote some years of a boy's time to getting such information, at the
cost of much more valuable information which he might else have got.

And if here the test of relative value is appealed to and held
conclusive, then should it be appealed to and held conclusive throughout. Had we time to master all subjects we need not be particular. To
quote the old song:

> Could a man be secure
> That his days would endure
> As of old, for a thousand long years,
> What things might he know!
> What deeds might he do!
> And all without hurry or care.

"But we that have but span-long lives" must ever bear in mind our
limited time for acquisition. And remembering how narrowly this time is
limited, not only by the shortness of life but also still more by the
business of life, we ought to be especially solicitous to employ what time
we have to the greatest advantage. Before devoting years to some subject
which fashion or fancy suggests, it is surely wise to weigh with great
care the worth of various alternative results which the same years might
bring if otherwise applied.

In education, then, this is the question of questions, which it is high
time we discussed in some methodic way. The first in importance, though
the last to be considered, is the problem how to decide among the
conflicting claims of various subjects on our attention. Before there can
be a rational *curriculum,* we must settle which things it most concerns us
to know; or, to use a word of Bacon's, now unfortunately obsolete, we
must determine the relative values of knowledges.

To this end a measure of value is the first requisite. And happily,
respecting the true measure of value, as expressed in general terms, there
can be no dispute. Every one in contending for the worth of any

particular order of information, does so by showing its bearing upon some part of life. In reply to the question, "Of what use is it?" the mathematician, linguist, naturalist, or philosopher explains the way in which his learning beneficially influences action—saves from evil or secures good—conduces to happiness. When the teacher of writing has pointed out how great an aid writing is to success in business—that is, to the obtaining of sustenance—that is, to satisfactory living—he is held to have proved his case. And when the collector of dead facts (say a numismatist) fails to make clear any appreciable effects which these facts can produce on human welfare, he is obliged to admit that they are comparatively valueless. All then, either directly or by implication, appeal to this as the ultimate test.

How to live?—that is the essential question for us. Not how to live in the mere material sense only, but in the widest sense. The general problem which comprehends every special problem is the right ruling of conduct in all directions under all circumstances. In what way to treat the body; in what way to treat the mind; in what way to manage our affairs; in what way to bring up a family; in what way to behave as a citizen; in what way to utilize all those sources of happiness which nature supplies—how to use our faculties to the greatest advantage of ourselves and others—how to live completely? And this being the great thing needful for us to learn, is, by consequence, the great thing which education has to teach. To prepare us for complete living is the function which education has to discharge; and the only rational mode of judging of any educational course is to judge in what degree it discharges such function.

This test, never used in its entirety, but rarely even partially used, and used then in a vague, half-conscious way, has to be applied consciously, methodically, and throughout all cases. It behooves us to set before ourselves, and ever to keep clearly in view, complete living as the end to be achieved; so that in bringing up our children we may choose subjects and methods of instruction with deliberate reference to this end. Not only ought we to cease from the mere unthinking adoption of the current fashion in education, which has no better warrant than any other fashion, but we must also rise above that rude, empirical style of judging displayed by those more intelligent people who do bestow some care in overseeing the cultivation of their children's minds. It must not suffice simply to *think* that such or such information will be useful in after life, or that this kind of knowledge is of more practical value than that; but we must seek out some process of estimating their respective values, so that as far as possible we may positively *know* which are most deserving of attention.

Doubtless the task is difficult—perhaps never to be more than

:ly achieved. But considering the vastness of the interests at fficulty is no reason for pusillanimously passing it by, but evoting every energy to its mastery. And if we only proceed systematically, we may very soon get at results of no small moment.

Our first step must obviously be to classify, in the order of their importance, the leading kinds of activity which constitute human life. They may naturally be arranged into, 1. Those activities which directly minister to self-preservation 2. Those activities which, by securing the necessaries of life, indirectly minister to self-preservation; 3. Those activities which have for their end the rearing and discipline of offspring; 4. Those activities which are involved in the maintenance of proper social and political relations; 5. Those miscellaneous activities which make up the leisure part of life, devoted to the gratification of the tastes and feelings.

That these stand in something like their true order of subordination, it needs no long consideration to show. The actions and precautions by which, from moment to moment, we secure personal safety must clearly take precedence of all others. Could there be a man, ignorant as an infant of all surrounding objects and movements, or how to guide himself among them, he would pretty certainly lose his life the first time he went into the street, notwithstanding any amount of learning he might have on other matters. And as entire ignorance in all other directions would be less promptly fatal than entire ignorance in this direction, it must be admitted that knowledge immediately conductive to self-preservation is of primary importance.

That next after direct self-preservation comes the indirect self-preservation, which consists in acquiring the means of living, none will question. That a man's industrial functions must be considered before his parental ones is manifest from the fact that, speaking generally, the discharge of the parental functions is made possible only by the previous discharge of the industrial ones. The power of self-maintenance necessarily preceding the power of maintaining offspring, it follows that knowledge needful for self-maintenance has stronger claims than knowledge for family welfare —is second in value to none save knowledge needful for immediate self-preservation.

As the family comes before the state in order of time—as the bringing up of children is possible before the state exists, or when it has ceased to be, whereas the state is rendered possible only by the bringing up of children —it follows that the duties of the parent demand closer attention than those of the citizen. Or, to use a further argument, since the goodness of a society ultimately depends on the nature of its citizens, and since the nature of its citizens is more modifiable by early training than by anything else, we must conclude that the welfare of the family underlies the welfare of society. And hence knowledge directly conducing to the first must take precedence of knowledge directly conducing to the last.

Those various forms of pleasurable occupation which fill up the leisure left by graver occupations—the enjoyments of music, poetry, painting, etc.—manifestly imply a pre-existing society. Not only is a considerable development of them impossible without a long-established social union, but their very subject matter consists in great part of social sentiments and sympathies. Not only does society supply the conditions to their growth, but also the ideas and sentiments they express. And consequently that part of human conduct which constitutes good citizenship is of more moment than that which goes out in accomplishments or exercise of the tastes; and, in education, preparation for the one rank before preparation for the other.

Such then, we repeat, is something like the rational order of subordination: that education which prepares for direct self-preservation; that which prepares for indirect self-preservation; that which prepares for parenthood; that which prepares for citizenship; that which prepares for the miscellaneous refinements of life. We do not mean to say that these divisions are definitely separable. We do not deny that they are intricately entangled with each other in such way that there can be no training for any that is not in some measure a training for all. Nor do we question that of each division there are portions more important than certain portions of the preceding divisions: that, for instance, a man of much skill in business, but little other faculty, may fall farther below the standard of complete living than one of but moderate power of acquiring money but great judgment as a parent; or that exhaustive information bearing on right social action, joined with entire want of general culture in literature and the fine arts, is less desirable than a more moderate share of the one joined with some of the other. But after making all qualifications, there still remain these broadly-marked divisions: and it still continues substantially true that these divisions subordinate one another in the foregoing order, because the corresponding divisions of life make one another *possible* in that order.

Of course the ideal of education is complete preparation in all these divisions. But failing this ideal, as in our phase of civilization every one must do more or less, the aim should be to maintain *a due proportion* between the degrees of preparation in each. Not exhaustive cultivation in any one, supremely important though it may be—not even an exclusive attention to the two, three, or four divisions of greatest importance; but an attention to all—greatest where the value is greatest, less where the value is less, least where the value is least. For the average man (not to forget the cases in which peculiar aptitude for some one department of knowledge rightly makes that one the bread-winning occupation)—for the average man, we say, the desideratum is a training that approaches nearest to perfection in the things which most subserve complete living, and falls more and more below perfection in the things that have more and more remote bearings on complete living.

In regulating education by this standard there are some general considerations that should be ever present to us. The worth of any kind of culture, as aiding complete living, may be either necessary or more or less contingent. There is knowledge of intrinsic value, knowledge of quasi-intrinsic value, and knowledge of conventional value. Such facts as that sensations of numbness and tingling commonly precede paralysis, that the resistance of water to a body moving through it varies as the square of the velocity, that chlorine is a disinfectant—these, and the truths of science in general, are of intrinsic value: they will bear on human conduct ten thousand years hence as they do now. The extra knowledge of our own language, which is given by an acquaintance with Latin and Greek, may be considered to have a value that is quasi-intrinsic; it must exist for us and for other races whose languages owe much to these sources, but will last only as long as our languages last. While that kind of information which, in our schools, usurps the name History—the mere tissue of names and dates and dead unmeaning events —has a conventional value only, it has not the remotest bearing upon any of our actions, and it is of use only for the avoidance of those unpleasant criticisms which current opinion passes upon its absence. Of course, as those facts which concern all mankind throughout all time must be held of greater moment than those which concern only a portion of them during a limited era, and of far greater moment than those which concern only a portion of them during the continuance of a fashion, it follows that in a rational estimate, knowledge of intrinsic worth must, other things equal, take precedence of knowledge that is of quasi-intrinsic or conventional worth.

One further preliminary. Acquirement of every kind has two values— value as *knowledge* and value as *discipline*. Besides its use for guidance in conduct, the acquisition of each order of facts has also its use as mental exercise; and its effects as a preparative for complete living have to be considered under both these heads.

These, then, are the general ideas with which we must set out in discussing a *curriculum*: life as divided into several kinds of activity of successively decreasing importance; the worth of each order of facts as regulating these several kinds of activity, intrinsically, quasi-intrinsically, and conventionally; and their regulative influences estimated both as knowledge and discipline.

And now we come to that remaining division of human life which includes the relaxations, pleasures, and amusements filling leisure hours.

After considering what training best fits for self-preservation, for the obtaining of sustenance, for the discharge of parental duties, and for the regulation of social and political conduct, we have now to consider what training best fits for the miscellaneous ends not included in these—for the enjoyments of nature, of literature, and of the fine arts, in all their forms. Postponing them as we do to things that bear more vitally upon human welfare, and bringing everything, as we have, to the list of actual value, it will perhaps be inferred that we are inclined to slight these less essential things. No greater mistake could be made, however. We yield to none in the value we attach to aesthetic culture and its pleasures. Without painting, sculpture, music, poetry, and the emotions produced by natural beauty of every kind, life would lose half its charm. So far from thinking that the training and gratification of the tastes are unimportant, we believe that the time will come when they will occupy a much larger share of human life than now. When the forces of nature have been fully conquered to man's use—when the means of production have been brought to perfection—when labor has been economized to the highest degree—when education has been so systematized that a preparation for the more essential activities may be made with comparative rapidity— and when, consequently, there is a great increase of spare time, then will the poetry, both of art and nature, rightly fill a large space in the minds of all.

But it is one thing to admit that aesthetic culture is in a high degree conducive to human happiness, and another thing to admit that it is a fundamental requisite to human happiness. However important it may be, it must yield precedence to those kinds of culture which bear more directly upon the duties of life. As before hinted, literature and the fine arts are made possible by those activities which make individual and social life possible; and manifestly, that which is made possible must be postponed to that which makes it possible. A florist cultivates a plant for the sake of its flower, and regards the roots and leaves as of value chiefly because they are instrumental in producing the flower. But while, as an ultimate product, the flower is the thing to which everything else is subordinate, the florist very well knows that the root and leaves are intrinsically of greater importance, because on them the evolution of the flower depends. He bestows every care in rearing a healthy plant, and knows it would be folly if, in his anxiety to obtain the flower, he were to neglect the plant. Similarly in the case before us. Architecture, sculpture, painting, music, poetry, etc., may be truly called the efflorescence of civilized life. But even supposing them to be of such transcendent worth as to subordinate the civilized life out of which they grow (which can hardly be asserted), it will still be admitted that the production of a healthy civilized life must be the first consideration, and that the knowledge conducing to this must occupy the highest place.

And here we see most distinctly the vice of our educational system. It neglects the plant for the sake of the flower. In anxiety for elegance it forgets substance. While it gives no knowledge conducive to self-preservation—while of knowledge that facilitates gaining a livelihood it gives but the rudiments, and leaves the greater part to be picked up anyhow in after life—while for the discharge of parental functions it makes not the slightest provision—and while for the duties of citizenship it prepares by imparting a mass of facts, most of which are irrelevant, and the rest without a key, it is diligent in teaching everything that adds to refinement, polish, eclat. However fully we may admit that extensive acquaintance with modern languages is a valuable accomplishment, which, through reading, conversation, and travel, aids in giving a certain finish, it by no means follows that this result is rightly purchased at the cost of that vitally important knowledge sacrificed to it. Supposing it true that classical education conduces to elegance and correctness of style, it can not be said that elegance and correctness of style are comparable in importance to a familiarity with the principles that should guide the rearing of children. Grant that the taste may be greatly improved by reading all the poetry written in extinct languages, yet it is not to be inferred that such improvement of taste is equivalent in value to an acquaintance with the laws of health. Accomplishments, the fine arts, *belles-lettres,* and all those things which, as we say, constitute the efflorescence of civilization, should be wholly subordinate to that knowledge and discipline in which civilization rests. *As they occupy the leisure part of life, so should they occupy the leisure part of education.*

Thus far our question has been the worth of knowledge of this or that kind for purposes of guidance. We have now to judge the relative values of different kinds of knowledge for purposes of discipline. This division of our subject we are obliged to treat with comparative brevity; and happily no very lengthened treatment of it is needed. Having found what is best for the one end, we have by implication found what is best for the other. We may be quite sure that the acquirement of those classes of facts which are most useful for regulating conduct involves a mental exercise best fitted for strengthening the faculties. It would be utterly contrary to the beautiful economy of nature if one kind of culture were needed for the gaining of information and another kind were needed as a mental gymnastic. Everywhere throughout creation we find faculties developed through the performance of those functions which it is their office to perform, not through the performance of artificial exercises devised to fit them for these functions. The red Indian acquires the swiftness and agility which make him a successful hunter by the actual pursuit of animals; and by the miscellaneous activities of his life he gains a better balance of physical powers than gymnastics ever give. That skill in tracking enemies and prey which he has reached by long practice implies a subtlety of perception far exceeding anything produced by artificial training. And similarly throughout. From the Bushman, whose eye, which being habitually employed in identifying distant objects that are to be pursued or fled from, has acquired a quite telescopic range, to the accountant whose daily practice enables him to add up several columns of figures simultaneously, we find that the highest power of a faculty results from the discharge of those duties which the conditions of life require it to discharge. And we may be certain, *a priori,* that the same law holds throughout education. The education of most value for guidance must at the same time be the education of most value for discipline.

We conclude, then, that for discipline as well as for guidance, science is of chiefest value. In all its effects, learning the meaning of things is better than learning the meaning of words. Whether for intellectual, moral, or religious training, the study of surrounding phenomena is immensely superior to the study of grammars and lexicons.

Thus to the question with which we set out, What knowledge is of most worth? the uniform reply is—science. This is the verdict on all the counts. For direct self-preservation, or the maintenance of life and health, the all-important knowledge is—science. For that indirect self-preservation which we call gaining a livelihood, the knowledge of greatest value is—science. For the due discharge of parental functions, the proper guidance is to be found only in—science. For that interpretation of national life, past and present, without which the citizen can not rightly regulate his conduct, the indispensable key is—science. Alike for the most perfect production and highest enjoyment of art in all its forms, the needful preparation is still—science. And for purposes of discipline— intellectual, moral, religious—the most efficient study is, once more— science. The question which at first seemed so perplexed has become, in the course of our inquiry, comparatively simple. We have not to estimate the degrees of importance of different orders of human activity, and different studies as severally fitting us for them, since we find that the study of science, in its most comprehensive meaning, is the best preparation for all these orders of activity. We have not to decide between the claims of knowledge of great though conventional value, and knowledge of less though intrinsic value, seeing that the knowledge which we find to be of most value in all other respects is intrinsically most valuable: its worth is not dependent upon opinion, but is as fixed as is the relation of man to the surrounding world. Necessary and eternal as are its truths, all science concerns all mankind for all time. Equally at present and in the remotest future must it be of incalculable importance for the regulation of their conduct that men should understand the science of life, physical, mental, and social, and that they should understand all other science as a key to the science of life.

And yet the knowledge which is of such transcendent value is that which, in our age of boasted education, receives the least attention. While this which we call civilization could never have arisen had it not been for science, science forms scarcely an appreciable element in what men consider civilized training. Though to the progress of science we owe it that millions find support where once there was food only for thousands, yet of these millions but a few thousand pay any respect to that which has made their existence possible. Though this increasing knowledge of the properties and relations of things has not only enabled wandering tribes to grow into populous nations, but has given to the countless members of those populous nations comforts and pleasures which their few naked ancestors never even conceived, or could have believed, yet is this kind of knowledge only now receiving a grudging recognition in our highest educational institutions. To the slowly growing acquaintance with the uniform coexistences and sequences of phenomena —to the establishment of invariable laws—we owe our emancipation from the grossest superstitions. But for science we should be still worshipping fetishes, or, with hecatombs of victims, propitiating diabolical deities.

Paraphrasing an Eastern fable, we may say that in the family of knowledges, science is the household drudge, who, in obscurity, hides unrecognized perfections. To her has been committed all the work; by her skill, intelligence, and devotion have all the conveniences and gratifications been obtained; and while ceaselessly occupied ministering to the rest, she has been kept in the background, that her haughty sisters might flaunt their fripperies in the eyes of the world. This parallel holds yet further. For we are fast coming to the *dénouement*, when the positions will be changed; and while these haughty sisters sink into merited neglect, science, proclaimed as highest alike in worth and beauty, will reign supreme.

2 / ROBERT M. HUTCHINS

The Basis of Education

The obvious failures of the doctrines of adaptation, immediate needs, social reform, and of the doctrine that we need no doctrine at all may suggest to us that we require a better definition of education. Let us concede that every society must have some system that attempts to adapt the young to their social and political environment. If the society is bad, in the sense, for example, in which the Nazi state was bad, the system will aim at the same bad ends. To the extent that it makes men bad in order that they may be tractable subjects of a bad state, the system may help to achieve the social ideals of the society. It may be what the society wants; it may even be what the society needs, if it is to perpetuate its form and accomplish its aims. In pragmatic terms, in terms of success in the society, it may be a "good" system.

But it seems to me clearer to say that, though it may be a system of training, or instruction, or adaptation, or meeting immediate needs, it is not a system of education. It seems clearer to say that the purpose of education is to improve men. Any system that tries to make them bad is not education, but something else. If, for example, democracy is the best form of society, a system that adapts the young to it will be an educational system. If despotism is a bad form of society, a system that adapts the young to it will not be an educational system, and the better it succeeds in adapting them the less educational it will be.

Every man has a function as a man. The function of a citizen or a subject may vary from society to society, and the system of training, or adaptation, or instruction, or meeting immediate needs may vary with it. But the function of a man as man is the same in every age and in every society, since it results from his nature as a man. The aim of an educational system is the same in every age and in every society where such a system can exist: it is to improve man as man.

If we are going to talk about improving men and societies, we have to

Robert M. Hutchins, "The Basis of Education," from *The Conflict in Education* (New York: Harper & Brothers, 1953), pp. 67–76. Reprinted with the permission of Harper & Row.

believe that there is some difference between good and bad. This difference must not be, as the positivists think it is, merely conventional. We cannot tell this difference by any examination of the effectiveness of a given program as the pragmatists propose; the time required to estimate these effects is usually too long and the complexity of society is always too great for us to say that the consequences of a given program are altogether clear. We cannot discover the difference between good and bad by going to the laboratory, for men and societies are not laboratory animals. If we believe that there is no truth, there is no knowledge, and there are no values except those which are validated by laboratory experiment, we cannot talk about the improvement of men and societies, for we can have no standard of judging anything that takes place among men or in societies.

Society is to be improved, not by forcing a program of social reform down its throat, through the schools or otherwise, but by the improvement of the individuals who compose it. As Plato said, "Governments reflect human nature. States are not made out of stone or wood, but out of the characters of their citizens: these turn the scale and draw everything after them." The individual is the heart of society.

To talk about making men better we must have some idea of what men are, because if we have none, we can have no idea of what is good or bad for them. If men are brutes like other animals, then there is no reason why they should not be treated like brutes by anybody who can gain power over them. And there is no reason why they should not be trained as brutes are trained. A sound philosophy in general suggests that men are rational, moral, and spiritual beings and that the improvement of men means the fullest development of their rational, moral, and spiritual powers. All men have these powers, and all men should develop them to the fullest extent.

Man is by nature free, and he is by nature social. To use his freedom rightly he needs discipline. To live in society he needs the moral virtues. Good moral and intellectual habits are required for the fullest development of the nature of man.

To develop fully as a social, political animal man needs participation in his own government. A benevolent despotism will not do. You cannot expect the slave to show the virtues of the free man unless you first set him free. Only democracy, in which all men rule and are ruled in turn for the good life of the whole community, can be an absolutely good form of government.

The community rests on the social nature of men. It requires communication among its members. They do not have to agree with one another; but they must be able to understand one another. And their philosophy in general must supply them with a common purpose and a common concept of man and society adequate to hold the community together. Civilization is the deliberate pursuit of a common ideal. The good society is not just a society we happen to like or to be used to. It is a community of good men.

Education deals with the development of the intellectual powers of men. Their moral and spiritual powers are the sphere of the family and the church. All three agencies must work in harmony; for, though a man has three aspects, he is still one man. But the schools cannot take over the role of the family and the church without promoting the atrophy of those institutions and failing in the task that is proper to the schools.

We cannot talk about the intellectual powers of men, though we can talk about training them, or amusing them, or adapting them, and meeting their immediate needs, unless our philosophy in general tells us that there is knowledge and that there is a difference between true and false. We must believe, too, that there are other means of obtaining knowledge than scientific experimentation. If knowledge can be sought only in the laboratory, many fields in which we thought we had knowledge will offer us nothing but opinion or superstition, and we shall be forced to conclude that we cannot know anything about the most important aspects of man and society. If we are to set about developing the intellectual powers of men through having them acquire knowledge of the most important subjects, we have to begin with the proposition that experimentation and empirical data will be of only limited use to us, contrary to the convictions of many American social scientists, and that philosophy, history, literature, and art give us knowledge, and significant knowledge, on the most significant issues.

If the object of education is the improvement of men, then any system of education that is without values is a contradiction in terms. A system that seeks bad values is bad. A system that denies the existence of values denies the possibility of education. Relativism, scientism, skepticism, and anti-intellectualism, the four horsemen of the philosophical apocalypse, have produced that chaos in education which will end in the disintegration of the West.

The prime object of education is to know what is good for man. It is to know the goods in their order. There is a hierarchy of values. The task of education is to help us understand it, establish it, and live by it. This Aristotle had in mind when he said: "It is not the possessions but the desires of men that must be equalized, and this is impossible unless they have a sufficient education according to the nature of things."

Such an education is far removed from the triviality of that produced by the doctrines of adaptation, of immediate needs, of social reform, or of the doctrine of no doctrine at all. Such an education will not adapt the young to a bad environment, but it will encourage them to make it good.

It will not overlook immediate needs, but it will place these needs in their proper relationship to more distant, less tangible, and more important goods. It will be the only effective means of reforming society.

This is the education appropriate to free men. It is liberal education. If all men are to be free, all men must have this education. It makes no difference how they are to earn their living or what their special interests or aptitudes may be. They can learn to make a living, and they can develop their special interests and aptitudes, after they have laid the foundation of free and responsible manhood through liberal education. It will not do to say that they are incapable of such education. This claim is made by those who are too indolent or unconvinced to make the effort to give such education to the masses.

Nor will it do to say that there is not enough time to give everybody a liberal education before he becomes a specialist. In America, at least, the waste and frivolity of the educational system are so great that it would be possible through getting rid of them to give every citizen a liberal education and make him a qualified specialist, too, in less time than is now consumed in turning out uneducated specialists.

A liberal education aims to develop the powers of understanding and judgment. It is impossible that too many people can be educated in this sense, because there cannot be too many people with understanding and judgment. We hear a great deal today about the dangers that will come upon us through the frustration of educated people who have got educated in the expectation that education will get them a better job, and who then fail to get it. But surely this depends on the representations that are made to the young about what education is. If we allow them to believe that education will get them better jobs and encourage them to get educated with this end in view, they are entitled to a sense of frustration if, when they have got the education, they do not get the jobs. But, if we say that they should be educated in order to be men, and that everybody, whether he is a ditch-digger or a bank president, should have this education because he is a man, then the ditch-digger may still feel frustrated, but not because of his education.

Nor is it possible for a person to have too much liberal education, because it is impossible to have too much understanding and judgment. But it is possible to undertake too much in the name of liberal education in youth. The object of liberal education in youth is not to teach the young all they will ever need to know. It is to give them the habits, ideas, and techniques that they need to continue to educate themselves. Thus the object of formal institutional liberal education in youth is to prepare the young to educate themselves throughout their lives.

I would remind you of the impossibility of learning to understand and judge many of the most important things in youth. The judgment and understanding of practical affairs can amount to little in the absence of experience with practical affairs. Subjects that cannot be understood without experience should not be taught to those who are without experience. Or, if these subjects are taught to those who are without experience, it should be clear that these subjects can be taught only by way of introduction and that their value to the student depends on his continuing to study them as he acquires experience. The tragedy in America is that economics, ethics, politics, history, and literature are studied in youth, and seldom studied again. Therefore the graduates of American universities seldom understand them.

This pedagogical principle, that subjects requiring experience can be learned only by the experienced, leads to the conclusion that the most important branch of education is the education of adults. We sometimes seem to think of education as something like the mumps, measles, whooping-cough, or chicken-pox. If a person has had education in childhood, he need not, in fact he cannot, have it again. But the pedagogical principle that the most important things can be learned only in mature life is supported by a sound philosophy in general. Men are rational animals. They achieve their terrestrial felicity by the use of reason. And this means that they have to use it for their entire lives. To say that they should learn only in childhood would mean that they were human only in childhood.

And it would mean that they were unfit to be citizens of a republic.[1] A republic, a true *res publica,* can maintain justice, peace, freedom, and order only by the exercise of intelligence. When we speak of the consent of the governed, we mean, since men are not angels who seek the truth intuitively and do not have to learn it, that every act of assent on the part of the governed is a product of learning. A republic is really a common educational life in process. So Montesquieu said that, whereas the principle of a monarchy was honor, and the principle of a tyranny was fear, the principle of a republic was education.

Hence the ideal republic is the republic of learning. It is the utopia by which all actual political republics are measured. The goal toward which we started with the Athenians twenty-five centuries ago is an unlimited republic of learning and a world-wide political republic mutually supporting each other.

All men are capable of learning. Learning does not stop as long as a man lives, unless his learning power atrophies because he does not use it. Political freedom cannot endure unless it is accompanied by provision for the unlimited acquisition of knowledge. Truth is not long retained in human affairs without continual learning and relearning. Peace is

---

[1] I owe this discussion to the suggestions of Scott Buchanan.

unlikely unless there are continuous, unlimited opportunities for learning and unless men continuously avail themselves of them. The world of law and justice for which we yearn, the world-wide political republic, cannot be realized without the world-wide republic of learning. The civilization we seek will be achieved when all men are citizens of the world republic of law and justice and of the republic of learning all their lives long.

3 / EDWARD L. THORNDIKE and ARTHUR I. GATES

The Ultimate Aims of Education

Aims of Education in Terms of Human Wants

Need of Definite Formulation of Aims.   In the preceding chapter it was said that the effect of education is to produce changes in human nature and in other things in the world. It was said furthermore that by educating himself and others, man aims to produce those changes which result in improving his condition, in achieving a better relation between himself and the rest of the world, in increasing his welfare, or in making his life better and richer. Such statements obviously leave the purpose of education rather vague. The acute reader will at once inquire: "What do you mean by an improved condition, a better relation, an increase in welfare, or a richer life?" "On what basis are we to decide what is a bad, indifferent, or good condition of life?" These are very pertinent questions, which have long engaged the attention of thoughtful men. They are pertinent because every person interested or active in education should have some idea of its aims or objectives. Statements of these aims or objectives should express the ultimate purposes of education in such a way that they may be used as definite, intelligible principles of guidance by those who seek to educate effectively. They should be so stated as to be helpful in deciding on particular steps in education such as the desirability of teaching this fact, establishing that habit, encouraging the other skill, inculcating another ideal.

Edward L. Thorndike and Arthur I. Gates, "The Ultimate Aims of Education," from *Elementary Principles of Education* (New York: The Macmillan Company, 1929), pp. 15–30. Reprinted by permission.

What Determines Values. Education seeks to secure for men things that are good instead of bad, conditions that satisfy instead of annoy, activities that are right and beneficial instead of wrong and harmful. Things are not good or bad in and of themselves; a man's acts are neither right nor wrong apart from their effects; no condition is either satisfying or annoying in isolation. Things, conditions, and acts can be classified as good or bad, beneficial or harmful, satisfying or annoying, or as otherwise possessing value and significance only when viewed from some point of view. In the last analysis, decisions as to the value and significance of things with which education is concerned are based on desires, wants, cravings, or urges. To justify and explain this statement, we must take a short excursion into the field of psychology, the science which undertakes to explain human conduct as it is.

The Rôle of Human Wants. According to modern psychology, all human activity is initiated and sustained by some urge, craving, desire, or want. The young infant is largely immobile until it experiences the craving for food, or the urge of thirst, or the desire for physical activity, or some other want. It then becomes active and the activity continues until the infant's craving is satisfied, until it secures what it wants, unless the desire subsides or is overcome by some other urge such as the craving to rest from the effects of its own exertions. Unless the infant wants something, there is no occasion for striving. When it is actively seeking to satisfy one urge, such as hunger, the object of that urge, food, is supremely important, valuable, good, whereas other things such as noises, movements, toys are at the time relatively unimportant and undesired. To the infant, then, things take on value and importance as they serve to satisfy some childish want.

What is true of infancy is fundamentally true of all ages. Human cravings, in the last analysis, initiate and sustain action. Without them, "the human organism would become inert like a wonderful clockwork whose springs had been removed or an engine whose fires had been drawn." Wants, furthermore, are the final determinants of good and bad, useful and useless, right and wrong, beautiful and ugly. Things have value and importance only as they serve to satisfy the urges which lie back of somebody's strivings; they are called useless, bad, wrong, and the like only as they fail to contribute to, or positively thwart, some conscious being's efforts to satisfy his cravings.

A thing or event or act or condition is not then, in the last analysis, desirable because it is valuable. It is valuable because it is desirable— because it satisfies a want or craving or impulse of some man or other conscious being. Suppose, for instance, that all creatures had been, and now and in the future were to be, blind. The most beautiful painting would be no better than the ugliest; for it could make no difference to anybody. Suppose that all beings, past, present, and future, existed equally well and equally happily without, as with, food—that no one wanted food or drink. Temperance would be no longer a virtue, and gluttony no longer a sin. They would simply be accidental qualities like the color of one's eyes. For the temperate man would satisfy no want of his own or anyone else's, nor would the glutton's acts imply deprivation for anybody else. Value or worth or goodness means power to satisfy wants. One thing or condition or act is more valuable or more worthy or better than another because it satisfies wants more fully, or satisfies more wants, or causes less deprivation of wants.

Aim of Education Stated in Terms of Human Wants. Life is activity initiated and sustained to satisfy wants. Since this is the case, we may say provisionally that the ultimate aim of education for man[1] is to secure the fullest satisfaction of human wants. Observe that this statement contains the word *fullest;* this implication of this word we should emphasize and explain.

Conflict among Wants of Different Individuals. Every infant, child, or adult has many wants. Some of these cravings, like that for foods of certain tastes or for a certain amount of unhampered physical action, are native or inherited, born in the very structure of the organism. Others, like the desire for smoking, are acquired. Among both native and acquired wants of persons of all ages are some which, when satisfied in the most convenient manner by one person, tend to deprive another person of the means of satisfying one or more of his wants. If, to satisfy my hunger, I should eat all the berries in the patch, someone else may have to go hungry. If, to satisfy my urge to excel, I should follow fraudulent practices in athletics, business, or love, some more deserving person may be deprived of a satisfaction rightfully earned. If, to appease his craving for domination and power, a man should take advantage of his superiority in wealth to underpay and torment his employees, their wants will be less fully satisfied. Thus, in many cases, if one person secures the *fullest* satisfaction of his individual wants, others will be less able to satisfy their cravings.

Conflict among Wants of Different Groups. The situation is much the same when we replace the individual by the family, the local community, the members of a religious or political or social or occupational group, or

---

[1] We shall not attempt to decide what the aim of education should be for the entire universe of conscious beings; or how far man should perhaps sacrifice his wants to those of the universe as a whole.

even the nation or a league of nations. If one group, to satisfy its cravings for hoarding and domination, monopolizes all of a certain class of goods, such as coal, it may not only reduce the fullness with which the wants of other groups are satisfied but, in the end, it may also cause a diminution in its own satisfaction since the other group may retaliate by monopolizing some other material and the productivity of both may be thereby reduced. If the members of one nation, to enjoy the feeling of superiority, indulge in unreasonable emotional patriotism, the result is likely to be misunderstanding, distrust, rivalry in unessentials, even war, which may reduce the ability of both groups to satisfy the needs of their members. In short, by attempting solely to fulfill the needs of a particular individual, family, community, nation, or even a league of nations, we shall not achieve the fullest satisfaction of the wants of individuals on the whole. On the contrary, by attempting to satisfy the wants of all human beings, the desires of each of us will be most fully satisfied.

Education Seeks to Promote the Satisfying of the Wants of Humanity as a Whole.   Education, then, aims at satisfying the wants of all people in order to give each person the fullest realization of his own desires. A fundamental principle of education, then, is that the best in life is not to be achieved by strivings for the individual aggrandizement of a person, race, nation, or any other group, but, on the contrary, by striving for the advancement of mankind as a whole.

The aim of education is international or universal in scope not for sentimental but for practical reasons; for only by considering the wants of everyone can we satisfy our own desires most fully. If we accept this aim, it will help us to appraise all types of conditions and acts that we may encounter and to evaluate changes in the physical world and in man himself which education may produce.

The chief aim of education, then, is to realize the fullest satisfaction of human wants. To this end external things and conditions and human nature must both be changed. In the last analysis, changes in human nature, to be effective, must include changes in human wants, since satisfaction and activity alike spring from cravings. In general, education aims to diminish or abolish those cravings which are futile or antagonistic to the satisfaction of other wants and to cultivate those wants which do not reduce or which actually increase the satisfaction of others.

Now that a brief statement of the ultimate aims of education has been given it may be clarified and appraised more fully by considering it in comparison with other objectives of education that have received attention. Happiness, preparation for life, growth, reorganization of experience, perfection of oneself, and culture are various terms employed to indicate other objectives of education.

Happiness as an Aim of Education

It is sometimes stated that the ultimate aim of education is to increase human happiness. If this statement takes such a form as "the greatest happiness for the most people," it is substantially equivalent to our statement of the aim of education in terms of satisfying human wants. When we inquire what occasions human happiness, we shall find that it depends upon human wants. Activity which satisfies no need, striving which results in failure or the frustration of wants will not yield the fullest happiness and often will, on the contrary, lead to unhappiness. Happiness results from the full activity of fulfilling human wants. Since the process of satisfying human wants seems to be fundamental to happiness, it is better to define the aim of education in terms of wants.

Education as Preparation for Life

To state that education should always attempt to give children happiness by the most immediate and direct means would be as unwise as to say that by satisfying any individual want the welfare of society would be fostered. Many instances of immediate happiness may reduce or deny later satisfaction; many causes of individual happiness are very dangerous to the welfare of others. Happiness for the individual and society as a whole in the long run is often best attained by denying a person some tempting opportunity of the moment. Among children, who less skillfully conceal their joys and sorrows, inconsistencies between individual immediate happiness and happiness in general for the individual and the group are often apparent. Not all happy experiences are constructively educative and not all educative activities result in immediate happiness. Overimpressed with these obvious facts, some stern souls have declared it ignoble and misleading to define the aim of education as a process of increasing happiness. Education, they claim, is the serious business of preparing children for life. Attempts to make the school add to the store of children's happiness especially are decried as unsafe, "soft pedagogy," trifling with the serious work of education.

Dewey, our leading American in the philosophy of education, has brilliantly and steadfastly opposed this false doctrine. Education, he maintains, is not preparation for life, it *is* life. It is not merely a business of getting ready to live happily and fruitfully, it is the process of living happily and fruitfully at each moment from birth to death. This view is not based on a sentimental attitude toward children but on the hard-headed realization that it represents the best method of realizing the ultimate aims of all life.

The statement that education is not preparation for later life but living here and now does not mean *mere* living but *happy* living here and now. Happiness, as stated above, results from the full process of successfully striving to fulfill our wants. To live happily, then, means not merely preparing to live later, and not merely living, in any way, now. It means living in such a way as to be striving successfully to fulfill our present wants. What Professor Dewey and other modern philosophers contend, then, apparently, is that at all stages in the process of education we must consider the individual's wants.

We should consider the child's wants not merely to make him happy— although this is desirable—but also to make his development more fruitful. If we disregard his wants, we jeopardize his physical well-being, we reduce his interests and activities, we arouse his resistance to the educative process. If, on the contrary, we relate our educational methods and materials to the wants which he experiences, we shall find the learner more vigorous, active, attentive, interested; his activity will be better motivated and longer sustained. To give due concern to the wants of children, then, is one means of making education more effective and of increasing happiness. Fundamentally the dictum *education should be living, instead of mere preparation for life* is justified by the practical results obtained by educating in conformity with, rather than in opposition to, children's wants.

Although it has the practical defense just mentioned, happiness as a guide in education may be considered from other points of view. Children have as great a claim upon happiness as do the adults which they will in time become. If the direct present happiness of children does not conflict with the ultimate ends of education, it is wholly desirable, and even if it does conflict somewhat, it has a right to be put in the balance against future goods and chosen if it outweighs them. It would be folly to deny children happiness for no purpose.

Happiness is not a fiend to be exorcised. The thwarting of every natural impulse and the deprivation of every cherished joy are not necessary means of grace. In fact, if we free ourselves from our adult tendency to think of what is good for us as adults, and consider how cheaply innocent happiness can be given to the young, and consider also that frequently (not always, of course) the childish likes and dislikes are as good guides to later welfare as our artificial prescriptions are, we shall make happiness at the time by no means a small concern of school education.

The apparent conflict between "happy living here and now" and "preparation for life" as statements of the aim of education, then, in the main, reduces itself to a conflict about the chances of attaining happiness and the relative value of present and deferred satisfaction. The greatest happiness for the most people for the most time is an end to be sought by making children's lives as happy as possible and by not denying their wants unless demonstrable good may come from it. The strongest justification of this view is the fact that happiness usually is a good guide and always a symptom of vigorous and active participation in the educative process.

Growth and Reorganization of Experiences

Education aims at change. But to define education as the process of producing change is insufficient since change may take many directions, both desirable and undesirable. It is often said that the aim of education is that growth which is brought about by a continuous reorganization of experience. The difficulty with this statement, of education as growth, is that growth may take many forms and directions—it may be wholesome or cancerous. If we express growth and reorganization of experience in terms of our previously stated aim, namely to secure the fullest gratification of wants, we have a helpful concept. Education then becomes the process of so promoting happy living that conditions in the world and our own wants are changed to increase the fullness with which our desires, as a whole, may be satisfied. The direction of growth is now defined; growth comprises changes which lead to the fuller satisfaction of human wants. As the child lives, his experiences should be constantly reorganized and reintegrated so that his wants become increasingly those which, by promoting the welfare of others, rebound to satisfy his own desires. He must grow, too, in power to fulfill his constantly improving wants. Both wants and means of satisfying them, then, are modifiable and changes in the direction of increasing their fullness constitutes growth. Such growth is the aim of education.

Perfectionism

Vague and Inadequate as a Complete Aim. A generation ago one of the most popular statements of the aim of education was "The Perfection of All One's Powers," or, in Herbert Spencer's words, "Complete Living." These statements always needed qualification. For it is not desirable that life should complete itself by having all possible varieties of envy, jealousy, and cruelty; and it is certain that some features of the life process are more desirable than others. Completeness had to be interpreted as the fulfillment of certain selected features which could work together *harmoniously*—that is, without sacrificing worthy wants. Obviously, no one would advocate perfecting the power to worry or despair. Since certain powers conflict with others, it was necessary to change the phrasing to "harmonious development" or the like.

Specialization Is Necessary. But even if the misleading character of the term *complete* and the vagueness of *perfection* are corrected by qualifying statements, the doctrine itself—that education's business is to make the best possible specimen of humanity out of each man—is faulty. The aim of life is not to stock the world as a museum with perfected specimens for man or deity to contemplate. It is to make men vital parts of an organized force for the welfare of the group. Powers are not for possession and display, but for use. This requires specialization rather than general perfection. Men have to live together and depend one upon another, not each trying to be the best possible creature in all ways, but each being taught to perform, and take pleasure in, those services in which by excelling he can do the most for the common good. Nor is it desirable, even from the point of view of individuals taken singly, that education should develop equally in every respect. Each individual, by sex, race, hereditary equipment, and the circumstances of time and place in which he is born, is more likely to meet certain situations than others during life, and it is to be competent and happy in those situations that he particularly needs to be trained. It would be wasteful to train a genius and an idiot identically. It would have been stupid to have perfected Pasteur's powers to drive a good bargain, or Darwin's powers as a public speaker, or Aristotle's powers as a gardener. Perfecting the power to shoot with bow and arrow is unimportant in America now for the very reverse of the reason that it was important four hundred years ago.

The doctrine of individual perfection is inadequate because it gives an excuse for the too common tendency of men to educate themselves for competitive display instead of coöperative work, because it opposes the specialization which is necessary for mutual aid, and because it neglects the fact that education beyond certain fundamentals should narrow itself to fit every man for a certain probable course of life, not for all life's possibilities.

Specialization Will Become Increasingly Necessary. Perfectionism of individuals, one at a time, grows less significant as an aim in proportion as more knowledge is discovered, as the world's work is more divided, and as education is for a wider group. Even today such an ideal for the education of the million children attending the public schools of New York City seems a little absurd. Many of them early show special talents to which other powers should be sacrificed for the common good and their personal happiness. Most of them have some weakness which it would be folly to try to remedy. Efficiency in service grows more significant as we see more clearly the world's needs and how to meet them. With every decade it becomes more possible for a special line of action to be chosen beforehand for an individual with a very high probability that, if he prepares himself properly, he will by that career be of greatest value to himself and to the world.

Other Narrow Aims of Education

During the long history of discussion of the aims of education, various objectives have been suggested and tested, and usually discarded as too ambiguous or too narrow to serve as the one ultimate aim. Among the objectives suggested have been knowledge, skill, mental power, culture, morality, and character. Without doubt, education does aim to assist the child to acquire character, moral and cultural traits, knowledge, skill, and mental power of some kind and for certain purposes. Merely to say, however, that the aim of education is to develop culture, information, or skill is not useful since such a statement does not suggest what kinds of culture, information, or skill, or what types of character or moral traits are to be sought. To indicate more clearly the significance of these facts, let us consider merely the cases of culture and knowledge, as representative of this list of proposed objectives.

Limitations of Culture as a General Aim

Most educated persons think they know what culture means—and usually think that they have it! But there would be a great variation in such opinions and possessions. To some, culture means a body of knowledge and habits which distinguish its possessor as a member of the leisure class, which ornament his intellect much as tailor-made clothes adorn his body, and which satisfy the craving to display his superiority to others. To others culture means knowledge of *human affairs* as contrasted with science and technology, which are taken to be knowledge of *things*. Thus history, literature, the fine arts, psychology, and government would be regarded as more cultural than physics, chemistry, and geology. To others culture means primarily knowledge and skill in the *fine* arts such as music and painting as contrasted with the *practical* arts such as engineering, nursing, or cooking. According to another idea, culture is a body of knowledge, habits, and interest such as prepares a person to perform, not the special work of any trade or profession, but the general work of citizen, parent, friend, and human being. Culture is thus a name for the broad knowledge useful for being a man or woman in general, as opposed to "technical training" for being a physician, statesman, or carpenter.

The term *culture* is ambiguous. It has too many meanings to serve as a definition of the major aim of education. Culture, as defined by some persons, is an aim of education since the knowledge and skills described are means of increasing the sum of satisfaction of human wants. In so far as culture means the cultivation of impersonal pleasures, or of stainless wants, such as appreciation of beauty in nature and art, interests in human life, a sense of humor, satisfaction in knowledge, which may be satisfied without deprivations to others or, better, with benefits to the welfare of others, it is a worthy aim of education. But in so far as culture becomes synonymous with selfish display, waste, triviality, expense, or uselessness, it runs counter to the ultimate objective of education. To appraise the value of culture, then, we must apply some other criterion such as that embodied in our earlier definition of the aim of education—the increase of satisfaction of the wants of mankind as a whole.

Knowledge as an Aim of Education

Knowledge Essential to Education. There can be no doubt that to increase and diffuse knowledge constitute important aims of education. Although knowledge can be misused, it is in and of itself of utmost value. In the work of making use of the forces and laws of nature to satisfy human wants, knowledge of natural forces and laws is indispensable. In the work of improving our own wants, knowledge of the forces and laws of human nature is essential. If mean men are unwilling and stupid men unable to use knowledge for the best interests of society, the fault is not with knowledge. The cure for folly and ignorance is not less knowledge but more. And for the cure of evil intentions, knowledge is essential.

Examples of Usefulness of Knowledge. It is only by ignorance or forgetfulness of what man owes to the knowledge thus given to him that anyone can resist a holy enthusiasm in the spread of knowledge. Consider the miseries removed and satisfactions created by the spread of one small fraction of knowledge—preventive medicine—to one small group of men! Cholera, smallpox, and the plague are thereby exterminated. The end of yellow fever, malaria, and tuberculosis in a country becomes simply a matter of dollars and cents. Deaths from wounds, childbirth, and minor surgical operations dwindle to rarities. Consider the fears and suffering that have been undergone on account of purely imaginary gods and evils, whose tyranny over human happiness mere knowledge removes. Ghosts, evil spirits, witches, and demons made the life of many primitive peoples an almost incessant fear, and took tithes in labor and goods that could have added a large increment to human comfort.

Morality Based on Knowledge. Morality itself, though often contrasted with or set apart from knowledge, is, except for the good will and certain other noble and humane qualities of character and temperament, a creation of knowledge. It is chiefly knowledge that saves the mother of today from throwing her baby to an idol, the consumptive from poisoning his neighbors, or the ruler from ruining his country. Most of the greatest disasters have been due more to ignorance than to evil intent.

Thus, it appears that the development of knowledge, while not itself the supreme end of education, is nevertheless a most important means of promoting the aim of education. Knowledge is valuable because it is an essential means of promoting human welfare.

Education Requires Specialization in Pursuit of Knowledge. While the acquisition of knowledge—any knowledge—is useful it does not follow that it is desirable to teach everybody all available knowledge, even were such an achievement possible. For the teacher, a practical problem becomes: "What knowledge is of most worth for each of my pupils and how is it to be made to function?" As a general guide, we must refer to our most satisfactory general definition of the aim of education—the control of nature to increase the welfare of society at large. . . .

A detailed study of skills, habits, ideals, and attitudes, as well as of knowledge, must be made because not all of these can be given to all men, and what is most suitable for a given person at one stage in his development and in one environment and in one stage of civilization is often unsuitable at other ages or in other places and times. . . .

4 / JOHN DEWEY

Aims in Education

The Nature of an Aim

The account of education given in our earlier chapters virtually anticipated the results reached in a discussion of the purport of education in a democratic community. For it assumed that the aim of education is to enable individuals to continue their education—or that the object and reward of learning is continued capacity for growth. Now this idea cannot be applied to *all* the members of a society except where intercourse of man with man is mutual, and except where there is adequate provision for the reconstruction of social habits and institutions by means of wide stimulation arising from equitably distributed interests. And this means a democratic society. In our search for aims in education, we are not concerned, therefore, with finding an end outside of the educative process to which education is subordinate. Our whole conception forbids. We are rather concerned with the contrast which exists when aims belong within the process in which they operate and when they are set up from without. And the latter state of affairs must obtain when social relationships are not equitably balanced. For in that case, some portions of the whole social group will find their aims determined by an external dictation; their aims will not arise from the free growth of their own experience, and their nominal aims will be means to more ulterior ends of others than truly their own.

Our first question is to define the nature of an aim so far as it falls within an activity, instead of being furnished from without. We approach the definition by a contrast of mere *results* with *ends*. Any exhibition of energy has results. The wind blows about the sands of the desert; the position of the grains is changed. Here is a result, an effect, but not an *end*. For there is nothing in the outcome which completes or fulfills what went before it. There is mere spatial redistribution. One state of affairs is just as good as any other. Consequently there is no basis upon which to select an earlier state of affairs as a beginning, a later as an end, and to consider what intervenes as a process of transformation and realization.

Consider for example the activities of bees in contrast with the changes in the sands when the wind blows them about. The results of the bees' actions may be called ends not because they are designed or consciously intended, but because they are true terminations or completions of what has preceded. When the bees gather pollen and make wax and build cells, each step prepares the way for the next. When cells are built, the queen lays eggs in them; when eggs are laid, they are sealed and bees brood them and keep them at a temperature required to hatch them. When they are hatched, bees feed the young till they can take care of themselves. Now we are so familiar with such facts, that we are apt to dismiss them on the ground that life and instinct are a kind of miraculous thing anyway. Thus we fail to note what the essential characteristic of the event is; namely, the significance of the temporal place and order of each element; the way each prior event leads into its successor while the successor takes up what is furnished and utilizes it for some other stage, until we arrive at the end, which, as it were, summarizes and finishes off the process.

Since aims relate always to results, the first thing to look to when it is a question of aims, is whether the work assigned possesses intrinsic continuity. Or is it a mere serial aggregate of acts, first doing one thing and then another? To talk about an educational aim when approximately each act of a pupil is dictated by the teacher, when the only order in the sequence of his acts is that which comes from the assignment of lessons and the giving of directions by another, is to talk nonsense. It is equally fatal to an aim to permit capricious or discontinuous action in the name of spontaneous self-expression. An aim implies an orderly and ordered activity, one in which the order consists in the progressive completing of a process. Given an activity having a time span and cumulative growth within the time succession, an aim means foresight in advance of the end or possible termination. If bees anticipated the consequences of their activity, if they perceived their end in imaginative foresight, they would have the primary element in an aim. Hence it is nonsense to talk about the aim of education—or any other undertaking—where conditions do not permit of foresight of results, and do not stimulate a person to look ahead to see what the outcome of a given activity is to be.

In the next place the aim as a foreseen end gives direction to the activity; it is not an idle view of a mere spectator, but influences the steps taken to reach the end. The foresight functions in three ways. In the first place, it involves careful observation of the given conditions to see what are the means available for reaching the end, and to discover the hindrances in the way. In the second place, it suggests the proper order or sequence in the use of means. It facilitates an economical selection and arrangement. In the third place, it makes choice of alternatives possible. If we can predict the outcome of acting this way or that, we can then compare the value of the two courses of action; we can pass judgment upon their relative desirability. If we know that stagnant water breeds mosquitoes and that they are likely to carry disease, we can, disliking that anticipated result, take steps to avert it. Since we do not anticipate results as mere intellectual onlookers, but as persons concerned in the outcome, we are partakers in the process which produces the result. We intervene to bring about this result or that.

Of course these three points are closely connected with one another. We can definitely foresee results only as we make careful scrutiny of present conditions, and the importance of the outcome supplies the motive for observations. The more adequate our observations, the more varied is the scene of conditions and obstructions that presents itself, and the more numerous are the alternatives between which choice may be made. In turn, the more numerous the recognized possibilities of the situation, or alternatives of action, the more meaning does the chosen activity possess, and the more flexibly controllable is it. Where only a single outcome has been thought of, the mind has nothing else to think of; the meaning attaching to the act is limited. One only steams ahead toward the mark. Sometimes such a narrow course may be effective. But if unexpected difficulties offer themselves, one has not as many resources at command as if he had chosen the same line of action after a broader survey of the possibilities of the field. He cannot make needed readjustments readily.

The net conclusion is that acting with an aim is all one with acting intelligently. To foresee a terminus of an act is to have a basis upon which to observe, to select, and to order objects and our own capacities. To do these things means to have a mind—for mind is precisely intentional purposeful activity controlled by perception of facts and their relationships to one another. To have a mind to do a thing is to foresee a future possibility; it is to have a plan for its accomplishment; it is to note the means which make the plan capable of execution and the obstructions in the way,—or, if it is really a *mind* to do the thing and not a vague aspiration—it is to have a plan which takes account of resources and difficulties. Mind is capacity to refer present conditions to future results, and future consequences to present conditions. And these traits are just what is meant by having an aim or a purpose. A man is stupid or blind or unintelligent—lacking in mind—just in the degree in which in any activity he does not know what he is about, namely, the probable consequences of his acts. A man is imperfectly intelligent when he contents himself with looser guesses about the outcome than is needful, just taking a chance with his luck, or when he forms plans apart from study of the actual conditions, including his own capacities. Such relative absence of mind means to make our feelings the measure of what is to happen. To be intelligent we must "stop, look, listen" in making the plan of an activity.

To identify acting with an aim and intelligent activity is enough to show its value—its function in experience. We are only too given to making an entity out of the abstract noun "consciousness." We forget that it comes from the adjective "conscious." To be conscious is to be aware of what we are about; conscious signifies the deliberate, observant, planning traits of activity. Consciousness is nothing which we have which gazes idly on the scene around one or which has impressions made upon it by physical things; it is a name for the purposeful quality of an activity, for the fact that it is directed by an aim. Put the other way about, to have an aim is to act with meaning, not like an automatic machine; it is to *mean* to do something and to perceive the meaning of things in the light of that intent.

The Criteria of Good Aims

We may apply the results of our discussion to a consideration of the criteria involved in a correct establishing of aims. (1) The aim set up must be an outgrowth of existing conditions. It must be based upon a consideration of what is already going on; upon the resources and difficulties of the situation. Theories about the proper end of our activities—educational and moral theories—often violate this principle. They assume ends lying *outside* our activities; ends foreign to the concrete makeup of the situation; ends which issue from some outside source. Then the problem is to bring our activities to bear upon the realization of these externally supplied ends. They are something for which we *ought* to act. In any case such "aims" limit intelligence; they are not the expression of mind in foresight, observation, and choice of the better among alternative possibilities. They limit intelligence because, given ready-made, they must be imposed by some authority external to intelligence, leaving to the latter nothing but a mechanical choice of means.

(2) We have spoken as if aims could be completely formed prior to the attempt to realize them. This impression must now be qualified. The aim as it first emerges is a mere tentative sketch. The act of striving to realize it tests its worth. If it suffices to direct activity successfully, nothing more is required, since its whole function is to set a mark in advance; and at times a mere hint may suffice. But usually—at least in complicated situations—acting upon it brings to light conditions which had been overlooked. This calls for revision of the original aim; it has to be added to and subtracted from. An aim must, then, be *flexible;* it must be capable of alteration to meet circumstances. An end established externally to the process of action is always rigid. Being inserted or imposed from without, it is not supposed to have a working relationship to the concrete conditions of the situation. What happens in the course of action neither confirms, refutes, nor alters it. Such an end can only be insisted upon. The failure that results from its lack of adaptation is attributed simply to the perverseness of conditions, not to the fact that the end is not reasonable under the circumstances. The value of a legitimate aim, on the contrary, lies in the fact that we can use it to change conditions. It is a method for dealing with conditions so as to effect desirable alterations in them. A farmer who should passively accept things just as he finds them would make as great a mistake as he who framed his plans in complete disregard of what soil, climate, etc., permit. One of the evils of an abstract or remote external aim in education is that its very inapplicability in practice is likely to react into a haphazard snatching at immediate

conditions. A good aim surveys the present state of experience of pupils, and forming a tentative plan of treatment, keeps the plan constantly in view and yet modifies it as conditions develop. The aim, in short, is experimental, and hence constantly growing as it is tested in action.

(3) The aim must always represent a freeing of activities. The term *end in view* is suggestive, for it puts before the mind the termination or conclusion of some process. The only way in which we can define an activity is by putting before ourselves the objects in which it terminates —as one's aim in shooting is the target. But we must remember that the *object* is only a mark or sign by which the mind specifies the *activity* one desires to carry out. Strictly speaking, not the target but *hitting* the target is the end in view; one *takes* aim by means of the target, but also by the sight on the gun. The different objects which are thought of are means of *directing* the activity. Thus one aims at, say, a rabbit; what he wants is to shoot straight: a certain kind of activity. Or, if it is the rabbit he wants, it is not rabbit apart from his activity, but as a factor in activity; he wants to eat the rabbit, or to show it as evidence of his marksmanship—he wants to do something with it. The doing with the thing, not the thing in isolation, is his end. The object is but a phase of the active end— continuing the activity successfully. This is what is meant by the phrase, used above, "freeing activity."

In contrast with fulfilling some process in order that activity may go on, stands the static character of an end which is imposed from without the activity. It is always conceived of as fixed; it is *something* to be attained and possessed. When one has such a notion, activity is a mere unavoidable means to something else; it is not significant or important on its own account. As compared with the end it is but a necessary evil; something which must be gone through before one can reach the object which is alone worth while. In other words, the external idea of the aim leads to a separation of means from end, while an end which grows up within an activity as plan for its direction is always both ends and means, the distinction being only one of convenience. Every means is a temporary end until we have attained it. Every end becomes a means of carrying activity further as soon as it is achieved. We call it end when it marks off the future direction of the activity in which we are engaged; means when it marks off the present direction. Every divorce of end from means diminishes by that much the significance of the activity and tends to reduce it to a drudgery from which one would escape if he could. A farmer has to use plants and animals to carry on his farming activities. It certainly makes a great difference to his life whether he is fond of them, or whether he regards them merely as means which he has to employ to get something else in which alone he is interested. In the former case, his entire course of activity is significant; each phase of it has its own value.

He has the experience of realizing his end at every stage; the postponed aim, or end in view, being merely a sight ahead by which to keep his activity going fully and freely. For if he does not look ahead, he is more likely to find himself blocked. The aim is as definitely a *means* of action as is any other portion of an activity.

Applications in Education

There is nothing peculiar about educational aims. They are just like aims in any directed occupation. The educator, like the farmer, has certain things to do, certain resources with which to do, and certain obstacles with which to contend. The conditions with which the farmer deals, whether as obstacles or resources, have their own structure and operation independently of any purpose of his. Seeds sprout, rain falls, the sun shines, insects devour, blight comes, the seasons change. His aim is simply to utilize these various conditions; to make his activities and their energies work together, instead of against one another. It would be absurd if the farmer set up a purpose of farming, without any reference to these conditions of soil, climate, characteristic of plant growth, etc. His purpose is simply a foresight of the consequences of his energies connected with those of the things about him, a foresight used to direct his movements from day to day. Foresight of possible consequences leads to more careful and extensive observation of the nature and perform- ances of the things he had to do with, and to laying out a plan—that is, of a certain order in the acts to be performed.

It is the same with the educator, whether parent or teacher. It is as absurd for the latter to set up his "own" aims as the proper objects of the growth of the children as it would be for the farmer to set up an ideal of farming irrespective of conditions. Aims mean acceptance of responsi- bility for the observations, anticipations, and arrangements required in carrying on a function—whether farming or educating. Any aim is of value so far as it assists observation, choice, and planning in carrying on activity from moment to moment and hour to hour; if it gets in the way of the individual's own common sense (as it will surely do if imposed from without or accepted on authority) it does harm.

And it is well to remind ourselves that education as such has no aims. Only persons, parents, and teachers, etc., have aims, not an abstract idea like education. And consequently their purposes are indefinitely varied, differing with different children, changing as children grow and with the growth of experience on the part of the one who teaches. Even the most valid aims which can be put in words will, as words, do more harm than good unless one recognizes that they are not aims, but rather suggestions to educators as to how to observe, how to look ahead, and how to choose in liberating and directing the energies of the concrete situations in which they find themselves. As a recent writer has said: "To lead this boy to read Scott's novels instead of old Sleuth's stories; to teach this girl to sew; to root out the habit of bullying from John's make-up; to prepare this class to study medicine,—these are samples of the millions of aims we have actually before us in the concrete work of education."

Bearing these qualifications in mind, we shall proceed to state some of the characteristics found in all good educational aims. (1) An educational aim must be founded upon the intrinsic activities and needs (including original instincts and acquired habits) of the given individual to be educated. The tendency of such an aim as preparation is, as we have seen, to omit existing powers, and find the aim in some remote accomplishment or responsibility. In general, there is a disposition to take considerations which are dear to the hearts of adults and set them up as ends irrespective of the capacities of those educated. There is also an inclination to propound aims which are so uniform as to neglect the specific powers and requirements of an individual, forgetting that all learning is something which happens to an individual at a given time and place. The larger range of perception of the adult is of great value in observing the abilities and weaknesses of the young, in deciding what they may amount to. Thus the artistic capacities of the adult exhibit what certain tendencies of the child are capable of; if we did not have the adult achievements we should be without assurance as to the significance of the drawing, reproducing, modeling, coloring activities of childhood. So if it were not for adult language, we should not be able to see the import of the babbling impulses of infancy. But it is one thing to use adult accomplishments as a context in which to place and survey the doings of childhood and youth; it is quite another to set them up as a fixed aim without regard to the concrete activities of those educated.

(2) An aim must be capable of translation into a method of cooperating with the activities of those undergoing instruction. It must suggest the kind of environment needed to liberate and to organize *their* capacities. Unless it lends itself to the construction of specific procedures, and unless these procedures test, correct, and amplify the aim, the latter is worthless. Instead of helping the specific task of teaching, it prevents the use of ordinary judgment in observing and sizing up the situation. It operates to exclude recognition of everything except what squares up with the fixed end in view. Every rigid aim just because it is rigidly given seems to render it unnecessary to give careful attention to concrete conditions. Since it *must* apply anyhow, what is the use of noting details which do not count?

The vice of externally imposed ends has deep roots. Teachers receive them from superior authorities; these authorities accept them from what is current in the community. The teachers impose them upon children. As a first consequence, the intelligence of the teacher is not free; it is

confined to receiving the aims laid down from above. Too rarely is the
individual teacher so free from the dictation of authoritative supervisor,
textbook on methods, prescribed course of study, etc., that he can let his
mind come to close quarters with the pupil's mind and the subject
matter. This distrust of the teacher's experience is then reflected in lack
of confidence in the responses of pupils. The latter receive their aims
through a double or treble external imposition, and are constantly
confused by the conflict between the aims which are natural to their own
experience at the time and those in which they are taught to acquiesce.
Until the democratic criterion of the intrinsic significance of every
growing experience is recognized, we shall be intellectually confused by
the demand for adaptation to external aims.

(3) Educators have to be on their guard against ends that are alleged
to be general and ultimate. Every activity, however specific, is, of course,
general in its ramified connections, for it leads out indefinitely into other
things. So far as a general idea makes us more alive to these connections,
it cannot be too general. But "general" also means "abstract," or detached
from all specific context. And such abstractness means remoteness, and
throws us back, once more, upon teaching and learning as mere means of
getting ready for an end disconnected from the means. That education is
literally and all the time its own reward means that no alleged study or
discipline is educative unless it is worth while in its own immediate
having. A truly general aim broadens the outlook; it stimulates one to
take more consequences (connections) into account. This means a wider
and more flexible observation of means. The more interacting forces, for
example, the farmer takes into account, the more varied will be his
immediate resources. He will see a greater number of possible starting
places, and a greater number of ways of getting at what he wants to do.
The fuller one's conception of possible future achievements, the less his
present activity is tied down to a small number of alternatives. If one
knew enough, one could start almost anywhere and sustain his activities
continuously and fruitfully.

Understanding then the term general or comprehensive aim simply in
the sense of a broad survey of the field of present activities, we shall take
up some of the larger ends which have currency in the educational
theories of the day, and consider what light they throw upon the
immediate concrete and diversified aims which are always the educator's
real concern. We premise (as indeed immediately follows from what has
been said) that there is no need of making a choice among them or
regarding them as competitors. When we come to act in a tangible way
we have to select or choose a particular act at a particular time, but any
number of comprehensive ends may exist without competition, since they
mean simply different ways of looking at the same scene. One cannot

climb a number of different mountains simultaneously, but the views had when different mountains are ascended supplement one another: they do not set up incompatible, competing worlds. Or, putting the matter in a slightly different way, one statement of an end may suggest certain questions and observations, and another statement another set of questions, calling for other observations. Then the more general ends we have, the better. One statement will emphasize what another slurs over. What a plurality of hypotheses does for the scientific investigator, a plurality of stated aims may do for the instructor. . . .

Questions for Discussion

SPENCER and Hutchins differ about the basis or rationale for constructing the aims of education. Spencer believes that the function of education is to prepare for complete living and that any course of study must evolve from this criterion. He then classifies, in the order of importance, the leading kinds of activities which constitute human life. Hutchins, on the other hand, looks to the nature of man for the basis of education. Which of these approaches do you believe is more desirable or effective in establishing educational aims? Why?

Spencer and Hutchins also differ about the importance of a scientific education, and they disagree as to the amount of emphasis that vocational preparation should receive. Explain their differences and the bases of their disagreements. Are these important issues today? How would you handle them?

Thorndike and Gates state that human cravings initiate and sustain action. Wants are the final determiners of good and bad, right and wrong. Things or conditions are desirable not because they are valuable but because they are held to be desirable. Value or worth or goodness means the power to satisfy wants. The ultimate aim of education, then, is to secure the fullest satisfaction of human wants. Compare this position with the positions of others in this section. Notice also that Thorndike and Gates offer criticisms of the positions of Spencer, Hutchins, and Dewey. Are these criticisms sound?

Dewey warns us not to seek an end outside the educative process to which education is subordinate, for aims fall within an activity rather than being imposed from without. He distinguishes between aims and results, and shows how aims give direction to activity. Dewey's statement that aims must be established in relation to conditions themselves is in conflict with Hutchins' assertion that the aim of education is the same in every age and in every society. If aims are not ultimate or absolute, must they be based on subjective desires? Can you defend your position?

CHAPTER TWO /

HUMAN NATURE

IT is no accident that for centuries discussions of human nature have loomed large in metaphysics, theology, and political and educational philosophy. In religion, for example, Christianity has been influenced by the notion of original sin. Metaphysicians have had to consider the nature of *being* and man's place in the universe before they could formulate a systematic philosophy. Political philosophers of the past have tended to establish the foundation of the state on their conceptions of human nature and the limitations which they believed such conceptions impose upon human relations.

A systematic philosophy of education is also concerned with man's nature. Since education is designed to change individuals, we should first know what man *can* become before we prescribe what he *ought* to become. Prescriptive statements in education, in order to be realistic, must take into consideration human potentialities. Educational aims, too, must make similar considerations.

The study of human nature is not just an academic concern; it makes a difference in educational practice. Within the history of education it has made a difference whether man is looked upon as basically good or inherently evil; whether his distinguishing trait is thought to be his reason or some other feature. There have been many controversies relative to the nature of man. One controversy centers on whether man is nothing more than a highly complex animal, or whether he is essentially unique and discontinuous with the animal kingdom. To take the former view does not automatically commit us to Thomas Hobbes's belief that man's life in a state of nature is "solitary, poor, nasty, brutish, and short." One could hold that, within the temporal backdrop of human progress, man's origin is not as important as what he is today and what he can become. Is the task of education, then, to shape man into what he can become?

To hold that man is discontinuous with the animal kingdom is to advance the claim that he has certain unique characteristics found in no other form of life. Through his memory he can relive events in time, and he can profit from past experiences; through his self-consciousness he can become an object to himself and see himself from a point of detachment; and through self-transcendence the self can rise above itself. Should schooling be a process of teaching self-transcendence? How can this be accomplished?

The claim is frequently made that the essentially distinguishing trait of man is his reason and that the purpose of education is to develop reason. Therefore, if reason is the defining characteristic of man, could it not be held that human nature everywhere is basically the same and an education which would develop and nurture reason should also be basically the same everywhere? One might conclude then that the aims of education can be derived from a knowledge of man's essence, although along with man's reason is his unique ability to wreak destruction on an almost undreamed of scale. How should the schools deal with this trait? Does man have a fixed essence, or can it be shaped for his own ends? Should education cultivate man's essential nature, work to change it, or nurture individuality rather than common generic characteristics?

For his own purposes man designs social institutions; they, in turn, shape man. These social institutions are formed to serve certain ends, but there are disagreements as to what these ends should be. Some hold that existing social arrangements are established to keep people from exploiting and abusing one another, while others claim that social arrangements are designed only to promote happiness. It has also been asserted that our institutions are devised to exploit the weak while satisfying the rapacious appetites of the strong. Should education attempt to fulfill human wants or try to teach youth how to sublimate or suppress them? Is there always a conflict between the wants and desires of individuals and society's restrictions on their expression and fulfillment?

Many theorists have influenced our understanding of human nature. The selections that follow represent the positions of four such theorists, and each has enjoyed a considerable following. In each case consider how subscribing to a particular position would incline one toward certain attitudes and beliefs regarding the individual and his education.

The selection by Thomas Hobbes is considered a major position in the history of political thought. He makes use of a mechanical model in developing his materialistic position. The provocative statements in this selection are especially effective in stimulating philosophical discussions. According to Hobbes, men in a state of nature, although approximately equal in strength, mental capacity, and experience, continue to exploit one another until a state of war ensues. Thus life would be "solitary, poor, nasty, brutish and short."

The writings of John Locke influenced Jefferson's thinking in writing the Declaration of Independence and imbedded themselves in the ideologies of many Americans. Selection 10 is from an important political treatise. Man—by nature—being free, equal, and independent, according to Locke, diverges from Hobbes' view.

Reinhold Niebuhr, a towering figure in Christian ethics and contemporary political philosophy, offers the student a philosophical view of man, one whose lineage can be traced from Saint Augustine. Niebuhr's position is important on two other accounts. If one contends that Locke's philosophy can be found in the Declaration of Independence, one may also argue that the very different philosophical assumptions underlying the Constitution and the Federalist papers have a modern counterpart in Niebuhr's political philosophy. Finally, Niebuhr's political philosophy has become a pragmatic guide to and source of interpretation in the formulation of liberal policies in the political arena.

It is doubtful that any single figure has exerted a greater influence on contemporary views of human nature than has Sigmund Freud. In Selection 8, Freud interprets man's inner life as it affects his behavior and explains the dynamic tension between the libido and the repressive nature of society or social controls. This leads the reader to explore a psychoanalytic interpretation of human nature and its import for education.

5 / THOMAS HOBBES

Leviathan

Nature, the art whereby God hath made and governs the world, is by the *art* of man, as in many other things, so in this also imitated, that it can make an artificial animal. For seeing life is but a motion of limbs, the

From Thomas Hobbs, *Leviathan or The Matter, Form and Power of a Commonwealth—Ecclesiastical and Civil,* reprinted in *Social and Political Philosophy,* edited by John Somerville and Ronald E. Santoni (Garden City, New York: Doubleday and Company, Inc.), chaps. XIII, XIV, and XVII.

beginning whereof is in some principal part within; why may we not say, that all *automata* (engines that move themselves by springs and wheels as doth a watch) have an artificial life? For what is the heart, but a spring; and the nerves, but so many strings, and the joints, but so many wheels, giving motion to the whole body, such as was intended by the artificer? Art goes yet further, imitating that rational and most excellent work of nature, *man*. For by art is created that great *Leviathan* called a *Commonwealth*, or *State*, in Latin *Civitas*, which is but an artificial man; though of greater stature and strength than the natural, for whose protection and defense it was intended; and in which the sovereignty is an artificial soul, as giving life and motion to the whole body; the magistrates, and other officers of judicature and execution, artificial joints; reward and punishment, by which fastened to the seat of the sovereignty every joint and member is moved to perform his duty, are the nerves, that do the same in the body natural; the wealth and riches of all the particular members, are the strength; *salus populi*, the people's safety, its business; counselors, by whom all things needful for it to know are suggested unto it, are the memory; equity and laws, an artificial reason and will; concord, health; sedition, sickness; and civil war, death. Lastly, the pacts and covenants, by which the parts of this body politic were at first made, set together, and united, resemble that *fiat*, or the *let us make man*, pronounced by God in the creation.

To describe the nature of this artificial man, I will consider:

First, the *matter* thereof, and the *artificer*; both which is *man*.

Secondly, *how*, and by what *covenants* it is made; what are the *rights* and just *power* or *authority* of a *sovereign*; and what it is that preserveth or dissolveth it.

Thirdly, what is a *Christian commonwealth*.

Lastly, what is the *kingdom of darkness*.

Concerning the first, there is a saying much usurped of late, that wisdom is acquired, not by reading of books, but of men. Consequently whereunto, those persons that for the most part can give no other proof of being wise, take great delight to show what they think they have read in men, by uncharitable censures of one another behind their backs. But there is another saying not of late understood, by which they might learn truly to read one another if they would take the pains: that is, *nosce teipsum*, Read thyself; which was not meant, as it is now used, to countenance either the barbarous state of men in power towards their inferiors, or to encourage men of low degree to a saucy behavior towards their betters; but to teach us that from the similitude of the thoughts and passions of one man to the thoughts and passions of another, whosoever looketh into himself, and considereth what he doth when he does think, opine, reason, hope, fear, etc. and upon what grounds; he shall thereby read and know what are the thoughts and passions of all other men upon the like occasions. I say the similitude of *passions*, which are the same in all men, desire, fear, hope, etc.; not the similitude of the *objects* of the passions, which are the things desired, feared, hoped, etc.: for these the constitution individual, and particular education, do so vary, and they are so easy to be kept from our knowledge, that the characters of man's heart, blotted and confounded as they are with dissembling, lying, counterfeiting, and erroneous doctrines, are legible only to him that searcheth hearts. And though by men's actions we do discover their design sometimes; yet to do it without comparing them with our own, and distinguishing all circumstances by which the case may come to be altered, is to decipher without a key, and be for the most part deceived, by too much trust or by too much diffidence, as he that reads is himself a good or evil man.

But let one man read another by his actions never so perfectly, it serves him only with his acquaintance, which are but few. He that is to govern a whole nation, must read in himself not this or that particular man, but mankind; which though it be hard to do, harder than to learn any language or science, yet when I shall have set down my own reading orderly and perspicuously, the pains left another will be only to consider if he also find not the same in himself. For this kind of doctrine admitteth no other demonstration. . . .

Chapter XIII. Of the Natural Condition of Mankind as Concerning Their Felicity, and Misery

Nature hath made men so equal, in the faculties of the body and mind; as that, though there be found one man sometimes manifestly stronger in body or of quicker mind than another, yet when all is reckoned together, the difference between man and man is not so considerable, as that one man can thereupon claim to himself any benefit, to which another may not pretend as well as he. For as to the strength of body, the weakest has strength enough to kill the strongest, either by secret machination, or by confederacy with others that are in the same danger with himself.

And as to the faculties of the mind—setting aside the arts grounded upon words, and especially that skill of proceeding upon general and infallible rules, called science; which very few have, and but in few things; as being not a native faculty, born with us; nor attained, as prudence, while we look after somewhat else—I find yet a greater equality amongst men, than that of strength. For prudence is but experience, which equal time equally bestows on all men, in those things they equally apply themselves unto. That which may perhaps make such equality incredible, is but a vain conceit of one's own wisdom, which almost all men think they have in greater degree than the vulgar; that is, than all men but themselves, and a few others, whom by fame, or for concurring with themselves, they approve. For such is the nature of men, that howsoever they may acknowledge many others to be more witty, or more eloquent, or more learned, yet they will hardly believe there be many so wise as themselves; for they see their own wit at hand, and other men's at a distance. But this proveth rather that men are in that point equal, than unequal. For there is not ordinarily a greater sign of the equal distribution of anything, than that every man is contented with his share.

From this equality of ability, ariseth equality of hope in the attaining of our ends. And therefore if any two men desire the same thing, which nevertheless they cannot both enjoy, they become enemies; and in the way to their end, which is principally their own conservation, and sometimes their delectation only, endeavor to destroy, or subdue one another. And from hence it comes to pass that where an invader hath no more to fear than another man's single power; if one plant, sow, build, or possess a convenient seat, others may probably be expected to come prepared with forces united, to dispossess and deprive him, not only of the fruit of his labor, but also of his life or liberty. And the invader again is in the like danger of another.

And from this diffidence of one another, there is no way for any man to secure himself so reasonable as anticipation; that is, by force or wiles to master the persons of all men he can, so long, till he see no other power great enough to endanger him: and this is no more than his own conservation requireth, and is generally allowed. Also because there be some, that taking pleasure in contemplating their own power in the acts of conquest, which they pursue farther than their security requires; if others, that otherwise would be glad to be at ease within modest bounds, should not by invasion increase their power, they would not be able long time, by standing only on their defense, to subsist. And by consequence, such augmentation of dominion over men being necessary to a man's conservation, it ought to be allowed him.

Again, men have no pleasure, but on the contrary a great deal of grief, in keeping company, where there is no power able to overawe them all. For every man looketh that his companion should value him at the same rate he sets upon himself; and upon all signs of contempt, or undervaluing, naturally endeavors, as far as he dares (which amongst them that have no common power to keep them in quiet, is far enough to make them destroy each other), to extort a greater value from his contemners by damage, and from others by the example.

So that in the nature of man, we find three principal causes of quarrel. First, competition; second, diffidence; thirdly, glory.

The first maketh men invade for gain; the second, for safety; and the third, for reputation. The first use violence to make themselves masters of other men's persons, wives, children, and cattle; the second, to defend them; the third, for trifles, as a word, a smile, a different opinion, and any other sign of undervalue, either direct in their persons, or by reflection in their kindred, their friends, their nation, their profession, or their name.

Hereby it is manifest that during the time men live without a common power to keep them all in awe, they are in that condition which is called war; and such a war as is of every man against every man. For *war* consisteth not in battle only, or the act of fighting, but in a tract of time wherein the will to contend by battle is sufficiently known, and therefore the notion of *time* is to be considered in the nature of war, as it is in the nature of weather. For as the nature of foul weather lieth not in a shower or two of rain, but in an inclination thereto of many days together; so the nature of war consisteth not in actual fighting, but in the known disposition thereto, during all the time there is no assurance to the contrary. All other time is *peace*.

Whatsoever therefore is consequent to a time of war, where every man is enemy to every man; the same is consequent to the time, wherein men live without other security than what their own strength and their own invention shall furnish them withal. In such condition there is no place for industry, because the fruit thereof is uncertain: and consequently no culture of the earth; no navigation, nor use of the commodities that may be imported by sea; no commodious building; no instruments of moving, and removing, such things as require much force; no knowledge of the face of the earth; no account of time; no arts; no letters; no society; and which is worst of all, continual fear, and danger of violent death; and the life of man, solitary, poor, nasty, brutish, and short.

It may seem strange to some man that has not well weighed these things, that nature should thus dissociate, and render men apt to invade and destroy one another; and he may therefore, not trusting to this inference, made from the passions, desire perhaps to have the same confirmed by experience. Let him therefore consider with himself, when taking a journey, he arms himself and seeks to go well accompanied; when going to sleep, he locks his doors; when even in his house he locks his chests; and this when he knows there be laws, and public officers, armed, to revenge all injuries shall be done him: what opinion he has of his fellow-subjects, when he rides armed; of his fellow-citizens, when he locks his doors; and of his children, and servants, when he locks his chests. Does he not there as much accuse mankind by his actions, as I do by my words? But neither of us accuse man's nature in it. The desires, and other passions of man, are in themselves no sin. No more are the actions that proceed from those passions, till they know a law that forbids them: which till laws be made they cannot know; nor can any law be made, till they have agreed upon the person that shall make it.

It may peradventure be thought, there was never such a time nor condition of war as this; and I believe it was never generally so, over all the world: but there are many places where they live so now. For the savage people in many places of America, except the government of small families, the concord whereof dependeth on natural lust, have no government at all; and live at this day in that brutish manner, as I said before. Howsoever, it may be perceived what manner of life there would be, where there were no common power to fear; by the manner of life which men that have formerly lived under a peaceful government, use to degenerate into a civil war.

But though there had never been any time wherein particular men were in a condition of war one against another; yet in all times, kings, and persons of sovereign authority, because of their independency, are in continual jealousies, and in the state and posture of gladiators; having their weapons pointing, and their eyes fixed on one another; that is, their forts, garrisons, and guns upon the frontiers of their kingdoms; and continual spies upon their neighbors; which is a posture of war. But because they uphold thereby the industry of their subjects, there does not follow from it that misery which accompanies the liberty of particular men.

To this war of every man against every man, this also is consequent: *that nothing can be unjust.* The notions of right and wrong, justice and injustice, have there no place. Where there is no common power, there is no law; where no law, no injustice. Force and fraud are in war the two cardinal virtues. Justice and injustice are none of the faculties neither of the body nor mind. If they were, they might be in a man that were alone in the world, as well as his senses and passions. They are qualities that relate to men in society, not in solitude. It is consequent also to the same condition, that there be no propriety, no dominion, no *mine* and *thine* distinct; but only that to be every man's, that he can get; and for so long as he can keep it. And thus much for the ill condition which man by mere nature is actually placed in; though with a possibility to come out of it, consisting partly in the passions, partly in his reason.

The passions that incline men to peace are fear of death, desire of such things as are necessary to commodious living, and a hope by their industry to obtain them. And reason suggesteth convenient articles of peace, upon which men may be drawn to agreement. These articles are they which otherwise are called the Laws of Nature whereof I shall speak more particularly in the two following chapters.

Chapter XIV. Of the First and Second Natural Laws, and of Contracts

The right of nature, which writers commonly call *jus naturale*, is the liberty each man hath to use his own power, as he will himself, for the preservation of his own nature; that is to say, of his own life; and consequently, of doing anything, which in his own judgment and reason, he shall conceive to be the aptest means thereunto.

By *liberty*, is understood, according to the proper signification of the word, the absence of external impediments: which impediments, may oft take away part of a man's power to do what he would; but cannot hinder him from using the power left him, according as his judgment and reason shall dictate to him.

A *law of nature, lex naturalis*, is a precept or general rule, found out by reason, by which a man is forbidden to do that which is destructive of his life, or taketh away the means of preserving the same; and to omit that by which he thinketh it may be best preserved. For though they that speak of this subject, use to confound *jus* and *lex, right* and *law;* yet they ought to be distinguished: because *right* consisteth in liberty to do or to forbear, whereas *law* determineth and bindeth to one of them; so that law, and right differ as much as obligation and liberty; which in one and the same matter are inconsistent.

And because the condition of man, as hath been declared in the precedent chapter, is a condition of war of everyone against everyone; in which case everyone is governed by his own reason, and there is nothing he can make use of that may not be a help unto him in preserving his life against his enemies: it followeth, that in such a condition every man has a right to everything; even to one another's body. And therefore, as long as this natural right of every man to everything endureth, there can be no security to any man, how strong or wise soever he be, of living out the time which nature ordinarily alloweth men to live. And consequently it is a precept, or general rule of reason, *that every man ought to endeavor peace, as far as he has hope of obtaining it; and when he cannot obtain it, that he may seek and use all helps and advantages of war.* The first branch of which rule containeth the first and fundamental law of nature; which is, *to seek peace and follow it.* The second, the sum of the right of nature; which is, *by all means we can, to defend ourselves.*

From this fundamental law of nature, by which men are commanded to endeavor peace, is derived this second law: *that a man be willing, when others are so too, as far forth as for peace and defense of himself he shall think it necessary, to lay down this right to all things; and be contented with so much liberty against other men, as he would allow other men against himself.* For as long as every man holdeth this right, of doing anything he liketh, so long are all men in the condition of war. But if other men will not lay down their right, as well as he, then there is no reason for anyone to divest himself of his: for that were to expose himself to prey, which no man is bound to, rather than to dispose himself to peace. This is that law of the Gospel: *whatsoever you require that others should do to you, that do ye to them.* And that law of all men, *quod tibi fieri non, vis, alteri ne feceris.*

To *lay down* a man's *right* to anything, is to *divest* himself of the *liberty,* of hindering another of the benefit of his own right to the same. For he that renounceth or passeth away his right, giveth not to any other man a right which he had not before; because there is nothing to which every man had not right by nature: but only standeth out of his way, that he may enjoy his own original right, without hindrance from him, not without hindrance from another. So that the effect which redoundeth to one man, by another man's defect of right, is but so much diminution of impediments to the use of his own right original.

Right is laid aside, either by simply renouncing it, or by transferring it to another. By *simply renouncing,* when he cares not to whom the benefit thereof redoundeth. By *transferring,* when he intendeth the benefit thereof to some certain person or persons. And when a man hath in either manner abandoned or granted away his right; then is he said to be *obliged,* or bound, not to hinder those to whom such right is granted or abandoned, from the benefit of it; and that he *ought,* and it is his *duty,* not to make void that voluntary act of his own; and that such hindrance is *injustice,* and *injury,* as being *sine jure;* the right being before renounced, or transferred. So that injury, or injustice, in the controversies of the world, is somewhat like to that, which in the disputations of scholars is called *absurdity.* For as it is there called an absurdity to contradict what one maintained in the beginning; so in the world, it is called injustice, and injury, voluntarily to undo that which from the beginning he had voluntarily done. The way by which a man either simply renounceth, or transferreth his right, is a declaration, or significa-tion, by some voluntary and sufficient sign or signs, that he doth so renounce or transfer, or hath so renounced or transferred the same, to him that accepteth it. And these signs are either words only, or actions only, or, as it happeneth most often, both words and actions. And the same are the *bonds,* by which men are bound and obliged—bonds that have their strength, not from their own nature, for nothing is more easily broken than a man's word, but from fear of some evil consequence upon the rupture.

Whensoever a man transferreth his right, or renounceth it; it is either in consideration of some right reciprocally transferred to himself, or for some other good he hopeth for thereby. For it is a voluntary act; and of the voluntary acts of every man, the object is some *good to himself*. And therefor there be some rights which no man can be understood by any words, or other signs, to have abandoned or transferred. As first a man cannot lay down the right of resisting them that assault him by force, to take away his life; because he cannot be understood to aim thereby, at any good to himself. The same may be said of wounds, and chains, and imprisonment: both because there is no benefit consequent to such patience, as there is to the patience of suffering another to be wounded or imprisoned; as also because a man cannot tell, when he seeth men proceed against him by violence, whether they intend his death or not. And lastly the motive, an end for which this renouncing and transferring of right is introduced, is nothing else but the security of a man's person, in his life, and in the means of so preserving life as not to be weary of it. And therefore if a man by words, or other signs, seem to despoil himself of the end for which those signs were intended, he is not to be understood as if he meant it, or that it was his will, but that he was ignorant of how such words and actions were to be interpreted.

The mutual transferring of right, is that which men call *contract*. . . .

Chapter XVII. Of the Causes, Generations, and Definition of a Commonwealth

The final cause, end, or design of men who naturally love liberty and dominion over others, in the introduction of that restraint upon themselves in which we see them live in commonwealths, is the foresight of their own preservation, and of a more contented life thereby; that is to say, of getting themselves out from that miserable condition of war, which is necessarily consequent, as hath been shown in Chapter XIII, to the natural passions of men, when there is no visible power to keep them in awe, and tie them by fear of punishment to the performance of their covenants and observation of those laws of nature set down in the fourteenth and fifteenth chapters.

For the laws of nature, as justice, equity, modesty, mercy, and, in sum, *doing to others as we would be done to,* of themselves, without the terror of some power to cause them to be observed, are contrary to our natural passions, that carry us to partiality, pride, revenge, and the like. And covenants, without the sword, are but words, and of no strength to secure a man at all. Therefore notwithstanding the laws of nature, which everyone hath then kept, when he has the will to keep them when he can do it safely; if there be no power erected, or not great enough for our security, every man will, and may, lawfully rely on his own strength and art, for caution against all other men. And in all places where men have lived by small families, to rob and spoil one another has been a trade, and so far from being reputed against the law of nature, that the greater spoils they gained, the greater was their honor; and men observed no other laws therein but the laws of honor; that is, to abstain from cruelty, leaving to men their lives, and instruments of husbandry. And as small families did then; so now do cities and kingdoms, which are but greater families, for their own security enlarge their dominions, upon all pretenses of danger and fear of invasion, or assistance that may be given to invaders, and endeavor as much as they can to subdue or weaken their neighbors, by open force and secret arts, for want of other caution, justly; and are remembered for it in after ages with honor.

Nor is it the joining together of a small number of men, that gives them this security; because in small numbers, small additions on the one side or the other make the advantage of strength so great, as is sufficient to carry the victory, and therefore gives encouragement to an invasion. The multitude sufficient to confide in for our security, is not determined by any certain number, but by comparison with the enemy we fear; and is then sufficient, when the odds of the enemy is not of so visible and conspicuous moment, to determine the event of war, as to move him to attempt.

And be there never so great a multitude, yet if their actions be directed according to their particular judgments and particular appetites, they can expect thereby no defense nor protection, neither against a common enemy nor against the injuries of one another. For being distracted in opinions concerning the best use and application of their strength, they do not help but hinder one another; and reduce their strength by mutual opposition to nothing: whereby they are easily, not only subdued by a very few that agree together; but also when there is no common enemy, they make war upon each other, for their particular interests. For if we could suppose a great multitude of men to consent in the observation of justice, and other laws of nature, without a common power to keep them all in awe, we might as well suppose all mankind to do the same; and then there neither would be, nor need to be any civil government or commonwealth at all, because there would be peace without subjection.

Nor is it enough for the security, which men desire should last all the time of their life, that they be governed and directed by one judgment for a limited time, as in one battle or one war. For though they obtain a victory by their unanimous endeavor against a foreign enemy; yet afterwards, when either they have no common enemy, or he that by one part is held for an enemy, is by another part held for a friend, they must needs by the difference of their interests dissolve, and fall again into a war amongst themselves.

It is true that certain living creatures, as bees and ants, live sociably one with another, which are therefore by Aristotle numbered amongst political creatures; and yet have no other direction than their particular judgments and appetites; nor speech, whereby one of them can signify to another what he thinks expedient for the common benefit: and therefore some man may perhaps desire to know why mankind cannot do the same. To which I answer:

First, that men are continually in competition for honor and dignity, which these creatures are not; and consequently amongst men there ariseth on that ground, envy and hatred, and finally war; but amongst these not so.

Secondly, that amongst these creatures, the common good differeth not from the private; and being by nature inclined to their private, they procure thereby the common benefit. But man, whose joy consisteth in comparing himself with other men, can relish nothing but what is eminent.

Thirdly, that these creatures, having not, as man, the use of reason, do not see, nor think they see, any fault in the administration of their common business; whereas amongst men, there are very many that think themselves wiser, and able to govern the public better, than the rest; and these strive to reform and innovate, one this way, another that way; and thereby bring it into distraction and civil war.

Fourthly, that these creatures, though they have some use of voice in making known to one another their desires and other affections; yet they want that art of words by which some men can represent to others, that which is good in the likeness of evil, and evil in the likeness of good, and augment or diminish the apparent greatness of good and evil; discontenting men and troubling their peace at their pleasure.

Fifthly, irrational creatures cannot distinguish between *injury* and *damage;* and therefore as long as they be at ease, they are not offended with their fellows: whereas man is then most troublesome when he is most at ease; for then it is that he loves to shew his wisdom, and control the actions of them that govern the commonwealth.

Lastly, the agreement of these creatures is natural; that of men is by covenant only, which is artificial: and therefore it is no wonder if there be somewhat else required, besides covenant, to make their agreement constant and lasting; which is a common power, to keep them in awe, and to direct their actions to the common benefit.

The only way to erect such a common power, as may be able to defend them from the invasion of foreigners and the injuries of one another, and thereby to secure them in such sort as that, by their own industry, and by the fruits of the earth, they may nourish themselves and live contentedly; is, to confer all their power and strength upon one man, or upon one assembly of men, that may reduce all their wills, by plurality of voices, unto one will: which is as much as to say, to appoint one man, or assembly of men, to bear their person; and everyone to own and acknowledge himself to be author of whatsoever he that so beareth their person, shall act or cause to be acted in those things which concern the common peace and safety; and therein to submit their wills, everyone to his will, and their judgments, to his judgment. This is more than consent, or concord; it is a real unity of them all, in one and the same person, made by covenant of every man with every man, in such manner as if every man should say to every man, "*I authorize and give up my right of governing myself to this man, or to this assembly of men, on this condition, that thou give up thy right to him, and authorize all his actions in like manner.*" This done, the multitude so united in one person, is called a *commonwealth*, in Latin *civitas*. This is the generation of that great LEVIATHAN, or rather, to speak more reverently, of that *mortal god*, to which we owe under the *immortal God*, our peace and defense. For by this authority, given him by every particular man in the commonwealth, he hath the use of so much power and strength conferred on him, that by terror thereof he is enabled to perform the wills of them all, to peace at home and mutual aid against their enemies abroad. And in him consisteth the essence of the commonwealth; which, to define it, is *one person, of whose acts a great multitude, by mutual covenants one with another, have made themselves every one the author, to the end he may use the strength and means of them all, as he shall think expedient, for their peace and common defense.*

And he that carrieth this person, is called *sovereign*, and said to have sovereign power; and everyone besides, his *subject*.

The attaining to this sovereign power is by two ways. One, by natural force; as when a man maketh his children to submit themselves and their children to his government, as being able to destroy them if they refuse; or by war subdueth his enemies to his will, giving them their lives on that condition. The other, is when men agree amongst themselves to submit to some man, or assembly of men, voluntarily, on confidence to be protected by him against all others. This latter, may be called a political commonwealth, or commonwealth by *institution;* and the former, a commowealth by *acquisition.* And first, I shall speak of a commonwealth by institution.

6 / JOHN LOCKE

Of Civil Government: Second Treatise

Chapter II. Of the State of Nature

To understand political power aright, and derive it from its original, we must consider what state all men are naturally in, and that is a state of perfect freedom to order their actions and dispose of their possessions and persons as they think fit, within the bounds of the law of nature, without asking leave, or depending upon the will of any other man.

A state also of equality, wherein all the power and jurisdiction is reciprocal, no one having more than another; there being nothing more evident than that creatures of the same species and rank, promiscuously born to all the same advantages of nature, and the use of the same faculties, should also be equal one amongst another without subordination or subjection, unless the Lord and Master of them all should by any manifest declaration of His will set one above another, and confer on him by an evident and clear appointment an undoubted right to dominion and sovereignty.

This equality of men by nature the judicious Hooker looks upon as so evident in itself and beyond all question, that he makes it the foundation of that obligation to mutual love amongst men on which he builds the duties they owe one another, and from whence he derives the great maxims of justice and charity. His words are:—

"The like natural inducement hath brought men to know that it is no less their duty to love others than themselves; for seeing those things which are equal must needs all have one measure, if I cannot but wish to receive good, even as much at every man's hands as any man can wish unto his own soul, how should I look to have any part of my desire herein satisfied, unless myself be careful to satisfy the like desire, which is undoubtedly in other men weak, being of one and the same nature? To have anything offered them repugnant to this desire, must needs in all respects grieve them as much as me, so that, if I do harm, I must look to

John Locke, *Of Civil Government: Second Treatise,* reprinted in *Social and Political Philosophy* (Garden City, New York: Doubleday and Company, Inc., 1963), Chaps. II, VIII and IX.

suffer, there being no reason that others should show greater measures of love to me than they have by me showed unto them. My desire, therefore, to be loved of my equals in nature as much as possible may be, imposeth upon me a natural duty of bearing to themward fully the like affection; from which relation of equality between ourselves and them that are as ourselves, what several rules and canons natural reason hath drawn for direction of life no man is ignorant."—(Eccl. Pol., lib. i).

But though this be a state of liberty, yet it is not a state of license; though man in that state have an uncontrollable liberty to dispose of his person or possessions, yet he has not liberty to destroy himself, or so much as any creature in his possession, but where some nobler use than its bare preservation calls for it. The state of nature has a law of nature to govern it, which obliges everyone; and reason, which is that law, teaches all mankind who will but consult it, that, being all equal and independent, no one ought to harm another in his life, health, liberty, or possessions. For men being all the workmanship of one omnipotent and infinitely wise Maker—all the servants of one sovereign Master, sent into the world by His order, and about His business—they are His property, whose workmanship they are, made to last during His, not one another's pleasure; and being furnished with like faculties, sharing all in one community of nature, there cannot be supposed any such subordination among us, that may authorize us to destroy one another, as if we were made for one another's uses, as the inferior ranks of creatures are for ours. Everyone, as he is bound to preserve himself, and not to quit his station willfully, so, by the like reason, when his own preservation comes not in competition, ought he, as much as he can, to preserve the rest of mankind, and not, unless it be to do justice on an offender, take away or impair the life, or what tends to the preservation of the life, the liberty, health, limb, or goods of another.

And that all men may be restrained from invading others' rights, and from doing hurt to one another, and the law of nature be observed, which willeth the peace and preservation of all mankind, the execution of the law of nature is in that state put into every man's hand, whereby everyone has a right to punish the transgressors of that law to such a degree as may hinder its violation. For the law of nature would, as all other laws that concern men in this world, be in vain if there were nobody that, in the state of nature, had a power to execute that law, and thereby preserve the innocent and restrain offenders. And if anyone in the state of nature may punish another for any evil he has done, everyone may do so. For in that state of perfect equality, where naturally there is no superiority or jurisdiction of one over another, what any may do in prosecution of that law, everyone must needs have a right to do.

And thus in the state of nature one man comes by a power over another; but yet no absolute or arbitrary power, to use a criminal, when he has got him in his hands, according to the passionate heats or boundless extravagance of his own will; but only to retribute to him so far as calm reason and conscience dictate what is proportionate to his transgression, which is so much as may serve for reparation and restraint. For these two are the only reasons why one man may lawfully do harm to another, which is that we call punishment. In transgressing the law of nature, the offender declares himself to live by another rule than that of common reason and equity, which is that measure God has set to the actions of men, for their mutual security; and so he becomes dangerous to mankind, the tie which is to secure them from injury and violence being slighted and broken by him. Which, being a trespass against the whole species, and the peace and safety of it, provided for by the law of nature, every man upon this score, by the right he hath to preserve mankind in general, may restrain, or, where it is necessary, destroy things noxious to them, and so may bring such evil on anyone who hath transgressed that law, as may make him repent the doing of it, and thereby deter him, and by his example others, from doing the like mischief. And in this case, and upon this ground, every man hath a right to punish the offender, and be executioner of the law of nature.

I doubt not but this will seem a very strange doctrine to some men: but before they condemn it, I desire them to resolve me by what right any prince or state can put to death or punish an alien, for any crime he commits in their country. 'Tis certain their laws, by virtue of any sanction they receive from the promulgated will of the legislative, reach not a stranger: they speak not to him, nor, if they did, is he bound to hearken to them. The legislative authority, by which they are in force over the subjects of that commonwealth, hath no power over him. Those who have the supreme power of making laws in England, France, or Holland, are to an Indian but like the rest of the world—men without authority. And, therefore, if by the law of nature every man hath not a power to punish offenses against it, as he soberly judges the case to require, I see not how the magistrates of any community can punish an alien of another country; since in reference to him they can have no more power than what every man naturally may have over another.

Besides the crime which consists in violating the law, and varying from the right rule of reason, whereby a man so far becomes degenerate, and declares himself to quit the principles of human nature, and to be a noxious creature, there is commonly injury done, and some person or other, some other man receives damage by his transgression, in which case he who hath received any damage, has, besides the right of punishment common to him with other men, a particular right to seek reparation from him that has done it. And any other person who finds it just, may also join with him that is injured, and assist him in recovering from the offender so much as may make satisfaction for the harm he has suffered.

From these two distinct rights—the one of punishing the crime, for restraint and preventing the like offense, which right of punishing is in everybody; the other of taking reparation, which belongs only to the injured party—comes it to pass that the magistrate, who by being magistrate hath the common right of punishing put into his hands, can often, where the public good demands not the execution of the law, remit the punishment of criminal offenses by his own authority, but yet cannot remit the satisfaction due to any private man for the damage he has received. That he who has suffered the damage has a right to demand in his own name, and he alone can remit. The damnified person has this power of appropriating to himself the goods or service of the offender, by right of self-preservation, as every man has a power to punish the crime, to prevent its being committed again, by the right he has of preserving all mankind, and doing all reasonable things he can in order to that end. And thus it is that every man in the state of nature has a power to kill a murderer, both to deter others from doing the like injury, which no reparation can compensate, by the example of the punishment that attends it from everybody, and also to secure men from the attempts of a criminal who having renounced reason, the common rule and measure God hath given to mankind, hath by the unjust violence and slaughter he hath committed upon one, declared war against all mankind, and therefore may be destroyed as a lion or a tiger, one of those wild savage beasts with whom men can have no society nor security. And upon this is grounded that great law of nature. "Whoso sheddeth man's blood, by man shall his blood be shed." And Cain was so fully convinced that everyone had a right to destroy such a criminal, that after the murder of his brother he cries out, "Every one that findeth me shall slay me;" so plain was it writ in the hearts of mankind.

By the same reason may a man in the state of nature punish the lesser breaches of that law. It will perhaps be demanded, With death? I answer, each transgression may be punished to that degree, and with so much severity, as will suffice to make it an ill bargain to the offender, give him cause to repent, and terrify others from doing the like. Every offense that can be committed in the state of nature, may in the state of nature be also punished equally, and as far forth as it may, in a commonwealth. For thought it would be beside my present purpose to enter here into the particulars of the law of nature, or its measures of punishment, yet it is certain there is such a law, and that, too, as intelligible and plain to a rational creature and a studier of that law as the positive laws of commonwealths; nay, possibly plainer, as much as reason is easier to be understood than the fancies and intricate contrivances of men, following contrary and hidden interests put into words; for truly so are a great part of the municipal laws of countries, which are only so far right as they are founded on the law of nature, by which they are to be regulated and interpreted.

To this strange doctrine—viz., that in the state of nature everyone has the executive power of the law of nature—I doubt not but it will be objected that it is unreasonable for men to be judges in their own cases, that self-love will make men partial to themselves and their friends. And on the other side, that ill-nature, passion, and revenge will carry them too far in punishing others; and hence nothing but confusion and disorder will follow; and that therefore God hath certainly appointed government to restrain the partiality and violence of men. I easily grant that civil government is the proper remedy for the inconveniences of the state of nature, which must certainly be great where men may be judges in their own case, since 'tis easy to be imagined that he who was so unjust as to do his brother an injury, will scarce be so just as to condemn himself for it. But I shall desire those who make this objection, to remember that absolute monarchs are but men, and if government is to be the remedy of those evils which necessarily follow from men's being judges in their own cases, and the state of nature is therefore not to be endured, I desire to know what kind of government that is, and how much better it is than the state of nature, where one man commanding a multitude, has the liberty to be judge in his own case, and may do to all his subjects whatever he pleases, without the least question or control of those who execute his pleasure; and in whatsoever he doth, whether led by reason, mistake, or passion, must be submitted to, which men in the state of nature are not bound to do one to another? And if he that judges, judges amiss in his own or any other case, he is answerable for it to the rest of mankind.

'Tis often asked as a mighty objection, Where are, or ever were there, any men in such a state of nature? To which it may suffice as an answer at present: That since all princes and rulers of independent governments all through the world are in a state of nature, 'tis plain the world never was, nor ever will be, without numbers of men in that state. I have named all governors of independent communities, whether they are or are not in league with others. For 'tis not every compact that puts an end to the state of nature between men, but only this one of agreeing together mutually to enter into one community, and make one body politic; other promises and compacts men may make one with another, and yet still be in the state of nature. The promises and bargains for truck, etc., between the two men in Soldania, in or between a Swiss and an Indian, in the woods of America, are binding to them, though they are perfectly in a state of nature in reference to one another. For truth and keeping of faith belong to men as men, and not as members of society.

To those that say there were never any men in the state of nature, I will not only oppose the authority of the judicious Hooker—(Eccl. Pol., lib. i., sect. 10), where he says, "The laws which have been hitherto mentioned," i.e., the laws of nature, "do bind men absolutely, even as they are men, although they have never any settled fellowship, and never any solemn agreement amongst themselves what to do or not to do; but forasmuch as we are not by ourselves sufficient to furnish ourselves with competent store of things needful for such a life as our nature doth desire —a life fit for the dignity of man—therefore to supply those defects and imperfections which are in us, as living single and solely by ourselves, we are naturally induced to seek communion and fellowship with others; this was the cause of men's uniting themselves at first in politic societies"— but I moreover affirm that all men are naturally in that state, and remain so, till by their own consents they make themselves members of some politic society; and I doubt not, in the sequel of this discourse, to make it very clear.

Chapter VIII. Of the Beginning of Political Societies

Men being, as has been said, by nature all free, equal, and independent, no one can be put out of this estate, and subjected to the political power of another, without his own consent, which is done by agreeing with other men to join and unite into a community for their comfortable, safe, and peaceable living one amongst another, in a secure enjoyment of their properties, and a greater security against any that are not of it. This any number of men may do, because it injures not the freedom of the rest; they are left as they were in the liberty of the state of nature. When any number of men have so consented to make one community or government, they are thereby presently incorporated, and make one body politic, wherein the majority have a right to act and conclude the rest.

For when any number of men have, by the consent of every individual, made a community, they have thereby made that community one body, with a power to act as one body, which is only by the will and determination of the majority. For that which acts any community being only the consent of the individuals of it, and it being one body must move one way, it is necessary the body should move that way whither the greater force carries it, which is the consent of the majority; or else it is impossible it should act or continue one body, one community, which the consent of every individual that united into it agreed that it should; and so everyone is bound by that consent to be concluded by the majority. And therefore we see that in assemblies empowered to act by positive laws, where no number is set by that positive law which empowers them, the act of the majority passes for the act of the whole, and of course determines, as having by the law of nature and reason the power of the whole.

And thus every man, by consenting with others to make one body politic under one government, puts himself under an obligation to every one of that society, to submit to the determination of the majority, and to be concluded by it; or else this original compact, whereby he with others incorporates into one society, would signify nothing, and be no compact, if he be left free and under no other ties than he was in before in the state of nature. For what appearance would there be of any compact? What new engagement if he were no farther tied by any decrees of the society, than he himself thought fit, and did actually consent to? This would be still as great a liberty as he himself had before his compact, or anyone else in the state of nature hath, who may submit himself and consent to any acts of it if he thinks fit.

For if the consent of the majority shall not in reason be received as the act of the whole and conclude every individual, nothing but the consent of every individual can make anything to be the act of the whole, which considering the infirmities of health and avocations of business, which in a number, though much less than that of a commonwealth, will necessarily keep many away from the public assembly, and the variety of opinions, and contrariety of interest, which unavoidably happen in all collections of men, 'tis next to impossible ever to be had. And therefore if the coming into society be upon such terms it will be only like Cato's coming into the theater, *tantum ut exiret.* Such a constitution as this would make the mighty leviathan of a shorter duration than the feeblest creatures, and not let it outlast the day it was born in; which cannot be supposed till we can think that rational creatures should desire and constitute societies only to be dissolved. For where the majority cannot conclude the rest, there they cannot act as one body, and consequently will be immediately dissolved again.

Whosoever therefore out of a state of nature unite into a community must be understood to give up all the power necessary to the ends for which they unite into society, to the majority of the community, unless they expressly agreed in any number greater than the majority. And this is done by barely agreeing to unite into one political society, which is all the compact that is, or needs be, between the individuals that enter into or make up a commonwealth. And thus that which begins and actually constitutes any political society is nothing but the consent of any number of freemen capable of a majority to unite and incorporate into such a society. And this is that, and that only, which did or could give beginning to any lawful government in the world.

To this I find two objections made.

First: That there are no instances to be found in story of a company of men independent, and equal one amongst another, that met together and in this way began and set up a government.

Secondly: 'Tis impossible of right that men should do so, because all men being born under government, they are to submit to that, and are not at liberty to begin a new one.

To the first there is this to answer—That it is not at all to be wondered that history gives us but a very little account of men that lived together in the state of nature. The inconveniences of that condition, and the love and want of society, no sooner brought any number of them together, but they presently united and incorporated if they designed to continue together. And if we may not suppose men ever to have been in the state of nature, because we hear not much of them in such a state, we may as well suppose the armies of Salmanasser or Xerxes were never children, because we hear little of them till they were men, and embodied in armies. Government is everywhere antecedent to records, and letters seldom come in amongst a people, till a long continuation of civil society has, by other more necessary arts, provided for their safety, ease, and plenty. And then they begin to look after the history of their founders, and search into their original, when they have outlived the memory of it. For 'tis with commonwealths as with particular persons, they are commonly ignorant of their own birth and infancies. And if they know anything of their original, they are beholden for it to the accidental records that others have kept of it. And those that we have of the beginning of any polities in the world, excepting that of the Jews, where God Himself immediately interposed, and which favors not at all paternal dominion, are all either plain instances of such a beginning as I have mentioned, or at least have manifest footsteps of it.

He must show a strange inclination to deny evident matter of fact, when it agrees not with his hypothesis, who will not allow that the beginning of Rome and Venice were by the uniting together of several men, free and independent one of another, amongst whom there was no natural superiority or subjection. And if Josephus Acosta's word may be taken, he tells us that in many parts of America there was no government at all. "There are great and apparent conjectures," says he, "that these men (speaking of those of Peru) for a long time had neither kings nor commonwealths, but lived in troops, as they do this day in Florida—the Cheriquanas, those of Brazil, and many other nations, which have no certain kings, but, as occasion is offered in peace or war, they choose their captains as they please" (Lib. i. cap. 25). If it be said, that every man there was born subject to his father, or the head of his family, that the subjection due from a child to a father took not away his freedom of uniting into what political society he thought fit, has been already proved; but be that as it will, these men, it is evident, were actually free; and whatever superiority some politicians now would place in any of them, they themselves claimed it not; but, by consent, were all equal, till, by the same consent, they set rulers over themselves. So that their politic societies all began from a voluntary union, and the mutual agreement of men freely acting in the choice of their governors and forms of government.

And I hope those who went away from Sparta, with Palantus, mentioned by Justin, will be allowed to have been freemen independent one of another, and to have set up a government over themselves by their own consent. Thus I have given several examples out of history of people, free and in the state of nature, that, being met together, incorporated and began a commonwealth. And if the want of such instances be an argument to prove that governments were not nor could not be so begun, I suppose the contenders for paternal empire were better let it alone than urge it against natural liberty; for if they can give so many instances out of history of governments began upon paternal right, I think (though at least an argument from what has been to what should of right be of no great force) one might, without any great danger, yield them the cause. But if I might advise them in the case, they would do well not to search too much into the original of governments as they have begun *de facto,* lest they should find at the foundation of most of them something very little favorable to the design they promote, and such a power as they contend for.

But, to conclude: reason being plain on our side that men are naturally free; and the examples of history showing that the governments of the world, that were begun in peace, had their beginning laid on that foundation, and were made by the consent of the people; there can be little room for doubt, either where the right is, or what has been the opinion or practice of mankind about the first erecting of governments. . . .

Every man being, as has been shown, naturally free, and nothing being able to put him into subjection to any earthly power but only his own consent, it is to be considered what shall be understood to be sufficient declaration of a man's consent to make him subject to the laws of any government. There is a common distinction of an express and a tacit consent, which will concern our present case. Nobody doubts but an express consent of any man entering into any society makes him a perfect member of that society, a subject of that government. The difficulty is, what ought to be looked upon as a tacit consent, and how far it binds, i.e., how far anyone shall be looked on to have consented, and thereby submitted to any government, where he has made no expressions of it at all. And to this I say that every man that hath any possession or enjoyment of any part of the dominions of any government doth thereby give his tacit consent, and is as far forth obliged to obedience to the laws of that government during such enjoyment as anyone under it; whether this his possession be of land to him and his heirs for ever, or a lodging only for a week; or whether it be barely traveling freely on the highway; and in effect it reaches as far as the very being of anyone within the territories of that government.

To understand this the better, it is fit to consider that every man when he at first incorporates himself into any commonwealth, he, by his uniting himself thereunto, annexed also, and submits to the community those possessions which he has or shall acquire that do not already belong to any other government; for it would be a direct contradiction for anyone to enter into society with others for the securing and regulating of property, and yet to suppose his land, whose property is to be regulated by the laws of the society, should be exempt from the jurisdiction of that government to which he himself, and the property of the land, is a subject. By the same act, therefore, whereby anyone unites his person, which was before free, to any commonwealth, by the same he unites his possession, which was before free, to it also; and they become, both of them, person and possession, subject to the government and dominion of that commonwealth as long as it hath a being. Whoever therefore from thenceforth by inheritance, purchases, permission, or otherwise, enjoys any part of the land so annexed to, and under the government of that commonwealth, must take it with the condition it is under, that is, of submitting to the government of the commonwealth under whose jurisdiction it is as far forth as any subject of it.

But since the government has a direct jurisdiction only over the land, and reaches the possessor of it (before he has actually incorporated himself in the society), only as he dwells upon, and enjoys that: the obligation anyone is under, by virtue of such enjoyment, to submit to the government, begins and ends with the enjoyment; so that whenever the owner, who has given nothing but such a tacit consent to the government, will by donation, sale, or otherwise, quit the said possession, he is at liberty to go and incorporate himself into any other commonwealth, or to agree with others to begin a new one (*in vacuis locis*) in any part of the world they can find free and unpossessed. Whereas he that has once by actual agreement and any express declaration given his consent to be of any commonweal is perpetually and indispensably obliged to be and remain unalterably a subject to it, and can never be again in the liberty of the state of nature; unless, by any calamity, the government he was under comes to be dissolved, or else by some public acts cuts him off from being any longer a member of it.

But submitting to the laws of any country, living quietly and enjoying privileges and protection under them makes not a man a member of that society. This is only a local protection and homage due to and from all those who, not being in the state of war, come within the territories belonging to any government to all parts whereof the force of its law extends. But this no more makes a man a member of that society a perpetual subject of that commonwealth, than it would make a man a subject to another in whose family he found it convenient to abide for some time; though whilst he continued in it he were obliged to comply with the laws, and submit to the government he found there. And thus we see, that foreigners by living all their lives under another government, and enjoying the privileges and protection of it, though they are bound even in conscience to submit to its administration as far forth as any denizen, yet do not thereby come to be subjects or members of that commonwealth. Nothing can make any man so, but his actually entering into it by positive engagement, and express promise and compact. This is that, which I think, concerning the beginning of political societies, and that consent which makes anyone a member of any commonwealth.

Chapter IX. Of the Ends of Political Society and Government

If man in the state of nature be so free, as has been said, if he be absolute lord of his own person and possessions, equal to the greatest, and subject to nobody, why will he part with his freedom, this empire, and subject himself to the dominion and control of any other power? To which, it is obvious to answer, that though in the state of nature he hath such a right, yet the enjoyment of it is very uncertain, and constantly exposed to the invasions of others. For all being kings as much as he, every man his equal, and the greater part no strict observers of equity and justice, the enjoyment of the property he has in his state is very unsafe, very unsecure. This makes him willing to quit this condition, which, however free, is full of fears and continual dangers; and it is not without reason that he seeks out and is willing to join in society with others, who are already united, or have a mind to unite, for the mutual preservation of their lives, liberties, and estates, which I call by the general name, property.

The great and chief end, therefore, of men's uniting into commonwealths, and putting themselves under government, is the preservation of their property; to which in the state of nature there are many things wanting.

First, There wants an established, settled, known law, received and allowed by common consent to be the standard of right and wrong, and the common measure to decide all controversies between them. For though the law of nature be plain and intelligible to all rational creatures; yet men, being biased by their interest, as well as ignorant for want of study of it, are not apt to allow of it as a law binding to them in the application of it to their particular cases.

Secondly, In the state of nature there wants a known and indifferent judge, with authority to determine all differences according to the established law. For everyone in that state, being both judge and executioner of the law of nature, men being partial to themselves, passion and revenge is very apt to carry them too far, and with too much heat in their own cases, as well as negligence and unconcernedness, to make them too remiss in other men's.

Thirdly, In the state of nature there often wants power to back and support the sentence when right, and to give it due execution. They who by any injustice offend, will seldom fail, where they are able by force to make good their injustice; such resistance many times makes the punishment dangerous, and frequently destructive to those who attempt it.

Thus mankind, notwithstanding all the privileges of the state of nature, being but in an ill condition, while they remain in it, are quickly driven into society. Hence it comes to pass that we seldom find any number of men live any time together in this state. The inconveniences that they are therein exposed to by the irregular and uncertain exercise of the power every man has of punishing the transgressions of others, make them take sanctuary under the established laws of government, and therein seek the preservation of their property. It is this makes them so willingly give up everyone his single power of punishing, to be exercised by such alone, as shall be appointed to it amongst them; and by such rules as the community, or those authorized by them to that purpose, shall agree on. And in this we have the original right and rise of both the legislative and executive power, as well as of the governments and societies themselves.

For in the state of nature, to omit the liberty he has of innocent delights, a man has two powers.

The first is to do whatsoever he thinks fit for the preservation of himself, and others within the permission of the law of nature, by which law, common to them all, he and all the rest of mankind are of one community, make up one society, distinct from all other creatures. And were it not for the corruption and viciousness of degenerate men there would be no need of any other, no necessity that men should separate from this great and natural community, and associate into lesser combinations.

The other power a man has in the state of nature is the power to punish the crimes committed against that law. Both these he gives up when he joins in a private, if I may so call it, or particular political society, and incorporates into any commonwealth separate from the rest of mankind.

The first power, viz., of doing whatsoever he thought fit for the preservation of himself and the rest of mankind, he gives up to be regulated by laws made by the society, so far forth as the preservation of himself and the rest of that society shall require; which laws of the society in many things confine the liberty he had by the law of nature.

Secondly, The power of punishing he wholly gives up, and engages his natural force (which he might before employ in the execution of the law of nature, by his own single authority as he thought fit), to assist the executive power of the society, as the law thereof shall require. For being now in a new state, wherein he is to enjoy many conveniences, from the labor, assistance, and society of others in the same community, as well as protection from its whole strength; he has to part also with as much of his natural liberty, in providing for himself, as the good, prosperity and safety of the society shall require; which is not only necessary but just, since the other members of the society do the like.

But though men when they enter into society give up the equality, liberty and executive power they had in the state of nature into the hands of the society, to be so far disposed of by the legislative as the good of the society shall require; yet it being only with an intention in everyone the better to preserve himself, his liberty and property (for no rational creature can be supposed to change his condition with an intention to be worse), the power of the society, or legislative constituted by them, can never be supposed to extend farther than the common good, but is obliged to secure everyone's property by providing against those three defects above-mentioned that made the state of nature so unsafe and uneasy. And so whoever has the legislative or supreme power of any commonwealth is bound to govern by established standing laws, promulgated and known to the people, and not by extemporary decrees; by indifferent and upright judges, who are to decide controversies by those laws; and to employ the force of the community at home only in the execution of such laws, or abroad, to prevent or redress foreign injuries, and secure the community from inroads and invasion. And all this to be directed to no other end but the peace, safety, and public good of the people.

7 / REINHOLD NIEBUHR

Man and Society: The Art of Living Together

Though human society has roots which lie deeper in history than the beginning of human life, men have made comparatively but little progress in solving the problem of their aggregate existence. Each century originates a new complexity and each new generation faces a new vexation in it. For all the centuries of experience, men have not yet learned how to live together without compounding their vices and covering each other "with mud and with blood." The society in which each man lives is at once the basis for, and the nemesis of, that fulness of life which each man seeks. However much human ingenuity may increase the treasures which nature provides for the satisfaction of human needs, they can never be sufficient to satisfy all human wants; for man, unlike other creatures, is gifted and cursed with an imagination which extends his appetites beyond the requirements of subsistence. Human society will never escape the problem of the equitable distribution of the physical and cultural goods which provide for the preservation and fulfillment of human life.

Unfortunately the conquest of nature, and the consequent increase in nature's beneficences to man, have not eased, but rather accentuated, the problem of justice. The same technology, which drew the fangs of nature's enmity of man, also created a society in which the intensity and extent of social cohesion has been greatly increased, and in which power is so unevenly distributed, that justice has become a more difficult achievement. Perhaps it is man's sorry fate, suffering from ills which have their source in the inadequacies of both nature and human society, that the tools by which he eliminates the former should become the means of increasing the latter. That, at least, has been his fate up to the present hour; and it may be that there will be no salvation for the human spirit from the more and more painful burdens of social injustice until the ominous tendency in human history has resulted in perfect tragedy.

Reinhold Niebuhr, "Man and Society: The Art of Living Together," in *Moral Man and Immoral Society* (New York: Charles Scribner's Sons, 1932), renewal Copyright © 1960, Reinhold Niebuhr, pp. 1–22. Reprinted with the permission of the publisher.

Human nature is not wanting in certain endowments for the solution of the problem of human society. Man is endowed by nature with organic relations to his fellow-men; and natural impulse prompts him to consider the needs of others even when they compete with his own. With the higher mammals man shares concern for his offspring; and the long infancy of the child created the basis for an organic social group in the earliest period of human history. Gradually intelligence, imagination, and the necessities of social conflict increased the size of this group. Natural impulse was refined and extended until a less obvious type of consanguinity than an immediate family relationship could be made the basis of social solidarity. Since those early days the units of human co-operation have constantly grown in size, and the areas of significant relationships between the units have likewise increased. Nevertheless conflict between the national units remains as a permanent rather than a passing characteristic of their relations to each other; and each national unit finds it increasingly difficult to maintain either peace or justice within its common life.

While it is possible for intelligence to increase the range of benevolent impulse, and thus prompt a human being to consider the needs and rights of other than those to whom he is bound by organic and physical relationship, there are definite limits in the capacity of ordinary mortals which makes it impossible for them to grant to others what they claim for themselves. Though educators ever since the eighteenth century have given themselves to the fond illusion that justice through voluntary co-operation waited only upon a more universal or a more adequate educational enterprise, there is good reason to believe that the sentiments of benevolence and social goodwill will never be so pure or powerful, and the rational capacity to consider the rights and needs of others in fair competition with our own will never be so fully developed as to create the possibility for the anarchistic millennium which is the social utopia, either explicit or implicit, of all intellectual or religious moralists.

All social co-operation on a larger scale than the most intimate social group requires a measure of coercion. While no state can maintain its unity purely by coercion neither can it preserve itself without coercion. Where the factor of mutual consent is strongly developed, and where standardised and approximately fair methods of adjudicating and resolving conflicting interests within an organised group have been established, the coercive factor in social life is frequently covert, and becomes apparent only in moments of crisis and in the group's policy toward recalcitrant individuals. Yet it is never absent. Divergence of interest, based upon geographic and functional differences within a society, is bound to create different social philosophies and political attitudes which goodwill and intelligence may partly, but never completely, harmonise.

Ultimately, unity within an organised social group, or within a federation of such groups, is created by the ability of a dominant group to impose its will. Politics will, to the end of history, be an area where conscience and power meet, where the ethical and coercive factors of human life will interpenetrate and work out their tentative and uneasy compromises. The democratic method of resolving social conflict, which some romanticists hail as a triumph of the ethical over the coercive factor, is really much more coercive than at first seems apparent. The majority has its way, not because the minority believes that the majority is right (few minorities are willing to grant the majority the moral prestige of such a concession), but because the votes of the majority are a symbol of its social strength. Whenever a minority believes that it has some strategic advantage which outweighs the power of numbers, and whenever it is sufficiently intent upon its ends, or desperate enough about its position in society, it refuses to accept the dictates of the majority. Military and economic overlords and revolutionary zealots have been traditionally contemptuous of the will of majorities. Recently Trotsky advised the German communists not to be dismayed by the greater voting strength of the fascists since in the inevitable revolution the power of industrial workers, in charge of the nation's industrial process, would be found much more significant than the social power of clerks and other petty bourgeoisie who comprised the fascist movement.

There are, no doubt, rational and ethical factors in the democratic process. Contending social forces presumably use the forum rather than the battleground to arbitrate their differences in the democratic method, and thus differences are resolved by moral suasion and a rational adjustment of rights to rights. If political issues were really abstract questions of social policy upon which unbiased citizens were asked to commit themselves, the business of voting and the debate which precedes the election might actually be regarded as an educational programme in which a social group discovers its common mind. But the fact is that political opinions are inevitably rooted in economic interests of some kind or other, and only comparatively few citizens can view a problem of social policy without regard to their interest. Conflicting interests therefore can never be completely resolved; and minorities will yield only because the majority has come into control of the police power of the state and may, if the occasion arises, augment that power by its own military strength. Should a minority regard its own strength, whether economic or martial, as strong enough to challenge the power of the majority, it may attempt to wrest control of the state apparatus from the majority, as in the case of the fascist movement in Italy. Sometimes it will resort to armed conflict, even if the prospects of victory are none too bright, as in the instance of the American Civil War, in which the

Southern planting interests, outvoted by a combination of Eastern industrialists and Western agrarians, resolved to protect their peculiar interests and privileges by a forceful dissolution of the national union. The coercive factor is, in other words, always present in politics. If economic interests do not conflict too sharply, if the spirit of accommodation partially resolves them, and if the democratic process has achieved moral prestige and historic dignity, the coercive factor in politics may become too covert to be visible to the casual observer. Nevertheless, only a romanticist of the purest water could maintain that a national group ever arrives at a "common mind" or becomes conscious of a "general will" without the use of either force or the threat of force. This is particularly true of nations, but it is also true, though in a slighter degree, of other social groups. Even religious communities, if they are sufficiently large, and if they deal with issues regarded as vital by their members, resort to coercion to preserve their unity. Religious organisations have usually availed themselves of a covert type of coercion (excommunication and the interdict) or they have called upon the police power of the state.

The limitations of the human mind and imagination, the inability of human beings to transcend their own interests sufficiently to envisage the interests of their fellow-men as clearly as they do their own makes force an inevitable part of the process of social cohesion. But the same force which guarantees peace also makes for injustice. "Power," said Henry Adams, "is poison"; and it is a poison which blinds the eyes of moral insight and lames the will of moral purpose. The individual or the group which organises any society, however social its intentions or pretensions, arrogates an inordinate portion of social privilege to itself. The two most obvious types of power are the military and the economic, though in primitive society the power of the priest, partly because he dispenses supernatural benefits and partly because he establishes public order by methods less arduous than those of the soldier, vies with that of the soldier and the landlord. The chief difference between the agrarian civilisations, which lasted from the rise of ancient Babylon and Egypt to the fall of European feudalism, and the commercial and industrial civilisations of today is that in the former the military power is primary, and in the latter it has become secondary, to economic power. In agrarian civilisations the soldier becomes the landlord. In more primitive periods he may claim the land by his own military prowess. In later periods a grateful sovereign bestowed land upon the soldiers who defended his realm and consolidated his dominion. The soldier thus gained the economic security and the social prestige which could be exploited in further martial service to his sovereign. The business man and industrial overlord are gradually usurping the position of eminence and privilege once held by the soldier and the priest. In most European nations their ascendancy over the landed aristocrat of military traditions is not as complete as in America, which has no feudal traditions. In present-day Japan the military caste is still so powerful that it threatens to destroy the rising power of the commercial groups. On the pre-eminence of economic power in an industrial civilisation and its ability to make the military power its tool we shall have more to say later. Our interest at the moment is to record that any kind of significant social power develops social inequality. Even if history is viewed from other than equalitarian perspectives, and it is granted that differentials in economic rewards are morally justified and socially useful, it is impossible to justify the degree of inequality which complex societies inevitably create by the increased centralisation of power which develops with more elaborate civilisations. The literature of all ages is filled with rational and moral justifications of these inequalities, but most of them are specious. If superior abilities and services to society deserve special rewards it may be regarded as axiomatic that the rewards are always higher than the services warrant. No impartial society determines the rewards. The men of power who control society grant these perquisites to themselves. Whenever special ability is not associated with power, as in the case of the modern professional man, his excess of income over the average is ridiculously low in comparison with that of the economic overlords, who are the real centres of power in an industrial society. Most rational and social justifications of unequal privilege are clearly afterthoughts. The facts are created by the disproportion of power which exists in a given social system. The justifications are usually dictated by the desire of the men of power to hide the nakedness of their greed, and by the inclination of society itself to veil the brutal facts of human life from itself. This is a rather pathetic but understandable inclination; since the facts of man's collective life easily rob the average individual of confidence in the human enterprise. The inevitable hypocrisy, which is associated with all of the collective activities of the human race, springs chiefly from this source: that individuals have a moral code which makes the actions of collective man an outrage to their conscience. They therefore invent romantic and moral interpretations of the real facts, preferring to obscure rather than reveal the true character of their collective behavior. Sometimes they are as anxious to offer moral justifications for the brutalities from which they suffer as for those which they commit. The fact that the hypocrisy of man's group behavior, about which we shall have much more to say later, expresses itself not only in terms of self-justification but in terms of moral justification of human behavior in general, symbolises one of the tragedies of the human spirit: its inability to conform its collective life to its individual ideals. As individuals, men believe that they ought to love and serve each other and establish justice between each other. As racial, economic and national groups they take for themselves, whatever their power can command.

The disproportion of power in a complex society began with the transmutation of the pastoral to the agrarian economy, and which destroyed the simple equalitarianism and communism of the hunting and nomadic social organisation, has perpetuated social injustice in every form through all the ages. Types of power have changed, and gradations of social inequality have varied, but the essential facts have remained unchanged. In Egypt the land was divided into three parts, respectively claimed by the king, the soldiers and the priests. The common people were landless. In Peru, where a rather remarkable despotic communism developed, the king owned all the land but gave the use of one third to the people, another third to the priests and kept one third for himself and his nobles. Needless to say, the commoners were expected to till not only their third but the other two thirds of the lands. In China, where the emperor maintained the right of eminent domain for many centuries, defeating the experiment in feudalism in the third century A.D., and giving each family inalienable rights in the soil which nominally belonged to him, there has probably been less inequality than in any other ancient empire. Nevertheless slavery persisted until a very recent day. In Japan the emperor gave the land to feudal princes, who again sublet it to the inferior nobility. The power of the feudal clans, originating in martial prowess and perpetuated through land ownership, has remained practically unbroken to this day, though the imperial power was ostensibly restored in the latter part of the last century, and growing industry has developed a class of industrial overlords who were partly drawn from the landed aristocracy. In Rome the absolute property rights of the *pater familias* of the patrician class gave him power which placed him on top of the social pyramid. All other classes, beginning with his own women and children, then the plebeians and finally the slaves, took their places in the various lower rungs of the social ladder. The efforts of the Gracchi to destroy the ever growing inequality, which resulted from power breeding more power, proved abortive, as did the land reforms of Solon and Lycurgus in Greece. Military conquest gave the owners of the Roman *latifundia* hundreds of slaves by the labor of which they reduced the small freeholders to penury. Thus the decay of the Roman Empire was prepared; for a state which has only lords and slaves lacks the social cement to preserve it from internal disintegration and the military force to protect it from external aggression.

All through history one may observe the tendency of power to destroy its very *raison d'être*. It is suffered because it achieves internal unity and creates external defenses for the nation. But it grows to such proportions that it destroys the social peace of the state by the animosities which its exactions arouse, and it enervates the sentiment of patriotism by robbing the common man of the basic privileges which might bind him to his nation. The words attributed by Plutarch to Tiberius Gracchus reveal the hollowness of the pretensions by which the powerful classes enlist their slaves in the defense of their dominions: "The wild beasts in Italy had at least their lairs, dens and caves whereto they might retreat; whereas the men who fought and died for that land had nothing in it save air and light, but were forced to wander to and fro with their wives and children, without resting place or house wherein they might lodge. . . . The poor folk go to war, to fight and to die for the delights, riches and superfluities of others."[1] In the long run these pretensions are revealed and the sentiment of patriotism is throttled in the breasts of the disinherited. The privileged groups who are outraged by the want of patriotism among modern proletarians could learn the cause of proletarian internationalism by a little study of history. "It is absurd," says Diodorus Siculus, speaking of Egypt, "to entrust the defence of a country to people who own nothing in it,"[2] a reflection which has applicability to other ages and other nations than his own. Russian communists of pure water pour their scorn upon European socialists, among whom patriotism outweighed class loyalty in the World War. But there is a very simple explanation for the nationalism of European socialists. They were not as completely, or at least not as obviously, disinherited as their Russian comrades.

The history of slavery in all ancient civilisations offers an interesting illustration of the development of social injustice with the growing size and complexity of the social unit. In primitive tribal organisation rights are essentially equal within the group, and no rights, or only very minimum rights are recognised outside of the group. The captives of war are killed. With the growth of agriculture the labor of captives becomes useful, and they are enslaved rather than destroyed. Since rightless individuals are introduced into the intimate life of the group, equality of rights disappears; and the inequality remains even after the slaves are no longer regarded as enemies and have become completely organic to the life of the group. The principle of slavery once established, is enlarged to include debt slaves, victims of the growing property system. The membership of the debt slaves in the original community at first guarantees them rights which the captive slaves do not enjoy. But the years gradually wipe out these distinctions and the captive slaves are finally raised to the status of debtor slaves. Thus the more humane attitudes which men practice within their social groups gains a slight

---

[1] Plutarch, *The Parallel Lives*, see "Tiberius Gracchus," Loeb Classical Library, Vol. X.

[2] Quoted by C. J. M. Letourneau, *Property; Its Origin and Development*, p. 277.

victory over the more brutal attitudes towards individuals in other groups. But the victory is insignificant in comparison with the previous introduction of the morals of inter-group relations into the intimate life of the group by the very establishment of slavery. Barbarism knows little or nothing of class distinctions. These are created and more and more highly elaborated by civilisation. The social impulses, with which men are endowed by nature are not powerful enough, even when they are extended by a growing intelligence, to apply with equal force toward all members of a large community. The distinction between slave and freeman is only one of the many social gradations which higher societies develop. They are determined in every case by the disproportion of power, military and economic, which develops in the more complex civilisations and in the larger social units. A growing social intelligence may be affronted by them and may protest against them, but it changes them only slightly. Neither the prophets of Israel nor the social idealists of Egypt and Babylon, who protested against social injustice, could make their vision of a just society effective. The man of power, though humane impulse may awaken in him, always remains something of the beast of prey. He may be generous within his family, and just within the confines of the group which shares his power and privilege. With only rare exceptions, his highest moral attitude toward members of other groups is one of warlike sportsmanship toward those who equal his power and challenge it, and one of philanthropic generosity toward those who possess less power and privilege. His philanthropy is a perfect illustration of the curious compound of the brutal and the moral which we find in all human behavior; for his generosity is at once a display of his power and an expression of his pity. His generous impulses freeze within him if his power is challenged or his generosities are accepted without grateful humility. If individual men of power should achieve more ethical attitudes than the one described, it remains nevertheless typical for them as a class; and is their practically unvarying attitude when they express themselves not as individuals but as a group.

The rise of modern democracy, beginning with the Eighteenth Century, is sometimes supposed to have substituted the consent of the governed for the power of royal families and aristocratic classes as the cohesive force of national society. This judgment is partly true but not nearly as true as the uncritical devotees of modern democracy assume. The doctrine that government exists by the consent of the governed, and the democratic technique by which the suffrage of the governed determines the policy of the state, may actually reduce the coercive factor in national life, and provide for peaceful and gradual methods of resolving conflicting social interests and changing political institutions. But the creeds and institutions of democracy have never become fully divorced from the special interests of the commercial classes who conceived and developed them. It was their interest to destroy political restraint upon economic activity, and they therefore weakened the authority of the state and made it more pliant to their needs. With the increased centralisation of economic power in the period of modern industrialism, this development merely means that society as such does not control economic power as much as social well-being requires; and that the economic, rather than the political and military, power has become the significant coercive force of modern society. Either it defies the authority of the state or it bends the institutions of the state to its own purposes. Political power has been made responsible, but economic power has become irresponsible in society. The net result is that political power has been made more responsible to economic power. It is, in other words, again the man of power or the dominant class which binds society together, regulates its processes, always paying itself inordinate rewards for its labors. The difference is that owners of factories, rather than owners of land, exert the power, and that it is more purely economic and less military than that which was wielded by the landed aristocrats. Needless to say, it is not completely divorced from military power. It may on occasion appropriate the police and the army of the state to defend its interests against internal and external foes. The military power has become the hired servant and is no longer the progenitor of economic ownership.

There will be opportunity to discuss these modern developments in the growth and use of power in society at greater length in another chapter. At the same time it will be possible to do justice to those aspects of the democratic creed which transcend the interests of the commercial and industrial classes and add a permanent contribution to the history of social life. At present it must suffice to discount a still widely held conviction that the democratic movement has given society a permanent solution for its vexing problems of power and justice.

Society is perennially harassed not only by the fact that the coercive factors in social life (which the limitations of human intelligence and imagination make inevitable) create injustice in the process of establishing peace; but also by the tendency of the same factors, which make for an uneasy peace within a social group, to aggravate inter-group conflict. Power sacrifices justice to peace within the community and destroys peace between communities. It is not true that only kings make war. The common members of any national community, while sentimentally desiring peace, nevertheless indulge impulses of envy, jealousy, pride, bigotry, and greed which make for conflict between communities. Neither is it true that modern wars are caused solely by the modern capitalistic system with its disproportion of economic power and privilege. Without an almost miraculous increase in human intelligence it will not be easy to resolve the conflicts of interest between various national communities even after the special privilege and the unequal power, which now aggravate international conflicts, have been destroyed. Nevertheless the whole history of mankind bears testimony to the fact that the power which prevents anarchy in intra-group relations encourages anarchy in intergroup relations. The kings of old claimed the loyalty and the sacrifices of their subjects in conflicts with other tyrants, in which the interests of the state and the welfare of the people were completely subordinated to the capricious purposes of the monarch. No personal whim, which a human being might indulge, is excluded from the motives, which have prompted monarchs to shed the blood of their unhappy subjects. Pride, jealousy, disappointed love, hurt vanity, greed for greater treasures, lust for power over larger dominions, petty animosities between royal brothers or between father and son, momentary passions and childish whims, these all have been, not the occasional but the perennially recurring, causes and occasions of international conflict. The growing intelligence of mankind and the increased responsibility of monarchs to their people have placed a check upon the caprice, but not upon the self-interest, of the men of power. They may still engage in social conflict for the satisfaction of their pride and vanity provided they can compound their personal ambitions with, and hallow them by, the ambitions of their group, and the pitiful vanities and passions of the individuals who compose the group. The story of Napoleon belongs to modern and not to ancient history. He could bathe Europe in blood for the sake of gratifying his overweening lust for power, as long as he could pose as the tool of French patriotism and as the instrument of revolutionary fervor. The fact that the democratic sentiment, opposed to the traditional absolutisms of Europe, could be exploited to create a tyranny more sanguinary and terrible than those which it sought ostensibly to destroy; and that the dream of equality, liberty and fraternity of the French Revolution could turn so quickly into the nightmare of Napoleonic imperialism is a tragic revelation of the inadequacies of the human resources with which men must try to solve the problems of their social life. The childish vanity of the German Emperor, who wanted a large navy so that he could stand on equal footing with his royal English uncle at naval manœuvres, helped to make the World War inevitable.[3] He would not have been permitted to indulge this vanity however had it not seemed compatible with the prejudices of his people and the economic necessities of a growing empire. Theodore Roosevelt belonged to a little junta which foisted the Spanish-American War upon the American

---

[3] See *Memoirs of Prince Von Bülow*, Vol. III, p. 204.

people. The ambition and vanity which prompted him could be veiled and exalted because the will-to-power of an adolescent nation and the frustrated impulses of pugnacity and martial ardor of the pitiful little "men in the street" could find in him symbolic expression and vicarious satisfaction. The need of the modern industrial overlord for raw materials and markets, and rivalry over control of the undeveloped and unexploited portions of the earth are the occasion of modern wars. Yet the ambitions and greed of dominant economic groups within each nation are not the only cause of international conflict. Every social group tends to develop imperial ambitions which are aggravated, but not caused solely, by the lusts of its leaders and privileged groups. Every group, as every individual, has expansive desires which are rooted in the instinct of survival and soon extend beyond it. The will-to-live becomes the will-to-power. Only rarely does nature provide armors of defense which cannot be transmuted into instruments of aggression. The frustrations of the average man, who can never realise the power and the glory which his imagination sets as the ideal, makes him the more willing tool and victim of the imperial ambitions of his group. His frustrated individual ambitions gain a measure of satisfaction in the power and the aggrandisement of his nation. The will-to-power of competing national groups is the cause of the international anarchy which the moral sense of mankind has thus far vainly striven to overcome. Since some nations are more powerful than others, they will at times prevent anarchy by effective imperialism, which in our industrial period has become more covert than overt. But the peace is gained by force and is always an uneasy and an unjust one. As powerful classes organise a nation, so powerful nations organise a crude society of nations. In each case the peace is a tentative one because it is unjust. It has been achieved only partially by a mutual accommodation of conflicting interests and certainly not by a rational and moral adjustment of rights. It will last only until those, who feel themselves too weak to challenge strength, will become, or will feel themselves, powerful enough to do so. It is not necessary to discount the moral influence of the League of Nations completely or to deny that it represents certain gains in the rational and moral organisation of society, to recognise that the peace of contemporary Europe is maintained by the force of French arms and that it will last only as long as the ingenuities of French statesmanship can maintain the combination of political and military forces which holds the people, who feel themselves defrauded by the Versailles Treaty, in check. Significantly the same power, which prompts the fear that prevents immediate action, also creates the mounting hatred which guarantees ultimate rebellion.

Thus society is in a perpetual state of war. Lacking moral and rational resources to organise its life, without resort to coercion, except in the most immediate and intimate social groups, men remain the victims of the individuals, classes and nations by whose force a momentary coerced unity is achieved, and further conflicts are as certainly created. The fact that the coercive factor in society is both necessary and dangerous seriously complicates the whole task of securing both peace and justice. History is a long tale of abortive efforts toward the desired end of social cohesion and justice in which failure was usually due either to the effort to eliminate the factor of force entirely or to an undue reliance upon it. Complete reliance upon it means that new tyrants usurp the places of eminence from which more traditional monarchs are cast down. Tolstoian pacifists and other advocates of non-resistance, noting the evils which force introduces into society, give themselves to the vain illusion that it can be completely eliminated, and society organised upon the basis of anarchistic principles. Their conviction is an illusion, because there are definite limits of moral goodwill and social intelligence beyond which even the most vital religion and the most astute educational programme will not carry a social group, whatever may be possible for individuals in an intimate society. The problem which society faces is clearly one of reducing force by increasing the factors which make for a moral and rational adjustment of life to life; of bringing such force as is still necessary under responsibility of the whole of society; of destroying the kind of power which cannot be made socially responsible (the power which resides in economic ownership for instance); and of bringing forces of moral self-restraint to bear upon types of power which can never be brought completely under social control. Every one of these methods has its definite limitations. Society will probably never be sufficiently intelligent to bring all power under its control. The stupidity of the average man will permit the oligarch, whether economic or political, to hide his real purposes from the scrutiny of his fellows and to withdraw his activities from effective control. Since it is impossible to count on enough moral goodwill among those who possess irresponsible power to sacrifice it for the good of the whole, it must be destoryed by coercive methods and these will always run the peril of introducing new forms of injustice in place of those abolished. There is, for instance, as yet power to sacrifice it for the good of the whole, it must be destroyed by means less rigorous than communism has employed; but there is also no proof that communistic oligarchs, once the idealistic passion of a revolutionary period is spent, will be very preferable to the capitalistic oligarchs, whom they are to displace. Since the increasing complexity of society makes it impossible to bring all those who are in charge of its intricate techniques and processes, and who are therefore in possession of social power, under complete control, it will always be necessary to rely partly upon the honesty and self-restraint of those who are not socially restrained. But here again, it will never be possible to insure moral antidotes sufficiently potent to destroy the deleterious effects of the poison of power upon character. The future peace and justice of society therefore depend upon, not one but many, social strategies, in all of which moral and coercive factors are compounded in varying degrees. So difficult is it to avoid the Scylla of despotism and the Charybdis of anarchy that it is safe to hazard the prophecy that the dream of perpetual peace and brotherhood for human society is one which will never be fully realised. It is a vision prompted by the conscience and insight of individual man, but incapable of fulfillment by collective man. It is like all true religious visions, possible of approximation but not of realisation in actual history. The vitality of the vision is the measure of man's rebellion against the fate which binds his collective life to the world of nature from which his soul recoils. The vision can be kept alive only by permitting it to overreach itself. But meanwhile collective man, operating on the historic and mundane scene, must content himself with a more modest goal. His concern for some centuries to come is not the creation of an ideal society in which there will be uncoerced and perfect peace and justice, but a society in which there will be enough justice, and in which coercion will be sufficiently non-violent to prevent his common enterprise from issuing into complete disaster. That goal will seem too modest for the romanticists; but the romanticists have so little understanding for the perils in which modern society lives, and overestimate the moral resources at the disposal of the collective human enterprise so easily, that any goal regarded as worthy of achievement by them must necessarily be beyond attainment.

8 / SIGMUND FREUD

Civilization and Its Discontents

Psycho-analytic work has shown us that it is precisely these frustrations of sexual life which people known as neurotics cannot tolerate. The neurotic creates substitutive satisfactions for himself in his symptoms, and these either cause him suffering in themselves or become sources of suffering for him by raising difficulties in his relations with his environment and the society he belongs to. The latter fact is easy to understand;

the former presents us with a new problem. But civilization demands other sacrifices besides that of sexual satisfaction.

We have treated the difficulty of cultural development as a general difficulty of development by tracing it to the inertia of the libido, to its disinclination to give up an old position for a new one.[1] We are saying much the same thing when we derive the antithesis between civilization and sexuality from the circumstance that sexual love is a relationship between two individuals in which a third can only be superfluous or disturbing, whereas civilization depends on relationships between a considerable number of individuals. When a love-relationship is at its height there is no room left for any interest in the environment; a pair of lovers are sufficient to themselves, and do not even need the child they have in common to make them happy. In no other case does Eros so clearly betray the core of his being, his purpose of making one out of more than one; but when he has achieved this in the proverbial way through the love of two human beings, he refuses to go further.

So far, we can quite well imagine a cultural community consisting of double individuals like this, who, libidinally satisfied in themselves, are connected with one another through the bonds of common work and common interests. If this were so, civilization would not have to withdraw any energy from sexuality. But this desirable state of things does not, and never did, exist. Reality shows us that civilization is not content with the ties we have so far allowed it. It aims at binding the members of the community together in a libidinal way as well and employs every means to that end. It favours every path by which strong identifications can be established between the members of the community, and it summons up aim-inhibited libido on the largest scale so as to strengthen the communal bond by relations of friendship. In order for these aims to be fulfilled, a restriction upon sexual life is unavoidable. But we are unable to understand what the necessity is which forces civilization along this path and which causes its antagonism to sexuality. There must be some disturbing factor which we have not yet discovered.

The clue may be supplied by one of the ideal demands, as we have called them,[2] of civilized society. It runs: 'Thou shalt love thy neighbour as thyself.' It is known throughout the world and is undoubtedly older than Christianity, which puts it forward as its proudest claim. Yet it is certainly not very old; even in historical times it was still strange to

---

[1] [Sigmund Freud, selections from *Civilization and Its Discontents*, translated from the German and edited by James Strachey (New York: W. W. Norton and Company Inc., 1961), pp. 55–63. Reprinted with the permission of the publisher. For some remarks on Freud's use of the concept of 'psychical inertia' in general, see an Editor's footnote to Freud, 1915f, *Standard Ed.*, 14, 272.]

[2] [Cf. also ' "Civilized" Sexual Morality' (1908d), *Standard Ed.*, 9, 199.]

mankind. Let us adopt a naïve attitude towards it, as though we were hearing it for the first time; we shall be unable then to suppress a feeling of surprise and bewilderment. Why should we do it? What good will it do us? But, above all, how shall we achieve it? How can it be possible? My love is something valuable to me which I ought not to throw away without reflection. It imposes duties on me for whose fulfilment I must be ready to make sacrifices. If I love someone, he must deserve it in some way. (I leave out of account the use he may be to me, and also his possible significance for me as a sexual object, for neither of these two kinds of relationship comes into question where the precept to love my neighbour is concerned.) He deserves it if he is so like me in important ways that I can love myself in him; and he deserves it if he is so much more perfect than myself that I can love my ideal of my own self in him. Again, I have to love him if he is my friend's son, since the pain my friend would feel if any harm came to him would be my pain too—I should have to share it. But if he is a stranger to me and if he cannot attract me by any worth of his own or any significance that he may already have acquired for my emotional life, it will be hard for me to love him. Indeed, I should be wrong to do so, for my love is valued by all my own people as a sign of my preferring them, and it is an injustice to them if I put a stranger on a par with them. But if I am to love him (with this universal love) merely because he, too, is an inhabitant of this earth, like an insect, an earth-worm or a grass-snake, then I fear that only a small modicum of my love will fall to his share—not by any possibility as much as, by the judgement of my reason, I am entitled to retain for myself. What is the point of a precept enunciated with so much solemnity if its fulfilment cannot be recommended as reasonable?

On closer inspection, I find still further difficulties. Not merely is this stranger in general unworthy of my love; I must honestly confess that he has more claim to my hostility and even my hatred. He seems not to have the least trace of love for me and shows me not the slightest consideration. If it will do him any good he has no hesitation in injuring me, nor does he ask himself whether the amount of advantage he gains bears any proportion to the extent of the harm he does to me. Indeed, he need not even obtain an advantage; if he can satisfy any sort of desire by it, he thinks nothing of jeering at me, insulting me, slandering me and showing his superior power; and the more secure he feels and the more helpless I am, the more certainly I can expect him to behave like this to me. If he behaves differently, if he shows me consideration and forbearance as a stranger, I am ready to treat him in the same way, in any case and quite apart from any precept. Indeed, if this grandiose commandment had run 'Love thy neighbour as thy neighbour loves thee', I should not take exception to it. And there is a second commandment, which seems to me even more incomprehensible and arouses still stronger opposition in me. It is 'Love thine enemies'. If I think it over, however, I see that I am wrong in treating it as a greater imposition. At bottom it is the same thing.[3]

I think I can now hear a dignified voice admonishing me: 'It is precisely because your neighbour is not worthy of love, and is on the contrary your enemy, that you should love him as yourself.' I then understand that the case is one like that of *Credo quia absurdum*.[4]

Now it is very probable that my neighbour, when he is enjoined to love me as himself, will answer exactly as I have done and will repel me for the same reasons. I hope he will not have the same objective grounds for doing so, but he will have the same idea as I have. Even so, the behaviour of human beings shows differences, which ethics, disregarding the fact that such differences are determined, classifies as 'good' or 'bad'. So long as these undeniable differences have not been removed, obedience to high ethical demands entails damage to the aims of civilization, for it puts a positive premium on being bad. One is irresistibly reminded of an incident in the French Chamber when capital punishment was being debated. A member had been passionately supporting its abolition and his speech was being received with tumultuous applause, when a voice from the hall called out: 'Que messieurs les assassins commencent!'[5]

The element of truth behind all this, which people are so ready to disavow, is that men are not gentle creatures who want to be loved, and who at the most can defend themselves if they are attacked; they are, on the contrary, creatures among whose instinctual endowments is to be reckoned a powerful share of aggressiveness. As a result, their neighbour is for them not only a potential helper or sexual object, but also someone who tempts them to satisfy their aggressiveness on him, to exploit his capacity for work without compensation, to use him sexually without his consent, to seize his possessions, to humiliate him, to cause him pain, to torture and to kill him. *Homo homini lupus*.[6] Who, in the face of all his

---

[3] A great imaginative writer may permit himself to give expression—jokingly, at all events—to psychological truths that are severely proscribed. Thus Heine confesses: 'Mine is a most peaceable disposition. My wishes are: a humble cottage with a thatched roof, but a good bed, good food, the freshest milk and butter, flowers before my window, and a few fine trees before my door; and if God wants to make my happiness complete, he will grant me the joy of seeing some six or seven of my enemies hanging from those trees. Before their death I shall, moved in my heart, forgive them all the wrong they did me in their lifetime. One must, it is true, forgive one's enemies—but not before they have been hanged.' (*Gedanken und Einfälle* [Section I].)

[4] [See Chapter V of *The Future of an Illusion* (1927c).

[5] ['It's the murderers who should make the first move.']

[6] ['Man is a wolf to man.' Derived from Plautus, *Asinaria* II, iv, 88.]

experience of life and of history, will have the courage to dispute this assertion? As a rule this cruel aggressiveness waits for some provocation or puts itself at the service of some other purpose, whose goal might also have been reached by milder measures. In circumstances that are favourable to it, when the mental counter-forces which ordinarily inhibit it are out of action, it also manifests itself spontaneously and reveals man as a savage beast to whom consideration towards his own kind is something alien. Anyone who calls to mind the atrocities committed during the racial migrations or the invasions of the Huns, or by the people known as Mongols under Jenghiz Khan and Tamerlane, or at the capture of Jerusalem by the pious Crusaders, or even, indeed, the horrors of the recent World War—anyone who calls these things to mind will have to bow humbly before the truth of this view.

The existence of this inclination to aggression, which we can detect in ourselves and justly assume to be present in others, is the factor which disturbs our relations with our neighbour and which forces civilization into such a high expenditure [of energy]. In consequence of this primary mutual hostility of human beings, civilized society is perpetually threatened with disintegration. The interest of work in common would not hold it together; instinctual passions are stronger than reasonable interests. Civilization has to use its utmost efforts in order to set limits to man's aggressive instincts and to hold the manifestations of them in check by psychical reaction-formations. Hence, therefore, the use of methods intended to incite people into identifications and aim-inhibited relationships of love, hence the restriction upon sexual life, and hence too the ideal's commandment to love one's neighbour as oneself—a commandment which is really justified by the fact that nothing else runs so strongly counter to the original nature of man. In spite of every effort, these endeavours of civilization have not so far achieved very much. It hopes to prevent the crudest excesses of brutal violence by itself assuming the right to use violence against criminals, but the law is not able to lay hold of the more cautious and refined manifestations of human aggressiveness. The time comes when each one of us has to give up as illusions the expectations which, in his youth, he pinned upon his fellow-men, and when he may learn how much difficulty and pain has been added to his life by their ill-will. At the same time, it would be unfair to reproach civilization with trying to eliminate strife and competition from human activity. These things are undoubtedly indispensable. But opposition is not necessarily enmity; it is merely misused and made an *occasion* for enmity.

The communists believe that they have found the path to deliverance from our evils. According to them, man is wholly good and is well-disposed to his neighbour; but the institution of private property has corrupted his nature. The ownership of private wealth gives the individual power, and with it the temptation to ill-treat his neighbour; while the man who is excluded from possession is bound to rebel in hostility against his oppressor. If private property were abolished, all wealth held in common, and everyone allowed to share in the enjoyment of it, ill-will and hostility would disappear among men. Since everyone's needs would be satisfied, no one would have any reason to regard another as his enemy; all would willingly undertake the work that was necessary. I have no concern with any economic criticisms of the communist system; I cannot enquire into whether the abolition of private property is expedient or advantageous.[7] But I am able to recognize that the psychological premisses on which the system is based are an untenable illusion. In abolishing private property we deprive the human love of aggression of one of one of its instruments, certainly a strong one, though certainly not the strongest; but we have in no way altered the differences in power and influence which are misused by aggressiveness, nor have we altered anything in its nature. Aggressiveness was not created by property. It reigned almost without limit in primitive times, when property was still very scanty, and it already shows iteslf in the nursery almost before property has given up its primal, anal form; it forms the basis of every relation of affection and love among people (with the single exception, perhaps, of the mother's relation to her male child[8]). If we do away with personal rights over material wealth, there still remains prerogative in the field of sexual relationships, which is bound to become the source of the strongest dislike and the most violent hostility among men who in other respects are on an equal footing. If we were to remove this factor, too, by allowing complete freedom of sexual life and thus abolishing the family, the germ-cell of civilization, we cannot, it is true, easily foresee what new paths the development of civilization could take; but one thing we can expect, and that is that this indestructible feature of human nature will follow it there.

It is clearly not easy for men to give up the satisfaction of this inclination to aggression. They do not feel comfortable without it. The advantage which a comparatively small cultural group offers of allowing

---

[7] Anyone who has tasted the miseries of poverty in his own youth and has experienced the indifference and arrogance of the well-to-do, should be safe from the suspicion of having no understanding or good will towards endeavours to fight against the inequality of wealth among men and all that it leads to. To be sure, if an attempt is made to base this fight upon an abstract demand, in the name of justice, for equality for all men, there is a very obvious objection to be made—that nature, by endowing individuals with extremely unequal physical attributes and mental capacities, has introduced injustices against which there is no remedy.

[8] [Cf. a footnote to Chapter VI of Group Psychology (1921c), Standard Ed., 18, 101n. A rather longer discussion of the point occurs near the end of Lecture XXXIII of the New Introductory Lectures (1933a).]

this instinct an outlet in the form of hostility against intruders is not to be despised. It is always possible to bind together a considerable number of people in love, so long as there are other people left over to receive the manifestations of their aggressiveness. I once discussed the phenomenon that it is precisely communities with adjoining territories, and related to each other in other ways as well, who are engaged in constant feuds and in ridiculing each other—like the Spaniards and Portuguese, for instance, the North Germans and South Germans, the English and Scotch, and so on.[9] I gave this phenomenon the name of 'the narcissism of minor differences', a name which does not do much to explain it. We can now see that it is a convenient and relatively harmless satisfaction of the inclination to aggression, by means of which cohesion between the members of the community is made easier. In this respect the Jewish people, scattered everywhere, have rendered most useful services to the civilizations of the countries that have been their hosts; but unfortunately all the massacres of the Jews in the Middle Ages did not suffice to make that period more peaceful and secure for their Christian fellows. When once the Apostle Paul had posited universal love between men as the foundation of his Christian community, extreme intolerance on the part of Christendom towards those who remained outside it became the inevitable consequence. To the Romans, who had not founded their communal life as a State upon love, religious intolerance was something foreign, although with them religion was a concern of the State and the State was permeated by religion. Neither was it an unaccountable chance that the dream of a Germanic world-dominion called for antisemitism as its complement; and it is intelligible that the attempt to establish a new, communist civilization in Russia should find its psychological support in the persecution of the bourgeois. One only wonders, with concern, what the Soviets will do after they have wiped out their bourgeois.

If civilization imposes such great sacrifices not only on man's sexuality but on his aggressivity, we can understand better why it is hard for him to be happy in that civilization. In fact, primitive man was better off in knowing no restrictions of instinct. To counterbalance this, his prospects of enjoying this happiness for any length of time were very slender. Civilized man has exchanged a portion of his possibilities of happiness for a portion of security. We must not forget, however, that in the primal family only the head of it enjoyed this instinctual freedom; the rest lived in slavish suppression. In that primal period of civilization, the contrast between a minority who enjoyed the advantages of civilization and a majority who were robbed of those advantages was, therefore, carried to

---

[9] [See Chapter VI of *Group Psychology* (1921c), *Standard Ed.*, 18, 101, and 'The Taboo of Virginity' (1918a), ibid., 11, 199.]

extremes. As regards the primitive peoples who exist to-day, careful researches have shown that their instinctual life is by no means to be envied for its freedom. It is subject to restrictions of a different kind but perhaps of greater severity than those attaching to modern civilized man.

When we justly find fault with the present state of our civilization for so inadequately fulfilling our demands for a plan of life that shall make us happy, and for allowing the existence of so much suffering which could probably be avoided—when, with unsparing criticism, we try to uncover the roots of its imperfection, we are undoubtedly exercising a proper right and are not showing ourselves enemies of civilization. We may expect gradually to carry through such alterations in our civilization as will better satisfy our needs and will escape our criticisms. But perhaps we may also familiarize ourselves with the idea that there are difficulties attaching to the nature of civilization which will not yield to any attempt at reform. Over and above the tasks of restricting the instincts, which we are prepared for, there forces itself on our notice the danger of a state of things which might be termed 'the psychological poverty of groups'.[10] This danger is most threatening where the bonds of a society are chiefly constituted by the identification of its members with one another, while individuals of the leader type do not acquire the importance that should fall to them in the formation of a group.[11] The present cultural state of America would give us a good opportunity for studying the damage to civilization which is thus to be feared. But I shall avoid the temptation of entering upon a critique of American civilization; I do not wish to give an impression of wanting myself to employ American methods.

[10] [The German *'psychologisches Elend'* seems to be a version of Janet's expression *'misère psychologique'* applied by him to describe the incapacity for mental synthesis which he attributes to neurotics.]
[11] Cf. *Group Psychology and the Analysis of the Ego* (1921c).

Questions for Discussion

BOTH Hobbes and Locke agree that men are approximately equal in a state of nature; but in other respects they diverge in their thinking. Hobbes contends that without civil society strife ensues—from human desire, distrust, and ambition—and leads to a state of war in which there is no property, no justice or injustice. But men, through fear of death and desire for a long and pleasant life, may join forces by making contracts with one another. A sovereign power must be established to make it more painful to violate contracts than to live by them; and it is only then that man's basic nature can be controlled.

According to Locke, men have the rights of life, liberty, and property; government is instituted by men to protect these rights. In a state of nature men ought to live according to reason and God's commands, and each man is the judge of his own actions. Each person who enters into society does so by his own consent and transfers his power to the commonwealth, which is obligated to use the power for the ends determined by the majority.

Notice that Hobbes and Locke differ about man's basic nature and, as a consequence, hold that different forms of government must be instituted. As we compare these two systems of thought, what hope can we hold for man? What can he become? As an educator, would it make much difference whether one adopted the position of Hobbes rather than that of Locke? Can you think of any ways in which one's choice may affect his attitudes and his relations with others?

Niebuhr warns of the dangers arising from disproportions of power. Man is endowed with organic relations with his fellows, but he also possesses an imagination that multiplies his desires beyond his ability to satisfy them. Even man's great mastery over nature has precipitated a more uneven distribution of power, which has aggravated the problems of justice. And those with superior abilities who hold power take more rewards than their services warrant. Romantic and moral interpretations of society are invented to obscure the abuse of power. Niebuhr poses a dichotomy between the individual and the social when he claims that the individual cherishes high ideals but that in collective life these ideals are transmuted as man seeks to accumulate as much power as he can command. Power, he believes, should be brought under the greatest degree of social control.

Niebuhr also chastens educators when he says that they erroneously believe in the utopian notion that universal education will extend the bonds of benevolence and good will and will eventually bring about a peaceful and just world community. But educators fail to realize that all social cooperation on a large scale requires coercion, and even the democratic method of resolving social conflict is more coercive than many believe.

Do you think that Niebuhr has made a perceptive analysis of man and his social and political life, or is his interpretation somewhat erroneous? If we adopt Niebuhr's position, what would be the legitimate role of education and what could education hope to attain?

Freud's thesis is that civilization imposes restrictions on man's sexual life and asks him to "love thy neighbor." These demands and restrictions, he contends, run counter to man's basic nature. He endeavors to show why he believes that the Christian ethic is woefully unrealistic. Freud discusses the basic aggressiveness of all men and points out that man's mutual hostility continually threatens civilization. Even when a group is bound together by love, it must sustain itself by venting its hostility on another group.

Compare Freud's views on human nature with the preceding ones studied. What type of moral code would those who hold Freud's position teach their students? Does Freud's analysis help to clear away what some would call the "myths of civilization"?

CHAPTER THREE

EDUCATION AND THE
SOCIAL ORDER

Since an educational system has certain relationships with the larger society, we need to determine what these relationships should be. In a democracy education is expected to be in the hands of the people and ultimately subject to their control, even though some groups may have a disproportionate influence on the schools. However, in some other forms of government educational systems have frequently been controlled by the group in power and used as a tool to perpetuate the ideologies and values of that group. For example, the relationship between education and the state in a totalitarian society is predetermined by those in power; but in those societies where new ideas are acceptable and human rights are guaranteed, the role of education is more fluid and indeterminate, especially when technological innovations have brought about periods of rapid change.

Education is designed to serve a society in accordance with its educational and societal aims and the roles espoused by those in positions of power. Whenever a society experiences a rapid expansion of knowledge and a concomitant multiplication of specialties, it can no longer rely on informal arrangements for education. Formal educational provisions are instituted within a legal framework in order to provide a more permanent place for education and ensure that the growing body of knowledge and skills will be properly transmitted to future generations.

We still have not determined exactly what the schools should do in relation to society. A systematic philosophy of education would be incomplete without a discussion of this issue. It is known that whenever a society becomes technologically more advanced, the amount of knowledge that the schools are expected to deal with multiplies and the demands placed on the schools become increasingly more difficult to fulfill. For example, when society is confronted with innovations, it may expect schools to introduce new programs for developing special skills, such as driver training or computer programming. To complicate matters further, a period of great change has an unsettling effect on people when their cherished values and accepted ways of behavior are seriously questioned. At such times, the role of the school becomes confused and ambiguous as numerous and conflicting voices are raised to express divergent goals and values. The usual conflict in such time centers on whether education should re-emphasize eternal verities and cultural traditions, or concentrate on new and emerging values and modes in behavior.

As a result of such confusion, educators have formulated a number of different positions in an attempt to clarify the role of the school. One major position is that the school is designed to serve the state and should inculcate the values of patriotism and loyalty. The individual's source of sustenance and the direction for his life stems from his relation to his country and, therefore, it is incumbent upon the school to instill in him a sense of sacrifice and loyalty to the state. Changes in the school must always originate with the state, and not vice-versa.

A somewhat different position is that the purpose of education is to conserve the great cultural values of society and, at the same time, to encourage youth to seek their own identity within this heritage. The individual, however, is not subordinate to the state. The great role of education is to assure the continuity of society by transmitting and preserving cultural values. Moreover, those who adhere to this position feel that one cannot be a good citizen or a truly educated person without a sound knowledge and appreciation of this heritage. But would such an education enable youth to live in a greatly changing world?

Still another position is that schools should promote critical, inventive, and experimental modes of thought in which even society and its institutions are subject to scrutiny and appraisal. Schooling should be a great bastion for sanctioned non-conformity in thought wherein imaginative and novel explorations lead to the intelligent reconstruction of human experience. Adherents to this position may suggest that schools cannot ignore widespread social change but must teach reflective thinking in the face of such changes for the improvement of social life.

Social reconstructionists believe that the previous position does not go far enough. Education, they say, must commit itself to a clearly conceived program of social action and reform. We live in an age of crisis; a time in history when chauvinistic nationalism must be eschewed for the development of a world civilization as the last best hope of man in a world teetering on the brink of self-annihilation. It is imperative that education commit itself to a democratic social order attuned to the highest values of our culture and in harmony with the emerging conditions of the modern world. The school should be future-oriented toward educating youth to live in and refashion the social order.

In the selections that follow, leading educators develop their own inimitable expressions of these positions. Notice how greatly the entire scope and direction of education is influenced by the issues raised in these essays.

Giovanni Gentile, a leading Italian educator and philosopher, takes the position (Selection 9) of Socrates in the dialogue "Crito"—that man is bound by the laws of the state and must obey. Gentile goes further and asserts that the citizen should want only that which the state wills, and that the laws of the state should become part of one's being. Although Gentile conceives spiritual freedom in education, it can not run counter to the will of the state.

I. L. Kandel, who was a pioneer in comparative education, takes basically a conservative view in Selection 10 of the role of education in society. He holds that the basic function of the school is to transmit the cultural heritage in order to assure the stability of society. He frankly recognizes social change, but sees the school's task as a stabilizing influence on society during times when society is undergoing rapid transformation. Kandel adds that the school has a knowledge-function to perform in acquainting pupils with the social changes in society. This is as far as the school should go.

The essay by John Dewey (Selection 11) makes a number of important distinctions in several alternate positions which Dewey subjects to criticism. He sees the school as providing youth with the insight and understanding and the requisite reflective ability to deal with problems and to take steps in the construction and organization needed in a society undergoing rapid social change. He neither falls back to Kandel's position nor moves on to the reconstructionist position of Rugg in the next selection. This essay, roughly speaking, is the liberal's position on the relation of school and society.

Harold Rugg, who was a leading figure in the reconstructionist movement, presents a view in Selection 12 that is in sharp contrast with the three preceding selections. He contends that the schools should be an agent for social regeneration, but before this can be done, the schools must undergo a thorough reconstruction. Considering that when the essay was written America was basically isolationist in outlook, his view of American society and education in the world perspective is particularly remarkable.

9 / GIOVANNI GENTILE

Education and Nationality

We shall first point out the inutility of distinguishing science from culture, education from instruction. Those who insist on these distinctions maintain that though a school is never national in virtue of the content of its scientific teaching, it must nevertheless be national in that it transforms science into culture, makes it over into an instrument with which to shape consciousness and conscience, and uses it as a tool for the making of men and for the training of citizens. Thus we have as an integral part of science a form of action directed on the character and the will of the young generations that are being nurtured and raised in accordance with national traditions and in view of the ends which the state wants to attain. Such distinctions however complicate but do not resolve the controversy. They entangle it with other questions which it were better to leave untouched at this juncture. For it might be said of questions what Manzoni said of books: one at a time is enough—if it isn't too much.

We shall therefore try to simplify matters, and begin by clarifying the two concepts of nationality and of knowledge, in order to define the concept of the "nationality of knowledge." What, then, is the nation? A very intricate question, indeed, over which violent discussions are raging, and all the more passionately because the premises and conclusions of this controversy are never maintained in the peaceful seclusion of abstract speculative theories, but are dragged at every moment in the very midst of the concrete interests of the men themselves who affirm or deny the value of nationalities. So that serious difficulties are encountered every time an attempt is made to determine the specific and concrete content of this concept of the nation, which is ever present, and yet ever elusive. Proteus-like, it appears before us, but as we try to grasp it, it changes semblance and breaks away. It is visible to the immediate intuition of every national consciousness, but it slips from thought as we strive to fix its essence.

Is it common territory that constitutes nationality? or is it common

From *The Reform of Education* by Giovanni Gentile, translated by Dino Bigongiari (New York: Harcourt, Brace and World, Inc., 1922), pp. 7–17, 27–31. Reprinted with permission of the publisher.

language? or political life led in common? or the accumulation of memories, of traditions, and of customs by which a people looks back to *one* past where it never fails to find itself? Or is it perhaps the relationship which binds together all the individuals of a community into a strong and compact structure, assigning a mission and an apostolate to a people's faith? One or the other of these elements, or all of them together, have in turn been proposed and rejected with equally strong arguments. For in each case it may be true or it may be false that the given element constitutes the essence of a people's nationality, or of any historical association whatsoever. All these elements, whether separately or jointly, may have two different meanings, one of which makes them a mere accidental content of the national consciousness, whereas the other establishes them as necessary, essential, and unfailing constituents. For they may have a merely natural value, or they may have a moral and spiritual one. Our birth-land, which nourished us in our infancy, and now shelters the bodies of our parents, the mountains and the shores that surround it and individualise it, these are natural entities. They are not man-made; we cannot claim them, nor can we fasten our existence to them. Even our speech, our religion itself, which do indeed live in the human mind, may yet be considered as natural facts similar to the geographical accidents which give boundaries and elevation to the land of a people. We may, abstractly, look upon our language as that one which was spoken before we were born, by our departed ancestors who somehow produced this spiritual patrimony of which we now have the use and enjoyment, very much in the same way that we enjoy the sunlight showered upon us by nature. In this same way a few, perhaps many, conceive of religion: they look upon it as something bequeathed and inherited, and not therefore as the fruit of our own untiring faith and the correlate of our actual personality. All these elements in so far as they are natural are evidently extraneous to our personality. We do dwell within this peninsula cloistered by the Alps; we delight in this luminous sky, in our charming shores smiled upon by the waters of the Mediterranean. But if we emigrate from this lovely abode, if under the stress of economic motives we traverse the ocean and gather, a number of us, somewhere across the Atlantic; and there, united by the natural tie of common origin, and fastened by the identity of speech, we maintain ourselves as a special community, with common interests and peculiar moral affinities, then, in spite of the severance from our native peninsula, we have preserved our nationality: Italy has crossed the ocean in our wake. Not only can we sunder ourselves from our land, but we may even relinquish our customs, forget our language, abandon our religion; or we may, within our own fatherland, be kept separate by peculiar historical traditions, by differences of dialects or even of language, by religion, by clashing interests, and yet respond with the same sentiment and the same soul to the sound of one Name, to the colours of one flag, to the summons of common hopes, to the alarm of common dangers.

And it is then that we feel ourselves to be a people; then are we a nation. It is not what we put within this concept that gives consistency and reality to the concept itself; it is the act of spiritual energy whereby we cling to a certain element or elements in the consciousness of that collective personality to which we feel we belong. Nationality consists not in content which may vary, but in the form which a certain content of human consciousness assumes when it is felt to constitute a nation's character.

But this truth is still far from being recognised. Its existence is not even suspected by those who utilise a materially constituted nationality as a title, that is, an antecedent, and a support for political rights claimed by more or less considerable ethnical aggregates that are more or less developed and more or less prepared to take on the form of free and independent states and to secure recognition of a *de facto* political personality on the strength of an assumed *de jure* existence.

This truth, however, was grasped by the profound intuition of Mazzini, the apostle of nationalities, the man who roused our national energies, and whose irresistible call awakened Italy and powerfully impelled her to affirm her national being. Even from the first years of the *Giovine Italia* he insisted that Italy, when still merely an idea, prior to her taking on a concrete and actual political reality, was not a people and was not a nation. For a nation, he maintained, is not something existing in nature, but a great spiritual reality. Therefore like all that is in and for the spirit, it is never a fact ready to be ascertained, but always a mission, a purpose, something that has to be realised—an action.

The Italians to whom Mazzini spoke were not the people around him. He was addressing that future people which the Italians themselves had to create. And they would create it by fixing their souls on one idea—the idea of a fatherland to be conquered—a sacred idea, so noble that people would live and die for it, as for that sovereign and ultimate Good for which all sacrifices are gladly borne, without which man can not live, outside of which he finds nothing that satisfies him, nothing that is conducive to a life's work. For Mazzini nationality is not inherited wealth, but it is man's own conquest. A people can not faint-heartedly claim from others recognition of their nation, but must themselves demonstrate its existence, realise it by their willingness to fight and die for its independence: independence which is freedom and unity and constitutes the nation. It is not true that first comes the nation and then follows the state; the nation is the state when it has triumphed over the enemy, and has overcome the oppression, which till then were hindering its formation. It is not therefore a vague aspiration or a faint wish, but an active faith, an energetic volition which creates, in the freed political Power, the reality of its own moral personality and of its collective consciousness. Hence the lofty aim of Mazzini in insisting that Italy should not be made with the help of foreigners but should be a product of the revolution, that is, of its own will.

And truly the nation is, substantially, as Mazzini saw and firmly believed, the common will of a people which affirms itself and thus secures self-realisation. A nation is a nation only when it wills to be one. I said, when it really wills, not when it merely says it does. It must therefore act in such a manner as to realise its own personality in the form of the State beyond which there is no collective will, no common personality of the people. And it must act seriously, sacrificing the individual to the collective whole, and welcoming martyrdom, which in every case is but the sacrifice of the individual to the universal, the lavishing of our own self to the ideal for which we toil.

From this we are not, however, to infer that a nation can under no circumstances exist prior to the formation of its State. For if this formation means the formal proclamation or the recognition by other States, it surely does pre-exist. But it does not if we consider that the proclamation of sovereignty is a moment in a previously initiated process, and the effect of pre-existing forces already at work; which effect is never definite because a State, even after it has been constituted, continues to develop in virture of those very forces which produced it; so that it is constantly renewing and continually reconstituting itself. Hence a State is always a future. It is that state which this very day we must set up, or rather at this very instant, and with all our future efforts bent to that political ideal which gleams before us, not only in the light of a beautiful thought, but as the irresistible need of our own personality.

The nation therefore is as intimately pertinent and native to our own being as the State, considered as Universal Will, is one with our concrete and actual ethical personality. Italy for us is the fatherland which lives in our souls as that complex and lofty moral idea which we are realising. We realise it in every instant of our lives, by our feelings, and by our thoughts, by our speech and by our imagination, indeed, by our whole life which concretely flows into that Will which is the State and which thus makes itself felt in the world. And this Will, this State is Italy, which has fought and won; which has struggled for a long time amid errors and sorrows, hopes and dejection, manifestations of strength and confessions of weakness, but always with a secret thought, with a deep-seated aspiration which sustained her throughout her entire ordeal, now exalting her in the flush of action, now, in the critical moment of resistance, confirming and fortifying her by the undying faith in ultimate triumph. This nation, which we all wish to raise to an ever loftier station of honour and of beauty, even though we differ as to the means of attaining this end, is it not the substance of our personality,—of that personality which we possess not as individuals who drift with the current, but as men who have a powerful self-consciousness and who look upward for their destiny?

If we thus understand the nation, it follows that not only every man must bear the imprint of his nationality, but that also there is no true science, no man's science, which is not national. The ancients believed, in conformity with the teachings of the Greeks, that science soars outside of the human life, above the vicissitudes of mortals, beyond the current of history, which is troubled by the fatal conflicts of error, by falterings and doubts, and by the unsatisfied thirst for knowledge. Truth, lofty, pure, motionless, and unchangeable, was to them the fixed goal toward which the human mind moved, but completely severed from it and transcendent. This concept, after two thousand years of speculation, was to reveal itself as abstract and therefore fallacious,—abstract from the human mind, which at every given instance mirrors itself in such an image of truth, ever gazing upon an eternal ideal but always intent on reshaping it in a new and more adequate form. The modern world, at first with dim consciousness, and guided rather by a fortunate intuition than by a clear concept of its own real orientation, then with an ever clearer, ever more critical conviction, has elaborated a concept which is directly antithetical to the classical idea of a celestial truth removed from the turmoil of earthly things. It has accordingly and by many ways reached the conclusion that reality, lofty though it be, and truth itself, which nourishes the mind and alone gives validity to human thought, are in life itself, in the development of the mind, in the growth of the human personality, and that this personality, though ideally beyond our grasp, is yet in the concrete always historical and actual, and realises itself in its immanent value. It therefore creates its truth and its world. Modern philosophy and modern consciousness no longer point to values which, transcending history, determine its movement and its direction by external finalities: they show to man that the lofty aim which is his law is within himself; that it is in his ever unsatisfied personality as it unceasingly strains upward towards its own ideal.

Science is no longer conceived to-day as the indifferent pure matter of the intellect. It is an interest which invests the entire person, extols it and with it moves onward in the eternal rhythm of an infinite development. Science is not for us the abstract contemplation of yore; it is self-consciousness that man acquires, and by means of which he actuates his own humanity. And therefore science is no longer an adornment or an equipment of the mind, considered as diverse to its content; it is culture, and the formation of this very mind. So that whenever science is as yet so abstract that it seems not to touch the person and fails to form it or transform it, it is an indication that it is not as yet true science.

So we conclude thus: he who distinguishes his person from his knowledge is ignorant of the nature of knowledge. The modern teacher knows of no science which is not an act of a personality. It knows no personality which admits of being sequestered from its ideas, from its ways of thinking and of feeling, from that greater life which is the nation. Concrete personality then is nationality, and therefore neither the school nor science possesses a learning which is not national.

And for this reason therefore our educational reforms which are inspired by the teachings of modern idealistic philosophy demand that the school be animated and vivified by the spiritual breath of the fatherland.

. . . But, then, when is it that my will really is effective, really *wills?* I am a citizen of a state which has power; this power, this will of the state expresses itself to me in laws which I must obey. The transgression of laws, if the state is in existence, bears with it the inevitable punishment of the transgressor, that is, the application of that law which the offender has refused to recognise. The state is supported by the inviolability of laws, of those sacred laws of the land which Socrates, as Plato tells us, taught his pupils to revere. I, then, as a citizen of my country, am bound by its Law in such a manner that to will its transgression is to aim at the impossible. If I did so, I should be indulging in vain velleities, in which my personality, far from realising itself, would on the contrary be disintegrated and scattered. I then want what the law wants me to will.

It makes no difference that, from a material and explicit point of view, a system of positive law does not coincide throughout with the sphere of my activity, and that therefore the major part of the standards of my conduct must be determined by the inner dictates of my particular conscience. For it is the Will of the State that determines the limits between the moral and the juridical, between what is imposed by the law of the land and what is demanded by the ethical conscience of the individual. And there is no limit which pre-exists to the line by which the constituent and legislative power of the State delimits the sphere subject to its sanctions. So that positively or negatively, either by command or by permission, our whole conduct is subject to that will by which the State establishes its reality.

But the Will of the State does not manifest itself solely by the enactments of positive legislation. It opens to private initiative such courses of action as may presumably be carried on satisfactorily without the impulse and the direct control of the sovereign power. But this concession has a temporary character, and the State is ever ready to intervene as soon as the private management ceases to be effective. So that even in the exercise of what seems the untrammelled will of the individual we discern the power of the State; and the individual is free to will something only because the sovereign power wants him to. So that in reality this apparently autonomous particular will is the will of the state not expressed in terms of positive legislation, there being no need of such an expression. But since the essence of law is not in the expression of it, but in the will which dictates it, or observes it, or enforces the observance of it, in the will, in short, that wills it, it follows that the law exists even though unwritten.

In the way of conclusion, then, it may be said that I, as a citizen, have indeed a will of my own; but that upon further investigation my will is found to coincide exactly with the will of the State, and I want anything only in so far as the State wants me to want it.

Could it possibly be otherwise? Such an hypothesis overwhelms me at the very thought of it. For it would come to this,—that I exist and my state does not:—the state in which I was born, which sustained and protected me before I saw the light of day, which formed and guaranteed to me this communion of life; the state in which I have always lived, which has constituted this spiritual substance, this world in which I support myself, and which I trust will never fail me even though it does change constantly. I could, it is true, ignore this close bond by which I am tied and united to that great will which is the will of my country. I might balk and refuse to obey its laws. But acting thus, I would be indulging in what I have called velleities. My personality, unable to transform the will of the state, would be overcome and suppressed by it.

Let us however assume for a moment that I might in the innermost depths of my being segregate myself. Averse to the common will and to the law of the land, I decide to proclaim over the boundless expanse of my thought the proud independence of my ego, as a lone, inaccessible summit rising out of the solitude. Up to a certain point this hypothesis is verified constantly by the manner in which my personality freely becomes actual. But even then I do not act as a particular being: it is the universal power that acts through my personal will.

For when we effectively observe the law, with true moral adhesion and in thorough sincerity, the law becomes part of ourselves, and our actions are the direct results of our convictions—of the necessity of our convictions. For every time we act, inwardly we see that such must be our course; we must have a clear intuition of this necessity. The Saint who has no will but the will of God intuitively sees necessity in his norm. So does the sinner in his own way: but his norm is erroneous and therefore destined to fail. Every criminal in transgressing the law obeys a precept of his own making which is in opposition to the enactments of the state. And in so doing he creates almost a state of his own, different from the one which historically exists and must exist because of certain good reasons, the excellence of which the criminal himself will subsequently realise. From the unfortunate point of view which he has taken, the transgressor is justified in acting as he does, and to such an extent that no one in his position, as he thinks, could possibly take exception to it. His will is also universal; if he were allowed to, if it were possible for him, he would establish new laws in place of the old ones: he would set up another state over the ruins of the one which he undermines. And what else does the tyrant when he destroys the freedom of the land and substitutes a new state for the crushed Commonwealth? In the same manner the rebel does away with the despot, starts a revolution and establishes liberty if he is successful; if not, he is overcome and must again conform his will to the will of that state which he has not been able to overthrow. So then, I exercise my true volition whenever the will of my state acts in my personal will, or rather when my will is the realisation of the will of a super-national group in which my state co-exists with other states, acting upon them, and being re-acted upon in reciprocal determinations. Or perhaps better still, when the entire world wills in me. For my will, I shall say it once again, is not individual but universal, and in the political community by which individuals are united into a higher individuality, historically distinct from other similar ones, we must see a form of universality.

10 / I. L. KANDEL

Education and Social Change

The general social and cultural unrest which can be traced back to the beginnings of the modern scientific movement and the consequent technological changes, an unrest which has grown in intensity since the War, has had its repercussions on educational thought. This has, indeed, been the history of education, for education has been most vigorous and vital in periods of great social changes, as, for example, in Athens, during

I. L. Kandel, "Education and Social Change," in *Conflicting Theories of Education* (New York: The Macmillan Company, 1938), pp. 77–88. Every possible effort was made to locate the Copyright holder.

the Renaissance and the Reformation, at the time of the early scientific movement of the seventeenth century, and at the beginning of the nineteenth century following the Industrial Revolution and the consolidation of nation-states. The period through which the world is passing in the present era is probably one of those nodal periods in which old ideas and ideals, standards and loyalties, are being questioned and modified, if not revolutionized. Science is remaking the world and bringing an economic upheaval in its train; political institutions are being questioned or overturned; a war of ideas is going on in every field that concerns human relationships. The conflicts are more profound and more widespread than those which have always existed between the older and younger generations.

Under these conditions unrest in education is inevitable, but in the discussions on education and social change it is not clear whether a formula is being sought whereby the rising generation shall be acquainted with the social changes going on about it or whether it is proposed that the school itself should be made an instrument for the reconstruction of society. These alternatives can be answered only in the light of the purposes for which society establishes schools.

The earliest and most persistent reason for the establishment of schools as formal agencies of education is the desire on the part of a group, society, or state to conserve and transmit its culture and heritage to the younger generation and to equip this generation with those habits, skills, knowledges, and ideals that will enable it to take its place in a society and contribute to the stability and perpetuation of that society. This purpose is based on faith in the possibilities of formal education during the formative and plastic period of childhood and adolescence. This is the principle in Plato's statement that the effectual functioning of the state depends upon the proper training of the young, and in Aristotle's insistence that the stability of systems of government has its basis in the adaptation of education to the form of government.

Education does not proceed in a vacuum; its character is determined by the group culture, and schools are institutions created by society to attain certain specific ends. These ends began to be defined when the national states at the beginning of the nineteenth century undertook to establish systems of education to initiate their future citizens into the national culture. Stability was to be secured by instructing the pupils in the schools in a common language, common history, common government and political ideals, common economic and social ideas and ideals, and common objects of social allegiance in order that there might emerge a common group, or national, self-consciousness. If the younger generation is to enter into meaningful partnership in and responsibility for its heritage the first function of the school is to initiate it into its common culture. Society is, in fact, prior to the individual, and the school is an agency for promoting stability and adapting the individual to the environment in which he lives. Without entering into other considerations which justify the transmission of the social heritage or the experiences of the race as a basis for understanding the present, it will be generally agreed that the function here described has received wide acceptance from the days of Plato down to modern times.

If, however, the school stops with the performance of this function, then a society either stagnates, as was the case in China, or its progress is determined by the will of the few who lead the rest, trained through the school to habits of duty, discipline, quiescent obedience, and uncritical acceptance of authority. The method of such a school is that of direct indoctrination and education becomes indistinguishable from propaganda. This was already the trend in authoritarian states of the last century; it is the principle definitely accepted in the totalitarian states of the present, in which education is directed by and to a common ideology. The social changes wrought by revolutions have produced patterns which know no compromise and are not open to question or criticism. Education has become adjustment to a fixed and unchanging environment, and national culture is something that is colored by a particular ideology and controlled by organizations created to prevent changes in it.

The situation is different in those countries in which culture is accepted as the spontaneous expression of individuals and the free interplay among individuals or groups. It is at this point that education and social change begin to be clothed with meaning and to challenge traditional practices. The procedure in the past was to impart a body of content, knowledge, and information representing selections from the group culture designed primarily to "train the mind." It tended to become stereotyped and formal and rarely came to grips with the present. The school was a cloistered institution which eschewed any contact with the environment into which the pupil was soon to pass. It must be remembered, however, that even this type of procedure did not ignore the changing environment and was not designed to maintain a static society, but it was conducted with the conviction that a mind trained by "academic" or "scholastic" material would have no difficulty in dealing with the realities of life. Nor was the procedure in the education of the masses differentiated from the procedure in the education of the potential leaders.

These practices were not accepted without protest. Since the days of Seneca educators have urged that education must be for life and not for the school, but it was not until the beginning of the present century that widespread efforts began to be made to bring school and society together. A better understanding of the process of child growth, a new interpretation of the concept of interest, a clearer realization of the meaning of democracy and the part to be played by the individual in it, and the rapid changes in the culture, due in the main to the progress of science—all these forces and many others contributed to the spread of the theory that if education is a social process, it must contribute to an understanding of the society which it serves. The influence of John Dewey's philosophy in bringing about the change of outlook not only in the United States but in other parts of the world is too well known to need further discussion. The vast body of educational literature which has grown up in the United States in the past three decades speaks eloquently of this influence. The educational trend in Germany during the period of the short-lived Republic was rooted in *Bodenständigkeit,* the relation of education to the environment. In England the latest edition of the *Handbook of Suggestions for Teachers* is inspired by the same principle, as is illustrated by a statement in the general introduction that "we feel more deeply the need of relating what is taught in the schools to what is happening in the world outside."

The new theory of education, in insisting that the work of the school must be related to the environment in which and for which its pupils are being educated, contains in its definition the suggestion that discussions of social change are implicit in the curriculum. It means that pupils should be taught to understand the world in which they live. Up to this point the problem is fairly simple. Difficulties arise, however, when it is suggested that change is the characteristic note of the present world— and change not merely in its material but in its ideational aspects. To what extent should or can the school concern itself with political and economic conflicts, with changes in the attitudes to authority, or with the general atmosphere that questions all traditions?

Changes in the material world are facts; political and economic theories are matters of opinion. If the teacher is an agent of the state, to what extent is he free to introduce controversial issues into the class-room? It is not necessary here to state that the issues should be relevant to the stage of development and the maturity of the pupils concerned and to the subject of instruction. But if the function of education is to develop an understanding of the problems of the environment in which the learner lives, the opportunity of discussing controversial issues in the school cannot be ignored. Indeed, one may argue that it is essential to train the pupil in recognizing the importance of accurate knowledge before reaching an opinion.

If the doors of the school are to be closed to the discussion of controversial issues, it might well be asked what the alternative would be; in a period of change the schools would be guilty of turning pupils out into the world ignorant of the problems that will confront them. There is, in fact, no choice but to bring those elements of conflict into the classroom. To adopt an ostrichlike attitude and ignore the existence of such issues, to deny the right to mention even the existence of what may be regarded as subversive ideas, is to follow the old practice of ignoring the existence of sex. Carried to its logical conclusion, such a policy could be used to justify the suppression of a free press and of freedom of opinion, and the arrest of anyone suspected of "harboring dangerous thoughts."

Any reference to the introduction of controversial issues in politics and economics arouses the fear that pupils will be exposed to the bias of the teachers. It may be true that no teacher can successfully conduct a discussion of controversial issues without the pupils' detecting his bias. Nevertheless, pupils pass through the hands of a large number of teachers during their school careers; to suspect that all teachers have the same bias has no justification in fact; nor are teachers the only educational influences that play upon the growing youth. The choice is whether the rising generation is to receive its political and economic education through informal agencies or through methods that are truly educative; whether the young are to be enlightened and trained through the scientific study of facts or whether they are to be exposed to deliberate propaganda without the support of accurate information on both sides of an issue. If the relationship between school and society or education and the environment means anything, then the schools must, at the appropriate stage, impart the realities of society. And if that society is in process of change, then all that the school can do is to place the pupils in possession of full knowledge of the facts in the issues involved and to give them that training which will enable them to make up their own minds on the basis of that knowledge.

The emphasis in this argument is on training in methods of thinking through issues that are real. There is some truth in the objection that solutions cannot be given to contemporary controversial issues; this objection is, however, not a valid argument for their exclusion from the schools. Neither the issues nor the solutions are likely to be the same when pupils now in school take their places in life as adult citizens; the detailed facts of an issue and the knowledge requisite to its solution will inevitably be different, but unless some training is given in the schools in the patterns of thinking with which a problem is to be approached, the intellectual equipment necessary to recognize even the existence of problems will have been withheld. If democracy depends for its survival upon the intelligence and understanding of the ordinary man, it is the function of the school to equip him in advance with the necessary knowledge and powers of clear thinking to discharge his duties as a citizen.

It is only in this sense that education and social change can be discussed. Education must go beyond its task of imparting a knowledge and appreciation of the common interests, or what Dewey has called the objects of that social allegiance which makes common social understanding and consciousness of group membership possible. It must help men and women to think for themselves, unless they are to succumb to the will of an authority which claims omniscience and infallibility.

There has, however, been injected into discussions of education and social change the suggestion that schools should, in a period of change, educate for a new social order, and that teachers should ally themselves with some political group and use their classrooms to propagate certain doctrines. Schools and teachers should, in other words, participate more directly and vitally in projecting particular ideas or patterns of social change and in their execution. The whole history of education emphasizes the impossibility of this idea, for society establishes schools to provide a firm basis for itself and to sustain the common interest. Schools are a part of the environment which they serve; they are not autonomous or insulated against the social forces and influences around them; nor can teachers on the basis of a guess as to the active forces of the day help to build a new social order. Society changes first and schools follow.

It is, however, becoming increasingly important that teachers should be more alive than they have been in the past and better informed about the environment in and for which they are educating their pupils. Only in this way can they give meaning to the subjects for which they are responsible, for subjects, if they are to have any significance, must be saturated with social meaning. To attempt to instill ready-made ideas on controversial issues or to influence pupils to accept one doctrine rather than another is to adopt the methods of totalitarian states and to confuse education with propaganda.

In a democracy the only acceptable aim in bringing the school and society more closely together is to develop the knowledge and understanding that make for enlightened citizenship. But the acquisition of knowledge, facts, and information about the environment in all those aspects that concern the conduct of the citizen is not the sole end of education; such an acquisition must be made the vehicle for training in scientific methods of thinking and for cultivating free and disciplined minds. To educate for a new social order is to close the minds of the pupils, for, in a society in transition, no one can have a final answer concerning the issues that are involved. True education would help to put the pupils in a position to appreciate the urgent necessity of acquiring knowledge, to discriminate between facts and prejudices, to weigh and judge evidence, to reach conclusions warranted by the information secured, and to recognize the issues involved in a period of social transition or crisis. If this end is to be achieved, if the aim of education is to develop free and enlightened citizens, then the teachers who are to be entrusted with carrying out this aim must themselves be enlightened and free. The problem, like all other problems in education, becomes one of teacher preparation and of the status of teachers. In the words of a former president of the English Board of Education, "The standards of the teaching profession itself are the only sure protection" against the abuse of the teachers' positions in discussing educational and social change.

The problem of education and social change solves itself if education is defined as the process of bringing pupils to an understanding of the environment in and for which they are being educated. That environment is a constantly expanding one; to concentrate on change alone is to deal only with the immediate present and to avoid the development of an understanding of the rich heritage which the environment carries with it. But understanding must lead to conduct, and if democracy is to survive, the schools must cultivate in their pupils ideals of freedom, tolerance, and open-mindedness, a critical attitude and intellectual sensitiveness based on ascertained facts and knowledge, a spirit of inquiry and insight, and those emotional qualities in addition which make for a sense of responsibility and co-operation. For democracy, in the words of Santayana, is a blind, groping adventure which implies open-mindedness and sensitiveness to the need of flexibility and adaptation of social institutions. These are the qualities which education can cultivate as the basis of social change.

11 / JOHN DEWEY

Education and Social Change

Attention has been continually called of late to the fact that society is in process of change, and that the schools tend to lag behind. We are all familiar with the pleas that are urged to bring education in the schools

John Dewey, "Education and Social Change," *The Social Frontier*, III, No. 26 (May 1937), 235–238. Reprinted by permission.

into closer relation with the forces that are producing social change and with the needs that arise from these changes. Probably no question has received so much attention in educational discussion during the past few years as the problem of integration of the schools with social life. Upon these general matters, I could hardly do more than reiterate what has often been said.

Nevertheless, there is as yet little consensus of opinion as to what the schools can do in relation to the forces of social change and how they should do it. There are those who assert in effect that the schools must simply reflect social changes that have already occurred, as best they may. Some would go so far as to make the work of schools virtually parasitic. Others hold that the schools should take an active part in *directing* social change, and share in the construction of a new social order. Even among the latter there is, however, marked difference of attitude. Some think the schools should assume this directive role by means of indoctrination; others oppose this method. Even if there were more unity of thought than exists there would still be the practical problem of overcoming institutional inertia so as to realize in fact an agreed-upon program.

There is, accordingly, no need to justify further discussion of the problem of the relation of education to social change. I shall do what I can, then, to indicate the factors that seem to me to enter into the problem, together with some of the reasons that prove that the schools do have a role—and an important one—in *production* of social change.

One factor inherent in the situation is that schools *do* follow and reflect the social "order" that exists. I do not make this statement as a grudging admission, nor yet in order to argue that they should *not* to so. I make it rather as a statement of a *conditioning* factor which supports the conclusion that the schools thereby do take part in the determination of a future social order; and that, accordingly, the problem is not whether the schools *should* participate in the production of a future society (since they do so anyway) but whether they should do it blindly and irresponsibly or with the maximum possible of courageous intelligence and responsibility.

The grounds that lead me to make this statement are as follows: The existing state of society, which the schools reflect, is not something fixed and uniform. The idea that such is the case is a self-imposed hallucination. Social conditions are not only in process of change, but the changes going on are in different directions, so different as to produce social confusion and conflict. There is no single and clear-cut pattern that pervades and holds together in a unified way the social conditions and forces that operate. It requires a good deal of either ignorance or intellectual naivete to suppose that these changes have all been tending to one coherent social outcome. The plaint of the conservative about the imperiling of old and time-tried values and truths, and the efforts of reactionaries to stem the tide of changes that occur, are sufficient evidence, if evidence be needed to the contrary.

Of course the schools have mirrored the social changes that take place. The notion that the educational system has been static is too absurd for notice; it has been and still is in a state of flux.

The fact that it is possible to argue about the desirability of many of the changes that have occurred, and to give valid reasons for deploring aspects of the flux, is not relevant to the main point. For the stronger the arguments brought forth on these points, and the greater the amount of evidence produced to show that the educational system is in a state of disorder and confusion, the greater is the proof that the schools have responded to, and have reflected, social conditions which are themselves in a state of confusion and conflict.

Do those who hold the idea that the schools should not attempt to give direction to social change accept complacently the confusion that exists, because the schools *have* followed in the track of one social change after another? They certainly do not, although the logic of their position demands it. For the most part they are severe critics of the existing state of education. They are as a rule opposed to the studies called modern and the methods called progressive. They tend to favor return to older types of studies and to strenuous "disciplinary" methods. What does this attitude mean? Does it not show that its advocates in reality adopt the position that the schools can do something to affect positively and constructively social conditions? For they hold in effect that the school should discriminate with respect to the social forces that play upon it; that instead of accepting the latter *in toto*, education should select and organize in a given direction. The adherents of this view can hardly believe that the effect of selection and organization will stop at the doors of school rooms. They must expect some ordering and healing influence to be exerted sooner or later upon the structure and movement of life outside. What they are really doing when they deny directive social effect to education is to express their opposition to some of the directions social change is actually taking, and their choice of other social forces as those with which education should throw in its lot so as to promote as far as may be their victory in the strife of forces. They are conservatives in education because they are socially conservative and vice-versa.

This is as it should be in the interest of clearness and consistency of thought and action. If these conservatives in education were more aware of what is involved in their position, and franker in stating its implications, they would help bring out the real issue. It is not whether the schools shall or shall not influence the course of future social life, but in what direction they shall do so and how. In some fashion or other, the schools will influence social life anyway. But they can exercise such influence in different ways and to different ends, and the important thing is to become conscious of these different ways and ends, so that an intelligent choice may be made, and so that if opposed choices are made, the further conflict may at least be carried on with understanding of what is at stake, and not in the dark.

There are three possible directions of choice. Educators may act so as to perpetuate the present confusion and possibly increase it. That will be the result of drift, and under present conditions to drift is in the end to make a choice. Or they may select the newer scientific, technological, and cultural forces that are producing change in the old order; may estimate the direction in which they are moving and their outcome if they are given freer play, and see what can be done to make the schools their ally. Or, educators may become intelligently conservative and strive to make the schools a force in maintaining the old order intact against the impact of new forces.

If the second course is chosen—as of course I believe it should be—the problem will be other than merely that of accelerating the rate of the change that is going on. The problem will be to develop the insight and understanding that will enable the youth who go forth from the schools to take part in the great work of construction and organization that will have to be done, and to equip them with the attitudes and habits of action that will make their understanding and insight practically effective.

There is much that can be said for an intelligent conservatism. I do not know anything that can be said for perpetuation of a wavering, uncertain, confused condition of social life and education. Nevertheless, the easiest thing is to refrain from fundamental thinking and let things go on drifting. Upon the basis of any other policy than drift—which after all is a policy, though a blind one—every special issue and problem, whether that of selection and organization of subject-matter of study, of methods of teaching, of school buildings and equipment, of school administration, is a special phase of the inclusive and fundamental problem: What movement of social forces, economic, political, religious, cultural, shall the school take to be controlling in its aims and methods, and with which forces shall the school align itself?

Failure to discuss educational problems from this point of view but intensifies the existing confusion. Apart from this background, and outside of this perspective, educational questions have to be settled *ad hoc* and are speedily unsettled. What is suggested does not mean that the schools shall throw themselves into the political and economic arena and take sides with some party there. I am not talking about parties; I am talking about social forces and their movement. In spite of absolute claims that are made for this party or that, it is altogether probable that existing parties and sects themselves suffer from existing confusions and conflicts, so that the understanding, the ideas, and attitudes that control their policies, need re-education and re-orientation. I know that there are some who think that the implications of what I have said point to abstinence and futility; that they negate the stand first taken. But I am surprised when educators adopt this position, for it shows a profound lack of faith in their own calling. It assumes that education as education has nothing or next to nothing to contribute; that formation of under-standing and disposition counts for nothing; that only immediate overt action counts and that it can count equally whether or not it has been modified by education.

Before leaving this aspect of the subject, I wish to recur to the utopian nature of the idea that the schools can be completely neutral. This idea sets up an end incapable of accomplishment. So far as it is acted upon, it has a definite social effect, but that effect is, as I have said, perpetuation of disorder and increase of blind because unintelligent conflict. Practi-cally, moreover, the weight of such action falls upon the reactionary side. Perhaps the most effective way of re-inforcing reaction under the name of neutrality, consists in keeping the oncoming generation ignorant of the conditions in which they live and the issues they have to face. This effect is the more pronounced because it is subtle and indirect; because neither teachers nor those taught are aware of what they are doing and what is being done to them. Clarity can develop only in the extent to which there is frank acknowledgment of the basic issue: Where shall the social emphasis of school life and work fall, and what are the educational policies which correspond to this emphasis?

12 / HAROLD RUGG

Social Reconstruction through Education

Industrial civilization is on trial. Its leaders are asking frankly: Can an interdependent civilization that ramifies around the earth manage itself? The current chaos throws out boldly the opportunity and obligation of educators. "Education for a changing society" implies that we shall

Harold Rugg, "Social Reconstruction through Education," *Progressive Education*, 10 (January 1933), 11–18. Reprinted by permission.

introduce youth to the understanding of our rapidly changing civilization. But much more is needed than that. The world is on fire, and the
youth of the world must be equipped to combat the conflagration.
Nothing less than thoroughgoing social reconstruction is demanded, and
there is no institution known to the mind of man that can compass that
problem except education.

In every changing culture of the world today, two insistent problems
should engage the attention of educators: (1) What are the concepts and
problems of our changing civilization which should constitute both the
needed social program of action and the outline of the educational
program? (2) What are the elements of a creative philosophy which shall
be appropriate for the new social order?

Before the school can be used as an agent for social regeneration, it
must undergo thorough reconstruction. In the past century, a system of
primary education has been set up in every industrial country. More than
ninety-five per cent of the people have been taught to read, write, and
reckon. The tabular contrast of the amount of illiteracy in the agricultural
and the industrial countries is a striking revelation of the success of this
first attempt to make the peoples of the earth literate. Certainly, we must
feel that this is a striking achievement.

But literacy must not be confused with education. There is grave
doubt, indeed, whether it should have been taken as the first objective of
education. In every country which has done so, there has been produced
a top-heavy, white-collar class, a false hierarchy of social classes; and the
literate masses of people have been made easy subjects for propaganda.
In England, France, Germany, Japan, America, and in the regions on
which they have imposed their scheme of intellectual education, has
already emerged a huge white-collar class, overcrowding the paper
occupations, imbued with contempt for nonintellectual work, discontented, looking down on their elders. I have just been an eyewitness of the
condition in one *hsien* in China. In that country, there are one hundred
and eighteen college graduates residing in tiny isolated farming villages,
unable to find work which they will accept, living on their families;
instead of leading China out of her difficulties, they are breeders of
unrest and mischief.

This is indicative of the dangerous social effects of a lopsided academic
education. For thus far, we of the West, have produced but a partial
education, an education which consists merely in the study of words and
abstractions. Furthermore, it is an education obsessed with the halo of
the past, blind to the insistent problems of the present, and impotent to
project alternative solutions.

This phenomenon of hyperintellectual education imposed upon peoples needing a handicraft-citizenship one is world-wide. We Americans have contributed to it in the Philippines, Porto Rico, and Hawaii, and in thousands of our own rural villages. The British, French, Germans, Dutch, Belgians, Italians have done it in India, in Malaya, in Africa, in Australia, in the islands of the seven seas.

Is it not clear that the leaders of the entire earth must join together in thoroughgoing educational reconstruction? Whatever their race or nationality, two great needs confront them: first, the construction of a realistic program of education directly from the problems and needs of the people; second, the development of a creative philosophy indigenous to our new civilization and constructed directly from the materials of each national culture. The educational leaders of this generation confront the first supreme test of modern civilization. They must answer such basic questions as these: Can a compact minority of the peoples of the earth be educated in the scientific attitude and habit of mind? Can they be informed concerning the chief characteristics and problems of our new civilization? Can they be practiced in tolerance? Can they be made critical of the propaganda of dominant economic groups? Can they be taught to see the superficialities of quack remedies for fundamental social ills?

Certainly these things cannot be done by fiat; they can be achieved only through a fundamental reconstruction in education. Only by uniting the educational workers of the world in a dynamic social program of action appropriate to world needs can the current impasse be managed.

How is the problem to be attacked? The first step is the building of a new program of work, a new content for the curriculum, directly out of the problems, issues, and characteristics of our changing society. The great central concepts which epitomize the characteristics of our society shall constitute the very skeleton of that program.

To do so will demand courage and concentrated study of modern problems. We must become students of economic, social, and political life, as well as students of artistic self-expression and of growing childhood. No longer can the educationist remain aloof from the frontiers of social and artistic life, for it is the problems on the frontier that constitute the nucleus of the educational program.

This first step is of such importance that I venture to consider it somewhat more fully. I shall state merely the basic concepts that should constitute the guiding skeleton of our new educational program.

First and foremost, the fragile interdependence of this world-mechanism of trade and culture that we have created. Youth in every land must grow up with the sense of responsibility for helping to carry on that mechanism, for preventing the cutting of any single nerve of the new economic-political organism.

Second, the accelerating change with which the cultures of the world are being transformed. The generation shortly to be given the responsibility of self-government must be practiced in the attitude of expectancy of change—change in industry and farming, change in transportation, communication and trade; and therefore change in standards and norms of life, in standards of morality, in family life. And correspondingly, of the need for change in political, economic and social government.

Third, the powerful role of the great economic concepts of private property, the desire for economic gain, and the doctrine of individual success through competition. Youth will learn that all group problems are colored by these prevailing concepts. They will be brought to see how the concept of *laissez-faire* in the marriage of politics and economics has produced enormous inequalities in wealth and social income, the export of large amounts of capital from Europe and America, the disastrous imperialistic exploitation of agrarian and non-militarized peoples, and thus to mad international rivalries and world war. They will understand that underneath most of the activities of individuals, and the political maneuverings of nations and groups, is the desire for economic gain; that throughout the history of the race the desire for trade has been the central thread of continuity; and that the political history of the past few centuries has been largely the story of the conflict between struggling economic classes.

Fourth, experiments in political democracy. Must we not build systematically the attitude among the young people of the world that the trend toward representative democracy has produced nothing more than important *experiments* in government? The need for understanding is two-fold: first, that the trend for two hundred years has been from autocracy toward democracy, from government by One Man to government by Many Men. Second, that every form of government on earth today must be regarded frankly as an experiment, tentative, and to be changed as new social and economic conditions develop. The trend has revealed scores of experiments, a great variety of forms and methods of collective living. The danger is that the young nationals of each of the sixty countries will grow up with the conviction that the form peculiar to his country is of proved superiority, rather than that it is one of many experiments and could very likely be greatly improved by the substitution of many foreign practices.

Fifth, it is equally important for youth to understand that effective democracy, whatever the form, postulates the adequate education of the people in understanding, and a dynamic interest in collective affairs. They should grasp the established fact that, as people have herded into cities, they have increasingly lost both interest in collective problems and ability to understand them. Nothing short of heroic efforts of mass education can successfully combat the new conditions of urban democracy.

Sixth, the utter lack of economic government in the modern world. Our new materials of instruction shall illustrate fearlessly and dramatically the inevitable consequence of the lack of planning and of central control over the production and distribution of physical things; namely, recurring cycles of unemployment of increasing intensity, and an unfair division of social wealth and income. Thus through the schools of the world, we shall disseminate a new conception of government—one that will embrace all of the collective activities of men; that will postulate the need for scientific control and operation of economic activities in the interest of all of the people; and one that will successfully adjust the psychological relations among men. Political government in a new connotation, then, including economic government and social government.

Seventh, the dangers inherent in growing economic nationalism. We shall illustrate clearly the manner in which gross differences in standards of living and in machine and military power have produced a destructive nationalism. One conspicuous example will be found in the mad erection of tariff barriers around nations that are almost completely interdependent. We shall introduce into our schools such a dramatic description of modes of living around the world that youth will respect the difficult endeavors of peoples of varying standards of economic life to exchange goods equitably.

Eighth, central world economic government. The recognition of these conditions will expedite the acceptance of the trend toward increasing centralized world control, allocation and exchange of basic commodities —especially foods, fuels, fibers, fertilizers, and metals. We shall illustrate the inevitable destructive effect of economic rivalries and the overproduction of all basic commodities and consequent unemployment of millions of workers under a nationalistic competitive system. Thus our youth of the world, while developing a warm loyalty for their native homeland, will hold to an equally strong loyalty for the brotherland of all men on the earth.

Ninth, dangerous overpopulation and crowding into cities. We shall teach the startling multiplication of the peoples of the earth since 1800 and their huddling together in steel-and-concrete cities; the great unnatural trends toward machine production, the raising of standards of living, the discovery and spread of scientific knowledge of sanitation, hygiene, and control of disease, and of universal education will be comprehended in close relationship. Correspondingly, the physical as well as social dangers inherent in this trend will be grasped by youth. Thus can direct education in the control and distribution of population develop.

Tenth, the roles of the promoter, the political, and the creative mind in our acquisitive society shall be made clear. The dangerous stratification of a society which minimizes or ignores the contribution of the creative mind of every frontier of thought and feeling, and puts into a position of power the exploiter and the aggrandizer, be he financial promoter or practical politician.

Eleventh, examples of the psychology of individual and group behavior shall pervade the dramatic content of our new program. Young people will study human conduct in action. They shall see the role of such deeplying fears as those of economic insecurity and social disapproval. They will learn that he who controls the formation of attitudes, opinions, and beliefs by social groups and by the non-personal agencies of communication is in a fair way to control the mind of the nation.

Twelfth, running through the entire program, from kindergarten to college and through all the adult agencies of education, shall be the attempt to build two great coordinate and controlling attitudes and methods of thought. The one is the attitude of experimental inquiry, the scientific attitude which is to control man and men in all the individual and group problem-solving situations of life. The other is the attitude of appreciative awareness, with which men shall adjust to all the personalized, expressive, non-problem-solving situations. These attitudes are coordinate in importance and no curriculum is complete that ignores either.

This, then, illustrates the first step in educational reconstruction—the construction of a new program of studies directly out of the content of our changing cultures. Phrased in another way, this step amounts to preparing and introducing into the schools of the world a courageous and intelligent description of our new society.

I have concentrated my attention on those parts of the curriculum known conventionally as the social sciences. Indeed, I am convinced that two great central themes will dominate the new curriculum—one broad strand of human and social science, and another of creative self-expression and aesthetic appreciation.

Thus we have illustrated the need of reconstruction for social action. But there must be equally far-reaching reconstruction in philosophy, and this leads us to our second great task—the development of a new and indigenous theory of life and education. This program of action must have an orienting and directing basis. To determine the content of our curriculum, we must know what manner of man we would produce. And it is at this point that I have found less hard thinking than upon the content of the new curriculum. There is much concern in America, in England, in Germany, in China with the questions: "What shall we teach?" but altogether too little concern with: "What kind of American? What kind of Chinese? What kind of world citizen shall we produce?"

That we need urgently a new theory of individual and group conduct is shown by the drastic changes in our culture in the past generation. The new industrial revolution, which has developed since 1890, has not only changed our external modes of living; it has also swept away the objects of allegiance in our inner culture. One by one the loyalties to which our fathers clung have disappeared, and less personalized ones have emerged to take their places. For the loyalty to the personal ruler, we are asked to substitute allegiance to abstract concepts—democracy . . . my country . . . liberty, equality, fraternity. For our religious loyalties, we are offered reason, personal initiative, and independence. In place of the authority of old age and governmental prestige, we are asked to set up the experimental attitude. Thus, as Waldo Frank first reminded us, the old objects of allegiance around which our fundamental institutions grew up—the family, the community, the church, the nation—are breaking down. A new culture is being produced in this first half of the twentieth century. New mores, new norms of conduct, are being precipitated by social trends. How shall we measure them? Which shall we deliberately build into our basic educational theory?

In China, and less drastically in the West, the old family system is breaking down; the one-generation family is taking the place of the three-and four-generation clan. As this happens, the older loyalties to parents, to elders, to the family group disappear. What shall the Chinese educators teach their children and youth? Are there not fine outcomes from the old family culture which should be kept, which could be kept by nationwide systematic preservation in the schools?

Similarly, we confront grave difficulties in determining the role of national and international loyalties. We know full well that selfish nationalism is dangerous, and history teaches clearly that present social trends are moving us all swiftly toward the need for world unity. But in laying our platform for internationalism, shall we ignore or negate national enthusiasm for our native fatherlands?

Thus we confront the problem of determining what the objects of allegiance of our new culture shall be. The question: "What kind of man shall we aim to produce?" becomes, "What attitudes and points of view, shall we definitely set ourselves to create?" What attitudes toward self, neighbor, family, nation? What attitudes toward our social relations, toward productive labor, the social classes? It is these psychological materials that constitute the very heart of our educational theory. Unless these are clearly thought through and clearly phrased, the educational program will drift aimlessly in no planned course, and social reconstruction will be impossible.

Our search for a new theory of life and education appropriate to the new and changing culture reveals the inadequacy of the pragmatic theories which are subscribed to by educators generally in the West. Indeed, careful study shows us that the pragmatism of Peirce and Dewey is not a philosophy; it is essentially a method of thought. It is a conspicuously fine phrasing of the experimental method of inquiry. It is an exposition of *"how we think" when solving problems*. It is an intellectual test, not a theory of life, and hence of education.

We need a philosophy, the loyalties of which shall be so inclusive as to guide men in all the situations of life. Our theory must embrace two attitudes, two outlooks on life. The first is the experimental attitude, the scientific outlook that has enabled men increasingly to master nature. It is education in this attitude that will enable men to devise economic government and to master social relations.

The second attitude is that of appreciative awareness. It is the all-embracing attitude of receptivity. These two attitudes are fundamentally different, and the techniques of mind that spring from them are equally different. Yet they are not different in the sense that they oppose each other; they are different in the sense that they complement each other. An educational system built upon either one or the other alone will be incomplete.

I should like to comment briefly here on one important factor or method in the development of the attitude of appreciative awareness. We have discussed one of the two fundamental ways in which social reconstruction shall take place; namely, the building of a new content for the educational program out of the culture of the people. But there is another and equally important one—the building of a new conception of labor and the method of its application in the school.

The new conception that I have in mind embraces two clear connotations—first, labor that is socially useful; second, labor that is creative. The old education denied labor of these types a place in its program. It recognized only intellectual activity, and assumed a hierarchy of social organization in which its product would have no contact with "labor." Under such an educational regime, and in cooperation with the growing mechanization of productive activities, the concept of labor came to emphasize manual skill and repetition. With the decline of the craftsman, the concept of creative labor steadily passed away.

Furthermore, other factors cooperate to urge upon us the reconsideration of our concept of labor and its place in education. These are the world-wide emergence of an unwieldy white-collar class, the aspiration of youth to enter the "paper" occupations, the increasing dislike, even contempt for hand labor, and the belittling of social and manual intelligence in the modern educational programs.

This two-fold concept of socially useful and creative labor is, in the hand of the educator, an effective instrument for social reconstruction. For, while it centers attention on the development of individual personality as the basis of a fine social life, it also recognizes definitely the role of the social group. The current nation-wide experiments of the Russians are bringing out clearly the intrinsic educational value of socially useful work. Correspondingly, the experiments of the child-centered schools in America and Europe have established the creative act as an indispensable factor in the complete education of the individual. And the astute studies of practical philosophers, such as Aaron Gordon, establish creative labor as an indispensable factor in the building of a sound national personality. Thus the new concept of labor, socially useful and creative, if incorporated in our educational theory, will have both individual and social implications.

In the past fifteen years of the new education, no event has been of more significance than that of the creative artist crossing the threshold of the classroom. As he has done so in increasing numbers, he has established beyond the possibility of doubt the fact that maximum appreciation and maximum personality eventuate only from participation in the creative act. Surround the young people with fine creative products, practice them in discriminating judgment, develop the thrill of rich aesthetic experience—all these steps we shall also employ. But for the finest production of persons—and that is our supreme goal, if we would produce a fine social order—we must employ the creative act.

I cannot escape the conclusion, therefore, that bodily education and especially creative handcraft, must come to have a place in the new education coordinate with that of literary education. Leaders and followers alike, the talented few as well as the mediocre mass, must be equipped with a respect for handcraft, as well as mindcraft, and practiced in appreciation of form with every medium of expression.

The production of craftsmen, then, is to be the supreme aim of the new education; not, in industrial countries, as the means of producing food, shelter, and clothing, but as the means of producing sound personalities. Especially is this demanded of us by the swiftly increasing mechanization of all the productive activities, and by the rapid decline of hours of labor and the consequent social danger of an idle and uncultured mass.

For the craftsman, working lovingly at his total product, not only molds his whole personality into it; his molding of it produces in him a new personality. Whatever the medium of expression, this is the process and the result. They work their wonders alike in the Japanese farmer tenderly nursing his garden plot, the Moro metal worker hammering a silver ring out of a Spanish peso, the New England cabinet-maker rubbing his wood surface, or Brancusi shaping his marble. In the process, product and laborer change together—if the labor is creative, that is, if it is an original, honest expression of the worker, of his moods, of his comprehension of and feeling for life. Thus the new educational program shall consist of a stream of activities, each of which, so far as possible, involves socially useful and crative labor.

Questions for Discussion

THE essays beginning with Gentile and ending with Rugg present the full spectrum of positions on the role of education in the social order. Gentile interprets national consciousness in terms of a collective spiritual energy rather than in terms of tangible material elements. The individual is realized through the State and the Will of the State is nourished by the thoughts and aspirations of its people. Science and other areas of knowledge are discovered or acquired by personalities that are part of a nation and, therefore, all schooling and learning have a national consciousness.

Gentile holds that for man to will that which runs counter to the state would be to disintegrate personality, for the personality and identity of all men are nationally derived. Education, too, is indigenous and derives its form and meaning from the state. In such a system, what do you believe education should attempt to do?

Kandel asks whether the school should be an instrument for the reconstruction of society. He notes that the most persistent reason for the establishment of schools has always been the preservation and trans- mission of the cultural heritage. The school is an agency for promoting stability and adapting the individual to society. And if the school ceases to perform these functions, it either stagnates or comes under the control of the will of a few. Schools should discuss controversial issues; but, it should be remembered, society changes first, and education follows.

What similarities and differences do you find in the position of Gentile and Kandel? Which one do you believe to be more defensible? Why?

According to Dewey, schools do reflect the existing social order and take part in the changes of society. Schools, like society itself, are in a state of flux. The question is not whether schools will influence social life, but in what direction and in what way they should do so. Do some of Dewey's criticisms of the conservative position apply to Kandel?

Rugg demands a thorough social reconstruction of education as the best means to deal with the unprecedented changes and conflicts in the modern world. He lays out a program to show how the educational leaders of the world can join forces in a dynamic program of social action to bring about the social reconstruction that the world solely needs.

How do the views of Dewey and Rugg differ? Which set of proposals do you believe will best meet the demands of contemporary life?

CHAPTER FOUR /

EDUCATIONAL VALUES

THERE is a pervasive quality about values; they can be found in all activities—individual or collective. Sometimes values are not recognized because they are assumed or are implicit; however, this makes them no less important, for frequently it is necessary to define and deal with the values that guide our decisions.

Our form of government rests on a system of values based on the rights of the individual. Systems of values are also found in our social institutions—family, economic, religious, and educational—as well as the various groups and agencies concerned with social relations. The fundamental bases and directions for the operations of social institutions stem from the values upon which they were established. For example, a basic value in the family is monogamy; in the economy it is private ownership; in religion it is freedom of conscience; in education it is equality of opportunity. These are just a few basic values. No doubt you can think of others.

Values are not fixed but undergo constant change and modification with the advent of new developments in government, technology, human relations, international affairs, the family, and other organized aspects of society. For instance, value changes occur in the economy with the advent of automation; in the family by the widespread dissemination of contraceptives; in international diplomacy with the general increase of nuclear weapons. In the face of uncertainty and confusion, some may search for eternal values which will provide a sense of direction; others may not believe that such values exist and prefer to use alternative sets of values as guides to action, believing that values should be flexible and adaptable.

It is readily apparent that decisions concerning values are of primary concern for educational institutions. Society expects the school to develop desirable behavior in youth as well as to provide them with skills and knowledge. The exact responsibility that the school has in this area is still a matter of debate, and it is not clearly defined where the duties of the family end and those of the school begin. This, however, is not a new problem. Effective teaching of moral values—so that the good citizen and the moral individual results—has been a source of perplexity and consternation in many civilizations of the past.

The confusion over values in our society frequently is mirrored in education. Educators must understand and be able to handle the many value conflicts that arise, for education is a value-infused process, in which the resolution of conflict situations frequently revolves around a reinterpretation or reconstruction of values. Some of the most important problems in education cannot be resolved without a serious attempt to adjudicate value conflicts. The process of education is designed to bring about certain desirable changes in youth, and the desirability of such changes can not be known apart from a consideration of the value questions involved. The process of developing a curriculum involves value decisions as to the forms of knowledge and materials that are to be chosen to secure certain ends. In like manner, other operations within an educational system, such as counseling and administration, can scarcely avoid a confrontation with values if decisions are to be made intelligently.

The great complexities involved in teaching moral values do not seem to have discouraged many from trying to clarify the process; but the same complexities seem to have caused much of what has been written to take the form of prescribing or proscribing certain values or advancing imperatives that entreat the reader to adopt a preferred system of norms. Writings on moral values, however, need to elucidate their nature, the logic of their use, and the modes of their justification. The selections that follow were chosen for these qualities and for their provocativeness related to the teaching of moral values. The essays raise exceedingly important questions and attempt to unravel some of the issues which have confounded educators for many generations.

Plato's *Protagoras* (the first selection) is a splendid piece of argumentation. This is one of the four great dialogues written during the height of Plato's literary activity, and it is probably surpassed in literary quality only by the *Symposium*. In the dialogue Socrates raises some doubts as to why good men have difficulty teaching goodness to children. He then wonders whether the virtues—justice, wisdom, temperance and courage —are identical. Both Protagoras and Socrates, holding opposite positions in the beginning, seem to reverse their positions in the end.

R. M. Hare, a leading English moral philosopher, deals with questions of moral training after considering the roles of decision and principle in conduct (Selection 14). Hare sees principles as necessary to moral education, but still recognizes the need for the overarching process of autonomous moral decision-making by youth. He provides an important analysis of teaching, moral conduct, and character. This is a lucid discussion that makes use of the tools of philosophical analysis.

Selection 15 is an important esasy on ethics and moral values by Dewey. He first takes an historical look at conceptions of moral values, explores their shortcomings, and offers a new perspective; then he develops the educational import of his new conception of morals. Some of Dewey's most famous quotations are to be found in this essay.

In Selection 16 William K. Frankena presents a host of problems that have confused and confounded educators for some time. Basically, he is concerned with the issue of moral and spiritual values in the public school. He makes some distinctions as to the meaning of "the good life," then examines the thesis that religion is essential to the good life. He then questions the necessity to teach religion in the public schools in order to have moral education for youth. His analysis is trenchant, and he discusses each issue with great care.

13 / PLATO

Protagoras

PERSONS OF THE DIALOGUE

SOCRATES, *who is the narrator of the Dialogue to his Companion*
HIPPOCRATES
ALCIBIADES

CRITIAS
PROTAGORAS
HIPPIAS
PRODICUS
} *Sophists*

CALLIAS, *a wealthy Athenian*

SCENE: The House of Callias.

Companion. Where do you come from, Socrates? And yet I need hardly ask the question, for I know that you have been in chase of the fair Alcibiades. I saw him the day before yesterday; and he had got a beard like a man,—and he is a man, as I may tell you in your ear. But I thought that he was still very charming.

Soc. What of his beard? Are you not of Homer's opinion, who says, "Youth is most charming when the beard appears"? And that is now the charm of Alcibiades.

Com. Well, and how do matters proceed? Have you been visiting him, and was he gracious to you?

Soc. Yes, I thought that he was very gracious; and especially today, for I have just come from him, and he has been helping me in an argument. But shall I tell you a strange thing? I paid no attention to him, and several times I quite forgot that he was present.

Com. What is the meaning of this? Has anything happened between you and him? For surely you cannot have discovered a fairer love than he is; certainly not in this city of Athens.

Soc. Yes, much fairer.

Com. What do you mean—a citizen or a foreigner?

Soc. A foreigner.

Com. Of what country?

Soc. Of Abdera.

Com. And is this stranger really in your opinion a fairer love than the son of Cleinias?

Soc. And is not the wiser always the fairer, sweet friend?

Com. But have you really met, Socrates, with some wise one?

Soc. Say rather, with the wisest of all living men, if you are willing to accord that title to Protagoras.

Com. What! Is Protagoras in Athens?

Soc. Yes; he has been here two days.

Com. And do you just come from an interview with him?

Soc. Yes; and I have heard and said many things.

Com. Then, if you have no engagement, suppose that you sit down and tell me what passed, and my attendant here shall give up his place to you.

Soc. To be sure; and I shall be grateful to you for listening.

Com. Thank you, too, for telling us.

Soc. That is thank you twice over. Listen then:—

Last night, or rather very early this morning, Hippocrates, the son of Apollodorus and the brother of Phason, gave a tremendous thump with his staff at my door; some one opened to him, and he came rushing in and bawled out: Socrates, are you awake or asleep?

I knew his voice, and said: Hippocrates, is that you? and do you bring any news?

Good news, he said; nothing but good.

Delightful, I said; but what is the news? and why have you come hither at this unearthly hour?

He drew nearer to me and said: Protagoras is come.

Yes, I replied; he came two days ago: have you only just heard of his arrival?

Yes, by the gods, he said; but not until yesterday evening.

At the same time he felt for the truckle-bed, and sat down at my feet, and then he said: Yesterday, quite late in the evening, on my return from Oenoe, whither I had gone in pursuit of my runaway slave Satyrus, as I meant to have told you, if some other matter had not come in the way;— on my return, when we had done supper and were about to retire to rest, my brother said to me: Protagoras is come. I was going to you at once, and then I thought that the night was far spent. But the moment sleep left me after my fatigue, I got up and came hither direct.

I, who knew the very courageous madness of the man, said: What is the matter? Has Protagoras robbed you of anything?

He replied, laughing: Yes, indeed he has, Socrates, of the wisdom which he keeps from me.

But, surely, I said, if you give him money, and make friends with him, he will make you as wise as he is himself.

Would to heaven, he replied, that this were the case! He might take all that I have, and all that my friends have, if he pleased. But that is why I have come to you now, in order that you may speak to him on my behalf; for I am young and also I have never seen nor heard him (when he visited Athens before I was but a child); and all men praise him, Socrates; he is reputed to be the most accomplished of speakers. There is no reason why we should not go to him at once, and then we shall find him at home. He lodges, as I hear, with Callias the son of Hipponicus: let us start.

I replied: Not yet, my good friend; the hour is too early. But let us rise and take a turn in the court and wait about there until daybreak; when the day breaks, then we will go. For Protagoras is generally at home, and we shall be sure to find him; never fear.

Upon this we got up and walked about in the court, and I thought that I would make trial of the strength of his resolution. So I examined him and put questions to him. Tell me, Hippocrates, I said, as you are going to Protagoras, and will be paying your money to him, what is he to whom you are going? and what will he make of you? If, for example, you had thought of going to Hippocrates of Cos, the Asclepiad, and were about to give him your money, and some one had said to you: You are paying money to your namesake Hippocrates, O Hippocrates; tell me, what is he that you give him money? how would you have answered?

I should say, he replied, that I gave money to him as a physician.

And what will he make of you?

A physician, he said.

And if you were resolved to go to Polycleitus the Argive, or Pheidias the Athenian, and were intending to give them money, and some one had asked you: What are Polycleitus and Pheidias? and why do you give them this money?—how would you have answered?

I should have answered, that they were statuaries.

And what will they make of you?

A statuary, of course.

Well, now, I said, you and I are going to Protagoras, and we are ready to pay him money on your behalf. If our own means are sufficient, and we can gain him with these, we shall be only too glad; but if not, then we are to spend the money of your friends as well. Now suppose that while we are thus enthusiastically pursuing our object some one were to say to us: Tell me, Socrates, and you Hippocrates, what is Protagoras, and why are you going to pay him money?—how should we answer? I know that Pheidias is a sculptor, and that Homer is a poet; but what appellation is given to Protagoras? how is he designated?

They call him a Sophist, Socrates, he replied.

Then we are going to pay our money to him in the character of a Sophist?

Certainly.

But suppose a person were to ask this further question: And how about yourself? What will Protagoras make of you, if you go to see him?

He answered, with a blush upon his face (for the day was just beginning to dawn, so that I could see him): Unless this differs in some way from the former instances, I suppose that he will make a Sophist of me.

By the gods, I said, and are you not ashamed at having to appear before the Hellenes in the character of a Sophist?

Indeed, Socrates, to confess the truth, I am.

But you should not assume, Hippocrates, that the instruction of Protagoras is of this nature: may you not learn of him in the same way that you learned the arts of the grammarian, or musician, or trainer, not with the view of making any of them a profession, but only as a part of education, and because a private gentleman and freeman ought to know them?

Just so, he said; and that, in my opinion, is a far truer account of the teaching of Protagoras.

I said: I wonder whether you know what you are doing?

And what am I doing?

You are going to commit your soul to the care of a man whom you call a Sophist. And yet I hardly think that you know what a Sophist is; and if not, then you do not even know to whom you are committing your soul and whether the thing to which you commit yourself be good or evil.

I certainly think that I do know, he replied.

Then tell me, what do you imagine that he is?

I take him to be one who knows wise things, he replied, as his name implies.

And might you not, I said, affirm this of the painter and of the carpenter also: Do not they, too, know wise things? But suppose a person were to ask us: In what are the painters wise? We should answer: In what relates to the making of likenesses, and similarly of other things. And if he were further to ask: What is the wisdom of the Sophist, and what is the manufacture over which he presides?—how should we answer him?

How should we answer him, Socrates? What other answer could there be but that he presides over the art which makes men eloquent?

Yes, I replied, that is very likely true, but not enough; for in the answer a further question is involved: Of what does the Sophist make a man talk eloquently? The player on the lyre may be supposed to make a man talk eloquently about that which he makes him understand, that is about playing the lyre. Is not that true?

Yes.

Then about what does the Sophist make him eloquent? Must not he make him eloquent in that which he understands?

Yes, that may be assumed.

And what is that which the Sophist knows and makes his disciples know?

Indeed, he said, I cannot tell.

Then I proceeded to say: Well, but are you aware of the danger which you are incurring? If you were going to commit your body to some one, who might do good or harm to it, would you not carefully consider and ask the opinion of your friends and kindred, and deliberate many days as to whether you should give him the care of your body? But when the soul is in question, which you hold to be of far more value than the body, and upon the good or evil of which depends the well-being of your all,— about this you never consulted either with your father or with your brother or with any one of us who are your companions. But no sooner does this foreigner appear, than you instantly commit your soul to his keeping. In the evening, as you say, you hear of him, and in the morning you go to him, never deliberating or taking the opinion of any one as to whether you ought to entrust yourself to him or not;—you have quite made up your mind that you will at all hazards be a pupil of Protagoras, and are prepared to expend all the property of yourself and of your friends in carrying out at any price this determination, although, as you admit, you do not know him, and have never spoken with him: and you call him a Sophist, but are manifestly ignorant of what a Sophist is; and yet you are going to commit yourself to his keeping.

When he heard me say this, he replied: No other inference, Socrates, can be drawn from your words.

I proceeded: Is not a Sophist, Hippocrates, one who deals wholesale or retail in the food of the soul? To me that appears to be his nature.

And what, Socrates, is the food of the soul?

Surely, I said, knowledge is the food of the soul; and we must take care, my friend, that the Sophist does not deceive us when he praises what he sells, like the dealers wholesale or retail who sell the food of the body; for they praise indiscriminately all their goods, without knowing what are really beneficial or hurtful: neither do their customers know, with the exception of any trainer or physician who may happen to buy of them. In like manner those who carry about the wares of knowledge, and make the round of the cities, and sell or retail them to any customer who is in want of them, praise them all alike; thought I should not wonder, O my friend, if many of them were really ignorant of their effect upon the soul; and their customers equally ignorant, unless he who buys of them happens to be a physician of the soul. If, therefore, you have understanding of what is good and evil, you may safely buy knowledge of Protagoras or of any one; but if not, then, O my friend, pause, and do not hazard your dearest interests at a game of chance. For there is far greater peril in buying knowledge than in buying meat and drink: the one you purchase of the wholesale or retail dealer, and carry them away in other vessels, and before you receive them into the body as food, you may deposit them at home and call in any experienced friend who knows what is good to be eaten or drunken, and what not, and how much, and when; and then the danger of purchasing them is not so great. But you cannot buy the wares of knowledge and carry them away in another vessel; when you have paid for them you must receive them into the soul and go your way, either greatly harmed or greatly benefited; and therefore we should deliberate and take counsel with our elders; for we are still young—too young to determine such a matter. And now let us go, as we were intending, and hear Protagoras; and when we have heard what he has to say, we may take counsel of others; for not only is Protagoras at the house of Callias, but there is Hippias of Elis, and, if I am not mistaken, Prodicus of Ceos, and several other wise men.

To this we agreed, and proceeded on our way until we reached the vestibule of the house; and there we stopped in order to conclude a discussion which had arisen between us as we were going along; and we stood talking in the vestibule until we had finished and come to an understanding. And I think that the doorkeeper, who was a eunuch, and who was probably annoyed at the great inroad of the Sophists, must have heard us talking. At any rate, when we knocked at the door, and he opened and saw us, he grumbled: They are Sophists—he is not at home; and instantly gave the door a hearty bang with both his hands. Again we knocked, and he answered without opening: Did you not hear me say that he is not at home, fellows? But, my friend, I said, you need not be alarmed; for we are not Sophists, and we are not come to see Callias, but we want to see Protagoras; and I must request you to announce us. At last, after a good deal of difficulty, the man was persuaded to open the door.

When we entered, we found Protagoras taking a walk in the cloister; and next to him, on one side, were walking Callias, the son of Hipponicus, and Paralus, the son of Pericles, who, by the mother's side, is his half-brother, and Charmides, the son of Glaucon. On the other side of him were Xanthippus, the other son of Pericles, Philippides, the son of Philomeus; also Antimoerus of Mende, who of all the disciples of Protagoras is the most famous, and intends to make sophistry his profession. A train of listeners followed him; the greater part of them appeared to be foreigners, whom Protagoras had brought with him out of the various cities visited by him in his journeys, he, like Orpheus, attracting them by his voice, and they following. I should mention also that there were some Athenians in the company. Nothing delighted me more than the precision of their movements: they never got into his way at all; but when he and those who were with him turned back, then the band of listeners parted regularly on either side; he was always in front, and they wheeled round and took their places behind him in perfect order.

After him, as Homer says, "I lifted my eyes and saw" Hippias the Elean sitting in the opposite cloister on a chair of state, and around him were seated on benches Eryximachus, the son of Acumenus, and Phaedrus the Myrrhinusian, and Andron the son of Androtion, and there were strangers whom he had brought with him from his native city of Elis, and some others: they were putting to Hippias certain physical and astronomical questions, and he, *ex cathedra*, was determining their several questions to them, and discoursing of them.

Also, "my eyes beheld Tantalus"; for Prodicus the Cean was at Athens: he had been lodged in a room which, in the days of Hipponicus, was a storehouse; but, as the house was full, Callias had cleared this out and made the room into a guest chamber. Now Prodicus was still in bed, wrapped up in sheepskins and bedclothes, of which there seemed to be a great heap; and there was sitting by him on the couches near, Pausanias of the deme of Cerameis, and with Pausanias was a youth quite young, who is certainly remarkable for his good looks, and, if I am not mistaken, is also of a fair and gentle nature. I thought that I heard him called Agathon, and my suspicion is that he is the beloved of Pausanias. There was this youth, and also there were the two Adeimantuses, one the son of Cepis, and the other of Leucolophides, and some others. I was very anxious to hear what Prodicus was saying, for he seems to me to be an all-wise and inspired man; but I was not able to get into the inner circle, and his fine deep voice made an echo in the room which rendered his words inaudible.

No sooner had we entered than there followed us Alcibiades the beautiful, as you say, and I believe you; and also Critias the son of Callaeschrus.

On entering we stopped a little, in order to look about us, and then walked up to Protagoras, and I said: Protagoras, my friend Hippocrates and I have come to see you.

Do you wish, he said, to speak with me alone, or in the presence of the company?

Whichever you please, I said; you shall determine when you have heard the purpose of our visit.

And what is your purpose? he said.

I must explain, I said, that my friend Hippocrates is a native Athenian; he is the son of Apollodorus, and of a great and prosperous house, and he is himself in natural ability quite a match for anybody of his own age. I believe that he aspires to political eminence; and this he thinks that conversation with you is most likely to procure for him. And now you can determine whether you would wish to speak to him of your teaching alone or in the presence of the company.

Thank you, Socrates, for your consideration of me. For certainly a stranger finding his way into great cities, and persuading the flower of the youth in them to leave the company of their kinsmen or any other acquaintances, old or young, and live with him, under the idea that they will be improved by his conversation, ought to be very cautious; great jealousies are aroused by his proceedings, and he is the subject of many enmities and conspiracies. Now the art of the Sophist is, as I believe, of great antiquity; but in ancient times those who practised it, fearing this odium, veiled and disguised themselves under various names, some under that of poets, as Homer, Hesiod, and Simonides, some, of hierophants and prophets, as Orpheus and Musaeus, and some, as I observe, even under the name of gymnastic masters, like Iccus of Tarentum, or the more recently celebrated Herodicus, now of Selymbria and formerly of Megara, who is a first-rate Sophist. Your own Agathocles pretended to be a musician, but was really an eminent Sophist; also Pythocleides the Cean; and there were many others; and all of them, as I was saying, adopted these arts as veils or disguises because they were afraid of the odium which they would incur. But that is not my way, for I do not believe that they effected their purpose, which was to deceive the government, who were not blinded by them; and as to the people, they have no understanding, and only repeat what their rulers are pleased to tell them. Now to run away, and to be caught in running away, is the very height of folly, and also greatly increases the exasperation of mankind; for they regard him who runs away as a rogue, in addition to any other objections which they have to him; and therefore I take an entirely opposite course, and acknowledge myself to be a Sophist and instructor of mankind; such an open acknowledgment appears to me to be a better sort of caution than concealment. Nor do I neglect other precautions, and therefore I hope, as I may say, by the favour of heaven that no harm will come of the acknowledgment that I am a Sophist. And I have been now many years in the profession—for all my years when added up are many: there is no one here present of whom I might not be the father. Wherefore I should much prefer conversing with you, if you want to speak with me, in the presence of the company.

As I suspected that he would like to have a little display and glorification in the presence of Prodicus and Hippias, and would gladly show us to them in the light of his admirers, I said: But why should we not summon Prodicus and Hippias and their friends to hear us?

Very good, he said.

Suppose, said Callias, that we hold a council in which you may sit and discuss.—This was agreed upon, and great delight was felt at the prospect of hearing wise men talk; we ourselves took the chairs and benches, and arranged them by Hippias, where the other benches had been already placed. Meanwhile Callias and Alcibiades got Prodicus out of bed and brought in him and his companions.

When we were all seated, Protagoras said: Now that the company are assembled, Socrates, tell me about the young man of whom you were just now speaking.

I replied: I will begin again at the same point, Protagoras, and tell you once more the purport of my visit: this is my friend Hippocrates, who is desirous of making your acquaintance; he would like to know what will happen to him if he associates with you. I have no more to say.

Protagoras answered: Young man, if you associate with me, on the very first day you will return home a better man than you came, and better on the second day than on the first, and better every day than you were on the day before.

When I heard this, I said: Protagoras, I do not at all wonder at hearing you say this; even at your age, and with all your wisdom, if any one were to teach you what you did not know before, you would become better no doubt: but please to answer in a different way—I will explain how by an example. Let me suppose that Hippocrates, instead of desiring your acquaintance, wished to become acquainted with the young man Zeuxippus of Heraclea, who has lately been in Athens, and he had come to him as he has come to you, and had heard him say, as he has heard you say, that every day he would grow and become better if he associated with him: and then suppose that he were to ask him, "In what shall I become better, and in what shall I grow?" Zeuxippus would answer, "In painting." And suppose that he went to Orthagoras the Theban, and heard him say the same thing, and asked him, "In what shall I become better day by day?" He would reply, "In flute-playing." Now I want you to make the same sort of answer to this young man and to me, who am asking questions on his account. When you say that on the first day on which he associates with you he will return home a better man, and on every day will grow in like manner,—in what, Protagoras, will he be better? and about what?

When Protagoras heard me say this, he replied: You ask questions fairly, and I like to answer a question which is fairly put. If Hippocrates comes to me he will not experience the sort of drudgery with which other Sophists are in the habit of insulting their pupils; who, when they have just escaped from the arts, are taken and driven back into them by these teachers, and made to learn calculation, and astronomy, and geometry, and music (he gave a look at Hippias as he said this); but if he comes to me, he will learn that which he comes to learn. And this is prudence in affairs private as well as public; he will learn to order his own house in the best manner, and he will be able to speak and act for the best in the affairs of the State.

Do I understand you, I said; and is your meaning that you teach the art of politics, and that you promise to make men good citizens?

That, Socrates, is exactly the profession which I make.

Then, I said, you do indeed possess a noble art, if there is no mistake about this; for I will freely confess to you, Protagoras, that I have a doubt whether this art is capable of being taught, and yet I know not how to disbelieve your assertion. And I ought to tell you why I am of opinion that this art cannot be taught or communicated by man to man. I say that the Athenians are an understanding people, and indeed they are esteemed to be such by the other Hellenes. Now I observe that when we are met together in the assembly, and the matter in hand relates to building, the builders are summoned as advisers; when the question is one of shipbuilding, then the shipwrights; and the like of other arts which they think capable of being taught and learned. And if some person offers to give them advice who is not supposed by them to have any more skill in the art than they, but to be good-looking, and rich, and noble, they don't listen to him, but laugh at him, and hoot him, until either he is clamoured down and retires of himself; or he persists, but is dragged away or put out by the constables at the command of the prytanes. This is their way of behaving about professors of the arts. But when the question is an affair of state, then everybody is free to have a say—carpenter, tinker, cobbler, sailor, passenger; rich and poor, high and low—any one who likes gets up, and no one reproaches him, as in the former case, with not having learned, and having no teacher, and yet giving advice; evidently because they are under the impression that this sort of knowledge cannot be taught. And not only is this true of the State, but of individuals; the best and wisest of our citizens are unable to impart their political wisdom to others: as for example, Pericles, the father of these young men, who gave them excellent instruction in all that could be learned from masters, in his own department of politics neither taught them, nor gave them teachers; but they were allowed to wander at their own free will in a sort of hope that they would light upon virtue of their own accord. Or take another example: there was Cleinias the younger brother of our friend Alcibiades, of whom this very same Pericles was the guardian; and he being in fact under the apprehension that Cleinias would be corrupted by Alcibiades, took him away, and placed him in the house of Ariphron to be educated; but before six months had elapsed, Ariphron sent him back, not knowing what to do with him. And I could mention numberless other instances of persons who were good themselves, and never yet made any one else good, whether friend or stranger. Now I, Protagoras, having these examples before me, am inclined to think that virtue cannot be taught. But then again, when I listen to your words, I waver; and am disposed to think that there must be something in what you say, because I know that you have great experience, and learning, and invention. And I wish that you would, if possible, show me a little more clearly that virtue can be taught. Will you be so good?

That I will, Socrates, and gladly. But what would you like? Shall I, as an elder, speak to you as younger men in an apologue or myth, or shall I argue out the question?

To this several of the company answered that he should choose for himself.

Well, then, he said, I think that the myth will be more interesting.

Once upon a time there were gods only, and no mortal creatures. But when the time came that these also should be created, the gods fashioned them out of earth and fire and various mixtures of both elements in the interior of the earth; and when they were about to bring them into the light of day, they ordered Prometheus and Epimetheus to equip them, and to distribute to them severally their proper qualities. Epimetheus said to Prometheus: "Let me distribute, and do you inspect." This was agreed, and Epimetheus made the distribution. There were some to whom he gave strength without swiftness, while he equipped the weaker with swiftness; some he armed, and others he left unarmed; and devised for the latter some other means of preservation, making some large, and having their size as a protection, and others small, whose nature was to fly in the air or burrow in the ground; this was to be their way of escape. Thus did he compensate them with the view of preventing any race from becoming extinct. And when he had provided against their destruction by one another, he contrived also a means of protecting them against the seasons of heaven; clothing them with close hair and thick skins sufficient to defend them against the winter cold and able to resist the summer heat, so that they might have a natural bed of their own when they wanted to rest; also he furnished them with hoofs and hair and hard and callous skins under their feet. Then he gave them varieties of food,—herb of the soil to some, to others fruits of trees, and to others roots, and to some again he gave other animals as food. And some he made to have few young ones, while those who were their prey were very prolific; and in this manner the race was preserved. Thus did Epimetheus, who, not being very wise, forgot that he had distributed among the brute animals all the qualities which he had to give,—and when he came to man, who was still unprovided, he was terribly perplexed. Now, while he was in this perplexity, Prometheus came to inspect the distribution, and he found that the other animals were suitably furnished, but that man alone was naked and shoeless, and had neither bed nor arms of defence. The appointed hour was approaching when man in his turn was to go forth into the light of day; and Prometheus, not knowing how he could devise his salvation, stole the mechanical arts of Hephaestus and Athene, and fire with them (they could neither have been acquired nor used without fire), and gave them to man. Thus man had the wisdom necessary to the support of life, but political wisdom he had not; for that was in the keeping of Zeus, and the power of Prometheus did not extend to entering into the citadel of heaven, where Zeus dwelt, who moreover had terrible sentinels; but he did enter by stealth into the common workshop of Athene and Hephaestus, in which they used to practise their favourite arts, and carried off Hephaestus' art of working by fire, and also the art of Athene, and gave them to man. And in this way man was supplied with the means of life. But Prometheus is said to have been afterwards prosecuted for theft, owing to the blunder of Epimetheus.

Now man, having a share of the divine attributes, was at first the only one of the animals who had any gods, because he alone was of their kindred; and he would raise altars and images of them. He was not long in inventing articulate speech and names; and he also constructed houses and clothes and shoes and beds, and drew sustenance from the earth. Thus provided, mankind at first lived dispersed, and there were no cities. But the consequence was that they were destroyed by the wild beasts, for they were utterly weak in comparison of them, and their art was only sufficient to provide them with the means of life, and did not enable them to carry on war against the animals: food they had, but not as yet the art of government, of which the art of war is a part. After a while the desire of self-preservation gathered them into cities; but when they were gathered together, having no art of government, they evil entreated one another, and were again in process of dispersion and destruction. Zeus feared that the entire race would be exterminated, and so he sent Hermes to them, bearing reverence and justice to be the ordering principles of cities and the bonds of friendship and conciliation. Hermes asked Zeus how he should impart justice and reverence among men:—Should he distribute them as the arts are distributed; that is to say, to a favoured few only, one skilled individual having enough of medicine or of any other art for many unskilled ones? "Shall this be the manner in which I am to distribute justice and reverence among men, or shall I give them to all?" "To all," said Zeus; "I should like them all to have a share; for cities cannot exist, if a few only share in the virtues, as in the arts. And further, make a law by my order, that he who has no part in reverence and justice shall be put to death, for he is a plague of the State."

And this is the reason, Socrates, why the Athenians and mankind in general, when the question relates to carpentering or any other mechanical art, allow but a few to share in their deliberations; and when any one else interferes, then, as you say, they object, if he be not of the favoured few; which, as I reply, is very natural. But when they meet to deliberate about political virtue, which proceeds only by way of justice and wisdom, they are patient enough of any man who speaks of them, as is also natural, because they think that every man ought to share in this sort of virtue, and that States could not exist if this were otherwise. I have explained to you, Socrates, the reason of this phenomenon.

And that you may not suppose yourself to be deceived in thinking that all men regard every man as having a share of justice or honesty and of every other political virtue, let me give you a further proof, which is this. In other cases, as you are aware, if a man says that he is a good flute-player, or skilful in any other art in which he has no skill, people either laugh at him or are angry with him, and his relations think that he is mad and go and admonish him; but when honesty is in question, or some other political virtue, even if they know that he is dishonest, yet if the man comes publicly forward and tells the truth about his dishonesty, then, what in the other case was held by them to be good sense, they now deem to be madness. They say that all men ought to profess honesty whether they are honest or not, and that a man is out of his mind who says anything else. Their notion is, that a man must have some degree of honesty; and that if he has none at all he ought not to be in the world.

I have been showing that they are right in admitting every man as a counsellor about this sort of virtue, as they are of opinion that every man is a partaker of it. And I will now endeavour to show further that they do not conceive this virtue to be given by nature, or to grow spontaneously, but to be a thing which may be taught; and which comes to a man by taking pains. No one would instruct, no one would rebuke, or be angry with those whose calamities they suppose to be due to nature or chance; they do not try to punish or to prevent them from being what they are; they do but pity them. Who is so foolish as to chastise or instruct the ugly, or the diminutive, or the feeble? And for this reason. Because he knows that good and evil of this kind is the work of nature and of chance; whereas if a man is wanting in those good qualities which are attained by study and exercise and teaching, and has only the contrary evil qualities, other men are angry with him, and punish and reprove him—of these evil qualities one is impiety, another injustice, and they may be described generally as the very opposite of political virtue. In such cases any man will be angry with another, and reprimand him,—clearly because he thinks that by study and learning, the virtue in which the other is deficient may be acquired. If you will think, Socrates, of the nature of punishment, you will see at once that in the opinion of mankind virtue may be acquired; no one punishes the evil-doer under the notion, or for the reason, that he has done wrong,—only the unreasonable fury of a beast acts in that manner. But he who desires to inflict rational punishment does not retaliate for a past wrong which cannot be undone; he has regard to the future, and is desirous that the man who is punished, and he who sees him punished, may be deterred from doing wrong again. He punishes for the sake of prevention, thereby clearly implying that virtue is capable of being taught. This is the notion of all who retaliate upon others either privately or publicly. And the Athenians, too, your own citizens, like other men, punish and take vengeance on all whom they regard as evil-doers; and hence, we may infer them to be of the number of those who think that virtue may be acquired and taught. Thus far, Socrates, I have shown you clearly enough, if I am not mistaken, that your countrymen are right in admitting the tinker and the cobbler to advise about politics, and also that they deem virtue to be capable of being taught and acquired.

There yet remains one difficulty which has been raised by you about the sons of good men. What is the reason why good men teach their sons the knowledge which is gained from teachers, and make them wise in that, but do nothing towards improving them in virtues which distinguish themselves? And here, Socrates, I will leave the apologue and resume the argument. Please to consider: Is there or is there not some one quality of which all the citizens must be partakers, if there is to be a city at all? In the answer to this question is contained the only solution of your difficulty; there is no other. For if there be any such quality, and this quality or unity is not the art of the carpenter, or the smith, or the potter, but justice and temperance and holiness and, in a word, manly virtue—if this is the quality of which all men must be partakers, and which is the very condition of their learning or doing anything else, and if he who is wanting in this, whether he be a child only or a grown-up man or woman, must be taught and punished, until by punishment he becomes better, and he who rebels against instruction and punishment is either exiled or condemned to death under the idea that he is incurable—if what I am saying be true, good men have their sons taught other things and not this, do consider how extraordinary their conduct would appear to be. For we have shown that they think virtue capable of being taught and cultivated both in private and public; and, notwithstanding, they have their sons taught lesser matters, ignorance of which does not involve the punishment of death: but greater things, of which the ignorance may cause death and exile to those who have no training or knowledge of them— aye, and confiscation as well as death, and, in a word, may be the ruin of families—those things, I say, they are supposed not to teach them,—not to take the utmost care that they should learn. How improbable is this, Socrates!

Education and admonition commence in the first years of childhood, and last to the very end of life. Mother and nurse and father and tutor are vying with one another about the improvement of the child as soon as ever he is able to understand what is being said to him: he cannot say or do anything without their setting forth to him that this is just and that is unjust; this is honourable, that is dishonourable; this is holy, that is unholy; do this and abstain from that. And if he obeys, well and good; if not, he is straightened by threats and blows, like a piece of bent or warped wood. At a later stage they send him to teachers, and enjoin them to see to his manners even more than to his reading and music; and the teachers do as they are desired. And when the boy has learned his letters and is beginning to understand what is written, as before he understood only what was spoken, they put into his hands the works of great poets, which he reads sitting on a bench at school; in these are contained many admonitions, and many tales, and praises, and encomia of ancient famous men, which he is required to learn by heart, in order that he may imitate or emulate them and desire to become like them. Then, again, the teachers of the lyre take similar care that their young disciple is temperate and gets into no mischief; and when they have taught him the use of the lyre, they introduce him to the poems of other excellent poets, who are the lyric poets; and these they set to music, and make their harmonies and rhythms quite familiar to the children's souls, in order that they may learn to be more gentle, and harmonious, and rhythmical, and so fitted for speech and action; for the life of man in every part has need of harmony and rhythm. Then they send them to the master of gymnastic, in order that their bodies may better minister to the virtuous mind, and that they may not be compelled through bodily weakness to play the coward in war or on any other occasion. This is what is done by those who have the means, and those who have the means are the rich; their children begin to go to school soonest and leave off latest. When they have done with masters, the State again compels them to learn the laws, and live after the pattern which they furnish, and not after their own fancies; and just as in learning to write, the writing master first draws lines with a style for the use of the young beginner, and gives him the tablet and makes him follow the lines, so the city draws the laws, which were the invention of good lawgivers living in the olden time; these are given to the young man, in order to guide him in his conduct whether he is commanding or obeying; and he who transgresses them is to be corrected, or, in other words, called to account, which is a term used not only in your country, but also in many others, seeing that justice calls men to account. Now, when there is all this care about virtue private and public, why, Socrates, do you still wonder and doubt whether virtue can be taught? Cease to wonder, for the opposite would be far more surprising.

But why then do the sons of good fathers often turn out ill? There is nothing very wonderful in this; for, as I have been saying, the existence of a State implies that virtue is not any man's private possession. If so— and nothing can be truer—then I will further ask you to imagine, as an illustration, some other pursuit or branch of knowledge which may be assumed equally to be the condition of the existence of a State. Suppose that there could be no state unless we were all flute-players, as far as each had the capacity, and everybody was freely teaching everybody the art, both in private and public, and reproving the bad player as freely and openly as every man now teaches justice and the laws, not concealing them as he would conceal the other arts, but imparting them—for all of us have a mutual interest in the justice and virtue of one another, and this is the reason why every one is so ready to teach justice and the laws;— suppose, I say, that there were the same readiness and liberality among us in teaching one another flute-playing, do you imagine, Socrates, that the sons of good flute-players would be more likely to be good than the sons of bad ones? I think not. Would not their sons grow up to be distinguished or undistinguished according to their own natural capacities as flute-players, and the son of a good player would often turn out to be a bad one, and the son of a bad player to be a good one, and all flute-players would be good enough in comparison of those who were ignorant and unacquainted with the art of flute-playing? In like manner I would have you consider that he who appears to you to be the worst of those who have been brought up in laws and humanities, would appear to be a just man and a master of justice if he were to be compared with men who had no education, or courts of justice, or laws, or any restraints upon them which compelled them to practise virtue—with the savages, for example, whom the poet Pherecrates exhibited on the stage at the last year's Lenaean festival. If you were living among men such as the man-haters in his chorus, you would be only too glad to meet with Eurybates and Phrynondas, and you would sorrowfully long to revisit the rascality of this part of the world. And you, Socrates, are discontented, and why? Because all men are teachers of virtue, each one according to his ability; and you say, Where are the teachers? You might as well ask, Who teaches Greek? For of that too there will not be any teachers found. Or you might ask, Who is to teach the sons of our artisans this same art which they have learned of their fathers? He and his fellow-workmen have taught them to the best of their ability,—but who will carry them further in their arts? And you would certainly have a difficulty, Socrates, in finding a teacher of them; but there would be no difficulty in finding a teacher of those who are wholly ignorant. And this is true of virtue or of anything else; if a man is better able than we are to promote virtue ever so little, we must be content with the result. A teacher of this sort I believe myself to be, and above all other men to have the knowledge which makes a man noble and good; and I give my pupils their money's worth, and even more, as they themselves confess. And therefore I have introduced the following mode of payment:—When a man has been my pupil, if he likes he pays my price, but there is no compulsion; and if he does not like, he has only to go into a temple and take an oath of the value of the instructions, and he pays no more than he declares to be their value.

Such is my apologue, Socrates, and such is the argument by which I endeavour to show that virtue may be taught, and that this is the opinion of the Athenians. And I have also attempted to show that you are not to wonder at good fathers having bad sons, or at good sons having bad fathers, of which the sons of Polycleitus afford an example, who are the companions of our friends here, Paralus and Xanthippus, but are nothing in comparison with their father; and this is true of the sons of many other artists. As yet I ought not to say the same of Paralus and Xanthippus themselves, for they are young and there is still hope of them.

Protagoras ended, and in my ear

> "So charming left his voice, that I the while
> Thought him still speaking; still stood fixed to hear."[1]

At length, when the truth dawned upon me, that he had really finished, not without difficulty I began to collect myself, and looking at Hippocrates, I said to him: O son of Apollodorus, how deeply grateful I am to you for having brought me hither; I would not have missed the speech of

---

[1] Borrowed by Milton, *Paradise Lost*, viii, 2, 3.

Protagoras for a great deal. For I used to imagine that no human care could make men good; but I know better now. Yet I have still one very small difficulty which I am sure that Protagoras will easily explain, as he has already explained so much. If a man were to go and consult Pericles or any of our great speakers about these matters, he might perhaps hear as fine a discourse; but then when one has a question to ask of any of them, like books, they can neither answer nor ask; and if any one challenges the least particular of their speech, they go ringing on in a long harangue, like brazen pots, which when they are struck continue to sound unless some one puts his hand upon them: whereas our friend Protagoras cannot only make a good speech, as he has already shown, but when he is asked a question he can answer briefly; and when he asks he will wait and hear the answer; and this is a very rare gift. Now I, Protagoras, want to ask you a little question, which if you will only answer, I shall be quite satisfied. You were saying that virtue can be taught;—that I will take upon your authority, and there is no one to whom I am more ready to trust. But I marvel at one thing about which I should like to have my mind set at rest. You were speaking of Zeus sending justice and reverence to men; and several times while you were speaking, justice, and temperance, and holiness, and all these qualities, were described by you as if together they made up virtue. Now I want you to tell me truly whether virtue is one whole, of which justice and temperance and holiness are parts; or whether all these are only the names of one and the same thing: that is the doubt which still lingers in my mind.

There is no difficulty, Socrates, in answering that the qualities of which you are speaking are the parts of virtue which is one.

And are they parts, I said, in the same sense in which mouth, nose, and eyes, and ears, are the parts of a face; or are they like parts of gold, which differ from the whole and from one another only in being larger or smaller?

I should say that they differed, Socrates, in the first way; they are related to one another as the parts of a face are related to the whole face.

And do men have some one part and some another part of virtue? Or if a man has one part, must he also have all the others?

By no means, he said; for many a man is brave and not just, or just and not wise.

You would not deny, then, that courage and wisdom are also parts of virtue?

Most undoubtedly they are, he answered; and wisdom is the noblest of the parts.

And they are all different from one another? I said.

Yes.

And has each of them a distinct function like the parts of the face;—
the eye, for example, is not like the ear, and has not the same functions;
and the other parts are none of them like one another, either in their
functions, or in any other way? I want to know whether the comparison
holds concerning the parts of virtue. Do they also differ from one another
in themselves and in their functions? For that is clearly what the simile
would imply.

Yes, Socrates, you are right in supposing that they differ.

Then, I said, no other part of virtue is like knowledge, or like justice, or
like courage, or like temperance, or like holiness?

No, he answered.

Well, then, I said, suppose that you and I enquire into their natures.
And first, you would agree with me that justice is of the nature of a thing,
would you not? That is my opinion: would it not be yours also?

Mine also, he said.

And suppose that some one were to ask us, saying, "O Protagoras, and
you, Socrates, what about this thing which you were calling justice, is it
just or unjust?"—and I were to answer, just: would you vote with me or
against me?

With you, he said.

Thereupon I should answer to him who asked me, that justice is of the
nature of the just: would not you?

Yes, he said.

And suppose that he went on to say: "Well, now, is there also such a
thing as holiness?"—we should answer, "Yes," if I am not mistaken?

Yes, he said.

Which you would also acknowledge to be a thing—should we not say
so?

He assented.

"And is this sort of thing which is of the nature of the holy, or of the
nature of the unholy?" I should be angry at his putting such a question,
and should say, "Peace, man; nothing can be holy if holiness is not holy."
What would you say? Would you answer in the same way?

Certainly, he said.

And then after this suppose that he came and asked us, "What were
you saying just now? Perhaps I may not have heard you rightly, but you
seemed to me to be saying that the parts of virtue were not the same as
one another." I should reply, "You certainly heard that said, but not, as
you imagine, by me; for I only asked the question; Protagoras gave the
answer." And suppose that he turned to you and said, "Is this true,
Protagoras? and do you maintain that one part of virtue is unlike another,
and is this your position?"—how would you answer him?

I could not help acknowledging the truth of what he said, Socrates.

Well, then, Protagoras, we will asume this; and now supposing that he proceeded to say further, "Then holiness is not of the nature of justice, nor justice of the nature of holiness, but of the nature of unholiness; and holiness is of the nature of the not just, and therefore of the unjust, and the unjust is the unholy"; how shall we answer him? I should certainly answer him on my own behalf that justice is holy, and that holiness is just; and I would say in like manner on your behalf also, if you would allow me, that justice is either the same with holiness, or very nearly the same; and above all I would assert that justice is like holiness and holiness is like justice; and I wish that you would tell me whether I may be permitted to give this answer on your behalf, and whether you would agree with me.

He replied, I cannot simply agree, Socrates, to the proposition that justice is holy and that holiness is just, for there appears to me to be a difference between them. But what matter? if you please I please; and let us assume, if you will, that justice is holy, and that holiness is just.

Pardon me, I replied; I do not want this "if you wish" or "if you will" sort of conclusion to be proven, but I want you and me to be proven: I mean to say that the conclusion will be best proven if there be no "if."

Well, he said, I admit that justice bears a resemblance to holiness, for there is always some point of view in which everything is like every other thing; white is in a certain way like black, and hard is like soft, and the most extreme opposites have some qualities in common; even the parts of the face which, as we were saying before, are distinct and have different functions, are still in a certain point of view similar, and one of them is like another of them. And you may prove that they are like one another on the same principle that all things are like one another; and yet things which are alike in some particular ought not to be called alike, nor things which are unlike in some particular, however slight, unlike.

And do you think, I said in a tone of surprise, that justice and holiness have but a small degree of likeness?

Certainly not; any more than I agree with what I understand to be your view.

Well, I said, as you appear to have a difficulty about this, let us take another of the examples which you mentioned instead. Do you admit the existence of folly?

I do.

And is not wisdom the very opposite of folly?

That is true, he said.

And when men act rightly and advantageously they seem to you to be temperate?

Yes, he said.

And temperance makes them temperate?

Certainly.

And they who do not act rightly act foolishly, and in acting thus are not temperate?

I agree, he said.

Then to act foolishly is the opposite of acting temperately?

He assented.

And foolish actions are done by folly, and temperate actions by temperance?

He agreed.

And that is done strongly which is done by strength, and that which is weakly done, by weakness?

He assented.

And that which is done with swiftness is done swiftly, and that which is done with slowness, slowly?

He assented again.

And that which is done in the same manner, is done by the same; and that which is done in an opposite manner by the opposite?

He agreed.

Once more, I said, is there anyting beautiful?

Yes.

To which the only opposite is the ugly?

There is no other.

And is there anything good?

There is.

To which the only opposite is the evil?

There is no other.

And there is the acute in sound?

True.

To which the only opposite is the grave?

There is no other, he said, but that.

Then every opposite has one opposite only and no more?

He assented.

Then now, I said, let us recapitulate our admissions. First of all we admitted that everything has one opposite and not more than one?

We did so.

And we admitted also that what was done in opposite ways was done by opposites?

Yes.

And that which was done foolishly, as we further admitted, was done in the opposite way to that which was done temperately?

Yes.

And that which was done temperately was done by temperance, and that which was done foolishly by folly?

He agreed.

And that which is done in opposite ways is done by opposites?

Yes.

And one thing is done by temperance, and quite another thing by folly?

Yes.

And in opposite ways?

Certainly.

And therefore by opposites:—then folly is the opposite of temperance?

Clearly.

And do you remember that folly has already been acknowledged by us to be the opposite of wisdom?

He assented.

And we said that everything has only one opposite?

Yes.

Then, Protagoras, which of the two assertions shall we renounce? One says that everything has but one opposite; the other that wisdom is distinct from temperance, and that both of them are parts of virtue; and that they are not only distinct, but dissimilar, both in themselves and in their functions, like the parts of a face. Which of these two assertions shall we renounce? For both of them together are certainly not in harmony; they do not accord or agree: for how can they be said to agree if everything is assumed to have only one opposite and not more than one, and yet folly, which is one, has clearly the two opposites—wisdom and temperance? Is not that true, Protagoras? What else would you say?

He assented, but with great reluctance.

Then temperance and wisdom are the same, as before justice and holiness appeared to us to be nearly the same. And now, Protagoras, I said, we must finish the enquiry, and not faint. Do you think that an unjust man can be temperate in his unjustice?

I should be ashamed, Socrates, he said, to acknowledge this, which nevertheless many may be found to assert.

And shall I argue with them or with you? I replied.

I would rather, he said, that you should argue with the many first, if you will.

Whichever you please, if you will only answer me and say whether you are of their opinion or not. My object is to test the validity of the argument; and yet the result may be that I who ask and you who answer may both be put on our trial.

Protagoras at first made a show of refusing, as he said that the argument was not encouraging; at length, he consented to answer.

Now then, I said, begin at the beginning and answer me. You think that some men are temperate, and yet unjust?

Yes, he said; let that be admitted.

And temperance is good sense?

Yes.

And good sense is good counsel in doing injustice?

Granted.

If they succeed, I said, or if they do not succeed?

If they succeed.

And you would admit the existence of good?

Yes.

And is the good that which is expedient for man?

Yes, indeed, he said: and there are some things which may be inexpedient, and yet I call them good.

I thought that Protagoras was getting ruffled and excited; he seemed to be setting himself in an attitude of war. Seeing this, I minded my business, and gently said:—

When you say, Protagoras, that things inexpedient are good, do you mean inexpedient for man only, or inexpedient altogether? and do you call the latter good?

Certainly not the last, he replied; for I know of many things,—meats, drinks, medicines, and ten thousand other things, which are inexpedient for man, and some which are expedient; and some which are neither expedient nor inexpedient for man, but only for horses; and some for oxen only, and some for dogs; and some for no animals, but only for trees; and some for the roots of trees and not for their branches, as for example, manure, which is a good thing when laid about the roots of a tree, but utterly destructive if thrown upon the shoots and young branches; or I may instance olive oil, which is mischievous to all plants, and generally most injurious to the hair of every animal with the exception of man, but beneficial to human hair and to the human body generally; and even in this application (so various and changeable is the nature of the benefit), that which is the greatest good to the outward parts of a man, is a very great evil to his inward parts: and for this reason physicians always forbid their patients the use of oil in their food, except in very small quantities, just enough to extinguish the disagreeable sensation of smell in meats and sauces.

When he had given this answer, the company cheered him. And I said: Protagoras, I have a wretched memory, and when any one makes a long speech to me I never remember what he is talking about. As then, if I had been deaf, and you were going to converse with me, you would have had to raise your voice; so now, having such a bad memory, I will ask you to cut your answers shorter, if you would take me with you.

What do you mean? he said: how am I to shorten my answers? shall I make them too short?

Certainly not, I said.

But short enough?

Yes, I said.

Shall I answer what appears to me to be short enough, or what appears to you to be short enough?

I have heard, I said, that you can speak and teach others to speak about the same things at such length that words never seemed to fail, or with such brevity that no one could use fewer of them. Please therefore, if you talk with me, to adopt the latter or more compendious method.

Socrates, he replied, many a battle of words have I fought, and if I had followed the method of disputation which my adversaries desired, as you want me to do, I should have been no better than another, and the name of Protagoras would have been nowhere.

I saw that he was not satisfied with his previous answers, and that he would not play the part of answerer any more if he could help; and I considered that there was no call upon me to continue the conversation; so I said: Protagoras, I do not wish to force the conversation upon you if you had rather not, but when you are willing to argue with me in such a way that I can follow you, then I will argue with you. Now you, as is said of you by others and as you say yourself, are able to have discussions in shorter forms of speech as well as in longer, for you are a master of wisdom; but I cannot manage these long speeches: I only wish that I could. You, on the other hand, who are capable of either, ought to speak shorter as I beg you, and then we might converse. But I see that you are disinclined, and as I have an engagement which will prevent my staying to hear you at greater length (for I have to be in another place), I will depart; although I should have liked to have heard you.

Thus I spoke, and was rising from my seat, when Callias seized me by the right hand, and in his left hand caught hold of this old cloak of mine. He said: We cannot let you go, Socrates, for if you leave us there will be an end of our discussions: I must therefore beg you to remain, as there is nothing in the world that I should like better than to hear you and Protagoras discourse. Do not deny the company this pleasure.

Now, I had got up, and was in the act of departure. Son of Hipponicus, I replied, I have always admired, and do now heartily applaud and love your philosophical spirit, and I would gladly comply with your request, if I could. But the truth is that I cannot. And what you ask is as great an impossibility to me, as if you bade me run a race with Crison of Himera, when in his prime, or with some one of the long or day course runners. To such a request I should reply that I would fain ask the same of my own legs; but they refuse to comply. And therefore if you want to see Crison and me in the same stadium, you must bid him slacken his speed to mine, for I cannot run quickly, and he can run slowly. And in like manner if you want to hear me and Protagoras discoursing, you must ask him to shorten his answers, and to keep to the point, as he did at first; if not, how can there be any discussion? For discussion is one thing, and making an oration is quite another, in my humble opinion.

But you see, Socrates, said Callias, that Protagoras may fairly claim to speak in his own way, just as you claim to speak in yours.

Here Alcibiades interposed, and said: That, Callias, is not a true statement of the case. For our friend Socrates admits that he cannot make a speech—in this he yields the palm to Protagoras; but I should be greatly surprised if he yielded to any living man in the power of holding and apprehending an argument. Now, if Protagoras will make a similar admission, and confess that he is inferior to Socrates in argumentative skill, that is enough for Socrates; but if he claims superiority in argument as well, let him ask and answer—not, when a question is asked, slipping away from the point, and instead of answering, making a speech at such length that most of his hearers forget the question at issue (not that Socrates is likely to forget—I will be bound for that, although he may pretend in fun that he has a bad memory). And Socrates appears to me to be more in the right than Protagoras; that is my view, and every man ought to say what he thinks.

When Alcibiades had done speaking, some one—Critias, I believe—went on to say: O Prodicus and Hippias, Callias appears to me to be a partisan of Protagoras: and this led Alcibiades, who loves opposition, to take the other side. But we should not be partisans either of Socrates or of Protagoras; let us rather unite in entreating both of them not to break up the discussion.

Prodicus added: That, Critias, seems to me to be well said, for those who are present at such discussions ought to be impartial hearers of both the speakers; remembering, however, that impartiality is not the same as equality, for both sides should be impartially heard, and yet an equal meed should not be assigned to both of them; but to the wiser a higher meed should be given, and a lower to the less wise. And I as well as Critias would beg you, Protagoras and Socrates, to grant our request, which is, that you will argue with one another and not wrangle; for friends argue with friends out of good-will, but only adversaries and enemies wrangle. And then our meeting will be delightful; for in this way you, who are the speakers, will be most likely to win esteem, and not praise only, among us who are your audience; for esteem is a sincere conviction of the hearers' souls, but praise is often an insincere expression of men uttering falsehoods contrary to their conviction. And thus we who are the hearers will be gratified and not pleased; for gratification is of the mind when receiving wisdom and knowledge, but pleasure is of the body when eating or experiencing some other bodily delight. Thus spoke Prodicus, and many of the company applauded his words.

Hippias the sage spoke next. He said: All of you who are here present I reckon to be kinsmen and friends and fellow-citizens, by nature and not by law; for by nature like is akin to like, whereas law is the tyrant of mankind, and often compels us to do many things which are against nature. How great would be the disgrace then, if we, who know the nature of things, and are the wisest of the Hellenes, and such are met together in this city, which is the metropolis of wisdom, and in the greatest and most glorious house of this city, should have nothing to show worthy of this height of dignity, but should only quarrel with one another like the meanest of mankind! I do pray and advise you, Protagoras, and you, Socrates, to agree upon a compromise. Let us be your peacemakers. And do not you, Socrates, aim at this precise and extreme brevity in discourse, if Protagoras objects, but loosen and let go the reins of speech, that your words may be grander and more becoming to you. Neither do you, Protagoras, go forth on the gale with every sail set out of sight of land into an ocean of words, but let there be a mean observed by both of you. Do as I say. And let me also persuade you to choose an arbiter or overseer or president; he will keep watch over your words and will prescribe their proper length.

This proposal was received by the company with universal approval; Callias said that he would not let me off, and they begged me to choose an arbiter. But I said that to choose an umpire of discourse would be unseemly; for if the person chosen was inferior, then the inferior or worse ought not to preside over the better; or if he was equal, neither would that be well; for he who is our equal will do as we do, and what will be the use of choosing him? And if you say, "Let us have a better then,"—to that I answer that you cannot have any one who is wiser than Protagoras. And if you choose another who is not really better, and whom you only say is better, to put another over him as though he were an inferior person would be an unworthy reflection on him; not that, as far as I am concerned, any reflection is of much consequence to me. Let me tell you then what I will do in order that the conversation and discussion may go as you desire. If Protagoras is not disposed to answer let him ask and I will answer; and I will endeavour to show at the same time how, as I maintain, he ought to answer: and when I have answered as many questions as he likes to ask, let him in like manner answer me; and if he seems to be not very ready at answering the precise question asked of him, you and I will unite in entreating him, as you entreated me, not to spoil the discussion. And this will require no special arbiter—all of you shall be arbiters.

This was generally approved, and Protagoras, though very much against his will, was obliged to agree that he would ask questions; and when he had put a sufficient number of them, that he would answer in his turn those which he was asked in short replies. He began to put his questions as follows:—

I am of opinion, Socrates, he said, that skill in poetry is the principal part of education; and this I conceive to be the power of knowing what compositions of the poets are correct, and what are not, and how they are to be distinguished, and of explaining when asked the reason of the difference. And I propose to transfer the question which you and I have been discussing to the domain of poetry; we will speak as before of virtue, but in reference to a passage of a poet. Now Simonides says to Scopas the son of Creon the Thessalian:—

> "Hardly on the one hand can a man become truly good, built four-square in hands and feet and mind, a work without a flaw."

Do you know the poem? or shall I repeat the whole?

There is no need, I said; for I am perfectly well acquainted with the ode,—I have made a careful study of it.

Very well, he said. And do you think that the ode is a good composition, and true?

Yes, I said, both good and true.

But if there is a contradiction, can the composition be good or true?

No, not in that case, I replied.

And is there not a contradiction? he asked. Reflect.

Well, my friend, I have reflected.

And does not the poet proceed to say, "I do not agree with the word of Pittacus, albeit the utterance of a wise man: Hardly can a man be good"? Now you will observe that this is said by the same poet.

I know it.

And do you think, he said, that the two sayings are consistent?

Yes, I said, I think so (at the same time I could not help fearing that there might be something in what he said). And you think otherwise?

Why, he said, how can he be consistent in both? First of all, premising as his own thought, "Hardly can a man become truly good"; and then a little further on in the poem, forgetting, and blaming Pittacus and refusing to agree with him, when he says, "Hardly can a man be good," which is the very same thing. And yet when he blames him who says the same with himself, he blames himself; so that he must be wrong either in his first or his second assertion.

Many of the audience cheered and applauded this. And I felt at first giddy and faint, as if I had received a blow from the hand of an expert boxer, when I heard his words and the sounds of cheering; and to confess the truth, I wanted to get time to think what the meaning of the poet really was. So I turned to Prodicus and called him. Prodicus, I said, Simonides is a countryman of yours, and you ought to come to his aid. I must appeal to you, like the river Scamander in Homer, who, when beleaguered by Achilles, summons the Simoïs to aid him, saying:

"Brother dear, let us both together stay the force of the hero."

And I summon you, for I am afraid that Protagoras will make an end of Simonides. Now is the time to rehabilitate Simonides, by the application of your philosophy of synonyms, which enables you to distinguish "will" and "wish," and make other charming distinctions like those which you drew just now. And I should like to know whether you would agree with me; for I am of opinion that there is no contradiction in the words of Simonides. And first of all I wish that you would say whether, in your opinion, Prodicus, "being" is the same as "becoming."

Not the same, certainly, replied Prodicus.

Did not Simonides first set forth, as his own view, that "Hardly can a man become truly good"?

Quite right, said Prodicus.

And then he blames Pittacus, not, as Protagoras imagines, for repeating that which he says himself, but for saying something different from himself. Pittacus does not say as Simonides says, that hardly can a man become good, but hardly can a man be good: and our friend Prodicus would maintain that being, Protagoras, is not the same as becoming; and if they are not the same, then Simonides is not inconsistent with himself. I dare say that Prodicus and many others would say, as Hesiod says,

> "On the one hand, hardly can a man become good,
> For the gods have made virtue the reward of toil;
> But on the other hand, when you have climbed the height,
> Then, to retain virtue, however difficult the acquisition,
>   is easy."

Prodicus heard and approved; but Protagoras said: Your correction, Socrates, involves a greater error than is contained in the sentence which you are correcting.

Alas! I said, Protagoras; then I am a sorry physician, and do but aggravate a disorder which I am seeking to cure.

Such is the fact, he said.

How so? I asked.

The poet, he replied, could never have made such a mistake as to say that virtue, which in the opinion of all men is the hardest of all things, can be easily retained.

Well, I said, and how fortunate are we in having Prodicus among us, at the right moment; for he has a wisdom, Protagoras, which, as I imagine, is more than human and of very ancient date, and may be as old as Simonides or even older. Learned as you are in many things, you appear to know nothing of this; but I know, for I am a disciple of his. And now, if I am not mistaken, you do not understand the word "hard" (χαλεπόν) in the sense which Simonides intended; and I must correct you, as Prodicus corrects me when I use the word "awful" (δεινόν) as a term of praise. If I say that Protagoras or any one else is an "awfully" wise man, he asks me if I am not ashamed of calling that which is good "awful"; and then he explains to me that the term "awful" is always taken in a bad sense, and that no one speaks of being "awfully" healthy or wealthy, or of "awful" peace, but of "awful" disease, "awful" war, "awful" poverty, meaning by the term "awful," evil. And I think that Simonides and his countrymen the Ceans, when they spoke of "hard" meant "evil," or something which you do not understand. Let us ask Prodicus, for he ought to be able to answer questions about the dialect of Simonides. What did he mean, Prodicus, by the term "hard"?

Evil, said Prodicus.

And therefore, I said, Prodicus, he blames Pittacus for saying, "Hard is the good" just as if that were equivalent to saying, Evil is the good.

Yes, he said, that was certainly his meaning; and he is twitting Pittacus with ignorance of the use of terms, which in a Lesbian, who has been accustomed to speak a barbarous language, is natural.

Do you hear, Protagoras, I asked, what our friend Prodicus is saying? And have you an answer for him?

You are entirely mistaken, Prodicus, said Protagoras; and I know very well that Simonides in using the word "hard" meant what all of us mean, not evil, but that which is not easy—that which takes a great deal of trouble: of this I am positive.

I said: I also incline to believe, Protagoras, that this was the meaning of Simonides, of which our friend Prodicus was very well aware, but he thought that he would make fun, and try if you could maintain your thesis; for that Simonides could never have meant the other is clearly proved by the context, in which he says that God only has this gift. Now, he cannot surely mean to say that to be good is evil, when he afterwards proceeds to say that God only has this gift, and that this is the attribute of him and of no other. For if this be his meaning, Prodicus would impute to Simonides a character of recklessness which is very unlike his countrymen. And I should like to tell you, I said, what I imagine to be the real meaning of Simonides in this poem, if you will test what, in your way of speaking, would be called my skill in poetry; or, if you would rather, I will be the listener.

To this proposal Protagoras replied: As you please;—and Hippias, Prodicus, and the others told me by all means to do as I proposed.

Then now, I said, I will endeavour to explain to you my opinion about this poem of Simonides. There is a very ancient philosophy which is more cultivated in Crete and Lacedaemon than in any other part of Hellas, and there are more philosophers in those countries than anywhere else in the world. This, however, is a secret which the Lacedaemonians deny; and they pretend to be ignorant, just because they do not wish to have it thought that they rule the world by wisdom, like the Sophists of whom Protagoras was speaking, and not by valour of arms; considering that if the reason of their superiority were disclosed, all men would be practising their wisdom. And this secret of theirs has never been discovered by the imitators of Lacedaemonian fashions in other cities, who go about with their ears bruised in imitation of them, and have the caestus bound on their arms and are always in training, and wear short cloaks; for they imagine that these are the practices which have enabled the Lacedaemonians to conquer the other Hellenes. Now, when the Lacedaemonians want to unbend and hold free conversation with their wise men, and are no longer satisfied with mere secret intercourse, they drive out all these laconizers, and any other foreigners who may happen to be in their country, and they hold a philosophical *séance* unknown to strangers; and they themselves forbid their young men to go out into other cities—in this they are like the Cretans—in order that they might not unlearn the lessons which they have taught them. And in Lacedaemon and Crete not only men but also women have a pride in their high cultivation. And hereby you may know that I am right in attributing to the Lacedaemonians this excellence in philosophy and speculation: If a man converses with the most ordinary Lacedaemonian, he will find him seldom good for much in general conversation, but at any point in the discourse he will be darting out some notable saying, terse and full of meaning, with unerring aim; and the person with whom he is talking seems to be like a child in his hands. And many of our own age and of former ages have noted that the true Lacedaemonian type of character has the love of philosophy even stronger than the love of gymnastics; they are conscious that only a perfectly educated man is capable of uttering such expressions. Such were Thales of Miletus, and Pittacus of Mitylene, and Bias of Priene, and our own Solon, and Cleobulus the Lindian, and Myson the Chenian; and seventh in the catalogue of wise men was the Lacedaemonian Chilo. All these were lovers and emulators and disciples of the culture of the Lacedaemonians, and any one may perceive that their wisdom was of this character; consisting of short memorable sentences, which they severally uttered. And they met together and dedicated in the temple of Apollo at Delphi, as the first fruits of their wisdom, the far-famed inscriptions, which are in all men's mouths,—"Know thyself," and "Nothing too much."

Why do I say all this? I am explaining that this Lacedaemonian brevity was the style of primitive philosophy. Now there was a saying of Pittacus which was privately circulated and received the approbation of the wise, "Hard is it to be good." And Simonides, who was ambitious of the fame of wisdom, was aware that if he could overthrow this saying, then, as if he had won a victory over some famous athlete, he would carry off the palm among his contemporaries. And if I am not mistaken, he composed the entire poem with the secret intention of damaging Pittacus and his saying.

Let us all unite in examining his words, and see whether I am speaking the truth. Simonides must have been a lunatic, if, in the very first words of the poem, wanting to say only that to become good is hard, he inserted μέν, "on the one hand" ["on the one hand to become good is hard"]; there would be no reason for the introduction of μέν, unless you suppose him to speak with a hostile reference to the words of Pittacus. Pittacus is saying "Hard is it to be good," and he, in refutation of this thesis, rejoins that the truly hard thing, Pittacus, is to become good, not joining "truly" with "good," but with "hard." Not, that the hard thing is to be truly good, as though there were some truly good men, and there were others who were good but not truly good (this would be a very simple observation, and quite unworthy of Simonides); but you must suppose him to make a trajection of the word "truly" (ἀλαθέως), construing the saying of Pittacus thus (and let us imagine Pittacus to be speaking and Simonides answering him): "O my friends," says Pittacus, "hard is it to be good," and Simonides answers, "In that, Pittacus, you are mistaken; the difficulty is not to be good, but on the one hand, to become good, four-square in hands and feet and mind, without a flaw—that is hard truly." This way of reading the passage accounts for the insertion of μέν, "on the one hand," and for the position at the end of the clause of the word "truly," and all that follows shows this to be the meaning. A great deal might be said in praise of the details of the poem, which is a charming piece of workmanship, and very finished, but such minutiae would be tedious. I should like, however, to point out the general intention of the poem, which is certainly designed in every part to be a refutation of the saying of Pittacus. For he speaks in what follows a little further on as if he meant to argue that although there is a difficulty in becoming good, yet this is possible for a time, and only for a time. But having become good, to remain in a good state and be good, as you, Pittacus, affirm, is not possible, and is not granted to man; God only has this blessing; "but man cannot help being bad when the force of circumstances overpowers him." Now, whom does the force of circumstances overpower in the command of a vessel? Not the private individual, for he is always overpowered; and as one who is already prostrate cannot be overthrown, and only he who is standing upright but not he who is prostrate can be laid prostrate, so the force of circumstances can only overpower him who, at some time or other, has resources, and not him who is at all times helpless. The descent of a great storm may make the pilot helpless, or the severity of the season the husbandman or the physician; for the good may become bad, as another poet witnesses:—

"The good are sometimes good and sometimes bad."

But the bad does not become bad; he is always bad. So that when the force of circumstances overpowers the man of resources and skill and virtue, then he cannot help being bad. And you, Pittacus, are saying, "Hard is it to be good." Now there is a difficulty in becoming good; and yet this is possible: but to be good is an impossibility—

"For he who does well is the good man, and he who does ill is the bad."

But what sort of doing is good in letters? and what sort of doing makes a man good in letters? Clearly the knowing of them. And what sort of well-doing makes a man a good physician? Clearly the knowledge of the art of healing the sick. "But he who does ill is the bad." Now, who becomes a bad physician? Clearly he who is in the first place a physician, and in the second place a good physician; for he may become a bad one also: but none of us unskilled individuals can by any amount of doing ill become physicians, any more than we can become carpenters or anything of that sort; and he who by doing ill cannot become a physician at all, clearly cannot become a bad physician. In like manner the good may become deteriorated by time, or toil, or disease, or other accident (the only real doing ill is to be deprived of knowledge), but the bad man will never become bad, for he is always bad; and if he were to become bad, he must previously have been good. Thus the words of the poem tend to show that on the one hand a man cannot be continuously good, but that he may become good and may also become bad; and again that

"They are the best for the longest time whom the gods love."

All this relates to Pittacus, as is further proved by the sequel. For he adds:—

"Therefore I will not throw away my span of life to no purpose in searching after the impossible, hoping in vain to find a perfectly faultless man among those who partake of the fruit of the broad-bosomed earth: if I find him, I will send you word."

(this is the vehement way in which he pursues his attack upon Pittacus throughout the whole poem):

"But him who does no evil, voluntarily I praise and love;—not even the gods war against necessity."

All this has a similar drift, for Simonides was not so ignorant as to say that he praised those who did no evil voluntarily, as though there were some who did evil voluntarily. For no wise man, as I believe, will allow that any human being errs voluntarily, or voluntarily does evil and dishonourable actions; but they are very well aware that all who do evil and dishonourable things do them against their will. And Simonides never says that he praises him who does no evil voluntarily; the word "voluntarily" applies to himself. For he was under the impression that a good man might often compel himself to love and praise another, and to be the friend and approver of another; and that there might be an involuntary love, such as a man might feel to an unnatural father or mother, or country, or the like. Now, bad men, when their parents or country have any defects, look on them with malignant joy, and find fault with them and expose and denounce them to others, under the idea that the rest of mankind will be less likely to take themselves to task and accuse them of neglect; and they blame their defects far more than they deserve, in order that the odium which is necessarily incurred by them may be increased: but the good man dissembles his feelings, and constrains himself to praise them; and if they have wronged him and he is angry, he pacifies his anger and is reconciled, and compels himself to love and praise his own flesh and blood. And Simonides, as is probable, considered that he himself had often had to praise and magnify a tyrant or the like, much against his will, and he also wishes to imply to Pittacus that he does not censure him because he is censorious.

> "For I am satisfied," he says, "when a man is neither bad nor very stupid; and when he knows justice (which is the health of states), and is of sound mind, I will find no fault with him, for I am not given to finding fault, and there are innumerable fools"

(implying that if he delighted in censure he might have abundant opportunity of finding fault).

> "All things are good with which evil is unmingled."

In these latter words he does not mean to say that all things are good which have no evil in them, as you might say "All things are white which have no black in them," for that would be ridiculous; but he means to say that he accepts and finds no fault with the moderate or intermediate state.

> ["I do not hope," he says, "to find a perfectly blameless man among those who partake of the fruits of the broad-bosomed earth (if I find him, I will send you word); in this sense I praise no man. But he who is moderately good, and does no evil, is good enough for me, who love and approve every one"]

(and here observe that he uses a Lesbian word, ἐπαίνημι [approve], because he is addressing Pittacus,—

"Who love and *approve* every one *voluntarily*, who does no evil":

and that the stop should be put after "voluntarily"); "but there are some whom I involuntarily praise and love. And you, Pittacus, I would never have blamed, if you had spoken what was moderately good and true; but I do blame you because, putting on the appearance of truth, you are speaking falsely about the highest matters."—And this, I said, Prodicus and Protagoras, I take to be the meaning of Simonides in this poem.

Hippias said: I think, Socrates, that you have given a very good explanation of the poem; but I have also an excellent interpretation of my own which I will propound to you, if you will allow me.

Nay, Hippias, said Alcibiades; not now, but at some other time. At present we must abide by the compact which was made between Socrates and Protagoras, to the effect that as long as Protagoras is willing to ask, Socrates should answer; or that if he would rather answer, then that Socrates should ask.

I said: I wish Protagoras either to ask or answer as he is inclined; but I would rather have done with poems and odes, if he does not object, and come back to the question about which I was asking you at first, Protagoras, and by your help make an end of that. The talk about the poets seems to me like a commonplace entertainment to which a vulgar company have recourse; who, because they are not able to converse or amuse one another, while they are drinking, with the sound of their own voices and conversation, by reason of their stupidity, raise the price of flute-girls in the market, hiring for a great sum the voice of a flute instead of their own breath, to be the medium of intercourse among them: but where the company are real gentlemen and men of education, you will see no flute-girls, nor dancing-girls, nor harp-girls; and they have no nonsense or games, but are contented with one another's conversation, of which their own voices are the medium, and which they carry on by turns in an orderly manner, even though they are very liberal in their potations. And a company like this of ours, and men such as we profess to be, do not require the help of another's voice, or of the poets whom you cannot interrogate about the meaning of what they are saying; people who cite them declaring, some that the poet has one meaning, and others that he has another, and the point which is in dispute can never be decided. This sort of entertainment they decline, and prefer to talk with one another, and put one another to the proof in conversation. And these are the models which I desire that you and I should imitate. Leaving the poets, and keeping to ourselves, let us try the mettle of one another and make proof of the truth in conversation. If you have a mind to ask, I am ready to answer; or if you would rather, do you answer, and give me the opportunity of resuming and completing our unfinished argument.

I made these and some similar observations; but Protagoras would not distinctly say which he would do. Thereupon Alcibiades turned to Callias, and said:—Do you think, Callias, that Protagoras is fair in refusing to say whether he will or will not answer? for I certainly think that he is unfair; he ought either to proceed with the argument, or distinctly to refuse to proceed, that we may know his intention; and then Socrates will be able to discourse with some one else, and the rest of the company will be free to talk with one another.

I think that Protagoras was really made ashamed by these words of Alcibiades, and when the prayers of Callias and the company were superadded, he was at last induced to argue, and said that I might ask and he would answer.

So I said: Do not imagine, Protagoras, that I have any other interest in asking questions of you but that of clearing up my own difficulties. For I think that Homer was very right in saying that

"When two go together, one sees before the other."

for all men who have a companion are readier in deed, word, or thought; but if a man

"Sees a thing when he is alone,"

he goes about straightway seeking until he finds some one to whom he may show his discoveries, and who may confirm him in them. And I would rather hold discourse with you than with any one, because I think that no man has a better understanding of most things which a good man may be expected to understand, and in particular of virtue. For who is there, but you?—who not only claim to be a good man and a gentleman, for many are this, and yet have not the power of making others good— whereas you are not only good yourself, but also the cause of goodness in others. Moreover, such confidence have you in yourself, that although other Sophists conceal their profession, you proclaim in the face of Hellas that you are a Sophist or teacher of virtue and education, and are the first who demanded pay in return. How then can I do otherwise than invite you to the examination of these subjects, and ask questions and consult with you? I must, indeed. And I should like once more to have my memory refreshed by you about the questions which I was asking you at first, and also to have your help in considering them. If I am not mistaken the question was this: Are wisdom and temperance and courage and justice and holiness five names of the same thing? or has each of the names a separate underlying essence and corresponding thing having a peculiar function, no one of them being like any other of them? And you replied that the five names were not the names of the same thing, but that each of them had a separate object, and that all these objects were parts of virtue, not in the same way that the parts of gold are like each other and the whole of which they are parts, but as the parts of the face are unlike the whole of which they are parts and one another, and have each of them a distinct function. I should like to know whether this is still your opinion; or if not, I will ask you to define your meaning, and I shall not take you to task if you now make a different statement. For I dare say that you may have said what you did only in order to make trial of me.

I answer, Socrates, he said, that all these qualities are parts of virtue, and that four out of the five are to some extent similar, and that the fifth of them, which is courage, is very different from the other four, as I prove in this way: You may observe that many men are utterly unrighteous, unholy, intemperate, ignorant, who are nevertheless remarkable for their courage.

Stop, I said; I should like to think about that. When you speak of brave men, do you mean the confident, or another sort of nature?

Yes, he said; I mean the impetuous, ready to go at that which others are afraid to approach.

In the next place, you would affirm virtue to be a good thing, of which good thing you assert yourself to be a teacher.

Yes, he said; I should say the best of all things, if I am in my right mind.

And is it partly good and partly bad, I said, or wholly good?

Wholly good, and in the highest degree.

Tell me, then, who are they who have confidence when diving into a well?

I should say, the divers.

And the reason of this is that they have knowledge?

Yes, that is the reason.

And who have confidence when fighting on horseback—the skilled horsemen or the unskilled?

The skilled.

And who when fighting with light shields—the peltasts or the nonpeltasts?

The peltasts. And that is true of all other things, he said, if that is your point: those who have knowledge are more confident than those who have no knowledge, and they are more confident after they have learned than before.

And have you not seen persons utterly ignorant, I said, of these things, and yet confident about them?

Yes, he said, I have seen such persons far too confident.

And are not these confident persons also courageous?

In that case, he replied, courage would be a base thing, for the men of whom we are speaking are surely madmen.

Then who are the courageous? Are they not the confident?

Yes, he said; to that statement I adhere.

And those, I said, who are thus confident without knowledge are really not courageous, but mad; and in that case the wisest are also the most confident, and being the most confident are also the bravest, and upon that view again wisdom will be courage.

Nay, Socrates, he replied, you are mistaken in your remembrance of what was said by me. When you asked me, I certainly did say that the courageous are the confident; but I was never asked whether the confident are the courageous; if you had asked me, I should have answered "Not all of them": and what I did answer you have not proved to be false, although you proceeded to show that those who have knowledge are more courageous than they were before they had knowledge, and more courageous than others who have no knowledge, and were then led on to think that courage is the same as wisdom. But in this way of arguing you might come to imagine that strength is wisdom. You might begin by asking whether the strong are able, and I should say "Yes"; and then whether those who know how to wrestle are not more able to wrestle than those who do not know how to wrestle, and more able after than before they had learned, and I should assent. And when I had admitted this, you might use my admissions in such a way as to prove that upon my view wisdom is strength; whereas in that case I should not have admitted, any more than in the other, that the able are strong, although I have admitted that the strong are able. For there is a difference between ability and strength; the former is given by knowledge as well as by madness or rage, but strength comes from nature and a healthy state of the body. And in like manner I say of confidence and courage, that they are not the same; and I argue that the courageous are confident, but not all the confident courageous. For confidence may be given to men by art, and also, like ability, by madness and rage; but courage comes to them from nature and the healthy state of the soul.

I said: You would admit, Protagoras, that some men live well and others ill?

He assented.

And do you think that a man lives well who lives in pain and grief?

He does not.

But if he lives pleasantly to the end of his life, will he not in that case have lived well?

He will.

Then to live pleasantly is a good, and to live unpleasantly an evil?

Yes, he said, if the pleasure be good and honourable.

And do you, Protagoras, like the rest of the world, call some pleasant things evil and some painful things good?—for I am rather disposed to say that things are good in as far as they are pleasant, if they have no consequences of another sort, and in as far as they are painful they are bad.

I do not know, Socrates, he said, whether I can venture to assert in that unqualified manner that the pleasant is the good and the painful the evil. Having regard not only to my present answer, but also the whole of my life, I shall be safer, if I am not mistaken, in saying that there are some pleasant things which are not good, and that there are some painful things which are good, and some which are not good, and that there are some which are neither good nor evil.

And you would call pleasant, I said, the things which participate in pleasure or create pleasure?

Certainly, he said.

Then my meaning is, that in as far as they are pleasant they are good; and my question would imply that pleasure is a good in itself.

According to your favourite mode of speech, Socrates, "let us reflect about this," he said; and if the reflection is to the point, and the result proves that the pleasure and good are really the same, then we will agree; but, if not, then we will argue.

And would you wish to begin the enquiry? I said; or shall I begin?

You ought to take the lead, he said; for you are the author of the discussion.

May I employ an illustration? I said. Suppose some one who is enquiring into the health or some other bodily quality of another:—he looks at his face and at the tips of his fingers, and then he says, Uncover your chest and back to me that I may have a better view:—that is the sort of thing which I desire in this speculation. Having seen what your opinion is about good and pleasure, I am minded to say to you: Uncover your mind to me, Protagoras, and reveal your opinion about knowledge, that I may know whether you agree with the rest of the world. Now, the rest of the world are of opinion that knowledge is a principle not of strength, or of rule, or of command: their notion is that a man may have knowledge, and yet that the knowledge which is in him may be over-mastered by anger, or pleasure, or pain, or love, or perhaps by fear, —just as if knowledge were a slave, and might be dragged about anyhow. Now, is that your view? or do you think that knowledge is a noble and commanding thing, which cannot be overcome, and will not allow a man, if he only knows the difference of good and evil, to do anything which is contrary to knowledge, but that wisdom will have strength to help him?

I agree with you, Socrates, said Protagoras; and not only so, but I, above all other men, am bound to say that wisdom and knowledge are the highest of human things.

Good, I said, and true. But are are you aware that the majority of the world are of another mind; and that men are commonly supposed to know the things which are best, and not to do them when they might? And most persons whom I have asked the reason of this have said that when men act contrary to knowledge they are overcome by pain, or pleasure, or some of those affections which I was just now mentioning.

Yes, Socrates, he replied; and that is not the only point about which mankind are in error.

Suppose, then, that you and I endeavour to instruct and inform them what is the nature of this affection which they call "being overcome by pleasure," and which they affirm to be the reason why they do not always do what is best. When we say to them: Friends, you are mistaken, and are saying what is not true, they would probably reply: Socrates and Protagoras, if this affection of the soul is not to be called "being overcome by pleasure," pray, what is it, and by what name would you describe it?

But why, Socrates, should we trouble ourselves about the opinion of the many, who just say anything that happens to occur to them?

I believe, I said, that they may be of use in helping us to discover how courage is related to the other parts of virtue. If you are disposed to abide by our agreement, that I should show the way in which, as I think, our recent difficulty is most likely to be cleared up, do you follow; but if not, never mind.

You are quite right, he said; and I would have you proceed as you have begun.

Well, then, I said, let me suppose that they repeat their question, What account do you give of that which, in our way of speaking, is termed being overcome by pleasure? I should answer thus: Listen, and Protagoras and I will endeavour to show you. When men are overcome by eating and drinking and other sensual desires which are pleasant, and they, knowing them to be evil, nevertheless indulge in them, would you not say that they were overcome by pleasure? They will not deny this. And suppose that you and I were to go on and ask them again: "In what way do you say that they are evil,—in that they are pleasant and give pleasure at the moment, or because they cause disease and poverty and other like evils in the future? Would they still be evil, if they had no attendant evil consequences, simply because they give the consciousness of pleasure of whatever nature?"—Would they not answer that they are not evil on account of the pleasure which is immediately given by them, but on account of the after consequences—diseases and the like?

I believe, said Protagoras, that the world in general would answer as you do.

And in causing diseases do they not cause pain? and in causing poverty do they not cause pain;—they would agree to that also, if I am not mistaken?

Protagoras assented.

Then I should say to them, in my name and yours: Do you think them evil for any other reason, except because they end in pain and rob us of other pleasures:—there again they would agree?

We both of us thought that they would.

And then I should take the question from the opposite point of view, and say: "Friends, when you speak of goods being painful, do you not mean remedial goods, such as gymnastic exercises, and military service, and the physician's use of burning, cutting, drugging and starving? Are these the things which are good but painful?" They would assent to me?

He agreed.

"And do you call them good because they occasion the greatest immediate suffering and pain; or because, afterwards, they bring health and improvement of the bodily condition and the salvation of States and power over others and wealth?"—they would agree to the latter alternative, if I am not mistaken?

He assented.

"Are these things good for any other reason except that they end in pleasure, and get rid of and avert pain? Are you looking to any other standard but pleasure and pain when you call them good?" They would acknowledge that they were not?

I think so, said Protagoras.

"And do you not pursue after pleasure as a good, and avoid pain as an evil?"

He assented.

"Then you think that pain is an evil and pleasure is a good: and even pleasure you deem an evil, when it robs you of greater pleasures than it gives, or causes pains greater than the pleasure. If, however, you call pleasure an evil in relation to some other end or standard, you will be able to show us that standard. But you have none to show."

I do not think that they have, said Protagoras.

"And have you not a similar way of speaking about pain? You call pain a good when it takes away greater pains than those which it has, or gives pleasures greater than the pains: then if you have some standard other than pleasure and pain to which you refer when you call actual pain a good, you can show what that is. But you cannot."

True, said Protagoras.

Suppose again, I said, that the world says to me: "Why do you spend many words and speak in many ways on this subject?" Excuse me, friends, I should reply; but in the first place there is a difficulty in explaining the meaning of the expression "overcome by pleasure"; and the whole argument turns upon this. And even now, if you see any possible way in which evil can be explained as other than pain, or good as other than pleasure, you may still retract. Are you satisfied, then, at having a life of pleasure which is without pain? If you are, and if you are unable to show any good or evil which does not end in pleasure and pain, hear the consequences:—If what you say is true, then the argument is absurd which affirms that a man often does evil knowingly, when he might abstain, because he is seduced and overpowered by pleasure; or again, when you say that a man knowingly refuses to do what is good because he is overcome at the moment by pleasure. And that this is ridiculous will be evident if only we give up the use of various names, such as pleasant and painful, and good and evil. As there are two things, let us call them by two names—first, good and evil, and then pleasant and painful. Assuming this, let us go on to say that a man does evil knowing that he does evil. But some one will ask, Why? Because he is overcome, is the first answer. And by what is he overcome? the enquirer will proceed to ask. And we shall not be able to reply "By pleasure," for the name of pleasure has been exchanged for that of good. In our answer, then, we shall only say that he is overcome. "By what?" he will reiterate. By the good, we shall have to reply; indeed we shall. Nay, but our questioner will rejoin with a laugh, if he be one of the swaggering sort, "This is too ridiculous, that a man should do what he knows to be evil when he ought not, because he is overcome by good. Is that," he will ask, "because the good was worthy or not worthy of conquering the evil?" And in answer to that we shall clearly reply, Because it was not worthy; for if it had been worthy, then he who, as we say, was overcome by pleasure, would not have been wrong. "But how," he will reply, "can the good be unworthy of the evil, or the evil of the good?" Is not the real explanation that they are out of proportion to one another, either as greater and smaller, or more and fewer? This we cannot deny. And when you speak of being overcome—"what do you mean," he will say, "but that you choose the greater evil in exchange for the lesser good?" Admitted. And now substitute the names of pleasure and pain for good and evil, and say, not as before, that a man does what is evil knowingly, but that he does what is painful knowingly, and because he is overcome by pleasure, which is unworthy to overcome. What measure is there of the relations of pleasure to pain other than excess and defect, which means that they become greater and smaller, and more and fewer, and differ in degree? For if any one says: "Yes, Socrates, but immediate pleasure differs widely from future pleasure and pain"—to that I should reply: And do they differ in anything but in pleasure and pain? There can be no other measure of them. And do you, like a skillful weigher, put into the balance the pleasures and the pains, and their nearness and distance, and weigh them, and then say which outweighs the other. If you weigh pleasures against pleasures, you of course take the more and greater; or if you weigh pains against pains, you take the fewer and the less; or if pleasures against pains, then you choose that course of action in which the painful is exceeded by the pleasant, whether the distant by the near or the near by the distant; and you avoid that course of action in which the pleasant is exceeded by the painful. Would you not admit, my friends, that this is true? I am confident that they cannot deny this.

He agreed with me.

Well, then, I shall say, if you agree so far, be so good as to answer me a question: Do not the same magnitudes appear larger to your sight when near, and smaller when at a distance? They will acknowledge that. And the same holds of thickness and number; also sounds, which are in themselves equal, are greater when near, and lesser when at a distance. They will grant that also. Now suppose happiness to consist in doing or choosing the greater, and in not doing or in avoiding the less, what would be the saving principle of human life? Would not the art of measuring be the saving principle; or would the power of appearance? Is not the latter that deceiving art which makes us wander up and down and take the things at one time of which we repent at another, both in our actions and in our choice of things great and small? But the art of measurement would do away with the effect of appearances, and, showing the truth, would fain teach the soul at last to find rest in the truth, and would thus save our life. Would not mankind generally acknowledge that the art which accomplishes this result is the art of measurement?

Yes, he said, the art of measurement.

Suppose, again, the salvation of human life to depend on the choice of odd and even, and on the knowledge of when a man ought to choose the greater or less, either in reference to themselves or to each other, and whether near or at a distance; what would be the saving principle of our lives? Would not knowledge?—a knowledge of measuring, when the question is one of excess and defect, and a knowledge of number, when the question is of odd and even? The world will assent, will they not?

Protagoras himself thought that they would.

Well, then, my friends, I say to them; seeing that the salvation of human life has been bound to consist in the right choice of pleasures and pains,—in the choice of the more and the fewer, and the greater and the less, and the nearer and remoter, must not this measuring be a consideration of their excess and defect and equality in relation to each other?

This is undeniably true.

And this, as possessing measure, must undeniably also be an art and science?

They will agree, he said.

The nature of that art or science will be a matter of future considera-tion; but the existence of such a science furnishes a demonstrative answer to the question which you asked of me and Protagoras. At the time when you asked the question, if you remember, both of us were agreeing that there was nothing mightier than knowledge, and that knowledge, in whatever existing, must have the advantage over pleasure and all other things; and then you said that pleasure often got the advantage even over a man who has knowledge; and we refused to allow this, and you rejoined: O Protagoras and Socrates, what is the meaning of being overcome by pleasure if not this?—tell us what you call such a state:—if we had immediately and at the time answered "Ignorance," you would have laughed at us. But now, in laughing at us, you will be laughing at yourselves: for you also admitted that men err in their choice of pleasures and pains; that is, in their choice of good and evil, from defect of knowledge; and you admitted further, that they err, not only from defect of knowledge in general, but of that particular knowledge which is called measuring. And you are also aware that the erring act which is done without knowledge is done in ignorance. This, therefore, is the meaning of being overcome by pleasure;—ignorance, and that the greatest. And our friends Protagoras and Prodicus and Hippias declare that they are the physicians of ignorance; but you, who are under the mistaken im-pression that ignorance is not the cause, and that the art of which I am speaking cannot be taught, neither go yourselves, nor send your children, to the Sophists, who are the teachers of these things—you take care of your money and give them none; and the result is, that you are the worse off both in public and private life:—Let us suppose this to be our answer to the world in general: And now I should like to ask you, Hippias, and you, Prodicus, as well as Protagoras (for the argument is to be yours as well as ours), whether you think that I am speaking the truth or not?

They all thought that what I said was entirely true.

Then you agree, I said, that the pleasant is the good, and the painful evil. And here I would beg my friend Prodicus not to introduce his distinction of names, whether he is disposed to say pleasurable, delight-ful, joyful. However, by whatever name he prefers to call them, I will ask you, most excellent Prodicus, to answer in my sense of the words.

Prodicus laughed and assented, as did the others.

Then, my friends, what do you say to this? Are not all actions honourable and useful, of which the tendency is to make life painless and pleasant? The honourable work is also useful and good?

This was admitted.

Then I said, if the pleasant is the good, nobody does anything under the idea or conviction that some other thing would be better and is also attainable, when he might do the better. And this inferiority of a man to himself is merely ignorance, as the superiority of a man to himself is wisdom.

They all assented.

And is not ignorance the having a false opinion and being deceived about important matters?

To this also they unanimously assented.

Then, I said, no man voluntarily pursues evil, or that which he thinks to be evil. To prefer evil to good is not in human nature; and when a man is compelled to choose one of two evils, no one will choose the greater when he may have the less.

All of us agreed to every word of this.

Well, I said, there is a certain thing called fear or terror; and here, Prodicus, I should particularly like to know whether you would agree with me in defining this fear or terror as expectation of evil.

Protagoras and Hippias agreed, but Prodicus said that this was fear and not terror.

Never mind, Prodicus, I said; but let me ask whether, if our former assertions are true, a man will pursue that which he fears when he is not compelled? Would not this be in flat contradiction to the admission which has been already made, that he thinks the things which he fears to be evil; and no one will pursue or voluntarily accept that which he thinks to be evil?

That also was universally admitted.

Then, I said, these, Hippias and Prodicus, are our premises; and I would beg Protagoras to explain to us how he can be right in what he said at first. I do not mean in what he said quite at first, for his first statement, as you may remember, was that whereas there were five parts of virtue none of them was like any other of them; each of them had a separate function. To this, however, I am not referring, but to the assertion which he afterwards made that of the five virtues four were nearly akin to each other, but that the fifth, which was courage, differed greatly from the others. And of this he gave me the following proof. He said: You will find, Socrates, that some of the most impious, and unrighteous, and intemperate, and ignorant of men are among the most courageous; which proves that courage is very different from the other parts of virtue. I was surprised at his saying this at the time, and I am still more surprised now that I have discussed the matter with you. So I asked him whether by the brave he meant the confident. Yes, he replied, and the impetuous or goers. (You may remember, Protagoras, that this was your answer.)

He assented.

Well, then, I said, tell us against what are the courageous ready to go —against the same dangers as the cowards?

No, he answered.

Then against something different?

Yes, he said.

Then do cowards go where there is safety, and the courageous where there is danger?

Yes, Socrates, so men say.

Very true, I said. But I want to know against what do you say that the courageous are ready to go—against dangers, believing them to be dangers, or not against dangers?

No, said he; the former case has been proved by you in the previous argument to be impossible.

That, again, I replied, is quite true. And if this has been tightly proven, then no one goes to meet what he thinks to be dangers, since the want of self-control, which makes men rush into dangers, has been shown to be ignorance.

He assented.

And yet the courageous man and the coward alike go to meet that about which they are confident; so that, in this point of view, the cowardly and the courageous go to meet the same things.

And yet, Socrates, said Protagoras, that to which the coward goes is the opposite of that to which the courageous goes; the one, for example, is ready to go to battle, and the other is not ready.

And is going to battle honourable or disgraceful? I said.

Honourable, he replied.

And if honourable, then already admitted by us to be good; for all honourable actions we have admitted to be good.

That is true; and to that opinion I shall always adhere.

True, I said. But which of the two are they who, as you say, are unwilling to go to war, which is a good and honourable thing?

The cowards, he replied.

And what is good and honourable, I said, is also pleasant?

It has certainly been acknowledged to be so, he replied.

And do the cowards knowingly refuse to go to the nobler, and pleasanter, and better?

The admission of that, he replied, would belie our former admissions.

But does not the courageous man also go to meet the better, and pleasanter, and nobler?

That must be admitted.

And the courageous man has no base fear or base confidence?

True, he replied.

And if not base, then honourable?

He admitted this.

And if honourable, then good?

Yes.

But the fear and confidence of the coward or foolhardy or madman, on the contrary, are base?

He assented.

And these base fears and confidences originate in ignorance and uninstructedness?

True, he said.

Then, as to the motive from which the cowards act, do you call it cowardice or courage?

I should say cowardice, he replied.

And have they not been shown to be cowards through their ignorance of dangers?

Assuredly, he said.

And because of that ignorance they are cowards?

He assented.

And the reason why they are cowards is admitted by you to be cowardice?

He again assented.

Then the ignorance of what is and is not dangerous is cowardice?

He nodded assent.

But surely courage, I said, is opposed to cowardice?

Yes.

Then the wisdom which knows what are and are not dangers is opposed to the ignorance of them?

To that again he nodded assent.

And the ignorance of them is cowardice?

To that he very reluctantly nodded assent.

And the knowledge of that which is and is not dangerous is courage, and is opposed to the ignorance of these things?

At this point he would no longer nod assent, but was silent.

And why, I said, do you neither assent nor dissent, Protagoras?

Finish the argument by yourself, he said.

I only want to ask one more question, I said. I want to know whether you still think that there are men who are most ignorant and yet most courageous?

You seem to have a great ambition to make me answer, Socrates, and therefore I will gratify you, and say, that this appears to me to be impossible consistently with the argument.

My only object, I said, in continuing the discussion, has been the desire to ascertain the nature and relations of virtue; for if this were clear, I am very sure that the other controversy which has been carried on at great length by both of us—you affirming and I denying that virtue can be taught—would also become clear. The result of our discussion appears to me to be singular. For if the argument had a human voice, that voice would be heard laughing at us and saying: "Protagoras and Socrates, you are strange beings; there are you, Socrates, who were saying that virtue cannot be taught, contradicting yourself now by your attempt to prove that all things are knowledge, including justice, and temperance, and courage,—which tends to show that virtue can certainly be taught; for if virtue were other than knowledge, as Protagoras attempted to prove, then clearly virtue cannot be taught; but if virtue is entirely knowledge, as you are seeking to show, then I cannot but suppose that virtue is capable of being taught. Protagoras, on the other hand, who started by saying that it might be taught, is now eager to prove it to be anything rather than knowledge; and if this is true, it must be quite incapable of being taught." Now I, Protagoras, perceiving this terrible confusion of our ideas, have a great desire that they should be cleared up. And I should like to carry on the discussion until we ascertain what virtue is, and whether capable of being taught or not, lest haply Epimetheus should trip us up and deceive us in the argument, as he forgot us in the story; I prefer your Prometheus to your Epimetheus, for of him I make use, whenever I am busy about these questions, in Promethean care of my own life. And if you have no objection, as I said at first, I should like to have your help in the enquiry.

Protagoras replied: Socrates, I am not of a base nature, and I am the last man in the world to be envious. I cannot but applaud your energy and your conduct of an argument. As I have often said, I admire you above all men whom I know, and far above all men of your age; and I believe that you will become very eminent in philosophy. Let us come back to the subject at some future time; at present we had better turn to something else.

By all means, I said, if that is your wish; for I too ought long since to have kept the engagement of which I spoke before, and only tarried because I could not refuse the request of the noble Callias. So the conversation ended, and we went our way.

14 / R. M. HARE

Decisions of Principle

There are two factors which may be involved in the making of any decision to do something. Of these, the first may at any rate theoretically be absent, the second is always present to some degree. They correspond to the major and minor premisses of the Aristotelian practical syllogism. The major premiss is a principle of conduct; the minor premiss is a statement, more or less full, of what we should in fact be doing if we did one or other of the alternatives open to us. Thus if I decide not to say something, because it is false, I am acting on a principle, 'Never (or never under certain conditions) say what is false', and I must know that this, which I am wondering whether to say, is false.

Let us take the minor premiss first, since it presents less difficulty. We plainly cannot decide what to do unless we know at least something about what we should be doing if we did this or that. For example, suppose that I am an employer, and am wondering whether or not to sack a clerk who habitually turns up at the office after the hour at which he has undertaken to turn up. If I sack him I shall be depriving his family of the money on which they live, perhaps giving my firm a reputation which will lead clerks to avoid it when other jobs are available, and so on; if I keep him, I shall be causing the other clerks to do work which otherwise would be done by this clerk; and the affairs of the office will not be transacted so quickly as they would if all the clerks were punctual. These would be the sorts of consideration that I should take into account in making my decision. They would be the effects on the total situation of the alternative actions, sacking him or not sacking him. It is the effects which determine what I should be doing; it is between the two sets of effects that I am deciding. The whole point about a decision is that it makes a difference to what happens; and this difference is the difference between the effects of deciding one way, and the effects of deciding the other.

It sometimes seems to be implied by writers on ethics that it is

R. M. Hare, "Decisions of Principle," in *The Language of Morals* (New York: Oxford University Press, 1952), pp. 56–78. Reprinted with permission of the publisher.

immoral, on certain sorts of occasion, to consider the effects of doing something. We ought, it is said, to do our duty no matter what the effects of doing it. As I am using the word 'effects', this cannot be maintained. I am not making a claim for 'expediency' (in the bad sense) as against 'duty'. Even to do our duty—in so far as it is *doing* something—is effecting certain changes in the total situation. It is quite true that, of the changes that it is possible to effect in the total situation, most people would agree that we ought to consider certain kinds more relevant than others (which than which, it is the purpose of moral principles to tell us). I do not think that the immediacy or remoteness of the effects makes any difference, though their certainty or uncertainty does. The reason why it is considered immoral to fail to right an injustice whose effects will maximize pleasure, is not that in such a choice the effects are considered when they should not have been; it is that certain of the effects—namely, the maximization of pleasure—are given a relevance which they should not have, in view of the prior claim of those other effects which should have consisted in the righting of the injustice.

For reasons which will become apparent when we have examined the logic of value-words, it is most important, in a verbal exposition of an argument about what to do, not to allow value-words in the minor premiss. In setting out the facts of the case, we should be as factual as we can. Those versed in the logic of these words, and therefore forewarned against its pitfalls, may in the interests of brevity neglect this precaution; but for the inexperienced it is very much better to keep value-expressions where they belong, in the major premiss. This will prevent the inadvertent admission of an ambiguous middle term, as in the example in 3. 3 *sub fine*. I do not mean that in discussing the facts of the case we should not admit any words which could possibly have an evaluative meaning; for this, in view of the way in which evaluative meaning pervades our language, would be well-nigh impossible. I only mean that we must be sure that, as we are using the words in the minor premiss, there are definite tests (not themselves involving evaluation) for ascertaining its truth or falsity. In the last paragraph I was using the word 'pleasure' in such a sense, though it is not always so used.

The relation between the two premisses may perhaps be made clearer by considering an artificial example. Let us suppose that a man has a peculiar kind of clairvoyance such that he can know everything about the effects of all the alternative actions open to him. But let us suppose that he has so far formed for himself, or been taught, no principles of conduct. In deciding between alternative courses of action, such a man would know, fully and exactly, between what he was deciding. We have to ask to what extent, if any, such a man would be handicapped, in coming to a decision, by not having any formed principles. It would seem beyond doubt that he could choose between two courses; it would be strange, even, to call such a choice necessarily arbitrary or ungrounded; for if a man knows to the last detail exactly what he is doing, and what he might otherwise have done, his choice is not arbitrary in the sense in which a choice would be arbitrary if made by the toss of a coin without any consideration of the effects. But suppose that we were to ask such a man 'Why did you choose this set of effects rather than that? Which of the many effects were they that led you to decide the way you did?' His answer to this question might be of two kinds. He might say 'I can't give any reasons; I just felt like deciding that way; another time, faced with the same choice, I might decide differently'. On the other hand, he might say 'It was this and this that made me decide; I was deliberately avoiding such and such effects, and seeking such and such'. If he gave the first of these two answers, we might in a certain sense of that word call his decision arbitrary (though even in that case he had *some* reason for his choice, namely, that he felt that way); but if he gave the second, we should not.

Let us see what is involved in this second type of answer. Although we have assumed that the man has no formed principles, he shows, if he gives the second answer, that he has started to form principles for himself; for to choose effects *because* they are such and such is to begin to act on a principle that such and such effects are to be chosen. We see in this example that in order to act on principle it is not necessary in some sense to have a principle already, before you act; it may be that the decision to act in a certain way, because of something about the effects of acting in that way, *is* to subscribe to a principle of action—though it is not necessarily to adopt it in any permanent sense.

Ordinary men are not so fortunate as the man in our artificial example. They start, indeed, without any knowledge of the future at all; and when they acquire knowledge it is not of this intuitive kind. The kind of knowledge that we have of the future—unless we are clairvoyant—is based upon principles of prediction which we are taught, or form for ourselves. Principles of prediction are one kind of principle of action; for to predict is to act in a certain way. Thus, although there is nothing logically to prevent someone doing entirely without principles, and making all his choices in the arbitrary manner exhibited in the first kind of answer, this never in fact occurs. Moreover, our knowledge of the future is fragmentary and only probable; and therefore in many cases the principles which we are taught or form for ourselves say, not 'Choose this kind of effect rather than that', but 'You do not know for certain what will be the effects; but do this rather than that, and the effects are most likely to be such as you would have chosen, if you had known them'. It is important to remember, in this connexion, that 'likely' and 'probable' are value-words; in many contexts 'It is probable (or likely) that P' is adequately rendered by 'There is *good* reason (or evidence) for holding that P'.

We may distinguish, so far, two reasons why we have principles. The first reason applies to anyone, even a man with complete insight into the future, who decides to choose something because it is of a certain character. The second reason applies to us because we do not in fact have complete knowledge of the future, and because such knowledge as we do have involves principles. To these reasons a third must now be added. Without principles, most kinds of teaching are impossible, for what is taught is in most cases a principle. In particular, when we learn *to do* something, what we learn is always a principle. Even to learn or be taught a fact (like the names of the five rivers of the Punjab) is to learn how to answer a question; it is to learn the principle 'When asked "What are the names of the five rivers of the Punjab?" answer "The Jhelum, the Chenab, &c.".' By this I do not of course mean, that to learn to do anything is to learn to recite by rote some universal imperative sentence. This would involve us in a vicious regress; for learning to recite is a kind of learning, and must have its principles; but in that case we should have to learn to recite the principles of reciting. The point is rather this, that to learn to do anything is never to learn to do an individual act; it is always to learn to do acts of a certain kind in a certain kind of situation; and this is to learn a principle. Thus, in learning to drive, I learn, not to change gear *now*, but to change gear when the engine makes a certain kind of noise. If this were not so, instruction would be of no use at all; for if all an instructor could do were to tell us to change gear *now*, he would have to sit beside us for the rest of our lives in order to tell us just when, on each occasion, to change gear.

Thus without principles we could not learn anything whatever from our elders. This would mean that every generation would have to start from scratch and teach itself. But even if each generation were able to teach itself, it could not do so without principles; for self-teaching, like all other teaching, is the teaching of principles. This may be seen by recurring to our artificial example. Let us suppose that our clairvoyant made all his choices on some principle, but always forgot, as soon as he had made the choice, what the principle had been. He would have, accordingly, each time he made a decision, to go over all the effects of the alternative actions. This would be so time-consuming that he would not have the leisure to make many decisions in the course of his life. He would spend his whole time deciding matters like whether to step off with the right or the left foot, and would never reach what we should call the more important decisions. But if he could remember the principles on which he acted, he would be in a much better position; he could *learn* how to act in certain kinds of circumstance; he could learn to single out quickly the relevant aspects of a situation, including the effects of the various possible actions, and so choose quickly, and in many cases habitually. Thus his powers of considered decision would be set free for more momentous decisions. When the cabinet-maker has learnt how to make a dovetail without thinking much about it, he will have time to think about such things as the proportions and aesthetic appearance of the finished product. And it is the same with our conduct in the moral sphere; when the performance of the lesser duties has become a matter of habit, we have time to think about the greater.

There is a limit in practice to the amount that can be taught to someone by someone else. Beyond this point, self-teaching is necessary. The limit is set by the variety of conditions which may be met with in doing whatever is being taught; and this variety is greater in some cases than in others. A sergeant can teach a recruit almost all there is to be known about fixing bayonets on parade, because one occasion of fixing bayonets on parade is much like another; but a driving instructor cannot do more than begin to teach his pupil the art of driving, because the conditions to be met with in driving are so various. In most cases, teaching cannot consist in getting the learner to perform faultlessly a fixed drill. One of the things that has to be included in any but the most elementary kinds of instruction is the opportunity for the learner to make decisions for himself, and in so doing to examine, and even modify to suit particular types of case, the principles which are being taught. The principles that are taught us initially are of a provisional kind (very like the principle 'Never say what is false' which I discussed in the last chapter). Our training, after the initial stages, consists in taking these principles, and making them less provisional; we do this by using them continually in our own decisions, and sometimes making exceptions to them; some of the exceptions are made because our instructor points out to us that certain cases are instances of classes of exceptions to the prin- ciple; and some of the exceptions we decide on for ourselves. This pre- sents no more difficulty than our clairvoyant had in deciding between two sets of effects. If we learn from experiment that to follow a certain principle would have certain effects, whereas to modify it in a certain way would have certain other effects, we adopt whichever form of the principle leads to the effects which we choose to pursue.

We may illustrate this process of modifying principles from the example already used, that of learning to drive. I am told, for instance, always to draw into the side of the road when I stop the car; but later I am told that this does not apply when I stop before turning into a side- road to the off-side—for then I must stop near the middle of the road until it is possible for me to turn. Still later I learn that in this manœuvre it is not necessary to stop at all if it is an uncontrolled junction and I can see that there is no traffic which I should obstruct by turning. When I have picked up all these modifications to the rule, and the similar modifications to all the other rules, and practice them habitually as so modified, then I am said to be a good driver, because my car is always in the right place on the road, travelling at the right speed, and so on. The good driver is, among other things, one whose actions are so exactly governed by principles which have become a habit with him, that he normally does not have to *think* just what to do. But road conditions are exceedingly various, and therefore it is unwise to let all one's driving become a matter of habit. One can never be certain that one's principles of driving are perfect—indeed, one can be very sure that they are not; and therefore the good driver not only drives well from habit, but constantly attends to his driving habits, to see whether they might not be improved; he never stops learning.

It is hardly necessary to point out that principles of driving, like other principles, are normally not inculcated by their verbal repetition, but by example, demonstration, and other practical means. We learn to drive, not by precept, but by being shown how to do particular bits of driving; the precepts are usually only explanatory or mnemonic of what we are being shown. Thereafter, we try to do the particular manœuvres ourselves, and are criticized for failures, commended when we do them well, and so gradually get the hang of the various principles of good driving. For although our instruction is far from being purely verbal, nevertheless what we are being taught are principles. The fact that the derivation of particular acts (or commands to do them) from principles is normally done non-verbally does not show that it is not a logical process, any more than the inference:

> The clock has just struck seven times
> The clock strikes seven times at seven o'clock only
> ∴ It is just after seven o'clock

is shown to be non-logical because it is never made explicitly in words.

Drivers often know just what to do in a certain situation without being able to enunciate in words the principle on which they act. This is a very common state of affairs with all kinds of principles. Trappers know just where to set their traps, but often cannot explain just why they have put a trap in a particular place. We all know how to use words to convey our meaning; but if a logician presses us for the exact definition of a word we have used, or the exact rules for its use, we are often at a loss. This does not mean that the setting of traps or the use of words or the driving of cars does not proceed according to principles. One may know how, without being able to say how—though if a skill is to be taught, it is easier if we *can* say how.

We must not think that, if we can decide between one course and another without further thought (it seems self-evident to us, which we should do), this necessarily implies that we have some mysterious intuitive faculty which tells us what to do. A driver does not know when to change gear by intuition; he knows it because he has learnt and not forgotten; what he knows is a principle, though he cannot formulate the principle in words. The same is true of moral decisions which are sometimes called 'intuitive'. We have moral 'intuitions' because we have learnt how to behave, and have different ones according to how we have learnt to behave.

It would be a mistake to say that all that had to be done to a man to make him into a good driver was to tell him, or otherwise inculcate into him, a lot of general principles. This would be to leave out the factor of decision. Very soon after he begins to learn, he will be faced with situations to deal with which the provisional principles so far taught him require modification; and he will then have to decide what to do. He will very soon discover which decisions were right and which wrong, partly because his instructor tells him, and partly because having seen the effects of the decisions he determines in future not to bring about such effects. On no account must we commit the mistake of supposing that decisions and principles occupy two separate spheres and do not meet at any point. All decisions except those, if any, that are completely arbitrary are to some extent decisions of principle. We are always setting precedents for ourselves. It is not a case of the principle settling everything down to a certain point, and decision dealing with everything below that point. Rather, decision and principles interact throughout the whole field. Suppose that we have a principle to act in a certain way in certain circumstances. Suppose then that we find ourselves in circumstances which fall under the principle, but which have certain other peculiar features, not met before, which make us ask 'Is the principle really intended to cover cases like this, or is it incompletely specified—is there here a case belonging to a class which should be treated as exceptional?' Our answer to this question will be a decision, but a decision of principle, as is shown by the use of the value-word 'should'. If we decide that this should be an exception, we thereby modify the principle by laying down an exception to it.

Suppose, for example, that in learning to drive I have been taught always to signal before I slow down or stop, but have not yet been taught what to do when stopping in an emergency; if a child leaps in front of my car, I do not signal, but keep both hands on the steering-wheel; and thereafter I accept the former principle with this exception, that in cases of emergency it is better to steer than to signal. I have, even on the spur of the moment, made a decision of principle. To understand what happens in cases like this is to understand a great deal about the making of value-judgements.

I do not wish to seem to be pressing too far my comparison, in respect of the way in which they are learnt, between principles of driving and principles of conduct. It is necessary also to bear in mind some distinctions. In the first place, the expression 'good driver' is itself ambiguous in that it is not immediately clear what standard is being applied. It might be simply a standard of expertness; we might call a person a good driver if he were able to do just what he wanted with his car; we might say 'Although a very good driver, he is most inconsiderate to other road users'. On the other hand, we sometimes expect a good driver to have moral qualities as well; we do not, according to this criterion, call a man a good driver if he drives expertly, but without the slightest heed for the convenience or safety of other people. The line between these two standards of good driving is not easy to draw in practice. There is also a third standard, according to which a driver is said to be good if he conforms to the accepted principles of good driving as laid down, for example, in the *Highway Code*. Since the *Highway Code* is compiled with a definite purpose in view, this standard coincides to a great extent with the second.

Secondly, there are two ways of looking at driving instruction:

    (1) We establish at the beginning certain ends, for example the avoidance of collisions, and instruction consists in teaching what practices are conducive to those ends. According to this way of looking at them, the principles of good driving are hypothetical imperatives.

    (2) We teach at first simple rules of thumb, and the learner only gradually comes to see what the ends are, at which the instruction is aimed.

It must not be thought that either (1) or (2) by itself gives a complete account of our procedure. Which method we adopt depends to a great extent on the maturity and intelligence of the learner. In teaching African soldiers to drive, we might incline more to the second method; if I had to teach my two-year-old son to drive, I should have to adopt the same methods as I now adopt for teaching him to refrain from interfering with the controls when I am driving myself. With a highly intelligent learner, on the other hand, we may adopt a method which has more of (1) in it than of (2).

It must not be thought, however, that method (2) is ever entirely without a place even in the case of the most rational of learners. It may be that the desirability of avoiding collisions is at once understood and accepted even by comparatively stupid learners; but there are a great many more ends than this which a good driver has to aim at. He has to avoid causing many kinds of avoidable inconvenience both to himself and to others; he has to learn not to do things which result in damage to his vehicle, and so on. It is of no use to establish at the beginning a general end, 'the avoidance of avoidable inconvenience'; for 'inconvenience' is a value-word, and until he has had experience of driving, the learner will not know what sorts of situation are to count as avoidable inconvenience. The general end or principle is vacuous until by our detailed instruction we have given it content. Therefore it is always necessary to start, to some extent, by teaching our learner *what* to do, and leaving it for him to find out later *why*. We may therefore say that although moral principles, which are normally taught us when we are immature, are taught largely by method (2), and principles of driving preponderantly by method (1), there is not an absolute division between the two sorts of principle in this respect. What I have just said about first learning *what* to do, and about the initial vacuity of the general end, is borrowed from Aristotle.[1] The one fundamental distinction between principles of driving and principles of conduct is that the latter are, in Aristotle's term, 'architectonic' of the former; for the ends of good driving (safety, the avoidance of inconvenience to others, the preservation of property, and so on) are justified ultimately, if justification is sought, by appeal to moral considerations.[2]

It would be folly, however, to say that there is only one way of learning a skill or any other body of principles, or of justifying a particular decision made in the practice of it. There are many ways, and I have tried to make the above account sufficiently general to cover all of them. It is sometimes said by writers on morals that we have to justify an act by reference to its effects, and that we tell which effects are to be sought, which avoided, by reference to some principle. Such a theory is that of the utilitarians, who bid us look at the effects, and examine these in the light of the principle of utility, to see which effects would maximize pleasure. Sometimes, on the other hand, it is said (as by Mr. Toulmin)[3] that an act is justified directly by reference to the principles which it observes, and these principles in their turn by reference to the effects of always observing them. Sometimes it is said that we should observe principles and ignore the effects—though for the reasons given above 'effects' cannot be here intended in the sense in which I have been using

---

[1] *Nicomachean Ethics*, i. 4.

[2] Op. cit. i. 1, 2.

[3] *Reason in Ethics*, pp. 144ff.

it. What is wrong with these theories is not what they say, but their assumption that they are telling us the only way to justify actions, or decide what actions to do. We do, indeed, justify and decide on actions in all these ways; for example, sometimes, if asked why we did A, we say, 'Because it was a case falling under principle P', and if asked to justify P in turn, we go into the effects of observing it and of not observing it. But sometimes, when asked the same question 'Why did you do A?' we say 'Because if I hadn't, E would have happened', and if asked what was wrong about E happening, we appeal to some principle.

The truth is that, if asked to justify as completely as possible any decision, we have to bring in both effects—to give content to the decision —and principles, and the effects in general of observing those principles, and so on, until we have satisfied our inquirer. Thus a complete justification of a decision would consist of a complete account of its effects, together with a complete account of the principles which it observed, and the effects of observing those principles—for, of course, it is the effects (what obeying them in fact consists in) which give content to the principles too. Thus, if pressed to justify a decision completely, we have to give a complete specification of the way of life of which it is a part. This complete specification it is impossible in practice to give; the nearest attempts are those given by the great religions, especially those which can point to historical persons who carried out the way of life in practice. Suppose, however, that we can give it. If the inquirer still goes on asking 'But why *should* I live like that?' then there is no further answer to give him, because we have already, *ex hypothesi,* said everything that could be included in this further answer. We can only ask him to make up his own mind which way he ought to live; for in the end everything rests upon such a decision of principle. He has to decide whether to accept that way of life or not; if he accepts it, then we can proceed to justify the decisions that are based upon it; if he does not accept it, then let him accept some other, and try to live by it. The sting is in the last clause. To describe such ultimate decisions as arbitrary, because *ex hypothesi* everything which could be used to justify them has already been included in the decision, would be like saying that a complete description of the universe was utterly unfounded, because no further fact could be called upon in corroboration of it. This is not how we use the words 'arbitrary' and 'unfounded'. Far from being arbitrary, such a decision would be the most well-founded of decisions, because it would be based upon a consideration of everything upon which it could possibly be founded.

It will be noticed how, in talking of decisions of principle, I have inevitably started talking value-language. Thus we decide that the principle *should* be modified, or that it is *better* to steer than to signal.

This illustrates the very close relevance of what I have been saying in the first part of this book to the problems of the second part; for to make a value-judgement is to make a decision of principle. To ask whether I ought to do A in these circumstances is (to borrow Kantian language with a small though important modification) to ask whether or not I will that doing A in such circumstances should become a universal law.[4] It may seem a far cry from Kant to Professor Stevenson; but the same question could be put in other words by asking 'What attitude shall I adopt and recommend towards doing A in such circumstances?'; for 'attitude', if it means anything, means a principle of action. Unfortunately Stevenson, unlike Kant, devotes very little space to the examination of this first-person question; had he paid due attention to it, and avoided the dangers of the word 'persuasive', he might have reached a position not unlike that of Kant.

As Kant points out in the important passage on the Autonomy of the Will, to which I referred earlier, we have to make our own decisions of principle.[5] Other people cannot make them for us unless we have first decided to take their advice or obey their orders. There is an interesting analogy here with the position of the scientist, who also has to rely on his own observations. It might be said that there is a difference here between decisions and observations, to the detriment of the former, in that an observation, once made, is public property, whereas decisions have to be made by the agent himself on each occasion. But the difference is only apparent. A scientist would not have become a scientist unless he had convinced himself that the observations of other scientists were in general reliable. He did this by making some observations of his own. When we learnt elementary chemistry at school, we had some theoretical periods and some practical. In the theoretical periods we studied books; in the practical periods we made experiments, and found, if we were lucky, that the results tallied with what the books said. This showed us that what the books said was not all nonsense; so that even if, by reason of disturbing factors ignored by us, our experiments came out wrong, we were inclined to trust the books and acknowledge that we had made a mistake. We were confirmed in this assumption by the fact that we often discovered later what the mistake had been. If our observations, however carefully we did them, were always at variance with the textbooks, we should not be tempted to make science our profession. Thus the confidence of the scientist in other people's observations is ultimately based, among other things, on his own observations and his own judgements about what is reliable. He has in the end to rely on himself.

---

[4] Cf. *Groundwork of the Metaphysic of Morals*, tr. H. J. Paton, p. 88.

[5] Op. cit., pp. 108ff.

The case of the moral agent is not dissimilar. When in our early days we are given our elementary moral instruction, there are some things that we are told, and some things that we do. If, when we did as we were told, the total effects of our so doing, when they happened, were always such as we would not have chosen, had we known, then we should seek better advice, or, if prevented from so doing, either work out our own salvation or become moral defectives. If we are in general given what we subsequently come to see to have been good advice, we decide in general to follow the advice and adopt the principles of those who have given us this good advice in the past. This is what happens to any child who is well brought up. Just as the scientist does not try to rewrite all that is in the textbooks, but takes that for granted and sticks to his own particular researches, so this fortunate child will take over bodily the principles of his elders and adapt them in detail, by his own decisions, to suit his own circumstances from time to time. This is how in a well-ordered society morality remains stable, and at the same time gets adapted to changing circumstances.

There are, however, many ways in which this happy state of affairs can deteriorate. Let us consider a process that seems to occur quite often in history; it occurred in Greece during the fifth and fourth centuries, and it has occurred in our own time. Suppose that the people of a certain generation—I will call it the first generation—have got very settled principles, inherited from their fathers. Suppose that they have become so settled as to be second nature, so that generally speaking people act on the principles without thinking, and their power of making considered decisions of principle becomes atrophied. They act always by the book, and come to no harm, because the state of the world in their time remains much the same as that for which the principles were thought out. But their sons, the second generation, as they grow up, find that conditions have changed (e.g. through a protracted war or an industrial revolution), and that the principles in which they have been brought up are no longer adequate. Since, in their education, much stress has been laid on observing principles, and very little on making the decisions on which these principles are ultimately based, their morality has no roots, and becomes completely unstable. Books on 'The Whole Duty of Man' are no longer written or read. Often, when they do what it says in such books, they subsequently find cause to regret their decisions; and there are too many cases of this kind for any confidence in the old principles, as a body, to remain. No doubt there are among these old principles certain very general ones, which will remain acceptable unless human nature and the state of the world undergo a most fundamental change; but the second generation, not having been brought up to make decisions of principle, but to do what it says in the book, will not, most of them, be able to make those crucial decisions which would determine which principles to keep, which to modify, and which to abandon. Some people, the Polemarchuses of the second generation, will have been so steeped in the old principles that they just follow them come what may; and these will on the whole be more fortunate than the others, for it is better to have some principles, even if they sometimes lead to decisions which we regret, than to be morally adrift. The bulk of the second generation, and still more perhaps of the third, will not know which of the principles to keep and which to reject; and so they will come more and more to live from day to day—not a bad thing, because it trains their powers of decision, but it is an unpleasant and dangerous state to be in. A few among them, the rebels, will shout from the house-tops that some or all of the old moral principles are worthless; some of these rebels will advocate new principles of their own; some will have nothing to offer. Though they increase the confusion, these rebels perform the useful function of making people decide between their rival principles; and if they not only advocate new principles, but sincerely try to live by them, they are conducting a moral experiment which may be of the utmost value to man (in which case they go down in history as great moral teachers), or may, on the other hand, prove disastrous both to them and to their disciples.

It may take several generations for this disease to play itself out. Morality regains its vigour when ordinary people have learnt afresh to decide for themselves what principles to live by, and more especially what principles to teach their children. Since the world, though subject to vast material changes, changes only very slowly in matters that are fundamental from the moral point of view, the principles which win the acceptance of the mass of people are not likely to differ enormously from those which their fathers came to distrust. The moral principles of Aristotle resemble those of Aeschylus more than they differ from them, and we ourselves shall perhaps come back to something recognizably like the morality of our grandfathers. But there will be some changes; some of the principles advocated by the rebels will have been adopted. That is how morality progresses—or retrogresses. The process is, as we shall see, reflected by very subtle changes in the uses of value-words; the impossibility of translating Aristotle's catalogue of virtues into modern English may serve as an example, and the disappearance without trace of the word 'righteous' may serve as another.

The question 'How shall I bring up my children?' which we have mentioned, is one to the logic of which, since ancient times, few philosophers have given much attention. A child's moral upbringing has an effect upon him which will remain largely untouched by anything that happens to him thereafter. If he has had a stable upbringing, whether on good principles or on bad ones, it will be extremely difficult for him to abandon those principles in later life—difficult but not impossible. They will have for him the force of an objective moral law; and his behaviour will seem to give much evidence in support of intuitionist ethical theories, provided that it is not compared with the behaviour of those who stick just as firmly to quite different principles. But nevertheless, unless our education has been so thorough as to transform us into automata, we can come to doubt or even reject these principles; that is what makes human beings, whose moral systems change, different from ants, whose 'moral system' does not. Therefore, even if for me the question 'What shall I do in such and such a situation?' is almost invariably answered without ambiguity by the moral intuition which my upbringing has given me, I may, if I ask myself 'How shall I bring up my children?' pause before giving an answer. It is here that the most fundamental moral decisions of all arise; and it is here, if only moral philosophers would pay attention to them, that the most characteristic uses of moral words are to be found. Shall I bring up my children *exactly* as I was brought up, so that they have the same intuitions about morals as I have? Or have circumstances altered, so that the moral character of the father will not provide a suitable equipment for the children? Perhaps I shall try to bring them up like their father, and shall fail; perhaps their new environment will be too strong for me, and they will come to repudiate my principles. Or I may have become so bewildered by the strange new world that, although I still act from force of habit on the principles that I have learnt, I simply do not know what principles to impart to my children, if, indeed, one in my condition can impart any settled principles at all. On all these questions, I have to make up my mind; only the most hide-bound father will try to bring up his children, without thinking, in exactly the way that he himself was brought up; and even he will usually fail disastrously.

Many of the dark places of ethics become clearer when we consider this dilemma in which parents are liable to find themselves. We have already noticed that, although principles have in the end to rest upon decisions of principle, decisions as such cannot be taught; only principles can be taught. It is the powerlessness of the parent to make for his son those many decisions of principle which the son during his future career will make, that gives moral language its characteristic shape. The only instrument which the parent possesses is moral education—the teaching of principles by example and precept, backed up by chastisement and other more up-to-date psychological methods. Shall he use these means, and to what extent? Certain generations of parents have had no doubts about this question. They have used them to the full; and the result has been to turn their children into good intuitionists, able to cling to the rails, but bad at steering round corners. At other times parents—and who shall blame them?—suffer from lack of confidence; they are not sure enough what they themselves think, to be ready to impart to their children a stable way of life. The children of such a generation are likely to grow up opportunists, well able to make individual decisions, but without the settled body of principles which is the most priceless heritage that any generation can leave to its successors. For, though principles are in the end built upon decisions of principle, the building is the work of many generations, and the man who has to start from the beginning is to be pitied; he will not be likely, unless he is a genius, to achieve many conclusions of importance, any more than the average boy, turned loose without instruction upon a desert island, or even in a laboratory, would be likely to make any of the major scientific discoveries.

The dilemma between these two extreme courses in education is plainly a false one. Why it is a false one is apparent, if we recall what was said earlier about the dynamic relation between decisions and principles. It is very like learning to drive. It would be foolish, in teaching someone to drive, to try to inculcate into him such fixed and comprehensive principles that he would never have to make an independent decision. It would be equally foolish to go to the other extreme and leave it to him to find his own way of driving. What we do, if we are sensible, is to give him a solid basis of principles, but at the same time ample opportunity of making the decisions upon which these principles are based, and by which they are modified, improved, adapted to changed circumstances, or even abandoned if they become entirely unsuited to a new environment. To teach only the principles, without giving the opportunity of subjecting them to the learner's own decisions of principle, is like teaching science exclusively from textbooks without entering a laboratory. On the other hand, to abandon one's child or one's driving-pupil to his own self-expression is like putting a boy into a laboratory and saying 'Get on with it'. The boy may enjoy himself or kill himself, but will probably not learn much science.

The moral words, of which we may take 'ought' as an example, reflect in their logical behaviour this double nature of moral instruction—as well they may, for it is in moral instruction that they are most typically used. The sentences in which they appear are normally the expression of decisions of principle—and it is easy to let the decisions get separated, in our discussion of the subject, from the principles. This is the source of the controversy between the 'objectivists', as intuitionists sometimes call themselves, and the 'subjectivists', as they often call their opponents. The former lay stress on the fixed principles that are handed down by the father, the latter on the new decisions which have to be made by the son. The objectivist says 'Of course you know what you ought to do; look at what your conscience tells you, and if in doubt go by the consciences of the vast majority of men'. He is able to say this, because our consciences are the product of the principles which our early training has indelibly planted in us, and in one society these principles do not differ much from one person to another. The subjectivist, on the other hand, says 'But surely, when it comes to the point—when I have listened to what other people say, and given due weight to my own intuitions, the legacy of my upbringing—I have in the end to decide for myself what I ought to do. To deny this is to be a conventionalist; for both common moral notions and my own intuitions are the legacy of tradition, and—apart from the fact that there are so many different traditions in the world—traditions cannot be started without someone doing what I now feel called upon to do, decide. If I refuse to make my own decisions, I am, in merely copying my fathers, showing myself a lesser man than they; for whereas they must have initiated, I shall be merely accepting.' This plea of the subjectivist is quite justified. It is the plea of the adolescent who wants to be adult. To become morally adult is to reconcile these two apparently conflicting positions by learning to make decisions of principle; it is to learn to use 'ought'-sentences in the realization that they can only be verified by reference to a standard or set of principles which we have by our own decision accepted and made our own. This is what our present generation is so painfully trying to do.

15 / JOHN DEWEY

Reconstruction in Moral Conceptions

The impact of the alteration in methods of scientific thinking upon moral ideas is, in general, obvious. Goods, ends are multiplied. Rules are softened into principles, and principles are modified into methods of understanding. Ethical theory began among the Greeks as an attempt to find a regulation for the conduct of life which should have a rational basis and purpose instead of being derived from custom. But reason as a substitute for custom was under the obligation of supplying objects and laws as fixed as those of custom had been. Ethical theory ever since has

From *Reconstruction in Philosophy*, Chap. VII, 161–186. Copyright 1920, by Henry Holt & Co. Copyright renewed, 1947 by John Dewey. Reproduced by permission of Mrs. John Dewey.

been singularly hypnotized by the notion that its business is to discover some final end or good or some ultimate and supreme law. This is the common element among the diversity of theories. Some have held that the end is loyalty or obedience to a higher power or authority; and they have variously found this higher principle in Divine Will, the will of the secular ruler, the maintenance of institutions in which the purpose of superiors is embodied, and the rational consciousness of duty. But they have differed from one another because there was one point in which they were agreed: a single and final source of law. Others have asserted that it is impossible to locate morality in conformity to law-giving power, and that it must be sought in ends that are goods. And some have sought the good in self-realization, some in holiness, some in happiness, some in the greatest possible aggregate of pleasures. And yet these schools have agreed in the assumption that there is a single, fixed and final good. They have been able to dispute with one another only because of their common premise.

The question arises whether the way out of the confusion and conflict is not to go to the root of the matter by questioning this common element. Is not the belief in the single, final and ultimate (whether conceived as good or as authoritative law) an intellectual product of that feudal organization which is disappearing historically and of that belief in a bounded, ordered cosmos, wherein rest is higher than motion, which has disappeared from natural science? It has been repeatedly suggested that the present limit of intellectual reconstruction lies in the fact that it has not as yet been seriously applied in the moral and social disciplines. Would not this further application demand precisely that we advance to a belief in a plurality of changing, moving, individualized goods and ends, and to a belief that principles, criteria, laws are intellectual instruments for analyzing individual or unique situations?

The blunt assertion that every moral situation is a unique situation having its own irreplaceable good may seem not merely blunt but preposterous. For the established tradition teaches that it is precisely the irregularity of special cases which makes necessary the guidance of conduct by universals, and that the essence of the virtuous disposition is willingness to subordinate every particular case to adjudication by a fixed principle. It would then follow that submission of a generic end and law to determination by the concrete situation entails complete confusion and unrestrained licentiousness. Let us, however, follow the pragmatic rule, and in order to discover the meaning of the idea ask for its consequences. Then it surprisingly turns out that the primary significance of the unique and morally ultimate character of the concrete situation is to transfer the weight and burden of morality to intelligence. It does not destroy responsibility; it only locates it. A moral situation is one in which judgment and choice are required antecedently to overt action. The practical meaning of the situation—that is to say the action needed to satisfy it—is not self-evident. It has to be searched for. There are conflicting desires and alternative apparent goods. What is needed is to find the right course of action, the right good. Hence, inquiry is exacted: observation of the detailed makeup of the situation; analysis into its diverse factors; clarification of what is obscure; discounting the more insistent and vivid traits; tracing the consequences of the various modes of action that suggest themselves; regarding the decision reached as hypothetical and tentative until the anticipated or supposed conse- quences which led to its adoption have been squared with actual consequences. This inquiry is intelligence. Our moral failures go back to some weakness of disposition, some absence of sympathy, some onesided bias that makes us perform the judgment of the concrete case carelessly or perversely. Wide sympathy, keen sensitiveness, persistence in the face of the disagreeable, balance of interests enabling us to undertake the work of analysis and decision intelligently are the distinctively moral traits—the virtues or moral excellencies.

It is worth noting once more that the underlying issue is, after all, only the same as that which has been already threshed out in physical inquiry. There too it long seemed as if rational assurance and demonstration could be attained only if we began with universal conceptions and subsumed particular cases under them. The men who initiated the methods of inquiry that are now everywhere adopted were denounced in their day (and sincerely) as subverters of truth and foes of science. If they have won in the end, it is because, as has already been pointed out, the method of universals confirmed prejudices and sanctioned ideas that had gained currency irrespective of evidence for them; while placing the initial and final weight upon the individual case, stimulated painstaking inquiry into facts and examination of principles. In the end, loss of eternal truths was more than compensated for in the accession of quotidian facts. The loss of the system of superior and fixed definitions and kinds was more than made up for by the growing system of hypotheses and laws used in classifying facts. After all, then, we are only pleading for the adoption in moral reflection of the logic that has been proved to make for security, stringency and fertility in passing judgment upon physical phenomena. And the reason is the same. The old method in spite of its nominal and esthetic worship of reason discouraged reason, because it hindered the operation of scrupulous and unremitting in- quiry.

More definitely, the transfer of the burden of the moral life from following rules or pursuing fixed ends over to the detection of the ills that need remedy in a special case and the formation of plans and methods for dealing with them, eliminates the causes which have kept moral theory controversial, and which have also kept it remote from helpful contact with the exigencies of practice. The theory of fixed ends inevitably leads thought into the bog of disputes that cannot be settled. If there is one *summum bonum*, one supreme end, what is it? To consider this problem is to place ourselves in the midst of controversies that are as acute now as they were two thousand years ago. Suppose we take a seemingly more empirical view, and say that while there is not a single end, there also are not as many as there are specific situations that require amelioration; but there are a number of such natural goods as health, wealth, honor or good name, friendship, esthetic appreciation, learning and such moral goods as justice, temperance, benevolence, etc. What or who is to decide the right of way when these ends conflict with one another, as they are sure to do? Shall we resort to the method that once brought such disrepute upon the whole business of ethics: Casuistry? Or shall we have recourse to what Bentham well called the *ipse dixit* method: the arbitrary preference of this or that person for this or that end? Or shall we be forced to arrange them all in an order of degrees from the highest good down to the least precious? Again we find ourselves in the middle of unreconciled disputes with no indication of the way out.

Meantime, the special moral perplexities where the aid of intelligence is required go unenlightened. We cannot seek or attain health, wealth, learning, justice or kindness in general. Action is always specific, concrete, individualized, unique. And consequently judgments as to acts to be performed must be similarly specific. To say that a man seeks health or justice is only to say that he seeks to live healthily or justly. These things, like truth, are adverbial. They are modifiers of action in special cases. How to live healthily or justly is a matter which differs with every person. It varies with his past experience, his opportunities, his temperamental and acquired weaknesses and abilities. Not man in general but a particular man suffering from some particular disability aims to live healthily, and consequently health cannot mean for him exactly what it means for any other mortal. Healthy living is not something to be attained by itself apart from other ways of living. A man needs to be healthy *in* his life, not apart from it, and what does life mean except the aggregate of his pursuits and activities? A man who aims at health as a distinct end becomes a valetudinarian, or a fanatic, or a mechanical performer of exercises, or an athlete so one-sided that his pursuit of bodily development injures his heart. When the endeavor to realize a so-called end does not temper and color all other activities, life is portioned out into strips and fractions. Certain acts and times are devoted to getting health, others to cultivating religion, others to seeking learning, to being a good citizen, a devotee of fine art and so on. This is the only logical alternative to subordinating all aims to the accomplishment of one alone—fanaticism. This is out of fashion at present, but who can say how much of distraction and dissipation in life, and how much of its hard and narrow rigidity is the outcome of men's failure to realize that each situation has its own unique end and that the whole personality should be concerned with it? Surely, once more, what a man needs is to live healthily, and this result so affects all the activities of his life that it cannot be set up as a separate and independent good.

Nevertheless the general notions of health, disease, justice, artistic culture are of great importance: Not, however, because this or that case may be brought exhaustively under a single head and its specific traits shut out, but because generalized science provides a man as physician and artist and citizen, with questions to ask, investigations to make, and enables him to understand the meaning of what he sees. Just in the degree in which a physician is an artist in his work he uses his science, no matter how extensive and accurate, to furnish him with tools of inquiry into the individual case, and with methods of forecasting a method of dealing with it. Just in the degree in which, no matter how great his learning, he subordinates the individual case to some classification of diseases and some generic rule of treatment, he sinks to the level of the routine mechanic. His intelligence and his action become rigid, dogmatic, instead of free and flexible.

Moral goods and ends exist only when something has to be done. The fact that something has to be done proves that there are deficiencies, evils in the existent situation. This ill is just the specific ill that it is. It never is an exact duplicate of anything else. Consequently the good of the situation has to be discovered, projected and attained on the basis of the exact defect and trouble to be rectified. It cannot intelligently be injected into the situation from without. Yet it is the part of wisdom to compare different cases, to gather together the ills from which humanity suffers, and to generalize the corresponding goods into classes. Health, wealth, industry, temperance, amiability, courtesy, learning, esthetic capacity, initiative, courage, patience, enterprise, thoroughness and a multitude of other generalized ends are acknowledged as goods. But the *value* of this systematization is intellectual or analytic. Classifications *suggest* possible traits to be on the lookout for in studying a particular case; they suggest methods of action to be tried in removing the inferred causes of ill. They are tools of insight; their value is in promoting an individualized response in the individual situation.

Morals is not a catalogue of acts nor a set of rules to be applied like drugstore prescriptions or cookbook recipes. The need in morals is for specific methods of inquiry and of contrivance: Methods of inquiry to locate difficulties and evils; methods of contrivance to form plans to be used as working hypotheses in dealing with them. And the pragmatic import of the logic of individualized situations, each having its own irreplaceable good and principle, is to transfer the attention of theory from preoccupation with general conceptions to the problem of developing effective methods of inquiry.

Two ethical consequences of great moment should be remarked. The belief in fixed values has bred a division of ends into intrinsic and instrumental, of those that are really worth while in themselves and those that are of importance only as means to intrinsic goods. Indeed, it is often thought to be the very beginning of wisdom, of moral discrimination, to make this distinction. Dialectically, the distinction is interesting and seems harmless. But carried into practice it has an import that is tragic. Historically, it has been the source and justification of a hard and fast difference between ideal goods on one side and material goods on the other. At present those who would be liberal conceive intrinsic goods as esthetic in nature rather than as exclusively religious or as intellectually contemplative. But the effect is the same. So-called intrinsic goods, whether religious or esthetic, are divorced from those interests of daily life which because of their constancy and urgency form the preoccupation of the great mass. Aristotle used this distinction to declare that slaves and the working class though they are necessary *for* the state—the commonweal—are not constituents of it. That which is regarded as *merely* instrumental must approach drudgery; it cannot command either intellectual, artistic or moral attention and respect. Anything becomes *unworthy* whenever it is thought of as intrinsically lacking worth. So men of "ideal" interests have chosen for the most part the way of neglect and escape. The urgency and pressure of "lower" ends have been covered up by polite conventions. Or, they have been relegated to a baser class of mortals in order that the few might be free to attend to the goods that are really or intrinsically worth while. This withdrawal, in the name of higher ends, has left, for mankind at large and especially for energetic "practical" people, the lower activities in complete command.

No one can possibly estimate how much of the obnoxious materialism and brutality of our economic life is due to the fact that economic ends have been regarded as *merely* instrumental. When they are recognized to be as intrinsic and final in their place as any others, then it will be seen that they are capable of idealization, and that if life is to be worth while, they must acquire ideal and intrinsic value. Esthetic, religious and other "ideal" ends are now thin and meagre or else idle and luxurious because of the separation from "instrumental" or economic ends. Only in connection with the latter can they be woven into the texture of daily life and made substantial and pervasive. The vanity and irresponsibility of values that are merely final and not also in turn means to the enrichment of other occupations of life ought to be obvious. But now the doctrine of "higher" ends gives aid, comfort and support to every socially isolated and socially irresponsible scholar, specialist, esthetic and religionist. It protects the vanity and irresponsibility of his calling from observation by others and by himself. The moral deficiency of the calling is transformed into a cause of admiration and gratulation.

The other generic change lies in doing away once for all with the traditional distinction between moral goods, like the virtues, and natural goods like health, economic security, art, science and the like. The point of view under discussion is not the only one which has deplored this rigid distinction and endeavored to abolish it. Some schools have even gone so far as to regard moral excellencies, qualities of character as of value only because they promote natural goods. But the experimental logic when carried into morals makes every quality that is judged to be good according as it contributes to amelioration of existing ills. And in so doing, it enforces the moral meaning of natural science. When all is said and done in criticism of present social deficiencies, one may well wonder whether the root difficulty does not lie in the separation of natural and moral science. When physics, chemistry, biology, medicine, contribute to the detection of concrete human woes and to the development of plans for remedying them and relieving the human estate, they become moral; they become part of the apparatus of moral inquiry or science. The latter then loses its peculiar flavor of the didactic and pedantic; its ultra-moralistic and hortatory tone. It loses its thinness and shrillness as well as its vagueness. It gains agencies that are efficacious. But the gain is not confined to the side of moral science. Natural science loses its divorce from humanity; it becomes itself humanistic in quality. It is something to be pursued not in a technical and specialized way for what is called truth for its own sake, but with the sense of its social bearing, its intellectual indispensableness. It is technical only in the sense that it provides the technique of social and moral engineering.

When the consciousness of science is fully impregnated with the consciousness of human value, the greatest dualism which now weighs humanity down, the split between the material, the mechanical, the scientific and the moral and ideal will be destroyed. Human forces that now waver because of this division will be unified and reinforced. As long as ends are not thought of as individualized according to specific needs and opportunities, the mind will be content with abstractions, and the adequate stimulus to the moral or social use of natural science and historical data will be lacking. But when attention is concentrated upon the diversified concretes, recourse to all intellectual materials needed to clear up the special cases will be imperative. At the same time that morals are made to focus in intelligence, things intellectual are moral-ized. The vexatious and wasteful conflict between naturalism and humanism is terminated.

These general considerations may be amplified. First: Inquiry, discov-ery take the same place in morals that they have come to occupy in sciences of nature. Validation, demonstration become experimental, a matter of consequences. Reason, always an honorific term in ethics, becomes actualized in the methods by which the needs and conditions, the obstacles and resources, of situations are scrutinized in detail, and intelligent plans of improvement are worked out. Remote and abstract generalities promote jumping at conclusions, "anticipations of nature." Bad consequences are then deplored as due to natural perversity and untoward fate. But shifting the issue to analysis of a specific situation makes inquiry obligatory and alert observation of consequences impera-tive. No past decision nor old principle can ever be wholly relied upon to justify a course of action. No amount of pains taken in forming a purpose in a definite case is final; the consequences of its adoption must be carefully noted, and a purpose held only as a working hypothesis until results confirm its rightness. Mistakes are no longer either mere unavoida-ble accidents to be mourned or moral sins to be expiated and forgiven. They are lessons in wrong methods of using intelligence and instructions as to a better course in the future. They are indications of the need of revision, development, readjustment. Ends grow, standards of judgment are improved. Man is under just as much obligation to develop his most advanced standards and ideals as to use conscientiously those which he already possesses. Moral life is protected from falling into formalism and rigid repetition. It is rendered flexible, vital, growing.

In the second place, every case where moral action is required becomes of equal moral importance and urgency with every other. If the need and deficiencies of a specific situation indicate improvement of health as the end and good, then for that situation health is the ultimate and supreme good. It is no means to something else. It is a final and intrinsic value. The same thing is true of improvement of economic status, of making a living, of attending to business and family demands—all of the things which under the sanction of fixed ends have been rendered of secondary and merely instrumental value, and so relatively base and unimportant. Anything that in a given situation is an end and good at all is of equal worth, rank and dignity with every other good of any other situation, and deserves the same intelligent attention.

We note thirdly the effect in destroying the roots of Phariseeism. We are so accustomed to thinking of this as deliberate hypocrisy that we overlook its intellectual premises. The conception which looks for the end of action within the circumstances of the actual situation will not have the same measure of judgment for all cases. When one factor of the situation is a person of trained mind and large resources, more will be expected than with a person of backward mind and uncultured experience. The absurdity of applying the same standard of moral judgment to savage peoples that is used with civilized will be apparent. No individual or group will be judged by whether they come up to or fall short of some fixed result, but by the direction in which they are moving. The bad man is the man who no matter how good he *has* been is beginning to deteriorate, to grow less good. The good man is the man who no matter how morally unworthy he *has* been is moving to become better. Such a conception makes one severe in judging himself and humane in judging others. It excludes that arrogance which always accompanies judgment based on degree of approximation to fixed ends.

In the fourth place, the process of growth, of improvement and progress, rather than the static outcome and result, becomes the significant thing. Not health as an end fixed once and for all, but the needed improvement in health—a continual process—is the end and good. The end is no longer a terminus or limit to be reached. It is the active process of transforming the existent situation. Not perfection as a final goal, but the ever-enduring process of perfecting, maturing, refining is the aim in living. Honesty, industry, temperance, justice, like health, wealth and learning, are not goods to be possessed as they would be if they expressed fixed ends to be attained. They are directions of change in the quality of experience. Growth itself is the only moral "end."

Although the bearing of this idea upon the problem of evil and the controversy between optimism and pessimism is too vast to be here discussed, it may be worth while to touch upon it superficially. The problem of evil ceases to be a theological and metaphysical one, and is perceived to be the practical problem of reducing, alleviating, as far as may be removing, the evils of life. Philosophy is no longer under obligation to find ingenious methods of proving that evils are only apparent, not real, or to elaborate schemes for explaining them away or, worse yet, for justifying them. It assumes another obligation:—That of contributing in however humble a way to methods that will assist us in discovering the causes of humanity's ills. Pessimism is a paralyzing doctrine. In declaring that the world is evil wholesale, it makes futile all efforts to discover the remediable causes of specific evils and thereby destroys at the root every attempt to make the world better and happier. Wholesale optimism, which has been the consequence of the attempt to explain evil away, is, however, equally an incubus.

After all, the optimism that says that the world is already the best possible of all worlds might be regarded as the most cynical of pessimisms. If this is the best possible, what would a world which was fundamentally bad be like? Meliorism is the belief that the specific conditions which exist at one moment, be they comparatively bad or comparatively good, in any event may be bettered. It encourages intelligence to study the positive means of good and the obstructions to their realization, and to put forth endeavor for the improvement of conditions. It arouses confidence and a reasonable hopefulness as optimism does not. For the latter in declaring that good is already realized in ultimate reality tends to make us gloss over the evils that concretely exist. It becomes too readily the creed of those who live at ease, in comfort, of those who have been successful in obtaining this world's rewards. Too readily optimism makes the men who hold it callous and blind to the sufferings of the less fortunate, or ready to find the cause of troubles of others in their personal viciousness. It thus co-operates with pessimism, in spite of the extreme nominal differences between the two, in benumbing sympathetic insight and intelligent effort in reform. It beckons men away from the world of relativity and change into the calm of the absolute and eternal.

The import of many of these changes in moral attitude focuses in the idea of happiness. Happiness has often been made the object of the moralists' contempt. Yet the most ascetic moralist has usually restored the idea of happiness under some other name, such as bliss. Goodness without happiness, valor and virtue without satisfaction, ends without conscious enjoyment—these things are as intolerable practically as they are self-contradictory in conception. Happiness is not, however, a bare possession; it is not a fixed attainment. Such a happiness is either the unworthy selfishness which moralists have so bitterly condemned, or it is, even if labelled bliss, an insipid tedium, a millennium of ease in relief from all struggle and labor. It could satisfy only the most delicate of mollycoddles. Happiness is found only in success; but success means succeeding, getting forward, moving in advance. It is an active process, not a passive outcome. Accordingly it includes the overcoming of obstacles, the elimination of sources of defect and ill. Esthetic sensitiveness and enjoyment are a large constituent in any worthy happiness. But the esthetic appreciation which is totally separated from renewal of spirit, from re-creation of mind and purification of emotion is a weak and sickly thing, destined to speedy death from starvation. That the renewal and re-creation come unconsciously not by set intention but makes them the more genuine.

Upon the whole, utilitarianism has marked the best in the transition from the classic theory of ends and goods to that which is now possible. It had definite merits. It insisted upon getting away from vague generalities, and down to the specific and concrete. It subordinated law to human achievement instead of subordinating humanity to external law. It taught that institutions are made for man and not man for institutions; it actively promoted all issues of reform. It made moral good natural, humane, in touch with the natural goods of life. It opposed unearthly and other-worldly morality. Above all, it acclimatized in human imagination the idea of social welfare as a supreme test. But it was still profoundly affected in fundamental points by old ways of thinking. It never questioned the idea of a fixed, final and supreme end. It only questioned the current notions as to the nature of this end; and then inserted pleasure and the greatest possible aggregate of pleasures in the position of the fixed end.

Such a point of view treats concrete activities and specific interests not as worthwhile in themselves, or as constituents of happiness, but as mere external means to getting pleasures. The upholders of the old tradition could therefore easily accuse utilitarianism of making not only virtue but art, poetry, religion and the state into mere servile means of attaining sensuous enjoyment. Since pleasure was an outcome, a result valuable on its own account independently of the active processes that achieve it, happiness was a thing to be possessed and held onto. The acquisitive instincts of man were exaggerated at the expense of the creative. Production was of importance not because of the intrinsic worth of invention and reshaping the world, but because its external results feed pleasure. Like every theory that sets up fixed and final aims, in making the end passive and possessive, it made all active operations *mere* tools. Labor was an unavoidable evil to be minimized. Security in possession was the chief thing practically. Material comfort and ease was magnified in contrast with the pains and risk of experimental creation.

These deficiencies, under certain conceivable conditions, might have remained merely theoretical. But the disposition of the times and the interests of those who propagated the utilitarian ideas, endowed them with power for social harm. In spite of the power of the new ideas in attacking old social abuses, there were elements in the teaching which operated or protected to sanction new social abuses. The reforming zeal was shown in criticism of the evils inherited from the class system of feudalism, evils economic, legal and political. But the new economic order of capitalism that was superseding feudalism brought its own social evils with it, and some of these ills utilitarianism tended to cover up or defend. The emphasis upon acquisition and possession of enjoyments took on an untoward color in connection with the contemporary enormous desire for wealth and the enjoyments it makes possible.

If utilitarianism did not actively promote the new economic material-ism, it had no means of combating it. Its general spirit of subordinating productive activity to the bare product was indirectly favorable to the cause of an unadorned commercialism. In spite of its interest in a thoroughly social aim, utilitarianism fostered a new class interest, that of the capitalistic property-owning interests, provided only property was obtained through free competition and not by governmental favor. The stress that Bentham put on security tended to consecrate the legal institution of private property provided only certain legal abuses in connection with its acquisition and transfer were abolished. *Beati possidentes*—provided possessions had been obtained in accord with the rules of the competitive game—without, that is, extraneous favors from government. Thus utilitarianism gave intellectual confirmation to all those tendencies which make "business" not a means of social service and an opportunity for personal growth in creative power but a way of accumulating the means of private enjoyment. Utilitarian ethics thus afford a remarkable example of the need of philosophic reconstruction which these lectures have been presenting. Up to a certain point, it reflected the meaning of modern thought and aspirations. But it was still tied down by fundamental ideas of that very order which it thought it had completely left behind: The idea of a fixed and single end lying beyond the diversity of human needs and acts rendered utilitarianism incapable of being an adequate representative of the modern spirit. It has to be reconstructed through emancipation from its inherited elements.

If a few words are added upon the topic of education, it is only for the sake of suggesting that the educative process is all one with the moral process, since the latter is a continuous passage of experience from worse to better. Education has been traditionally thought of as preparation: as learning, acquiring certain things because they will later be useful. The end is remote, and education is getting ready, is a preliminary to something more important to happen later on. Childhood is only a preparation for adult life, and adult life for another life. Always the future, not the present, has been the significant thing in education: Acquisition of knowledge and skill for future use and enjoyment; formation of habits required later in life in business, good citizenship and pursuit of science. Education is thought of also as something needed by some human beings merely because of their dependence upon others. We are born ignorant, unversed, unskilled, immature, and consequently in a state of social dependence. Instruction, training, moral discipline are processes by which the mature, the adult, gradually raise the helpless to the point where they can look out for themselves. The business of childhood is to grow into the independence of adulthood by means of the guidance of those who have already attained it. Thus the process of education as the main business of life ends when the young have arrived at emancipation from social dependence.

These two ideas, generally assumed but rarely explicitly reasoned out, contravene the conception that growing, or the continuous reconstruction of experience, is the only end. If at whatever period we choose to take a person, he is still in process of growth, then education is not, save as a by-product, a preparation for something coming later. Getting from the present the degree and kind of growth there is in it is education. This is a constant function, independent of age. The best thing that can be said about any special process of education, like that of the formal school period, is that it renders its subject capable of further education: more sensitive to conditions of growth and more able to take advantage of them. Acquisition of skill, possession of knowledge, attainment of culture are not ends: they are marks of growth and means to its continuing.

The contrast usually assumed between the period of education as one of social dependence and of maturity as one of social independence does harm. We repeat over and over that man is a social animal, and then confine the significance of this statement to the sphere in which sociality usually seems least evident, politics. The heart of the sociality of man is in education. The idea of education as preparation and of adulthood as a fixed limit of growth are two sides of the same obnoxious untruth. If the moral business of the adult as well as the young is a growing and developing experience, then the instruction that comes from social dependencies and interdependencies is as important for the adult as for the child. Moral independence for the adult means arrest of growth, isolation means induration. We exaggerate the intellectual dependence of childhood so that children are too much kept in leading strings, and then we exaggerate the independence of adult life from intimacy of contacts and communication with others. When the identity of the moral process with the processes of specific growth is realized, the more conscious and formal education of childhood will be seen to be the most economical and efficient means of social advance and reorganization, and it will also be evident that the test of all the institutions of adult life is their effect in furthering continued education. Government, business, art, religion, all social institutions have a meaning, a purpose. That purpose is to set free and to develop the capacities of human individuals without respect to race, sex, class or economic status. And this is all one with saying that the test of their value is the extent to which they educate every individual into the full stature of his possibility. Democracy has many meanings, but if it has a moral meaning, it is found in resolving that the supreme test of all political institutions and industrial arrangements shall be the contribution they make to the all-around growth of every member of society.

16 / WILLIAM K. FRANKENA

Public Education and the Good Life

This paper is an attempt to say something about the subject which usually goes under the title of "moral and spiritual values in the public schools" and sometimes under the clearer but still less lovely label "character education in state-supported institutions." More specifically, it will address itself to one of the problems about public education for the good life, namely the problem which is raised by the doctrine of the separation of church and state. It seems to me that this is one of the topics in the philosophy of education on which a philosopher, and in particular a moral philosopher, may be able to shed some light.

I

To get the problem stated let us assume, as Plato and Aristotle do, that the end of the state and of education is the good life of the members of society. As C. M. Bowra writes, however, "The Greeks distinguished between the good man and the good life."[1] A recent television speaker made the same distinction in saying of someone that "he was too good for his own good." The point is that there are two kinds of good life. One kind of good life is much described in funeral orations, for funeral orators are (or at least used to be) prone to say, and to say it loudest when it is least true, that the deceased person led a good and virtuous life, and that no one surpassed him in benevolence and justice. When we say that a man has led a good life in this sense (and notice, we say "led" not "had" here), we mean that he has led a *morally* good life, a life of honesty and service, a "good and useful" life. But the phrase "a good life" has another meaning also. During the war Richard Tregaskis told in his *Guadalcanal Diary* of being in a fox-hole watching the descent of a bomb which seemed certain to strike just where he was crouching. It did not, of

William K. Frankena, "Public Education and the Good Life," *Harvard Educational Review*, 31, No. 4 (Fall 1961), 413–426. Reprinted by permission of *Harvard Educational Review* and William K. Frankena.

[1] C. H. Bowra, *The Greek Experience* (Cleveland and New York: World Pub. Co., 1957), p. 85.

course, but in the brief moment during which Tregaskis expected it to, his past flashed before him, and he said to himself, "Well, it's been a good life; I would live it again." He did not mean that he had lived a morally good life. No doubt he had, but for him to say so would have been out of place. What he meant was that on the whole his life had been an enjoyable or happy one, which he would choose again if given a chance. It was good in the way Browning is lyrical about in the lines:

> How good is man's life, the mere living! how fit to employ
> All the heart and the soul and the senses for ever in joy!

There is, then, the good life in the sense of the morally good or virtuous life, and the good life in the sense of the happy or satisfying life. For convenience of reference in the rest of the paper, I shall call the former the *moral* life and the latter the *good* life. Now, when I said above that the end of education is the good life, I meant that education must promote both the good life in this narrower sense and the moral life, or in more traditional terms, both the happy and the virtuous life. It must do what it can to make men good, and it must do what it can to make their lives so satisfactory that they would be willing to live them again in preference to others they might be offered.

Perhaps no one will dispute the view that public education, formal or informal, if it exists at all, must be concerned to promote the good life. Not all would grant, however, that the public schools may properly seek to advance the moral life, though they give different reasons for their opinion. Nevertheless, I shall assume here that public education is and should be concerned to promote morality as well as happiness. But, while formal public education, on this assumption, has the same ends as education in general, it is in a special position. Just because it is supported by the state, it has a limitation which private education does not have. This limitation is not just a matter of constitutional law or of the intentions of our founding fathers, as many seem to think; it is a matter of philosophical principle which underlies, or at any rate should underlie, both the constitution and the thinking of our founders. The limitation, as I understand it, is that, in the interests of freedom of conscience, thought, and worship, the public schools, being organs of the state, cannot teach religion. Like the state itself, they must be neutral with respect to the various churches and religions; they must be neutral even as between religion and anti-religious philosophies of life. They can and should teach informative courses *about* religion—its history, beliefs, institutions, influences, etc.—but they may not seek to inculcate or propagate any particular kind of ultimate creed, religious or non-religious. What J. S. Mill says about universities applies to public education as a whole:

> . . . it is not the teacher's business to impose his own judgment, but to inform and discipline that of his students. . . . The proper business of a University is . . . not to tell us from authority what we ought to believe, and make us accept the belief as a duty, but to give us information and training, and help us to form our own belief in a manner worthy of intelligent beings . . .[2]

This neutralist, but not necessarily secularist, conception of the relation of state-supported institutions to religion has been subject to heavy attack during "the current upsurge of religiousness" which the events of our century have brought about. The spokesmen of religion are generally against it, and many public school teachers, themselves religious, are uncomfortable with it. In the rest of this paper, however, I shall take it for granted.[3]

At this point we come face to face with our problem. We have said both that public education should promote the good and the moral life, and that it should be neutral with respect to religion. But, from these two propositions taken together, it follows that public schools and colleges can promote the good life and the moral life only if and insofar as these do not require or rest on religion, i.e., on religious belief and observance. We must therefore try to determine whether, how, and to what degree public education can be concerned to advance the good life and morality when they cannot be concerned to advance religious faith and worship. Robert M. Hutchins raises this problem when he says:

> . . . public institutions seem required by the Constitution to be secular. Yet it must be admitted that religion is of the greatest moral importance. . . . Men, simply because they are men, are unlikely to find within themselves the power that can bring the good life and the good state to pass. . . . If a college cannot make its students religious, it cannot, to that extent, make them good.[4]

But his subsequent discussion does not help us very much, because he is concerned with higher education in general, not with public education as such, whether higher or lower. The drift of his thesis that religion is indispensable to the good and the moral life, however, must be noted, for one who accepts this thesis *without qualification* must conclude *either* that our public schools must teach religion, *or* that they cannot promote

[2] J. S. Mill, *Inaugural Address* (London: Longmans Green, n.d.), pp. 39–40.

[3] For a statement of my position see "A Point of View for the Future," in *Religion and the State University*, E. A. Walter, ed. (Ann Arbor: Univ. of Michigan Press, 1958), pp. 295–309.

[4] Robert M. Hutchins, *Freedom, Education, and the Fund* (New York: Meridian Books, 1956), pp. 91–92.

morality or the good life. Either way, as I see it, the upshot for him is that public education should go out of business. On the other hand, it need not go out of business, if there is any important extent or way in which the good and the moral lives are independent of specifically religious beliefs and experiences.

II

To deal with this problem we must now try to discern somewhat more clearly and fully just what the public schools, in their programs of education for the good and the moral life, are debarred from doing on the above view of their relation to religion. Let us look first at education for the good life, i.e., non-moral education. What is it that the school might possibly do here? (1) They might teach an individual, on the basis of human experience and reflection, what the ingredients of the good life —the values of human life—are. (2) They might provide him with an experience and an appreciation of some of these values, e.g., the enjoyment of music or poetry. (3) They might furnish him with knowledge, which is at once one of the great goods of life and a necessary means to the realization of the others. (4) They might train his intellect, imagination, and sensibility so as to enable him to discover further knowledge, perhaps even to discover new values or forms of satisfaction. (5) They might help him to work out a philosophy of life, which seems to be one of the things human beings need to be happy.

Now we can see what the *public* schools, by the fact that they are debarred from teaching religion, are precluded from doing with respect to the good life. They cannot advocate any specifically religious values, i.e., values whose realization is conditioned by religious belief or observance, as necessary for the good life. They cannot provide the student with any first-hand experience of such values, e.g., of the values of worship or of "the peace that passeth understanding," though they can through the teaching of art and literature give him an imaginative realization of these values, along with others. Whatever knowledge they may pass on to him, they cannot pass on any of the "truths" of religion, natural or revealed. The fear of the Lord may be the beginning of wisdom, as the author of *Proverbs* asserts, but the public school cannot teach the "wisdom" of which this "fear" is the beginning, though it may and should inform its pupils about the history, beliefs, and institutions of the religions which are inspired by this "fear." As for teaching its pupils a philosophy of life—this it cannot do for the same reason that it cannot teach a religion. As Mill says, all it can do is to give them "information and training" so that they may form their own belief "in a manner worthy of intelligent beings."

Coming to education for the moral life, we find that the case is similar.[5] As non-moral education must teach *values* and provide the knowledge and intellectual training necessary to realize them, so moral education must teach *principles* of conduct, together with the knowledge and intelligence needed to apply them. For we must know what to do, and, as Aristotle pointed out, the process of determining what we should do takes the form of a "practical syllogism." There is (a) the rule, e.g. that of keeping promises or of not harming anyone. There is (b) the factual knowledge that one has made a certain promise or that certain actions will cause harm to certain people. And there is (c) the conclusion that one should or should not do a certain deed. To begin with, at least, the principles and the factual knowledge which we use in such practical syllogisms must be taught us by our elders; we may revise or add to them later, but the ability to make such revisions and additions must also be a product of our education.

Here again there are some things that the public educator cannot do. Firstly, there are some principles which he cannot teach, even if they are valid, e.g., that we ought to worship God. Such principles depend on the truth of certain corresponding theological beliefs, and so may not be inculcated by the state or its agencies. Secondly, at least in our culture, we normally expect a moral rule to be supported by a reason; recent moral philosophers even go so far as to claim that "morality" means "the intelligent following of rules the point of which is understood."[6] And reasons for a rule may be of two kinds. They may be such as to *justify* the rule, or they may be such as to *motivate* people to act according to it. If a child asks "Why should I keep my promises?" and I answer, "Because people won't like you if you break them," I give a motivating reason; but if I reply, "Because you are taking unfair advantage if you don't keep them," I give a justifying one. So the moral teacher must teach reasons along with his principles; to parody another *Proverb*, with all our getting we must get understanding. *But,* if he is a public school teacher he cannot teach, as a reason for doing anything, whether justifying or motivating, any belief about God or about a hereafter. Such theological justifications and "religious sanctions" he must avoid. Hamlet was taught that the Almighty had set his canon 'gainst self-slaughter, as a reason for not making one's quietus with a bare bodkin, but that was before the day of proper public schools. The proper public school teacher, while he need not (in fact may not) deny the validity of theological reasons, must in his official teaching limit himself to more humanistic and this-worldly ones.

[5] For a discussion of some general problems of moral education see my "Toward a Philosophy of Moral Education," *Harv. Ed. Rev.,* 28 (1958), 300–313.

[6] R. S. Peters, *The Concept of Motivation* (London: Routledge, 1958), p. 87.

He may teach the tragedy of the Prince of Denmark, but cannot recommend his reasoning.

Moral education involves more than teaching *principles,* however; it also involves teaching *virtues,* that is, "right habits" or dispositions to act in accordance with moral principles. But just as there are certain widely accepted *values* and *principles,* so there are also certain highly regarded *virtues* which cannot be part of the content of public education, for example, what the ancients called piety or what the Christians call faith and hope (and at least part of what they call love). The public schools may seek to teach St. Thomas' human virtues but not his theological virtues—which indeed cannot be taught at all but only infused by divine operation.

Specifically religious values, principles, and virtues, then, as well as specifically religious reasons and sanctions, are not to be taught, inculcated, or employed in public schools, however concerned they may be to advance the good or the moral life. This may be disturbing to the proponents of religion, but the spokesmen of public education must insist on it, and its practitioners must remember it whenever they are acting in their official capacities. It may be remarked, however, that just as the public educator is debarred from teaching values, principles, or virtues which presuppose the acceptance of religious beliefs, so he is also debarred from teaching any values, principles, or virtues which presuppose the acceptance of anti-religious beliefs, e.g. such naturalistic ones as those of John Dewey. But it should be added at once that he may try to give his students an *understanding* of both the religious and the naturalistic ways of thinking, feeling, and living through a study of representative poems, paintings, and other works of art, as well as of representative religions and philosophies. He cannot seek to conduct them in either way, but he may and should try to show them what each way is like to one who follows it. In such imaginative realization of opposing ways of life, for which belief is not required but only a "willing suspension of disbelief," lies one of the chief contributions of the study of art and literature.

This seems a good place to speak of the vexed and vexing subject of "spiritual values." Is there a place for such values in the public schools? It is almost like asking if the public schools can be on the side of the angels or against sin? One cannot without qualification say *yes,* but one hesitates to say *no* even qualifiedly. For the phrase "spiritual values" is at once vague and emotionally charged. What does it mean? It is not only the term "spiritual" that is unclear. The word "values" is also used here in a confusing way. It is used not only to stand for what I have called *values* (i.e., things which are good), but also for what I have called *principles, virtues,* and even for *beliefs.* Let us for the moment allow it to keep this wide meaning. Then what does "spiritual values" mean? It might mean (and, I am inclined to say, should mean) "specifically religious values." In this sense, as I see it, public education cannot be concerned to promote spiritual values. But "spiritual values" is often used to include also values which are not so specifically religious—namely, aesthetic, moral, and intellectual ones. In this sense of the phrase there definitely is a place for some "spiritual values" in the public school.

III

In saying, as we have, that certain so-called values, principles, and virtues (namely, religious ones) cannot be part of the concern of public education even though its aim is to promote the good and the moral life, we have been implying that there are still others which do not depend on the acceptance of any religious belief and which may therefore be a part of its concern. Here, however, we run up against the contention, referred to earlier, that religion is indispensable both to the good and to the moral life. If this contention is true without qualification, then, as we saw before, public education must disown the endeavor to advance either the good life or the moral one—in short, must go out of business. We cannot here discuss it as fully as we should for a definitive answer, but we can try to make some clarifications and come at least to some partial or tentative answers.

Like the phrase "spiritual values," the thesis of the indispensability of religion is very unclear and emotionally charged. Those who maintain it rarely make clear just what they mean by "religion," just what they mean by "indispensable," or just what they think religion is indispensable to. Let us begin with a partial clarification of the term "religion." In discussions of the treatment of religion in state-supported institutions "religion" is sometimes used to mean any kind of ultimate creed, and sometimes to mean only such ultimate creeds as are typified by Judaism, Christianity, or Islam. In the former sense, even atheism and naturalism are religions; in the latter, however, they are anti-religions. I propose that we use "religion" in the latter or narrower sense, and have so been using it. Then the thesis that religion is necessary to the good and the moral life does not mean merely that *some* kind of ultimate commitment is required. This, I think, may be admitted. The thesis means, rather, that a specifically theistic kind of ultimate commitment is required. And, in this sense, it is not obviously true.

It may, of course, be admitted that such a religious commitment *is* required for *some* widely-accepted values, principles, and virtues, namely, the specifically religious ones of which we were speaking earlier. But it cannot simply be taken for granted that these values, principles, and virtues, widely-honored as they may be, are in fact genuine, valid, or well-founded. They may be, but to assert that they are presupposes the truth of the religious beliefs on which they depend, and the truth of these religious beliefs cannot simply be assumed, particularly not in a debate about any public functions. For, if these beliefs are not true, then the religious values, principles, and virtues in question have no sound basis, and need not be taken seriously. Some may still try to argue that they will have a beneficent effect if they are taken as regulative ideals, but others will reply that they are a snare and a delusion, distracting mankind from its proper study. To this debate the state and its schools can hardly be a party. Nor can we be a party to it here.

Even if we grant, however, that such *religious* values, principles and virtues are valid and are an indispensable *part* of the good and the moral life, it may still be that there are *others* to which religion is *not* indispensable. And, if there are important values, rules, and virtues which do not necessarily rest on specifically religious beliefs and observances, then it may well be contended that these are properly a concern of the state and its schools, and that the peculiarly religious ones are more properly the care of the individual, his church, or some other private and voluntary association to which he belongs. It is an old and respected principle that we must distinguish the temporal and the eternal, the natural and the spiritual. The same authority who said, "He who is not with me is against me," also said, "Render unto Caesar the things which are Caesar's, and unto God the things that are God's."

With these general remarks out of the way, we may divide the doctrine of the indispensability of religion into two parts: first, the claim that religion is indispensable to the good life, and, second, the assertion that it is indispensable to the moral life. In connection with the former we at once encounter the historic thesis that the supreme good and the highest happiness consist in the contemplation of, or communion with, God. If this thesis is correct, then a life which knows not God is at best a very incomplete and truncated good; it may be worthless, dust and ashes, a broken cistern that can hold no water; it may even be a snare and a delusion whose apparent values only serve to distract man fatally from his true long run interests. We cannot here try to determine the validity of the thesis; but we may note, that, whether it is true or false, it need be taken seriously only if there is a God, and that, even if true, it does not prove there is a God. I do not mean to question that there is a God. I doubt, however, that his existence can be proved in any publicly available way, and, if this is true, then we certainly cannot take it for granted in such a discussion as the present one. Nor can we take for granted the claim that man's true interests lie, not in any values he can enjoy in this life, but in his finding an assurance that he will know God in another.

The crucial question for our purposes, as was indicated a moment ago, is whether there are any important values or ingredients in the good life which are not dependent on any religious belief. To many people it seems clear that there are such goods as knowledge, artistic creation and appreciation, friendship, love, freedom, sense of achievement, etc., which do not have any religious faith as a necessary condition of their attainment or enjoyment. Some may reply that these goods are illusory or even delusive, but to say this presupposes a certain religious conception of the universe and so begs the question. In any case, not all religious thinkers have taken this hard line. It may be that the values mentioned gain an additional dimension if they are woven into a religious life, but it is at any rate plausible to hold that they do or at least may bring a genuine worthwhileness into the life of an unbeliever as well. Even if they do not constitute a good which is self-sufficient in Aristotle's sense, they may still be desirable in themselves.

If this is so, then it is also plausible to maintain that religion is not so indispensable to the good life that only a religious institution can minister to such a life. For then it is possible that there is a part or aspect of the good life for which a neutral institution such as the state may be concerned, even if there is also another part or aspect of it which is beyond the care or competence of such an institution. That is, there may be good things which are Caesar's, as well as good things that are God's. St. Thomas implies as much when he finds a place for natural as well as supernatural happiness.

IV

The question whether religion is necessary to morality is too large to deal with adequately in the space that remains. But perhaps we can accomplish something worthwhile if we make some distinctions. For those who answer the question in the affirmative usually neglect to make these distinctions, and so can be at least partly answered by making them. There are, in fact, several senses in which morality may be and has been said to be dependent on religion. (1) It is often held to be *causally* or *genetically* dependent on religion. This is asserted, for example, by those who argue that our democratic morality is a historical outgrowth of the Christian religion, coming into the world as a result of the advent of this religion. This contention is not unquestionable, but let us grant it for the sake of discussion. It does not follow that our morality is strictly dependent on religion. Even if historically our morality was a product of Christianity, it may still be that our morality could have arisen in some other way. History only happens once, and, as Hume pointed out, one instance does not prove a necessary connection or even a constant conjunction. In any event, even if part of our morality has religious faith as a necessary condition, it does not follow that all of it does.

(2) Morality may also be said to rest on religion in a *psychological* sense. That is, it may be held that the *motivation* to be moral presupposes certain religious or theological beliefs—in short, that morality requires religious sanctions or motivating reasons, as I called them earlier. This is what D. E. Trueblood means when he speaks of "the impotence of ethics" in *The Predicament of Modern Man,* and it seems to be what Hutchins has in mind in the passage quoted above. Now this contention is not in the least plausible if it is meant to say that *no* one *ever* has *any* motivation to do what is right which is not the result of some specifically religious conviction on his part. Many people have often been moved to do what is right by considerations which are not religious. Perhaps all who are moral have sometimes been moved by such considerations as a desire for peace or for a stable social order, even if St. Augustine talks in one place as if he would have been an Epicurean of the worst sort if he had not believed in God and a hereafter. For some moral persons religious considerations seem never to play a part at all. Trueblood himself allows that atheists like Dewey are often kind and good. So the contention must be modified to say either (a) that *some* people will only be moral if they have certain religious beliefs, or (b) that no one will be *completely* moral who does not have these beliefs, or (c) that *most* people will be adequately moral only if they have these beliefs.

Let us consider these three more qualified tenets. I should like to point out that it is very difficult to get conclusive empirical evidence for or against such assertions, and that those who make them seldom adduce such evidence in a form which cannot be challenged. Still, it does look as if (a) is true, i.e., that *some* people will be moral only if they have certain religious beliefs. But, notice, this fact does not prove that these religious beliefs are true or even that they should be taught. It certainly does not prove that there is no room in the schools for moral education which is non-religious; the most it would show is that such education must be supplemented, perhaps in the home or the church, by a religious one.

As for (b)—that only a religious person will be completely virtuous, or at least as virtuous as mortal man may—this too may be true. But, once more, it does not follow that all moral education must be pervaded by religion; at most it follows only that public education needs to be supplemented by a religious one—and this follows only if there is independent ground for believing that religion is true. For it will hardly do to offer religious beliefs as reasons for being moral, if the only reason for believing them is that they are necessary for being moral.

(C), which says that most people will perform their duties adequately only if they hold religious beliefs, is much more doubtful. It would be very difficult to find in history or to create in an experiment situations so controlled or so structured as to show it to be true. Trueblood and others have averred that the events and experiences of the twentieth century constitute "a great body of evidence . . . of the moral decay that follows a loss of theistic conviction."[7] Presumably they are thinking either that the conduct of Nazi Germany and of Communist Russia is a consequence of a loss of theistic conviction in those countries, or that there is moral decay on our own side which is due to such a loss. Let us suppose that there has been, on whatever side, a widespread decline of religious faith and also a widespread moral decay. This would by no means establish that the former was the cause of the latter. There are other developments in our century which might have caused whatever change in conduct there has been besides a decline in religious faith, e.g., nationalism, fear, etc. It may even be that something more basic is the cause of both the religious and the moral change. It can, in fact, be maintained with some plausibility that the present upsurge of religiosity is itself due to some pervasive economic, political, or social phenomenon of our time, and, if this is the case, it may be that some such phenomenon, and not the increase or decrease of religion as such, is what determines our moral behavior and thinking.

But suppose that (c) is true—that the average individual will be even adequately moral only if he has religious convictions. What follows? Even then all that follows is that a public or religiously neutral moral education must be supplemented, not that it should go out of business. And, once more, this need for religious supplementation follows only if religion is true on other grounds. For the only alternative would be to say that religion should be taught as a prop for morality even though it is not true. But to say this is to condone myth-making and propaganda; and, moreover, it hardly seems to comport with the spirit of religion itself.

(3) So far we have dealt, respectively, with the claims that morality is *historically* and *psychologically* dependent on religion. But the crucial issue is whether morality is *logically* dependent on religion, that is, whether theological premises are required to *justify* statements about our moral duties—not only about specifically religious duties but also about others, not only about so-called duties to God but also about duties to our fellow man. I made this distinction between *justifying* a moral judgment and *motivating* people to act on it earlier when I was talking about teaching reasons as well as moral rules, but must say a little more about it here, for the distinction is often neglected by religious as well as non-religious moralists. Take, for instance, the religious rule which many regard as a moral duty, "We ought to worship God." Suppose A asserts it and B asks, "Why?" Then A may give an answer which is intended to

[7] D. E. Trueblood, *The Predicament of Modern Man* (New York: Harper Bros., 1944), pp. 56–57.

convince B on intellectual grounds that he has a moral obligation to worship God, or he may give one which is calculated only to *motivate* B to worship God. He does the latter if he replies that the Lord is a jealous God and will not hold him guiltless who has other gods before Him, but shows mercy unto thousands that love Him and keep His commandments. But he does the former if he reasons as follows:

> We ought to be grateful to those who have been good to us.
> God has been good to us.
> Therefore we ought to be grateful to Him.
> But being grateful to Him entails worshipping Him.
> Therefore we ought to worship Him.

Here A is offering B a moral justification for his rule, not just a motive for obeying it.

Moreover, A's argument has at least one theological premise, viz., "God has been good to us," and so, in his reasoning, the duty to worship God is *logically* dependent on a religious proposition. I think we may say that the same thing is true of all specifically religious obligations—if they are duties at all, they logically presuppose at least one religious premise for their justification. Now I am not concerned to ask whether there are such duties, but whether the same thing is true of *all* of our moral obligations. Do they *all logically* presuppose some theological premise or other? Can one never *justify* a rule of duty without using such a premise? I see no reason for thinking so. It seems to me that I do give a moral justification of, say, the rule to keep promises, if I show that promise-keeping is necessary for the stability and well-being of society in the world. Of course, someone may still ask me why he should be concerned about the well-being of society, but then he seems to have switched the question from that of justification to that of motivation.

In fact, it cannot be true that *all* moral principles depend *logically* on a prior theological premise. Look at A's argument again. It does rest on a theological premise, as we saw. Its very first premise, however, is not a theological proposition, but a *moral* one, namely, "We ought to be grateful to those who have been good to us." And any argument to *justify* any moral rule must have a similar structure, i.e., it must begin with a basic moral principle. Else one cannot draw a moral conclusion. It follows that justifying arguments rest ultimately, at least in part, on moral principles which do *not* depend *logically* on theological or other premises. One of these ultimate moral premises may even be the rule that we ought to do what God commands; but this is a moral principle and not a theological proposition, and it does not follow logically from any theological proposition.[8] One may, of course, ask even in the case of such

---

[8] Of course, one might claim that the ultimate moral premise is a definition or true by definition, but then one must establish the acceptability of one's definition and one cannot do this simply by deducing it logically from theology.

an ultimate moral principle, "Why should I do what it enjoins?," but then one is asking, not for a moral argument, but for motivation or some kind of non-moral argument. And, as we saw before, the answer need not involve any religious considerations.

(4) At this point, it might be contended that the ultimate principles of morality must be matters of divine revelation, if what has just been said is true. Then it might be said that morality is at least *epistemologically* dependent on religion or rather on a faith that certain principles have been divinely revealed. But, if by this is meant that some such special revelation as Moses is supposed to have received on Mt. Sinai is required, the view can hardly be sustained. As St. Paul said, even "the Gentiles which have not the [revealed] law—are a law unto themselves," having "the [moral] law written in their hearts, their consciences also bearing witness."[9]

There is a different kind of "revelation" which is sometimes said to be necessary as a basis for morality, namely, the "realization" of other people as persons whose lives have the same "inner significance" that ours have. Josiah Royce describes this realization of our neighbor, which he calls "the moral insight," most vividly, and William James dramatizes it even more in the essay "On a Certain Blindness in Human Beings," where he speaks of this "higher vision" which pierces the "great cloudbank of ancestral blindness weighing down upon us" and "makes an epoch in [the] history" of the person to whom it comes. And he calls it a "religious insight." Now, I am inclined to agree that a morality without this insight is in some way truncated, as Henri Bergson holds.[10] But I find it misleading to call it a "religious" rather than a "moral" insight, for, while it may involve some kind of regeneration on the part of one who has it, it is not clear that it presupposes any belief of a specifically religious or theological nature, e.g., the belief that there is a God or that human beings have immortal souls. In any case, however, there seem to be forms of morality like F. H. Bradley's morality of "my station and its duties" or Bergson's "closed morality" which do not rest on such a "higher vision of an inner significance," and even if these moralities are truncated, they may be an important part of our moral education.

V

Well, much more might be said about the thesis of the indispensability of religion to morality. I might have pointed out that if one rests morality on religion, one encourages moral scepticism in those who find religion uncertain or false, e.g., the Sartrian existentialists. I might have shown

[9] *Romans* 2:14. See also Reinhold Niebuhr's criticism of Karl Barth in *The Nature and Destiny of Man* (New York: Charles Scribners Sons, 1941). II, pp. 254–256.

[10] See the article referred to in Note 5, p. 312.

that, if religious ideas have influenced moral ones, so have moral ideas influenced religious conceptions, as is illustrated by Plato's critique of Greek theology in the *Republic*. I might even have mentioned Matthew Arnold's view that religion is "morality touched by emotion," which John Dewey restated in *A Common Faith*. But it is not my intention to denigrate religion in any way, even if I have not been willing in this discussion to take its truth for granted. It may be that religion is necessary for certain reaches of both morality and the good life. This I have not been concerned to dispute. Nor have I been trying to justify the existence of public education. What I have been arguing is this: (1) that public education, if it exists at all, should be concerned to do what it can to promote the good and the moral life, (2) that, because it is publicly-supported, it cannot seek to inculcate any religious belief as part of its endeavor to advance the good or the moral life, and (3) that this fact does not mean that it must go out of business, since there are important values, principles, and virtues to which religion is not indispensable, logically, psychologically, or otherwise.

All this it is important to say now, when there is such strong pressure on the state-supported schools to do something more "positive" about religion. For one of the main grounds on which this pressure rests is the conviction that religious belief and experience are indispensable to both the good and the moral life whose promotion must be the concern of the state and its agencies—a conviction which is usually vaguely-formulated and inadequately supported, but which many feel so deeply that they are ready to give up the neutrality of the public schools and to jeopardize the freedom of thought which it was designed to protect. The thought behind this paper is that this conviction is only partly true at best, that the public schools may remain nonmalevolently neutral and yet have an important sphere of operation relative to morality and the good life, and that, if and insofar as religion is required for certain dimensions of happiness and virtue, these schools should rather be supplemented than subverted.

Questions for Discussion

IN Plato's dialogue Protagoras claims that he teaches his students to be better individuals and better citizens, but Socrates wonders whether this can be taught. They discuss whether the virtues are identical and whether whatever is good is also pleasant. A seeming shift of positions occurs at the end of the dialogue on the question whether virtue can be taught, although there is actually no fundamental change in Socrates' position. Socrates holds that a skill is acquired by practice, but since virtue is knowledge it can be taught.

Is there a separation between one's *knowing* what is good and consistently *doing* what is good? For Plato, knowledge is knowledge-action and to know the Good is to be able to do the Good. Do you believe Plato to be correct? Also in the dialogue arises the question why do some good men have difficulty teaching their own children moral values? Must one first exemplify the traits he is teaching before such instruction can be successful?

Hare shows the reasoning that underlies decisions of principle by examining the *form* that reasoning takes in moral decisions. He indicates how principles of action may be obscure, though present, and how principles of prediction are utilized in ascertaining the effects of action. Most forms of teaching, according to Hare, are impossible without the teaching of principles. We do not learn to perform individual acts; instead we learn certain acts in certain kinds of situations. And when we are freed by correct habits in performing our lesser duties, we can concentrate on the principles on which we base our higher duties. Hare notes that a point is reached when teaching becomes ineffectual; that is when the student must teach himself. Hare also states that it is first necessary to teach the student *what* he should do before we teach him to analyze *why* he should do it.

Contrast the views of Plato and Hare on the teaching of moral values. To which position would you subscribe and how would you defend your position?

Dewey objects to the long held view that ethics should seek some final end or ultimate good. He holds, instead, that principles and criteria are instruments for analyzing situations and every moral situation has its own irreplaceable good. Do you feel that Dewey effectively supports his position against the older views of ethics? What does Dewey mean when he claims that truth is "adverbial"? Why does he believe that the separation between intrinsic and instrumental ends is undesirable? Notice that Dewey strongly opposes the construction of dualisms. What is the source of his opposition? How would Dewey propose that we judge the individual, and what does he suggest is the goal of life? He also states that the educative process is all one with the moral process. Can you explain the meaning and significance of this statement?

Frankena raises the question whether the public schools must teach religion in order to promote morality and the good life. He asks whether there are important values in the good life which are not dependent on any religious belief and takes the position that there are such values.

Frankena next makes a careful examination of whether religion is necessary to morality. Can you state the major arguments that he uses and how he supports them? Do you agree or disagree with Frankena's position, and how would you support your beliefs?

PART TWO

PHILOSOPHICAL ANALYSIS AND EDUCATION

CHAPTER FIVE

KNOWLEDGE AND EDUCATION

In recent years we have witnessed a renewed interest in questions of knowledge and education. Philosophers have long been concerned with epistemological problems or problems of knowledge, and philosophers of education have lately investigated the logical structure of educational concepts with heightened intensity. Moreover, psychologists and curriculum specialists have joined the undertaking by exploring an area that has come to be known as "the structure of knowledge." As the expansion of knowledge exceeds the ability of any single individual to master much more than a limited segment, the problems imposed on education become serious, indeed. Educators have had to become more highly selective in establishing curricula, because that which can be taught within the formal school years has become very limited. Since the aim of many educators is to produce liberally educated students as well as specialized ones, the tasks confronting education are multiplied. How, then, can we make an intelligent choice?

There are a number of different approaches to this problem. If it is agreed that the most valuable knowledge is that which is most reliable and leads to the discovery of additional knowledge of the same type, then it is the duty of education to select such knowledge as the basis of the curriculum. It is generally believed that teaching exact knowledge equips future leaders with the ability to make careful inquiries in all lines of endeavor—those which advance society and move it away from reliance on dogma, myth, and superstition. It is usually thought that of all the disciplines mathematics epitomizes exact knowledge, with some arrangement of the natural sciences, following closely in descending order. This, then, is the beginning of a classification system for the curriculum in which priorities can be assigned and undesirable material eliminated. Once the classification system is developed, some of the major problems of selection can be brought under control. Much depends, however, on one's system of classification and the criteria on which it is based, for if the criteria are too limited the curriculum may become one-sided.

Another approach to selecting knowledge of greatest worth is to determine the tasks that youth will be expected to fulfill as citizens, and by making systematic, empirical studies of the nature and demands of these tasks, the requisite skills and abilities can be developed in school. There are tasks within the home, in vocations, and in one's citizenship role that can be catalogued and dissected to discover how they are performed; then they can be organized into a curriculum to prepare students for their respective roles in society. This approach would eliminate those courses of study which have no bearing on the tasks which individual students face. Some have argued, however, that what *is* done in society at large and the manner in which it is done is not necessarily what *ought* to be done and, thus, such an approach is unsuitable as a criterion for determining the basis of the curriculum.

Instead of seeking a classification for knowledge or cataloging the tasks youth will face as adults, one could look at the nature of man to determine what should be taught. One may observe with Aristotle that the distinguishing and most important trait of man is his reason and the duty of education is to develop that which differentiates man from animals and enables him to be human. It could further be noted that human knowledge falls into certain major classifications—Theoretical, Practical, and Productive—some of which are higher than others and more in accordance with man's nature. The Productive, which is concerned with the development of skills to produce artifacts, is lowest in the classificatory scheme and probably does not merit a place in the educational program. Theoretical knowledge pertains to such studies as the sciences and provides the most exact and highest form of knowledge; whereas Practical knowledge is of moral and political affairs, and although reason can be used to arrive at decisions, the exactness and certainty of the decisions can never rival Theoretical knowledge. It has been objected, however, that even if agreement could be reached as to man's nature (and there is still disagreement in some quarters), no direct inferences can logically be drawn from this nature as to what should be done with it.

Various attempts have been made to determine the structure of the disciplines and organized knowledge and to clarify the methodological procedures that each discipline uses in gaining new knowledge. Some believe that if students can grasp the structure of a discipline and gain some experience in using the modes of inquiry that have proved fruitful in research, the student will be in a position to interpret new knowledge, think with greater sophistication, and see relationships and situations in which he may use his new learning. Others have objected that this may not be the manner in which young minds operate best and that there may be merit in maintaining experimental curriculum patterns that were introduced during the progressive education movement so that the developmental characteristics of the learner will be given priority in the organization of the curriculum.

The selections in this section are drawn from two classical approaches to knowledge and curriculum that have been highly influential in the history of education, and from two contemporary outlooks that offer somewhat different interpretations and conclusions.

Aristotle in Selection 17 develops a classification of human knowledge: the Theoretical, the Practical, and the Productive. Much of our thinking today stems from interpretations and applications of this classification and, thus, it becomes exceedingly important to give it careful study.

Auguste Comte, called by some the "father of sociology," offers another landmark in the area. Comte's positive hierarchy of the sciences is based on the view that only subject matter should provide the basis for classification. Comte maintains that order of phenomena can be discerned, each order, consisting of members of the next lower order, organized into disciplines of more particular and complex structures. Thus a natural order of study arises. This hierarchy has exerted considerable influence on the structuring of the curriculum and the establishing of sequence.

The essay by Joseph J. Schwab (Selection 19) is an excellent overview of the present status and characteristics of the structure of knowledge in the disciplines. However, it is more than a survey. In it Schwab directly confronts some of the more obdurate problems and analyzes ways to approach them more fruitfully. Finally, he points out that subject matter alone should not be our only concern in organizing the curriculum. Schwab has written important papers on the structure of the disciplines; this particular essay helps the reader place the entire field in perspective.

Arno Bellack, who has worked extensively in curriculum, makes a survey in Selection 20 of the contemporary terrain in the structure of knowledge and finds a number of promising developments; yet he inveighs against the current tendency toward the atomization of knowledge and the lack of fruitful interchanges of ideas between scholars in the respective disciplines. He would encourage a rapprochement between present developments in the scholarly disciplines and the broad fields approach to the organization of knowledge that emerged from the progressive education movement.

17 / ARISTOTLE

Metaphysics

All men by nature desire to know. An indication of this is the delight
we taken in our senses; for even apart from their usefulness they are
loved for themselves; and above all others the sense of sight. For not only
with a view to action, but even when we are not going to do anything, we
prefer seeing (one might say) to everything else. The reason is that this,
most of all the senses, makes us know and brings to light many
differences between things.

By nature animals are born with the faculty of sensation, and from
sensation memory is produced in some of them, though not in others.
And therefore the former are more intelligent and apt at learning than
those which cannot remember; those which are incapable of hearing
sounds are intelligent though they cannot be taught, e.g. the bee, and any
other race of animals that may be like it; and those which besides
memory have this sense of hearing can be taught.

The animals other than man live by appearances and memories, and
have but little of connected experience; but the human race lives also by
art and reasonings. Now from memory experience is produced in men;
for the several memories of the same thing produce finally the capacity
for a single experience. And experience seems pretty much like science
and art, but really science and art come to men *through* experience; for
"experience made art," as Polus says, "but inexperience luck." Now art
arises when from many notions gained by experience one universal
judgement about a class of objects is produced. For to have a judgement
that when Callias was ill of this disease this did him good, and similarly
in the case of Socrates and in many individual cases, is a matter of
experience; but to judge that it has done good to all persons of a certain
constitution, marked off in one class, when they were ill of this disease,
e.g. to phlegmatic or bilious people when burning with fever,—this is a
matter of art.

With a view to action experience seems in no respect inferior to art,
and men of experience succeed even better than those who have theory

Aristotle, from *Metaphysics*, Book A, Chaps. 1 and 2, and *Nicomachean Ethics*,
Book VI, Chaps. 3–7, in the *Works of Aristotle*. Translation by W. D. Ross (Oxford:
The Clarendon Press, 1910–1952). Reprinted with permission of the publisher.

without experience. (The reason is that experience is knowledge of individuals, art of universals, and actions and productions are all concerned with the individual; for the physician does not cure *man*, except in an incidental way, but Callias or Socrates or some other called by some such individual name, who happens to be a man. If, then, a man has the theory without the experience, and recognizes the universal but does not know the individual included in this, he will often fail to cure; for it is the individual that is to be cured.) But yet we think that *knowledge* and *understanding* belong to art rather than to experience, and we suppose artists to be wiser than men of experience (which implies that Wisdom depends in all cases rather on knowledge); and this because the former know the cause, but the latter do not. For men of experience know that the thing is so, but do not know why, while the others know the 'why' and the cause. Hence we think also that the master-workers in each craft are more honourable and know in a truer sense and are wiser than the manual workers, because they know the causes of the things that are done (we think the manual workers are like certain lifeless things which act indeed, but act without knowing what they do, as fire burns,—but while the lifeless things perform each of their functions by a natural tendency, the labourers perform them through habit); thus we view them as being wiser not in virtue of being able to act, but of having the theory for themselves and knowing the causes. And in general it is a sign of the man who knows and of the man who does not know, that the former can teach, and therefore we think art more truly knowledge than experience is; for artists can teach, and men of mere experience cannot.

Again, we do not regard any of the senses as Wisdom; yet surely these give the most authoritative knowledge of particulars. But they do not tell us the 'why' of anything—e.g. why fire is hot; they only say *that* it is hot.

At first he who invented any art whatever that went beyond the common perceptions of man was naturally admired by men, not only because there was something useful in the inventions, but because he was thought wise and superior to the rest. But as more arts were invented, and some were directed to the necessities of life, others to recreation, the inventors of the latter were naturally always regarded as wiser than the inventors of the former, because their branches of knowledge did not aim at utility. Hence when all such inventions were already established, the sciences which do not aim at giving pleasure or at the necessities of life were discovered, and first in the places where men first began to have leisure. This is why the mathematical arts were founded in Egypt; for there the priestly caste was allowed to be at leisure.

We have said in the *Ethics* what the difference is between art and science and the other kindred faculties; but the point of our present discussion is this, that all men suppose what is called Wisdom to deal with the first causes and the principles of things; so that, as has been said before, the man of experience is thought to be wiser than the possessors of any sense-perception whatever, the artist wiser than the men of experience, the master-worker than the mechanic, and the theoretical kinds of knowledge to be more of the nature of Wisdom than the productive. Clearly then Wisdom is knowledge about certain principles and causes.

Since we are seeking this knowledge, we must inquire of what kind are the causes and the principles, the knowledge of which is Wisdom. If one were to take the notions we have about the wise man, this might perhaps make the answer more evident. We suppose first, then, that the wise man knows all things, as far as possible, although he has not knowledge of each of them in detail; secondly, that he who can learn things that are difficult, and not easy for man to know, is wise (sense-perception is common to all, and therefore easy and no mark of Wisdom); again, that he who is more exact and more capable of teaching the causes is wiser, in every branch of knowledge; and that of the sciences, also, that which is desirable on its own account and for the sake of knowing it is more of the nature of Wisdom than that which is desirable on account of its results, and the superior science is more of the nature of Wisdom than the ancillary; for the wise man must not be ordered but must order, and he must not obey another, but the less wise must obey *him*.

Such and so many are the notions, then, which we have about Wisdom and the wise. Now of these characteristics that of knowing all things must belong to him who has in the highest degree universal knowledge; for he knows in a sense all the instances that fall under the universal. And these things, the most universal, are on the whole the hardest for men to know; for they are farthest from the senses. And the most exact of the sciences are those which deal most with first principles; for those which involve fewer principles are more exact than those which involve additional principles, e.g. arithmetic than geometry. But the science which investigates causes is also *instructive*, in a higher degree, for the people who instruct us are those who tell the causes of each thing. And understanding and knowledge pursued for their own sake are found most in the knowledge of that which is most knowable (for he who chooses to know for the sake of knowing will choose most readily that which is most truly knowledge, and such is the knowledge of that which is most knowable); and the first principles and the causes are most knowable; for by reason of these, and from these, all other things come to be known, and not these by means of the things subordinate to them. And the science which knows to what end each thing must be done is the most authoritative of the sciences, and more authoritative than any ancillary science; and this end is the good of that thing, and in general the supreme good in the whole of nature. Judged by all the tests we have mentioned, then, the name in question falls to the same science; this must be a science that investigates the first principles and causes; for the good, i.e. the end, is one of the causes.

That it is not a science of production is clear even from the history of the earliest philosophers. For it is owing to their wonder that men both now begin and at first began to philosophize; they wondered originally at the obvious difficulties, then advanced little by little and stated difficulties about the greater matters, e.g. about the phenomena of the moon and those of the sun and of the stars, and about the genesis of the universe. And a man who is puzzled and wonders thinks himself ignorant (whence even the lover of myth is in a sense a lover of Wisdom, for the myth is composed of wonders); therefore since they philosophized in order to escape from ignorance, evidently they were pursuing science in order to know, and not for any utilitarian end. And this is confirmed by the facts; for it was when almost all the necessities of life and the things that make for comfort and recreation had been secured, that such knowledge began to be sought. Evidently then we do not seek it for the sake of any other advantage; but as the man is free, we say, who exists for his own sake and not for another's, so we pursue this as the only free science, for it alone exists for its own sake. . . .

Let us begin, then, from the beginning, and discuss these states once more. Let it be assumed that the states by virtue of which the soul possesses truth by way of affirmation or denial are five in number, i.e. art, scientific knowledge, practical wisdom, philosophic wisdom, intuitive reason; we do not include judgement and opinion because in these we may be mistaken.

Now what *scientific knowledge* is, if we are to speak exactly and not follow mere similarities, is plain from what follows. We all suppose that what we know is not even capable of being otherwise; of things capable of being otherwise we do not know, when they have passed outside our observation, whether they exist or not. Therefore the object of scientific knowledge is of necessity. Therefore it is eternal; for things that are of necessity in the unqualified sense are all eternal; and things that are eternal are ungenerated and imperishable. Again, every science is thought to be capable of being taught, and its object of being learned. And all teaching starts from what is already known, as we maintain in the *Analytics* also; for it proceeds sometimes through induction and sometimes by syllogism. Now induction is the starting-point which knowledge even of the universal presupposes, while syllogism proceeds *from* universals. There are therefore starting-points from which syllogism proceeds, which are not reached by syllogism; it is therefore by induction that they are acquired. Scientific knowledge is, then, a state of capacity to demonstrate, and has the other limiting characteristics which we specify in the *Analytics;* for it is when a man believes in a certain way and the starting-points are known to him that he has scientific knowledge, since if they are not better known to him than the conclusion, he will have his knowledge only incidentally.

Let this, then, be taken as our account of scientific knowledge.

In the variable are included both things made and things done; making and acting are different (for their nature we treat even the discussions outside our school as reliable); so that the reasoned state of capacity to act is different from the reasoned state of capacity to make. Hence too they are not included one in the other; for neither is acting making nor is making acting. Now since architecture is an art and is essentially a reasoned state of capacity to make, and there is neither any art that is not such a state nor any such state that is not an art, *art* is identical with a state of capacity to make, involving a true course of reasoning. All art is concerned with coming into being, i.e. with contriving and considering how something may come into being which is capable of either being or not being, and whose origin is in the maker and not in the thing made; for art is concerned neither with things that are, or come into being, by necessity, nor with things that do so in accordance with nature (since these have their origin in themselves). Making and acting being different, art must be a matter of making, not of acting. And in a sense chance and art are concerned with the same objects; as Agathon says, "art loves chance and chance loves art." Art, then, as has been said, is a state concerned with making, involving a true course of reasoning, and lack of art on the contrary is a state concerned with making, involving a false course of reasoning; both are concerned with the variable.

Regarding *practical wisdom* we shall get at the truth by considering who are the persons we credit with it. Now it is thought to be the mark of a man of practical wisdom to be able to deliberate well about what is good and expedient for himself, not in some particular respect, e.g. about what sorts of thing conduce to health or to strength, but about what sorts of thing conduce to the good life in general. This is shown by the fact that we credit men with practical wisdom in some particular respect when they have calculated well with a view to some good end which is one of those that are not the object of any art. It follows that in the general sense also the man who is capable of deliberating has practical wisdom. Now no one deliberates about things that are invariable, nor about things that it is impossible for him to do. Therefore, since scientific knowledge involves demonstration, but there is no demonstration of things whose first principles are variable (for all such things might actually be otherwise), and since it is impossible to deliberate about things that are of necessity, practical wisdom cannot be scientific knowledge nor art; not science because that which can be done is capable of being otherwise, not art because action and making are different kinds of thing. The remaining alternative, then, is that it is a true and reasoned state of capacity to act with regard to the things that are good or bad for man. For while making has an end other than itself, action cannot; for good action itself is its end. It is for this reason that we think Pericles and men like him have practical wisdom, viz. because they can see what is good for themselves and what is good for men in general; we consider that those can do this who are good at managing households or states. (This is why we call temperance (σωφροσύνη) by this name; we imply that it preserves one's practical wisdom (σῴζουσα τὴν φρόνησιν). Now what it preserves is a judgement of the kind we have described. For it is not any and every judgement that pleasant and painful objects destroy and pervert, e.g. the judgement that the triangle has or has not its angles equal to two right angles, but only judgements about what is to be done. For the originating causes of the things that are done consist in the end at which they are aimed; but the man who has been ruined by pleasure or pain forthwith fails to see any such originating cause—to see that for the sake of this or because of this he ought to choose and do whatever he chooses and does; for vice is destructive of the originating cause of action.)

Practical wisdom, then, must be a reasoned and true state of capacity to act with regard to human goods. But further, while there is such a thing as excellence in art, there is no such thing as excellence in practical wisdom; and in art he who errs willingly is preferable, but in practical wisdom, as in the virtues, he is the reverse. Plainly, then, practical wisdom is a virtue and not an art. There being two parts of the soul that can follow a course of reasoning, it must be the virtue of one of the two, i.e. of that part which forms opinions; for opinion is about the variable and so is practical wisdom. But yet it is not only a reasoned state; this is shown by the fact that a state of that sort may be forgotten but practical wisdom cannot.

Scientific knowledge is judgement about things that are universal and necessary, and the conclusions of demonstration, and all scientific knowledge, follow from first principles (for scientific knowledge involves apprehension of a rational ground). This being so, the first principle from which what is scientifically known follows cannot be an object of scientific knowledge, of art, or of practical wisdom; for that which can be scientifically known can be demonstrated, and art and practical wisdom deal with things that are variable. Nor are these first principles the objects of philosophic wisdom, for it is a mark of the philosopher to have *demonstration* about some things. If, then, the states of mind by which we have truth and are never deceived about things invariable or even variable are scientific knowledge, practical wisdom, philosophic wisdom, and intuitive reason, and it cannot be any of the three (i.e. practical wisdom, scientific knowledge, or philosophic wisdom), the remaining alternative is that it is *intuitive reason* that grasps the first principles.

Wisdom[1] (1) in the arts we ascribe to their most finished exponents, e.g. to Phidias as a sculptor and to Polyclitus as a maker of portrait-statues, and here we mean nothing by wisdom except excellence in art; but (2) we think that some people are wise in general, not in some particular field or in any other limited respect, as Homer says in the *Margites,*

> Him did the gods make neither a digger nor yet a ploughman
> Nor wise in anything else.

Therefore wisdom must plainly be the most finished of the forms of knowledge. It follows that the wise man must not only know what follows from the first principles, but must also possess truth about the first principles. Therefore wisdom must be intuitive reason combined with scientific knowledge—scientific knowledge of the highest objects which has received as it were its proper completion.

Of the highest objects, we say; for it would be strange to think that the art of politics, or practical wisdom, is the best knowledge, since man is not the best thing in the world. Now if what is healthy or good is different for men and for fishes, but what is white or straight is always the same, any one would say that what is wise is the same but what is practically wise is different; for it is to that which observes well the various matters concerning itself that one ascribes practical wisdom, and it is to this that one will entrust such matters. This is why we say that some even of the lower animals have practical wisdom,[2] viz. those which are found to have a power of foresight with regard to their own life. It is evident also that philosophic wisdom and the art of politics cannot be the same; for if the state of mind concerned with a man's own interests is to be called philosophic wisdom, there will be many philosophic wisdoms; there will not be one concerned with the good of all animals (any more than there is one art of medicine for all existing things), but a different philosophic wisdom about the good of each species.

But if the argument be that man is the best of the animals, this makes no difference; for there are other things much more divine in their nature

---

[1] In this chapter Aristotle restricts to a very definite meaning the word σοφία, which in ordinary Greek, as the beginning of the chapter points out, was used both of skill in a particular art or craft, and of wisdom in general.

[2] We do not say this in English; but we call them "intelligent" or "sagacious," which comes to the same thing.

even than man, e. g., most conspicuously, the bodies of which the heavens are framed. From what has been said it is plain, then, that philosophic wisdom is scientific knowledge, combined with intuitive reason, of the things that are highest by nature. This is why we say Anaxagoras, Thales, and men like them have philosophic but not practical wisdom, when we see them ignorant of what is to their own advantage, and why we say that they know things that are remarkable, admirable, difficult, and divine, but useless; viz. because it is not human goods that they seek.

Practical wisdom on the other hand is concerned with things human and things about which it is possible to deliberate; for we say this is above all the work of the man of practical wisdom, to deliberate well, but no one deliberates about things invariable, nor about things which have not an end, and that a good that can be brought about by action. The man who is without qualification good at deliberating is the man who is capable of aiming in accordance with calculation at the best for man of things attainable by action. Nor is practical wisdom concerned with universals only—it must also recognize the particulars; for it is practical, and practice is concerned with particulars. This is why some who do not know, and especially those who have experience, are more practical than others who know; for if a man knew that light meats are digestible and wholesome, but did not know which sorts of meat are light, he would not produce health, but the man who knows that chicken is wholesome is more likely to produce health.

Now practical wisdom is concerned with action; therefore one should have both forms of it, or the latter in preference to the former. But of practical as of philosophic wisdom there must be a controlling kind.

18 / AUGUSTE COMTE

Hierarchy of the Positive Sciences

In proceeding to offer a Classification of the Sciences, we must leave on one side all others that have as yet been attempted. Such scales as those of Bacon and D'Alembert are constructed upon an arbitrary division of the faculties of the mind; whereas, our principal faculties are often

From Auguste Comte, *Course on the Positive Philosophy*. Translation by Harriet Martineau (London: Trubner and Co., 1875), Chap. 2, pp. 15–27.

engaged at the same time in any scientific pursuit. As for other classifications, they have failed, through one fault or another, to command assent: so that there are almost as many schemes as there are individuals to propose them. The failure has been so conspicuous, that the best minds feel a prejudice against this kind of enterprise, in any shape.

Now, what is the reason of this?—For one reason, the distribution of the sciences, having become a somewhat discredited task, has of late been undertaken chiefly by persons who have no sound knowledge of any science at all. A more important and less personal reason, however, is the want of homogeneousness in the different parts of the intellectual system, —some having successively become positive, while others remain theological or metaphysical. Among such incoherent materials, classification is of course impossible. Every attempt at a distribution has failed from this cause, without the distributor being able to see why;—without his discovering that a radical contrariety existed between the materials he was endeavouring to combine. The fact was clear enough; if it had but been understood, that the enterprise was premature; and that it was useless to undertake it till our principal scientific conceptions should all have become positive. The preceding chapter seems to show that this indispensable condition may now be considered fulfilled: and thus the time has arrived for laying down a sound and durable system of scientific order.

We may derive encouragement from the example set by recent botanists and zoologists, whose philosophical labours have exhibited the true principle of classification; viz., that the classification must proceed from the study of the things to be classified, and must by no means be determined by *a priori* considerations. The real affinities and natural connections presented by objects being allowed to determine their order, the classification itself becomes the expression of the most general fact. And thus does the positive method apply to the question of classification itself, as well as to the objects included under it. It follows that the mutual dependence of the sciences,—a dependence resulting from that of the corresponding phenomena,—must determine the arrangement of the system of human knowledge. Before proceeding to investigate this mutual dependence, we have only to ascertain the real bounds of the classification proposed: in other words, to settle what we mean by human knowledge, as the subject of this work.

The field of human labour is either speculation or action: and thus, we are accustomed to divide our knowledge into the theoretical and the practical. It is obvious that, in this inquiry, we have to do only with the theoretical. We are not going to treat of all human notions whatever, but of those fundamental conceptions of the different orders of phenomena which furnish a solid basis to all combinations, and are not founded on any antecedent intellectual system. In such a study, speculation is our material, and not the application of it,—except where the application may happen to throw back light on its speculative origin. This is probably what Bacon meant by that First Philosophy which he declared to be an extract from the whole of Science, and which has been so differently and so strangely interpreted by his metaphysical commentators.

There can be no doubt that Man's study of nature must furnish the only basis of his action upon nature; for it is only by knowing the laws of phenomena, and thus being able to foresee them, that we can, in active life, set them to modify one another for our advantage. Our direct natural power over everything about us is extremely weak, and altogether disproportioned to our needs. Whenever we effect anything great it is through a knowledge of natural laws, by which we can set one agent to work upon another,—even very weak modifying elements producing a change in the results of a large aggregate of causes. The relation of science to art may be summed up in a brief expression:

From Science comes Prevision: from Prevision comes Action.

We must not, however, fall into the error of our time, of regarding Science chiefly as a basis of Art. However great may be the services rendered to Industry by science, however true may be the saying that Knowledge is Power, we must never forget that the sciences have a higher destination still;—and not only higher but more direct;—that of satisfying the craving of our understanding to know the laws of phenomena. To feel how deep and urgent this need is, we have only to consider for a moment the physiological effects of *consternation,* and to remember that the most terrible sensation we are capable of, is that which we experience when any phenomenon seems to arise in violation of the familiar laws of nature. This need of disposing facts in a comprehensible order (which is the proper object of all scientific theories) is so inherent in our organization, that if we could not satisfy it by positive conceptions, we must inevitably return to those theological and metaphysical explanations which had their origin in this very fact of human nature.—It is this original tendency which acts as a preservative, in the minds of men of science, against the narrowness and incompleteness which the practical habits of our age are apt to produce. It is through this that we are able to maintain just and noble ideas of the importance and destination of the sciences; and if it were not thus, the human understanding would soon, as Condorcet has observed, come to a stand, even as to the practical applications for the sake of which higher things had been sacrificed; for, if the arts flow from science, the neglect of science must destroy the consequent arts. Some of the most important arts are derived from speculations pursued during long ages with a purely scientific intention. For instance, the ancient Greek geometers delighted themselves with beautiful speculations of Conic Sections; those speculations wrought, after a long series of generations, the renovation of astronomy; and out of this has the art of navigation attained a perfection which it never could have reached otherwise than through the speculative labours of Archimedes and Apollonius: so that, to use Condorcet's illustration, "the sailor who is preserved from shipwreck by the exact observation of the longitude, owes his life to a theory conceived two thousand years before by men of genius who had in view simply geometrical speculations."

Our business, it is clear, is with theoretical researches, letting alone their practical application altogether. Though we may conceive of a course of study which should unite the generalities of speculation and application, the time is not come for it. To say nothing of its vast extent, it would require preliminary achievements which have not yet been attempted. We must first be in possession of appropriate Special conceptions, formed according to scientific theories; and for these we have yet to wait. Meantime, an intermediate class is rising up, whose particular destination is to organize the relations of theory and practice; such as the engineers, who do not labour in the advancement of science, but who study it in its existing state, to apply it to practical purposes. Such classes are furnishing us with the elements of a future body of doctrine on the theories of the different arts. Already, Monge, in his view of descriptive geometry, has given us a general theory of the arts of construction. But we have as yet only a few scattered instances of this nature. The time will come when out of such results, a department of Positive philosophy may arise: but it will be in a distant future. If we remember that several sciences are implicated in every important art,— that, for instance, a true theory of Agriculture requires a combination of physiological, chemical, mechanical, and even astronomical and mathematical science,—it will be evident that true theories of the arts must wait for a large and equable development of these constituent sciences.

One more preliminary remark occurs, before we finish the prescription of our limits,—the ascertainment of our field of inquiry. We must distinguish between the two classes of Natural science;—the abstract or general, which have for their object the discovery of the laws which regulate phenomena in all conceivable cases: and the concrete, particular, or descriptive, which are sometimes called Natural sciences in a restricted sense, whose function it is to apply these laws to the actual history of existing beings. The first are fundamental; and our business is with them alone, as the second are derived, and however important, not rising into the rank of our subjects of contemplation. We shall treat of physiology, but not of botany and zoology, which are derived from it. We shall treat of chemistry, but not of mineralogy, which is secondary to it.— We may say of Concrete Physics, as these secondary sciences are called, the same thing that we said of theories of the arts,—that they require a preliminary knowledge of several sciences, and an advance of those sciences not yet achieved; so that, if there were no other reason, we must leave these secondary classes alone. At a future time Concrete Physics will have made progress, according to the development of Abstract Physics, and will afford a mass of less incoherent materials than those which it now presents. At present, too few of the students of these secondary sciences appear to be even aware that a due acquaintance with the primary sciences is requisite to all successful prosecution of their own.

We have now considered,

First, that science being composed of speculative knowledge and of practical knowledge, we have to deal only with the first; and

Second, that theoretical knowledge, or science properly so called, being divided into general and particular, or abstract and concrete science, we have again to deal only with the first.

Being thus in possession of our proper subject, duly prescribed, we may proceed to the ascertainment of the true order of the fundamental sciences.

This classification of the sciences is not so easy a matter as it may appear. However natural it may be, it will always involve something, if not arbitrary, at least artificial; and in so far, it will always involve imperfection. It is impossible to fulfil, quite rigorously, the object of presenting the sciences in their natural connection, and according to their mutual dependence, so as to avoid the smallest danger of being involved in a vicious circle. It is easy to show why.

Every science may be exhibited under two methods or procedures, the Historical and the Dogmatic. These are wholly distinct from each other, and any other method can be nothing but some combination of these two. By the first method knowledge is presented in the same order in which it was actually obtained by the human mind, together with the way in which it was obtained. By the second, the system of ideas is presented as it might be conceived of at this day, by a mind which, duly prepared and placed at the right point of view, should begin to reconstitute the science as a whole. A new science must be pursued historically, the only thing to be done being to study in chronological order the different works which have contributed to the progress of the science. But when such materials have become recast to form a general system, to meet the demand for a more natural logical order, it is because the science is too far advanced for the historical order to be practicable or suitable. The more discoveries are made, the greater becomes the labour of the historical method of study, and the more effectual the dogmatic, because the new conceptions bring forward the earlier ones in a fresh light. Thus, the education of an ancient geometer consisted simply in the study, in their due order, of the very small number of original treatises then existing on the different parts of geometry. The writings of Archimedes and Apollonius were, in fact, about all. On the contrary, a modern geometer commonly finishes his education without having read a single original work dating further back than the most recent discoveries, which cannot be known by any other means. Thus the Dogmatic Method is for ever superseding the Historical, as we advance to a higher position in science. If every mind had to pass through all the stages that every predecessor in the study had gone through, it is clear that, however easy it is to learn rather than invent, it would be impossible to effect the purpose of education—to place the student on the vantage-ground gained by the labours of all the men who have gone before. By the dogmatic method this is done, even though the living student may have only an ordinary intellect, and the dead may have been men of lofty genius. By the dogmatic method therefore must every advanced science be attained, with so much of the historical combined with it as is rendered necessary by discoveries too recent to be studied elsewhere than in their own records. The only objection to the preference of the Dogmatic method is that it does not show how the science was attained; but a moment's reflection will show that this is the case also with the Historical method. To pursue a science historically is quite a different thing from learning the history of its progress. This last pertains to the study of human history, as we shall see when we reach the final division of this work. It is true that a science cannot be completely understood without a knowledge of how it arose; and again, a dogmatic knowledge of any science is necessary to an understanding of its history; and therefore we shall notice, in treating of the fundamental sciences, the incidents of their origin, when distinct and illustrative; and we shall use their history, in a scientific sense, in our treatment of Social Physics; but the historical study, important, even essential, as it is, remains entirely distinct from the proper dogmatic study of science. These considerations in this place, tend to define more precisely the spirit of our course of inquiry, while they more exactly determine the conditions under which we may hope to succeed in the construction of a true scale of the aggregate fundamental sciences. Great confusion would arise from any attempt to adhere strictly to historical order in our exposition of the sciences, for they have not all advanced at the same rate; and we must be for ever borrowing from each some fact to illustrate another, without regard to priority of origin. Thus, it is clear that, in the system of the sciences, astronomy must come before physics, properly so called: and yet, several branches of physics, above all, optics, are indispensable to the complete exposition of astronomy. Minor defects, if inevitable, cannot invalidate a classification which, on the whole, fulfils the principal conditions of the case. They belong to what is essentially artificial in our division of intellectual labour. In the main, however, our classification agrees with the history of science; the more general and simple sciences actually occurring first and advancing best in human history, and being followed by the more complex and restricted, though all were, since the earliest times, enlarging simultaneously.

A simple mathematical illustration will precisely represent the difficulty of the question we have to resolve, while it will sum up the preliminary considerations we have just concluded.

We propose to classify the fundamental sciences. They are six, as we shall soon see. We cannot make them less; and most scientific men would reckon them as more. Six objects admit of 720 different dispositions, or, in popular language, changes. Thus we have to choose the one right order (and there can be but one right) out of 720 possible ones. Very few of these have ever been proposed; yet we might venture to say that there is probably not one in favour of which some plausible reason might not be assigned; for we see the wildest divergences among the schemes which have been proposed,—the sciences which are placed by some at the head of the scale being sent by others to the further extremity. Our problem is, then, to find the one rational order, among a host of possible systems.

Now we must remember that we have to look for the principle of classification in the comparison of the different orders of phenomena, through which science discovers the laws which are her object. What we have to determine is the real dependence of scientific studies. Now, this dependence can result only from that of the corresponding phenomena. All observable phenomena may be included within a very few natural categories, so arranged as that the study of each category may be grounded on the principal laws of the preceding, and serve as the basis of the next ensuing. This order is determined by the degree of simplicity, or, what comes to the same thing, of generality of their phenomena. Hence results their successive dependence, and the greater or lesser facility for being studied.

It is clear, *a priori*, that the most simple phenomena must be the most general; for whatever is observed in the greatest number of cases is of course the most disengaged from the incidents of particular cases. We must begin then with the study of the most general or simple phenomena, going on successively to the more particular or complex. This must be the most methodical way, for this order of generality or simplicity fixes the degree of facility in the study of phenomena, while it determines the necessary connection of the sciences by the successive dependence of their phenomena. It is worthy of remark in this place that the most general and simple phenomena are the furthest removed from Man's ordinary sphere, and must thereby be studied in a calmer and more rational frame of mind than those in which he is more nearly implicated; and this constitutes a new ground for the corresponding sciences being developed more rapidly.

We have now obtained our rule. Next we proceed to our classification.

We are first struck by the clear division of all natural phenomena into two classes—of inorganic and of organic bodies. The organized are evidently, in fact, more complex and less general than the inorganic, and depend upon them, instead of being depended on by them. Therefore it is that physiological study should begin with inorganic phenomena; since the organic include all the qualities belonging to them, with a special order added, viz., the vital phenomena, which belong to organization. We have not to investigate the nature of either; for the positive philosophy does not inquire into natures. Whether their nature be supposed different or the same, it is evidently necessary to separate the two studies of inorganic matter and of living bodies. Our classification will stand through any future decision as to the way in which living bodies are to be regarded; for, on any supposition, the general laws of inorganic physics must be established before we can proceed with success to the examination of a dependent class of phenomena.

Each of these great halves of natural philosophy has subdivisions. Inorganic physics must, in accordance with our rule of generality and the order of dependence of phenomena, be divided into two sections—of celestial and terrestrial phenomena. Thus we have Astronomy, geometrical and mechanical, and Terrestrial Physics. The necessity of this division is exactly the same as in the former case.

Astronomical phenomena are the most general, simple, and abstract of all; and therefore the study of natural philosophy must clearly begin with them. They are themselves independent, while the laws to which they are subject influence all others whatsoever. The general effects of gravitation preponderate, in all terrestrial phenomena, over all effects which may be peculiar to them, and modify the original ones. It follows that the analysis of the simplest terrestrial phenomenon, not only chemical, but even purely mechanical, presents a greater complication than the most compound astronomical phenomenon. The most difficult astronomical question involves less intricacy than the simple movement of even a solid body, when the determining circumstances are to be computed. Thus we see that we must separate these two studies, and proceed to the second only through the first, from which it is derived.

In the same manner, we find a natural division of Terrestrial Physics into two, according as we regard bodies in their mechanical or their chemical character. Hence we have Physics, properly so called, and Chemistry. Again, the second class must be studied through the first. Chemical phenomena are more complicated than mechanical, and depend upon them, without influencing them in return. Every one knows that all chemical action is first submitted to the influence of weight, heat, electricity, etc., and presents moreover something which modifies all these. Thus, while it follows Physics, it presents itself as a distinct science.

Such are the divisions of the sciences relating to inorganic matter. An analogous division arises in the other half of Natural Philosophy—the science of organized bodies.

Here we find ourselves presented with two orders of phenomena; those which relate to the individual, and those which relate to the species, especially when it is gregarious. With regard to Man, especially, this distinction is fundamental. The last order of phenomena is evidently dependent on the first, and is more complex. Hence we have two great sections in organic physics—Physiology, properly so called, and Social Physics, which is dependent on it. In all Social phenomena we perceive the working of the physiological laws of the individual; and moreover something which modifies their effects, and which belongs to the influence of individuals over each other—singularly complicated in the case of the human race by the influence of generations on their successors. Thus it is clear that our social science must issue from that which relates to the life of the individual. On the other hand, there is no occasion to suppose, as some eminent physiologists have done, that Social Physics is only an appendage to physiology. The phenomena of the two are not identical, though they are homogeneous; and it is of high importance to hold the two sciences separate. As social conditions modify the operation of physiological laws, Social Physics must have a set of observations of its own.

It would be easy to make the divisions of the Organic half of Science correspond with those of the Inorganic, by dividing physiology into vegetable and animal, according to popular custom. But this distinction, however important in Concrete Physics (in that secondary and special class of studies before declared to be inappropriate to this work), hardly extends into those Abstract Physics with which we have to do. Vegetables and animals come alike under our notice, when our object is to learn the general laws of life—that is, to study physiology. To say nothing of the fact that the distinction grows ever fainter and more dubious with new discoveries, it bears no relation to our plan of research; and we shall therefore consider that there is only one division in the science of organized bodies.

Thus we have before us Five fundamental Sciences in successive dependence,—Astronomy, Physics, Chemistry, Physiology, and finally Social Physics. The first considers the most general, simple, abstract, and remote phenomena known to us, and those which affect all others without being affected by them. The last considers the most particular, compound, concrete phenomena, and those which are the most interesting to Man. Between these two, the degrees of speciality, of complexity, and individuality, are in regular proportion to the place of the respective sciences in the scale exhibited. This—casting out everything arbitrary— we must regard as the true filiation of the sciences; and in it we find the plan of this work.

As we proceed, we shall find that the same principle which gives this order to the whole body of science arranges the parts of each science; and its soundness will therefore be freshly attested as often as it presents itself afresh. There is no refusing a principle which distributes the interior of each science after the same method with the aggregate sciences. But this is not the place in which to do more than indicate what we shall contemplate more closely hereafter. We must now rapidly review some of the leading properties of the hierarchy of science that has been disclosed.

This gradation is in essential conformity with the order which has spontaneously taken place among the branches of natural philosophy, when pursued separately, and without any purpose of establishing such order. Such an accordance is a strong presumption that the arrangement is natural. Again, it coincides with the actual development of natural philosophy. If no leading science can be effectually pursued otherwise than through those which precede it in the scale, it is evident that no vast development of any science could take place prior to the great astronomical discoveries to which we owe the impulse given to the whole. The progression may since have been simultaneous; but it has taken place in the order we have recognized.

This consideration is so important that it is difficult to understand without it the history of the human mind. The general law which governs this history, as we have already seen, cannot be verified, unless we combine it with the scientific gradation just laid down: for it is according to this gradation that the different human theories have attained in succession the theological state, the metaphysical, and finally the positive. If we do not bear in mind the law which governs progression, we shall encounter insurmountable difficulties: for it is clear that the theological or metaphysical state of some fundamental theories must have temporarily coincided with the positive state of others which precede them in our established gradation, and actually have at times coincided with them; and this must involve the law itself in an obscurity which can be cleared up only by the classification we have proposed.

Again, this classification marks, with precision, the relative perfection of the different sciences, which consists in the degree of precision of knowledge, and in the relation of its different branches. It is easy to see that the more general, simple, and abstract any phenomena are, the less they depend on others, and the more precise they are in themselves, and the more clear in their relations with each other. Thus, organic phenomena are less exact and systematic than inorganic; and of these again terrestrial are less exact and systematic than those of astronomy. This fact is completely accounted for by the gradation we have laid down; and we shall see as we proceed, that the possibility of applying mathematical analysis to the study of phenomena is exactly in proportion to the rank which they hold in the scale of the whole.

There is one liability to be guarded against, which we may mention here. We must beware of confounding the degree of precision which we are able to attain in regard to any science, with the certainty of the science itself. The certainty of science, and our precision in the knowledge of it, are two very different things, which have been too often confounded; and are so still, though less than formerly. A very absurd proposition may be very precise; as if we should say, for instance, that the sum of the angles of a triangle is equal to three right angles; and a very certain proposition may be wanting in precision in our statement of it; as, for instance, when we assert that every man will die. If the different sciences offer to us a varying degree of precision, it is from no want of certainty in themselves, but of our mastery of their phenomena.

The most interesting property of our formula of gradation is its effect on education, both general and scientific. This is its direct and unquestionable result. It will be more and more evident as we proceed, that no science can be effectually pursued without the preparation of a competent knowledge of the anterior sciences on which it depends. Physical philosophers cannot understand Physics without at least a general knowledge of Astronomy; nor Chemists, without Physics and Astronomy; nor Physiologists, without Chemistry, Physics, and Astronomy; nor, above all, the students of Social philosophy, without a general knowledge of all the anterior sciences. As such conditions are, as yet, rarely fulfilled, and as no organization exists for their fulfillment, there is amongst us, in fact, no rational scientific education. To this may be attributed, in great part, the imperfection of even the most important sciences at this day. If the fact is so in regard to scientific education, it is no less striking in regard to general education. Our intellectual system cannot be renovated till the natural sciences are studied in their proper order. Even the highest understandings are apt to associate their ideas according to the order in which they were received: and it is only an intellect here and there, in any age, which in its utmost vigour can, like Bacon, Descartes, and Leibnitz, make a clearance in their field of knowledge, so as to reconstruct from the foundation their system of ideas.

Such is the operation of our great law upon scientific education through its effect on Doctrine. We cannot appreciate it duly without seeing how it affects Method.

As the phenomena which are homogeneous have been classed under one science, while those which belong to other sciences are heterogeneous, it follows that the Positive Method must be constantly modified in an uniform manner in the range of the same fundamental science, and will undergo modifications, different and more and more compound, in passing from one science to another. Thus, under the scale laid down, we shall meet with it in all its varieties; which could not happen if we were to adopt a scale which should not fulfil the conditions we have admitted. This is an all-important consideration; for if, as we have already seen, we cannot understand the positive method in the abstract, but only by its application, it is clear that we can have no adequate conception of it but by studying it in its varieties of application. No one science, however well chosen, could exhibit it. Though the Method is always the same, its procedure is varied. For instance, it should be Observation with regard to one kind of phenomena, and Experiment with regard to another; and different kinds of experiment, according to the case. In the same way, a general precept, derived from one fundamental science, however applicable to another, must have its spirit preserved by a reference to its origin; as in the case of the theory of Classifications. The best idea of the Positive Method would, of course, be obtained by the study of the most primitive and exalted of the sciences, if we were confined to one; but this isolated view would give no idea of its capacity of application to others in a modified form. Each science has its own proper advantages; and without some knowledge of them all, no conception can be formed of the power of the Method.

One more consideration must be briefly adverted to. It is necessary not only to have a general knowledge of all the sciences, but to study them in their order. What can come of a study of complicated phenomena, if the student have not learned, by the contemplation of the simpler, what a Law is, what it is to Observe; what a Positive conception is; and even what a chain of reasoning is? Yet this is the way our young physiologists proceed every day,—plunging into the study of living bodies, without any other preparation than a knowledge of a dead language or two, or at most a superficial acquaintance with Physics and Chemistry, acquired without any philosophical method, or reference to any true point of departure in Natural philosophy. In the same way, with regard to Social phenomena, which are yet more complicated, what can be effected but by the rectification of the intellectual instrument, through an adequate study of the range of anterior phenomena? There are many who admit this: but they do not see how to set about the work, nor understand the Method itself for want of the preparatory study; and thus, the admission remains barren, and social theories abide in the theological or metaphysical state, in spite of the efforts of those who believe themselves positive reformers.

These, then, are the four points of view under which we have recognized the importance of a Rational and Positive Classification.

It cannot but have been observed that in our enumeration of the sciences there is a prodigious omission. We have said nothing of Mathematical science. The omission was intentional; and the reason is no other than the vast importance of mathematics. This science will be the first of which we shall treat. Meantime, in order not to omit from our sketch a department so prominent, we may indicate here the general results of the study we are about to enter upon.

In the present state of our knowledge we must regard Mathematics less as a constituent part of natural philosophy than as having been, since the time of Descartes and Newton, the true basis of the whole of natural philosophy; though it is, exactly speaking, both the one and the other. To us it is of less value for the knowledge of which it consists, substantial and valuable as that knowledge is, than as being the most powerful instrument that the human mind can employ in the investigation of the laws of natural phenomena.

In due precision, Mathematics must be divided into two great sciences, quite distinct from each other—Abstract Mathematics, or the Calculus (taking the word in its most extended sense), and Concrete Mathematics, which is composed of General Geometry and of Rational Mechanics. The Concrete part is necessarily founded on the Abstract, and it becomes in its turn the basis of all natural philosophy; all the phenomena of the universe being regarded, as far as possible, as geometrical or mechanical.

The Abstract portion is the only one which is purely instrumental, it being simply an immense extension of natural logic to a certain order of deductions. Geometry and mechanics must, on the contrary, be regarded as true natural sciences, founded, like all others, on observation, though, by the extreme simplicity of their phenomena, they can be systematized to much greater perfection. It is this capacity which has caused the experimental character of their first principles to be too much lost sight of. But these two physical sciences have this peculiarity, that they are now, and will be more and more, employed rather as method than as doctrine.

It needs scarcely be pointed out that in placing Mathematics at the head of Positive Philosophy, we are only extending the application of the principle which has governed our whole Classification. We are simply carrying back our principle to its first manifestation. Geometrical and Mechanical phenomena are the most general, the most simple, the most abstract of all,—the most irreducible to others, the most independent of them; serving, in fact, as a basis to all others. It follows that the study of them is an indispensable preliminary to that of all others. Therefore must Mathematics hold the first place in the hierarchy of the sciences, and be the point of departure of all Education, whether general or special. In an empirical way, this has hitherto been the custom,—a custom which arose from the great antiquity of mathematical science. We now see why it must be renewed on a rational foundation.

We have now considered, in the form of a philosophical problem, the rational plan of the study of the Positive Philosophy. The order that results is this; an order which of all possible arrangements is the only one that accords with the natural manifestation of all phenomena. MATHEMATICS, ASTRONOMY, PHYSICS, CHEMISTRY, PHYSIOLOGY, SOCIAL PHYSICS.

19 / JOSEPH J. SCHWAB

Structure of the Disciplines: Meanings and Significances

We embark here on an exploration of one of the most difficult of terrains: investigation of the nature, variety, and extent of human knowledge; and the attempt to determine what that nature, variety, and extent have to tell us about teaching and learning. My share of this task is a specialized one and a preliminary one. It is simply to map that terrain. Later papers will explore the land itself.

What is meant by the structure of the disciplines? It means three things, three distinct but related sets of problems. Let us take a foretaste of all three together without discriminating them by name.

It has been widely supposed that there are indubitable grounds for recognizing basically different orders of phenomena, each requiring a different discipline for its investigation because of the differences in the character of the phenomena.

Joseph J. Schwab, "Structures of the Disciplines: Meanings and Significances," in G. W. Ford and L. Pugno (eds.), *The Structure of Knowledge and the Curriculum* (Chicago: Rand McNally and Company, 1964), pp. 6–30. Reprinted by permission of Joseph J. Schwab.

There are many different views based on such a premise. For example, many philosophers have insisted on a fundamental distinction between living phenomena and non-living, thus generating the notion that there are two fundamentally different sciences, the biological and the physio-chemical. These two sciences were supposed to differ in method, in guiding conceptions, in the kind of knowledge produced, and in degree of certainty, differing to precisely the same extent that their subject matters were supposed to differ.

Another such view is generated by a distinction between man and nature, a distinction in which nature is conceived as bound by inexorable laws while men are in some sense and in some degree free. In this view, two major areas of investigation are again discriminated: on the one hand, science, concerned with the inexorable laws that nature presumably obeys; and on the other hand, a discipline in the neighborhood of ethics and politics, which would investigate the freedom that man has and the ways in which men make their choices.

There is also a view that emphasizes the vast difference between the generality of "natural" phenomena (i.e., their predictability, the tendency of "natural" things to behave or be the same in instance after instance) and the particularity of human events (the essentially unique and non-repeating character of acts notable in the behavior of man). Again, two widely different bodies of investigation and study are generated: science on the one hand and history on the other. Science, in this view, would seek the general laws that characterize the repeating behavior of natural things, while history would seek to determine the precise, unique events that characterized each life, each era, each civilization or culture that it studied. Hence, again, there would be two basically different curriculum components, differing in method, principle, and warrantability.

There have been similar separations of other disciplines, notably mathematics and logic. Mathematics was long ago seen to differ radically from other disciplines, including the sciences, in that its subject matter appeared to have no material existence. The objects of physical or biological enquiry could be seen, touched, smelled, tasted. The objects of mathematics could not. The plane, the line, the point, unity, number, etc. existed in some way which was not material or did not exist at all. This peculiarity of mathematical objects continues to be a puzzle. No one view of the nature of mathematics has been developed which is satisfactory to all concerned, though most moderns are agreed that mathematics differs radically from the other sciences.

Logic has been set apart because of its unique relationship to other disciplines rather than because of something peculiar about its subject matter. To one degree or another, all other disciplines test the reliability of their conclusions by appealing to canons of reasoning and of evidence which are developed in the first place by the discipline of logic. Since logic is responsible for developing these canons, it cannot itself use them to check its own work. Logic thus stands as a sort of "queen of the sciences," dictating their rules but having for itself rules of some other and puzzling sort. Unlike the case of mathematics, this peculiarity of logic is no longer universally recognized. In some quarters, for example, it is held that logic does no more than formulate the methods and the canons of reasoning and of evidence which other sciences have developed, used, and bear witness to by their effectiveness. In this view, logic is not so much the queen of the sciences as their handmaiden.

Let us continue our foretaste of the problems of the structures of the disciplines by noting a peculiarity of the distinctions we have described. The peculiarity is that the differences among phenomena which appear at one period in the history of the disciplines to be radical and self-evident may at a later date disappear or become inconsequential as bases for differentiating disciplines. Take, for example, the differentiation of biology from the physical-chemical sciences. In early times and through the eighteenth century, fundamental differences between the living and the non-living could not be evaded. The living thing was "self-moving"; no other object was. The living thing reproduced itself; the living thing developed, had a personal history which no non-living thing could duplicate. Then, in the middle to late nineteenth century, some of these differences ceased to be notable, others disappeared entirely from human recognition. In this altered climate, the physiologist Claude Bernard pleaded for a study of living things strictly in terms of physics and chemistry. Since then, such an approach to living things has been so fruitful that it is now safe to say that it will be only a brief time before we shall synthesize living molecules in the laboratory. In recent years a still further shift in outlook has taken place: we now hear pleas from some physicists that certain physical phenomena be treated in much the way that living things were investigated *before* Bernard.

A similar shift is visible on a smaller scale in the history of the science of mechanics. Three hundred years ago the behavior of celestial bodies (the planets and the stars) and the behavior of terrestrial bodies in motion (things rolling on the surface of the earth and things thrown or propelled through the air) appeared to be radically different. Terrestrial bodies inevitably came to rest and fell to earth; celestial bodies inevitably continued in their regular motion without stop. Then, with Newton, these differences, though still visible, became entirely unimportant.

In brief, what we see of and in things changes from epoch to epoch. Differences that once appeared to be radical are seen later to be illusory or trivial; then, at another period, some of these differences reappear in a new guise. What can account for such changes in what appears to be objectively perceived? The answer is most easily exemplified in the case of mechanics, where in our own day the once radical difference between terrestrial and celestial bodies continues to be treated as illusory.

Granted that this difference was an illusion, what made the illusion disappear? The answer is this: Newton conceived an idea called universal gravitation. In the light of this idea, it became desirable and possible to examine the motion of the celestial bodies (in Newton's case, the moon) in a new way. Specifically, it became desirable and possible to measure the changing directions and changing velocities of the moon in such a fashion that it could be described as continually falling toward earth, while, at the same time, continually moving in a straight line at an angle to its fall. Thus its continuous orbit of the earth could be understood as the resultant of these two motions. In the same way it became possible to conceive of a terrestrial missile as falling to earth and coming to rest there only because its initial velocity in a straight line was not great enough to carry it straight forward beyond the bend of the earth before its fall brought it into contact with the earth. One could then see that as the initial velocity of a missile became greater and greater, it would not only go farther before it fell to earth, but at some point the increased velocity would be so great that the fall of the missile would be compensated by the falling away of the spherical surface of the earth. Such a missile would then become a satellite of the earth precisely like the moon. In brief, a new conception dictating new studies and a new way to interpret the data exhibited the movement of celestial bodies as nothing more than an extreme case of the motions of familiar terrestrial bodies moving at lower velocities.

In general, two collections of phenomena appear to be vastly different because we have used separate and distinct bodies of conceptions in studying them and discovering knowledge about them. Each such body of conceptions dictates what data we think we should seek, what experiments to perform, and what to make of our data by way of knowledge. If widely different conceptions are used to guide enquiries on two different collections of phenomena, we end inevitably with bodies of knowledge which exhibit few similarities and many differences. It is through the limiting or distorting lenses of these bodies of knowledge that we look at things. Hence, if the lenses distort or limit in different ways, we see things as different. The differences we see disappear if, but only if, a new conception is given birth which permits the study of both collections of phenomena in one set of terms and therefore makes for unity where diversity existed before.

Before we discriminate the problems of the structure of the disciplines, let us take note of a *caveat*. It is this: the integration of previously separate bodies of knowledge by new and unifying conceptions should not blind us to the possibility that some of the differences we recognize among phenomena may be genuine; some differentiation of disciplines may be perennial. There really may be joints in nature, a forearm, then an elbow, and then an upper arm. Science, ethics, and aesthetics may indeed represent three widely variant objects of enquiry. The doctrine of the unity of science, which insists on a unification of all knowledge, is either a dogma or a hope but not a fact. There are no data from which to conclude decisively that eventually all the disciplines will become or should become one.

Now let us step back and identify in this foretaste of knowledge and knowledge-seeking the three major but related sets of problems which define the area called structure of the disciplines.

Recall first our brief review of efforts to discriminate life from non-life, science from history, and so on. These efforts illustrate the first problem of the structure of the disciplines. It is the problem of determining the membership and organization of the disciplines, of identifying the significantly different disciplines, and of locating their relations to one another.

This set of problems is illustrated by the following questions. *Is* mathematical knowledge significantly different from knowledge of physical things? If so, how are the behaviors of mathematical objects related to the behaviors of physical objects? That is, how must we account for the extraordinary usefulness of mathematics to the sciences? Is it because we impose mathematical forms on our observation of physical things, or is it because, in some mysterious way, the objects of the external world behave according to patterns that we discover through mathematical enquiry into our own intellects? Similarly, we might raise questions about practical knowledge and scientific or theoretical knowledge. Are they much the same or truly different? Is practical knowledge merely the application of science? Or does science take hold of ideal objects extrapolated from experience of things while practical knowledge must supply the bridge for return from scientific knowledge of such ideal objects to the actual and practicable? This set of problems may properly be called a problem of the structure of the disciplines, if we keep in mind that by the plural "disciplines" we refer to them collectively rather than distributively, while "structure" is singular and refers to the organization of the disciplines *inter se.*

The significance of this set of problems to education is obvious enough. To identify the disciplines that constitute contemporary knowledge and mastery of the world, is to identify the subject matter of education, the material that constitutes both its resources and its obligations. To locate the relations of these disciplines to one another is to determine what may be joined together for purposes of instruction and what should be held apart; these same relations will also weigh heavily in determining our decisions about the sequence of instruction, for it will tell us what must come before what, or what is most desirably placed first, or second, or third.

The second set of problems of the structure of the disciplines is exemplified by the tremendous role of the concept of universal gravitation in supplying us with a more nearly universal mechanics. A similar role is played by other conceptions in the attainment and formulation of all scientific knowledge. Embedded in the knowledge we have of the workings of the human body lies one or another concept of the nature of an organism, of the character of the parts of such an organism and how they relate to one another. Back of our knowledge of heredity lies a conception of particles behaving as do the terms in the expansion of a binominal to the second or higher powers. Back of our ability to make decisions in playing games lie similar conceptions. Again, the conceptions happen to be mathematical: the expansion of the binominal or a more complex mathematical structure derived by taking the expansion of the binominal to its limit. These mathematical conceptions provide us with a body of probability theory with which we play poker, determine tactics in battle, plan the production and sale of the products of our industries. Similarly, knowledge of human behavior, both individual and social, has arisen only as the men concerned with enquiry in psychology, sociology, and anthropology have developed conceptions that have enabled them to plan their researches.

In general then, enquiry has its origin in a conceptual structure, often mathematical, but not necessarily so. It is this conceptual structure through which we are able to formulate a telling question. It is through the telling question that we know what data to seek and what experiments to perform to get those data. Once the data are in hand, the same conceptual structure tells us how to interpret them, what to make of them by way of knowledge. Finally, the knowledge itself is formulated in the terms provided by the same conception. Thus we formulate and convey some of the knowledge we discover about the body in terms of organs and functions; we formulate and communicate our knowledge of atomic structure in terms of a concept of particles and waves; we formulate some of our knowledge of human personality in terms of psychic organs and their functions and other portions of it in terms of interpersonal relations.

In each science and in many arts such conceptual structures prevail. The second problem of the structure of the disciplines is to identify these structures and understand the powers and limits of the enquiries that take place under their guidance. Let us call this set of problems the problem of the *substantive* structures of each discipline.

Again, the significance of this problem of the structure of the disciplines to education is obvious enough—or at least one part of it is. For to know what structures underlie a given body of knowledge is to know what problems we shall face in imparting this knowledge. Perhaps the conceptual structure is no more complex than that involved in the discrimination of two classes of things by a single criterion, such as color or shape. In that case, we may suppose that little difficulty would be encountered in teaching this body of knowledge even to the very young. Perhaps the conceptual structure is more complex but so firmly embedded in common-sense knowledge of things that the child at some early, given age will already have encountered it and become familiar with it. In that case, we should, again, have little difficulty in imparting our knowledge, provided that we impart it at the right time in the development of the child in our culture. However, suppose the conceptual structure is both complex and largely unused in common-sense knowledge? This would be the case at the moment for the physical conception of a wave-like particle. In such a case, to locate and identify the conception is to locate and identify a difficult problem of instruction requiring much experiment and study.

A second curricular significance of the problem of the substantive structures of each discipline is less obvious. It concerns a peculiar consequence of the role of conceptual structures on our knowledge, a consequence little noted until recently. The dependence of knowledge on a conceptual structure means that any body of knowledge is likely to be of only temporary significance. For the knowledge which develops from the use of a given concept usually discloses new complexities of the subject matter which call forth new concepts. These new concepts in turn give rise to new bodies of enquiry and, therefore, to new and more complete bodies of knowledge stated in new terms. The significance of this ephemeral character of knowledge to education consists in the fact that it exhibits the desirability if not the necessity for so teaching what we teach that students understand that the knowledge we possess is not mere literal, factual truth but a kind of knowledge which is true in a more complex sense. This in turn means that we must clarify for students the role of concepts in making knowledge possible (and limiting its validity) and impart to them some idea of the particular concepts that underlie present knowledge of each subject matter, together with the reasons for the appropriateness of these concepts and some hint of their limitations.[1]

The third problem of the structure of the disciplines we shall call the problem of the *syntactical* structure of the disciplines. This problem is

[1] See Joseph J. Schwab, "Enquiry, the Science Teacher, and the Educator," *School Review*, LXVIII (Summer 1960), for an elaboration of this point.

hidden in the fact that if different sciences pursue knowledge of their respective subject matters by means of different conceptual frames, it is very likely that there will be major differences between one discipline and another in the way and in the extent to which it can verify its knowledge. There is, then, the problem of determining for each discipline what it does by way of discovery and proof, what criteria it uses for measuring the quality of its data, how strictly it can apply canons of evidence, and in general, of determining the route or pathway by which the discipline moves from its raw data through a longer or shorter process of interpretation to its conclusion.

Again, certain obvious consequences to education accrue from such a study. For, unless we intend to treat all knowledge as literal, true dogma, and thereby treat students as mere passive, obedient servants of our current culture, we want our students to know, concerning each body of knowledge learned, how sound, how dependable it is.

In summary then, three different sets of problems constitute the general problem of the structure of the disciplines. First there is the problem of the organization of the disciplines: how many there are; what they are; and how they relate to one another. Second, there is the problem of the substantive conceptual structures used by each discipline. Third, there is the problem of the syntax of each discipline: what its canons of evidence and proof are and how well they can be applied. Let us turn now to a brief investigation of each of these problems.

The Problem of the Organization of the Disciplines

With the problem of the organization of the disciplines we must face at once one of the inevitable complexities of this terrain, the fact that it does not and cannot supply a single, authoritative answer to the question of what disciplines there are, how many there are, and how they are related to one another. The reason for this complexity is fairly obvious. The problem of organization is a problem of classification primarily. If we classify any group of complex things, we are faced with a wide choice of bases of classification. (Even with postage stamps, we could classify by country of origin, by color, by shape or size, or by some combination of two or more of these.) Disciplines are very complex, hence the diversity and variety of available modes of classification are great. Consequently, depending on what one emphasizes about the disciplines, one or another or still a third or a fifth or a tenth classification of them is generated.

Four bases of classification of disciplines have always demanded attention: (1) their subject matter, what they aim to investigate, or work upon; (2) their practitioners, what competences and habits are required to carry on their work; (3) their methods (syntax), and modes of enquiry by which the enquirer brings himself to bear on the subject matter; (4) their ends, the kinds of knowledge or other outcomes at which they aim. Let us, then, examine a few organizations of the disciplines which use one or more of these, choosing them for the light they may throw on current curriculum problems.

The basic organization of the sciences proposed by Aristotle is worth taking a brief look at nowadays because we have tended to forget what it emphasizes. In this organization, Aristotle made most use of the end or aim of the disciplines together with the character of the materials they work on, the subject matter. Using these two as bases of classification, Aristotle distinguished three major groups of disciplines, the names of which have survived even in our current common-sense knowledge of the disciplines—though the significance assigned them has altered or been lost. The three basic divisions are the *Theoretical,* the *Practical,* and the *Productive.*

The theoretical disciplines are those whose aim is to know. For Artistotle, "to know" meant to know indubitably. Therefore, the theoretical disciplines included only those whose subject matters exhibited such inexorable regularity that they could be considered proper objects of "knowing" enquiry. Aristotle thought there were three such "knowing" or theoretical disciplines: physics, mathematics, and metaphysics. Today, though we would be very doubtful about the possibility of indubitable knowledge, we would, nevertheless, recognize a group of "theoretical" disciplines whose aim was to know and whose subject matters were such that the knowledge these disciplines sought was as nearly stable as knowledge can be. We would include the physical and biological sciences in this group. We would include substantial portions of the social sciences. We would exclude metaphysics as doubtful indeed. We would exclude mathematics, not because it is doubtful, but because we would consider it very special.

The practical disciplines, for Aristotle, included those concerned with choice, decision, and action based on deliberate decision. Precisely because its aim was to do, and therefore to alter the course of things, its subject matter had to have the property that was exactly opposite to the property required for the theoretical sciences. The subject matters of the practical sciences by necessity, must be not inexorable in their behavior, but capable of alteration, not fixed and stable but changeable.

It is exceedingly important, if we are to appreciate the bearing of this Aristotelian classification on modern problems, that we realize that "deliberate action" meant for Aristotle actions undertaken for their *own sakes* and not actions undertaken merely as the necessary preliminaries to some other end. Such actions, undertaken for their own sakes, constitute, then, what we mean by "a good life." They are the activities that stem from and express the best of which each man is capable. The practical sciences were (and are) therefore, ethics and politics. For us in modern times, ethics and politics would include not only each individual effort to lead and examine a deliberate life and the governing and policymaking in high places, but also the difficult and terrifying business of being parents, of being teachers *deliberately* and not as automatons, and the responsible work of administration and policymaking at all levels, together with those parts of the social sciences which contribute to such activities. I need not add that of all the things the schools might do, they do least of this. A few nursery schools, a very few teachers at the elementary level, and some few men and women at the college level give thought and time and energy toward evoking in their students the competencies and habits that lead to the making of good choices and good decisions and help the person to act in ways commensurate with his decisions. But by and large, the time, the energy, and the resources of our public schools ignore the very existence of practical disciplines in the Aristotelian sense.

The productive disciplines in the Aristotelian scheme are what the work "productive" suggests. They are the disciplines devoted to *making:* the fine arts, the applied arts, engineering. In connection with the significance of the Aristotelian productive disciplines for modern curriculum problems, let us note a principal characteristic of the entire Aristotelian organization: it emphasizes the sharp differences among the three groups of disciplines. The theoretical disciplines, devoted to knowing, concern themselves with those aspects of things which are fixed, stable, enduring. Hence, the theoretical disciplines are concerned with precisely these aspects of things which we cannot alter by making or make use of by doing. The productive disciplines are concerned with what is malleable, capable of being changed. The practical disciplines are concerned with another sort of malleability of human character, its ability to deliberate on its future and (within limits) to do as it sees fit.

We, on the other hand, have tended to fall into the habit of treating all disciplines proper to the schools as if they were theoretical. We manage to maintain this preoccupation in the case of the practical disciplines by ignoring them. In the case of the productive disciplines, we ignore them in some cases and in others resort to the trick of treating them as if they were theoretical. Music appreciation is taught as if its purpose were to recognize obvious themes of symphonies or concertos and proudly announce the opus number and the composer's name. Performing music is taught as if the aim were merely to follow the notes and obey the teacher's instructions about the score. Literature is taught as if dramas and novels were windows looking out on life, or worse, as if, as in the case of music appreciation, the object of the game were to know choice tidbits about the character, the life, or the times of the author. Art is taught, like literature, as if its aim were to provide a true, a faithful photograph of life. Happily, the exceptions to these strictures are increasing. Music appreciation is more and more being taught as a mastery of those arts by which the ear and the mind creatively take in the form and content of music. Performing music is more and more being taught in such a way that the students learn the grounds by which to discover and select from alternative interpretations of the score. Poetry, literature, and drama are more and more the objects of the kind of scrutiny which permits their appreciation as works of art rather than as sources of vicarious experience. More and more teachers of art permit their students the freedom for creation which society has long since accorded the professional artist. Nevertheless, the theorizing of the productive disciplines is still prevalent enough to render this warning relevant.

Let us turn to another organization of the sciences, notable in that one version of it is reborn with every undergraduate generation. This is Auguste Comte's positive hierarchy of the sciences. This scheme is based on the view that subject matter, and only subject matter, should provide the basis for classification. It takes the further view that subject matters should be ordered in terms of *their* subject matters; that is, Comte maintains that orders of phenomena can be discerned, each order consisting of members of the next lower order organized into more complex structures. Using this Chinese box conception of the world, Comte locates physical things as the simplest of all orders (presumably something like our modern fundamental particles). Chemicals come next, as consisting of physicals organized in a new way. Then come biologicals as still higher organizations of chemicals. Finally, at the top, come socials as organizations of biologicals. Thus the Comtian hierarchy of the sciences runs: physics, chemistry, biology, the social sciences. Then Comte adds one last factor. At the bottom of the entire structure he places another "science"—mathematics, mathematics conceived as a kind of natural logic governing the study of all the sciences above it.

Perhaps because of its simplicity and its tendency to be reborn in every generation, this particular organization of the disciplines has been one of the most tyrannical and unexamined curriculum principles in our time. It has dictated, I suspect, at least thirty-five per cent of all the sequences and orders of study of the sciences at the high school and college level in the country. The biologist tries to make his task easier by insisting that chemistry precede his subject field. In turn, the chemist demands that physics precede his. The physicist demands that mathematics precede physics. And each appeals to the Comtian hierarchy as the principal reason for his demand.

There is some justice in this view but there is injustice too. For it is quite possible to read the Comtian hierarchy the other way around. The inverted reading can, indeed, be done without departing from Comte's own principles, as Comte himself well knew. The principle in question requires that each science in the hierarchy shall be well developed before the one above it can be developed. Thus an adequate sociology must wait upon a thoroughly adequate biology; biology, in turn, cannot become complete until chemistry is complete, and so on. This *seems* to suggest that physics ought to be developed by a study simply of physical things, postponing chemistry until the study of physicals is complete; in the same way chemistry would be developed by a study of chemicals, postponing biology until the chemistry is complete. However, if we look closely at the basic Comtian principles, we realize that a complete, positive knowledge of the constituents and the organization of chemicals can be developed only if we have sought out and identified all the behaviors of which chemicals are capable. At this point arises the startling corollary that leads to an inverted reading of the Comtian hierarchy. For, clearly, if biologicals are organizations of chemicals, biologicals constitute the place in which some large array of chemical potentialities becomes real and can be seen. It follows, then, that a study of biologicals must precede any completion of chemistry; a study of socials must, in the same way, precede complete knowledge of biologicals, and so on.

The developments of science since the days of Comte most certainly bear out this reading of his hierarchy. Organic chemistry has developed only as we have studied the complex chemistry of the living organism. The behavior of the human individual has become better understood as we have studied human culture and society. The development by physicists of adequate theories of atomic structure rests upon knowledge of chemicals. Thus we see that it is just as plausible to read the Comtian hierarchy downward from sociology through biology, chemistry, and physics to mathematics, as it is to read it upward from mathematics to physics, to chemistry, to biology, and finally to social science.

We cannot, then, rest our arguments for mathematics as prerequisite to physics, physics prerequisite to chemistry, and so on, on the assumption that the upward reading of the Comtian hierarchy constitutes an unequivocal curriculum principle. Rather, we might well argue that bits and portions of each of these alleged prerequisites should be taught as the need arises during the study of the higher sciences. For example, physics might well be taught by examining the obvious behaviors of physical things up to the point where it becomes clear to student and teacher alike that further progress in the physics requires mastery of certain mathematical conceptions or operations. At this point, the class would turn to the mastery of the mathematics required by the physics under study. In the same way, the complex study of the microchemistry of the living cell would not be taught as a prerequisite to study of the organism and its larger parts and functions; rather, the visible behaviors of the organism, of its organ systems and gross organs might well come first, with the biochemical materials so placed as to be meaningful to the students as the physio-chemical basis for the behaviors already known.

The curriculum sequence of prerequisites based on the upward reading of the Comtian hierarchy (i.e., mathematics to physics to chemistry, etc.) is often referred to as the "logical order" of instruction. The fact that the Comtian hierarchy can be read plausibly in either direction requires us to realize, however, that the phrase "logical order" applied only to one of them is a special pleading. Either order is "logical." The upward order from mathematics to the social sciences we might well call the dogmatic order, i.e., the order that runs from the current explanation to that which is explained. The downward order from, say, biology to chemistry, we might call the order of enquiry, i.e., the order that runs from a display of phenomena calling for explanation to the explanation the science has developed. A curriculum choice between the order of enquiry and the dogmatic order cannot be made on subject-matter criteria alone. Rather, we must look to the capacities of our students, to knowledge of ways in which learning takes place, and to our objectives, what we hope our students will achieve, in order to make our decision.

The Problem of the Syntax of the Disciplines

If all disciplines sought only to know and if the knowledge they sought were merely the simple facts, the syntax of the disciplines would be no problem. As we have seen, the disciplines are not this simple. Many are not, in the Aristotelian sense, theoretical at all: they seek ends that are not knowledge but something else—making, the appreciation of what is made, the arts and habits of deliberation, choice, and action. Those that are theoretical seek knowledge of different kinds (commensurate to their subject matters), hence use different methods and different canons of evidence and warrantability. For example, science seeks very general or even universal knowledge, while much history seeks the most detailed and particular knowledge. Each of these objects of enquiry poses problems peculiar to itself. Hence knowledge of each of them is sought in different ways. Even within the sciences there is much variability. Biologists find it necessary or desirable to seek knowledge in bits and pieces while physicists, at the other extreme, work hard to develop broad, comprehensive theories which embrace vast ranges of subject matter.

The evidence that justifies the acceptance of an isolated bit of knowledge and the evidence that justifies the acceptance of a broad, comprehensive theory are of different sorts. There is a problem, therefore, of determining for each discipline or for small groups of disciplines what pathway of enquiry they use, what they mean by verified knowledge and how they go about this verification.

To illustrate this diversity, let us take three "things" that are asserted to exist and to have certain defining properties and behaviors. Let us take, first, an automobile, second, an electron, third, a neutrino. Let the three statements read as follows:

The automobile in front of the house is black.

The electron is a particle with a small mass and a negative electrical charge.

The neutrino is a particle with neither charge nor rest mass.

All three statements, let us suppose, are "true." That they are "true" in different senses becomes plain when we consider the following points. We say that the car in front of the house is black and say it with confidence on two bases. First, we look at the car and its neighborhood and report what we see. Second, we invite a colleague to look at the car and its neighborhood; we repeat the statement that reports what we saw; our colleague nods agreement. This, then, is a very simple syntax of discovery, requiring only a naive, private experience of the objects we propose to make statements about plus a transaction between ourself, another enquirer, and the same objects.

By contrast, the syntax that leads us to assert that the electron is a particle with a small mass and a negative electrical charge is far more complex. The statement most certainly does not rest on the fact that I have looked at an electron and that my colleague has also looked and nodded agreement. It cannot arise from such a syntax because the electron is not visible. It rests, rather, on a syntax that involves looking at quite different things, seeking agreement about them, and then adding two further steps. We note certain phenomena; others note the same; then we seek an *explanation* for what we have seen. For explanation we conceive the existence of a minute particle. To it, we assign precisely the mass and precisely the magnitude and kind of charge which would permit this particle—if it existed—to give rise to the phenomena we have observed. The two additional steps are hidden in the additional process of seeking explanation. First, we conceive of something that would account for the phenomena we are concerned about. However, we are not satisfied to use just any conception that will account for it. Rather, we demand that the conception fulfill a second condition: that it fit in with, be coherent with, the rest of the body of knowledge that constitutes our science. In the case of our electron we meet this condition by choosing a particular mass and a particular charge as its important properties. The choice of a particular mass ties our electron to the entire body of physical knowledge called gravitational dynamics. The assignment of a certain electrical charge ties our particle to our knowledge of electricity and its dynamical laws.

The assertion about the neutrino rests on still a third kind of syntactical structure. For not only are neutrinos invisible by definition but they have been assigned a *lack* of such properties as charge and rest mass which characterize the electron. The assigned lack of such properties means that in the ordinary course of events the behavior of neutrinos would have no detectable consequences, would give rise to no phenomena such as we observed and accounted for by positing the existence of the electron. Instead, the ground for positing the existence of the neutrino was roughly as follows: certain effects were found in a phenomenon called beta decay which appeared to be exceptions to certain of the so-called conservation laws, laws that formed part of the very foundation of the body of physical knowledge. One way to account for these beta decay phenomena would be to treat them as "disproofs" of these conservation laws. Another way would have been to treat the decay phenomena as exceptions to the conservation laws and then to dream up an ad hoc explanation for the exception. Physicists preferred, however (for reasons I shall not go into now), to keep the conservation laws intact and universal, and the only conceived alternative enabling them to retain these laws was to suppose the existence of a well-nigh undetectable particle that carried off the quantities whose disappearance would otherwise have called the conservation laws into question.

We have here, then, three different senses in which statements are said to be "true" or warranted, differences of sense not revealed by the statements themselves. The statements are all of the same form—the automobile is black, the neutrino is such and such, the electron is something else. Only the context, the structure of problem, evidence, inference, and interpretation which constitutes the syntax of discovery behind each statement, would reveal to us the different senses in which each is true.

The significance of this variety of modes of enquiry, of patterns of discovery and verification, lies in this: most statements of most disciplines are like the single words of a sentence. They take their most telling meanings, not from their dictionary sense, not from their sense in isolation, but from their context, their place in the syntax. The meaning of $F = MA$ or of free fall, of electron or neutrino, is understood properly only in the context of the enquiry that produced them.

This need for context of enquiry wherewith to make teaching and learning clear has been almost universally overlooked because of a singular failure in the subject-matter preparation of teachers. They have been permitted to assume, or, indeed, have been flatly told, that "induction" or "scientific method" stands for something simple, single, and well defined. Quite the contrary is true: "induction" is not the name for some single, definite process but merely an honorific word attached by various philosophers to whatever mode of enquiry they favor. To a few philosophers, "induction" means the process of simple enumeration of a large number of instances of something or other by which we try to discern what is common among them. In this view, the outcome of "induction" is "generalization." To other philosophers, "induction" means the analysis of phenomena into unit events and the attempt to find out which events invariably precede which others. To still others, "induction" means the attempt to conceive ideas, however remote they may be from the possibility of direct verification, which will "explain," "account for," "embrace," the largest possible variety of phenomena with the greatest economy.

The Problem of the Substantive Structures of the Disciplines

Let us first redevelop the idea of substantive structures and their role in enquiry as sketched in our introduction.

The fact that we propose to investigate a given subject is to admit that we are, in large part, ignorant of it. We may have some superficial knowledge: we may have dealt with the subject matter as part of our round of practical problems; but the very fact that we propose to investigate the subject means that we mistrust our knowledge or consider it entirely inadequate. Thus, enquiry begins in virtual ignorance. Ignorance however, cannot originate an enquiry. Subjects complex enough to demand enquiry are subjects that confound us by the great variety of characteristics, qualities, behaviors, and interactions they present to our view. This richness paralyzes enquiry, for it is far too much to handle all at once and, in our ignorance, we have no way of discerning the greater from the lesser fact; we cannot discriminate the facts that are most "telling" about our subject matter from those that are trivial. In short, if data are to be collected, we must have some sort of guide to relevance and irrelevance, importance and unimportance.

This role of guide to the enquiry is played by a conception borrowed or invented by the enquirer. These conceptions constitute the substantive structures of a discipline.

Let us take, as an example of a primitive beginning of enquiry, the situation that prevailed in the study of animal behavior some sixty years ago. Our knowledge of the behavior of small aquatic animals at that time was no greater than might have been possessed by an alert, small boy who had watched the darting of fish, the play of tadpoles, and the movements of insect larvae in the ponds and streams of his farm. What, then, should we investigate about these dartings, movements, and plays? Should we ask what needs they serve? Perhaps. Yet we do not even know that needs are involved. Shall we ask what purposes the animals have in mind? We do not know whether they have purposes or not. Shall we then try to discover the patterns of these motions, the order in which they occur? The trouble with this is that when a vast number of movements are involved, we must suppose, by analogy to ourselves, that they do not all belong together. Hence the over-all order of them would be meaningless. Yet we cannot discern each coherent sub-group of motions because we do not yet know either the beginnings ("wants," "needs," "stimuli") or their terminations ("goals," "needs satisfied," "terminal response").

This frustration of enquiry was resolved by appealing to the then popular view that all things, including living things, were no more than simple machines, the pattern of which was the simple one known to nineteenth-century physics. This idea of a simple machine was applied to the study of behavior by supposing that every movement through space of an animal was a response to some single, specific, stimulating factor in the environment. It was further supposed that each such stimulated response could be one of only two possible kinds—a movement toward the stimulus or a movement away from it. Such a movement was dubbed a "tropism," "taxis"; movements toward the stimulus being called positive, those away from the stimulus, negative.

This naive and now obsolete conception removed the frustration of enquiry by giving us questions to ask. We were to determine for each organism what stimuli it responded to and whether it responded in the positive or negative sense. These identified questions in turn determined the pattern of experiment. We were to place our aquatic organism in a tank of water, make sure that all physical stimuli but one were uniform throughout the tank, let one stimulus, light, for example, be of high intensity at one end of the tank and low intensity at the other, and then note, as our important datum, which way the animal went. Then our knowledge of animal behavior was to be summed up in a catalogue of negative and positive tropisms characteristic of each species investigated.

Similar naive conceptions enabled us to begin enquiry in other complex fields. Chemistry was able to make great advances in the study of the array of substances of the world by imposing on them the notion of "element." By "element" was meant a substance of ultimate simplicity, a substance made only of itself and incapable of being changed into another such simple substance. This conception dictated the questions to be asked of matter by chemists and the patterns of experiment. The fundamental question was: into what simpler substance can this substance be decomposed? Hence the patterns of experiment were analysis and synthesis. Similar "elements" were devised to guide our earliest enquiries into human personality. We conceived of each human person as consisting of a greater or lesser quantity of each of a number of "traits." Like the chemical elements, each such "trait" (such as courage, imagination, logical reasoning, assiduity) was supposed to be simple (made of no further sub-traits) and independent of all other traits.

The substantive principles chosen to guide enquiry are controlled by two opposing criteria. One of these I shall call reliability. Reliability requires that the guiding principle be free of vagueness and ambiguity, that the referents of its terms have unequivocal location and limit, and that the measurements or manipulations of these referents can be made precisely and can be repeated with uniform results. The substantive structures cited as examples above meet this criterion as well as could be expected.

They do not, however, satisfactorily fulfill the second criterion, which I shall call validity. Note the failure in each case which illustrates the lack of adequate validity. Animal behavior is reduced to a catalogue of independent responses to independently acting stimuli. Yet our knowledge of ourselves and of higher animals makes it highly unlikely that any animal's behavior will be a repertory of separate and independent responses to stimuli. It is much more likely (we suspect) that previous responses modify later ones and that the response to two stimuli presented simultaneously will *not* be the algebraic sum of the responses to each when presented separately. The idea of simple and independent traits, which enabled us to make a start on a study of human personality, is similarly questionable. It is entirely likely that traits are not independent at all but, rather, affect one another. Further, traits may not be fixed quantities but products of experience, changing as our experience grows and changes. Indeed, it may be that a much richer and more complete understanding of human personality could be achieved by doing away entirely with a notion of traits in any form. The notion of chemical element and compound in its most primitive form we may also suspect to be highly incomplete. It supposes that the properties of a compound arise simply by juxtaposition or union of two or more elements. Yet our experience in art, architecture, and engineering tells us that it is not only the constituents of a compound which confer properties on the compound but the organization of these constituents as well.

In short, the criterion of validity asks that the data we use be not only reliable but representative. It asks that the substantive structure that points to these data as the appropriate data of enquiry reflect as much as possible of the richness and complexity of the subject matter to which it is applied.

The existence of these two criteria is important to us because they lead to two characteristics of knowledge which, in turn, have important implications for curriculum. In the first place, the play of these two criteria confer on scientific knowledge a distinctly revisionary character. In the second place, in some sciences the same interplay leads to the concurrent development of a number of bodies of knowledge of the same subject matter.

The revisionary character of scientific knowledge accrues from the continuing assessment and modification of substantive structures. As investigations proceed under the guidance of an early, naive structure, we begin to detect inconsistencies in our data and disparities between our conclusions and the behavior of our subject. These inconsistencies and disparities help us identify the invalidities in our conception. Meanwhile, the naive structure has enabled us nevertheless to gain some knowledge of our subject and to sharpen our techniques for study. Our new knowledge of the subject, our improved techniques, and our sharpened awareness of inadequacies in our substantive structures enable us to conceive new structures more complex than the old, more adequate to the richness of the subject matter. With the advent of a new structure, the knowledge contained in the older conceptions, though "right" enough in its own terms, is rendered obsolete and replaced by a new formulation which puts old facts and new ones together in more revealing ways.

While different substantive structures tend to succeed one another in physics, chemistry, and biology, other disciplines are characterized by the concurrent utilization of several sets of structures. In the recent study of human personality, for example, two bodies of knowledge competed in the market place at the same time. One body of knowledge had been developed by conceiving personality, after the analogy of the body, as consisting of psychic organs. The other body of knowledge had been developed by conceiving of personalities as arising from the need of persons for one another, as developing, for better or for worse, out of the experience of self and of others. Personality, this body of knowledge held, is best described in terms of the various relations the self can establish with others.

Such a pluralism of substantive structures and of bodies of knowl-edge is characteristic of the social sciences generally and of many humane studies. There is more than one body of economic knowledge; different anthropologists and different sociologists tackle their problems in different terms and in different ways; different critics use widely different conceptions of the art object in the analysis and evaluation of drama, poetry, music, and painting.

The curricular significances of the revisionary character of knowledge and the plural character of knowledge are too numerous to develop fully here. Let us be satisfied with three.

In the first place, both characteristics point to the danger of a purely dogmatic, inculcative curriculum. If we dogmatically select one of several bodies of theory in a given field and dogmatically teach this as the truth about its subject matter, we shall create division and failure of communication among our citizens. Students of different school systems in different regions who are dogmatically taught different histories of crucial moments in our nation's development are an obvious case in point. It is no less divisive, however, if our future citizens are barred from sharing enjoyment of literature and the arts by having been the victims of different dogmas, or barred from understanding each other by having been inculcated with different dogmatic views of the roots of human action or the origins of culture and civilization. The alternative is to avoid indoctrination. We may, if we like, choose but one of several pluralities of bodies of knowledge. But if we do, let it be taught in such a way that the student learns what substantive structures gave rise to the chosen body of knowledge, what the strengths and limitations of these structures are, and what some of the alternative structures are which give rise to alternative bodies of knowledge.

The revisionary character of knowledge assumes curriculum significance because revisions now take place so rapidly that they will probably occur not once but several times in the lives of our students. If they have been taught their physics, chemistry, or biology dogmatically, their discovery that revision has occurred can lead only to bewilderment and disaffection. Again, the alternative is the teaching of scientific knowledge in the light of the enquiry that produced it. If students discover how one body of knowledge succeeds another, if they are aware of the substantive structures that underlie our current knowledge, if they are given a little freedom to speculate on the possible changes in structures which the future may bring, they will not only be prepared to meet future revisions with intelligence but will better understand the knowledge they are currently being taught.

20 / ARNO A. BELLACK

The Structure of Knowledge and the Structure of the Curriculum

During the current period of curriculum reform, most of the debate hinges on an old and familiar question: "What shall the schools teach?" This is a perennial question, one that apparently every generation has to solve over again for itself in the light of changing conditions and changing needs. And it is a question that can be answered only by reference to one's view of the nature of knowledge, for by universal agreement knowledge is the stock-in-trade of the school. Few would deny that the fields of organized inquiry are significant aspects of our culture that the school is uniquely equipped to introduce to students.

But there is also general agreement that the school's responsibility extends beyond teaching the organized fields of learning and inquiry; the school must also serve a multitude of ends and needs created by our society and our culture. At different times in the history of our schools widely different views have been held regarding the way in which knowledge should be organized and taught to meet these ends and needs. The traditionalists, for example, taught the time-honored subjects as anthologies of separate topics, with the hope that the bits and pieces of information would somehow or other turn out to be useful in the lives of their students. History became a recital of "one damned thing after another" (the phrase is Toynbee's), civics turned out to be a collection of miscellaneous information about government, and geography was nothing more than a catalogue of facts about places scattered over the globe.

Convinced that this kind of teaching would not prepare students to face the increasingly complex problems of their society, the progressive reformers of the 1930's and '40's proposed a new curriculum—one centered on the personal and social problems of youth and drawing on the academic disciplines as they became relevant to the problems under study. The disciplines were viewed as reservoirs from which facts and

Arno A. Bellack, "The Structure of Knowledge and the Structure of the Curriculum," in *A Reassessment of the Curriculum* (New York: Bureau of Publications, Teachers College, Columbia University, 1964), pp. 25–40. Reprinted by permission.

ideas could be drawn as needed; emphasis was on the *practical* ordering
of knowledge with reference to problems to be solved.

Contemporary efforts to redefine the role of knowledge in the curriculum place emphasis on the *logical* order inherent in knowledge itself, on
the structure of concepts and principles of inquiry that characterize the
various fields of learning. Whereas formerly factual and descriptive
content was stressed, now the emphasis is on basic concepts and methods
which scholars use as intellectual tools to analyze and order their data.

Several claims are made for teaching the fundamental structures of the
disciplines, two of which are of central importance and are worth
considering here. The first is that understanding of fundamental ideas is
the main road to adequate transfer of training. Professor Bruner, who is
largely responsible for introducing the concept of structure into educational discourse, observes that

> knowledge is a model we construct to give meaning and structure
> to regularities in experience. The organizing ideas of any body of
> knowledge are inventions for rendering experience economical
> and connected. We invent concepts such as force in physics, the
> bond in chemistry, motives in psychology, style in literature as
> means to the end of comprehension. . . . The power of great
> organizing concepts is in large part that they permit us to
> understand and sometimes to predict or change the world in
> which we live. But their power lies also in the fact that ideas
> provide instruments for experience.

Therefore, he contends, "the structure of knowledge—its connectedness
and its derivations that make one idea follow another—is the proper
emphasis in education."[1]

The second important claim for emphasis on structure is that by
constantly re-examining material taught in the schools for its fundamental patterns of organization, the schools will be able to narrow the gap
between "advanced" knowledge and "elementary" knowledge. Since
scholars at the forefront of their disciplines are able to make the greatest
contribution to the substantive reorganization of their fields, current
curriculum projects place great emphasis on the participation of university researchers in continuing revision of the program of studies. Scholars
in the various disciplines and their professional organizations have in
recent years made proposals for revamping the curriculum in elementary
and secondary schools—first in mathematics, physics, chemistry, and
biology; then in English; and recently and belatedly in economics,
geography, anthropology, and history.

[1] Jerome Bruner, *On Knowing* (Cambridge, Mass., Harvard University Press,
1962), p. 120.

The focus of attention in each of these projects is an individual discipline. Little or no attention is given to the relationships of the individual fields to each other or to the program of studies within which they must find their place. National committees in the fields of chemistry, physics, and biology have proceeded independently of each other. The projects in economics, geography, and anthropology are unrelated to one another or to the other social sciences. Only in mathematics has there been a disposition to view the field as a whole, but this is a reflection of developments within the discipline of mathematics at the highest levels of scholarship.

The situation developing in the elementary and secondary schools thus begins to reflect, at least to some degree, the state of affairs in the universities with respect to the development and organization of knowledge, which Professor John Randall has described in this way:

As reflected in the microcosm of the modern university, the world of knowledge has today become radically plural. It is a world of many different knowledges, pursued in varied ways to diverse ends. These many inquiries are normally carried on with little thought for their relation to each other. The student of John Donne's poetry, the student of the structure of the atom—each gives little enough attention to what the others are doing, and none at all to any total picture of anything. Each has his own goals, his own methods, his own language for talking about what he is doing and what he has discovered. Each seems happiest when left to his own devices, glad indeed if he can keep others from treading on his toes. Each is convinced that what he himself is doing is worth while. But none has too much respect for the others, though he is willing enough to tolerate them. They have all little understanding of each other's pursuits—what they are trying to do, how they are doing it, and what they really mean when they talk about it.[2]

I emphasize this pluralism in the academic world not to deplore it but to call attention to the problem that it presents for those who are concerned with the organization of the entire curriculum. For the curriculum builder is concerned not only with the structures of the individual disciplines, but also with the structure of the instructional program within which the fields of knowledge find their place. The problem can be very simply stated, if not easily solved: What general structure of the curriculum can be developed so that autonomy of the parts does not result in anarchy in the program as a whole? This is the question I propose to discuss briefly here.

When one looks beyond the structure of the individual disciplines and asks about the structure of the curriculum, attention is focused on

[2] John H. Randall, Jr., "The World to be Unified," in Lewis Leary, ed., *The Unity of Knowledge* (Garden City, N.Y., Doubleday and Company, 1955), p. 63.

relationships among the various fields that comprise the program of studies. For just as relationships among ideas is at the heart of the concept of structure as applied to the individual disciplines, so relationships among the disciplines is at the heart of the notion of structure as applied to the curriculum as a whole.

The mathematics teacher, the science teacher, the music teacher, and so on through the list of specialized functionaries in the school—each tends typically to interpret the entire program of the school through his own specialized teaching field. This is probably inevitable, and it would not be undesirable except for one stubborn fact: each of the specialized aspects of the program deals with human beings, and since human beings are not infinitely plastic in adapting to particular situations, it follows that what goes on at one place in the system sets limiting conditions for the accomplishments of purposes elsewhere in the system. Hence the importance of giving attention not only to connections between ideas in an individual field, but also to relationships among the fields of knowledge included in the curriculum.

There are many ways in which one can conceive of these inter-connections. I should like to focus attention on three types of relationships that obtain (or *ought* to obtain) among the teaching fields that comprise the curriculum:

(1) *Relationships among cognate or allied disciplines that deal with similar problems or phenomena.* Here I have in mind, for example, relations among the social sciences, whose common objective is to describe and explain the social and cultural behavior of man; and connections among the natural sciences, whose common aim is to describe and explain physical and biological phenomena.

(2) *Relationships among the broad areas of knowledge—the sciences and mathematics on the one hand, and the humanities on the other.* Call to mind the problem raised by C. P. Snow in his *The Two Cultures and the Scientific Revolution,* the great gulf that lies between the literary world and the scientific world. Snow insists that the only way to close the gap between the two cultures is by rethinking our education.

(3) *Relationships of knowledge to human affairs.* Given the current emphasis on the role of organized knowledge in the curriculum, we do well to remind ourselves that the goal of general education is not to train students as specialists in mathematics, geography, biology, or whatever other subjects they might study. Rather, the goal is to make available to students the intellectual and aesthetic resources of their culture in such a way that they become guides for intelligent action and help students create meaning and order out of the complex world in which they find themselves.

Let us briefly examine these three types of relationships.

I. Relationships Among Allied Disciplines

According to long and honorable tradition, knowledge is grouped for pedagogical purposes in four major categories—the natural sciences, the social sciences, mathematics, and the humanities (the latter an omnibus term that includes art, literature, philosophy, and music). These broad groupings of organized disciplines are generally recognized as basic cultural interests of our society which constitute both the resources and the obligations of the schools. Each major field represents distinctive methods and conceptual schemes in which the world and man are viewed from quite different vantage points. Instruction in these areas has as its primary goal equipping students with key concepts and methods that inform and sustain intelligent choice in human affairs.

Although the four major areas of knowledge are generally recognized as important components of the curriculum, they are not currently used as the context or framework for curriculum building. Instead, as we have already noted, recent curriculum projects have focused attention on individual disciplines without concern for their relationships to allied fields. Thus the economists, the geographers, and the anthropologists have proceeded independently of each other, as have the biologists, chemists, and physicists. To be sure, economists suggest ways in which economic ideas can be taught in history; and anthropologists show how some of their generalizations can be woven into courses in geography. This is all to the good; it even seems to suggest that integration of a limited variety might be appropriate for teaching purposes. But scant attention is given to building a curriculum design within which the individual fields might find their place.

It is my contention that this approach has certain inherent shortcomings and that we would do well to shift the context for curriculum planning from the individual disciplines, as is now the vogue, to the broad groupings of knowledge represented by the natural sciences, the social sciences, mathematics, and the humanities. Let us briefly consider some of the problems involved in curriculum building in the social sciences to show why this proposed shift is desirable and necessary.

The social sciences—economics, social psychology, political science, sociology, anthropology, geography, and history—are all seeking explanations of the same phenomenon, man's social life. This common goal is what makes it reasonable to group them together as the *social* sciences. All of them have grown out of man's attempt to interpret, understand, and control the social environment. But each field formulates its own questions about this subject matter and develops its own system of concepts to guide its research. The economist is preoccupied with the concept of scarcity, the political scientist with the concepts of power and authority, the anthropologist with the notion of culture, and the sociologist with social functions and social systems. Each science is thus abstract, dealing with only certain facets of actual social relationships and institutions—facets that do not permit of physical separation but only of analytical separation.

Man's social life as it is actually lived is therefore far more complex than the limited image of it reflected in the concepts and generalizations of any one of the social disciplines. It follows then, as Professor Kingsley Davis has suggested, that "in so far as the prediction of actual events is concerned, the various social sciences are mutually interdependent, because only by combining their various points of view can anything approaching a complete anticipation of future occurrences be achieved."[3] Policies that are proposed and actions that are taken to deal with problems in social affairs are of necessity interdisciplinary, for concrete social reality is not mirrored in the findings of any one discipline.

Now this is a matter of central importance to those whose job it is to plan and organize the social studies curriculum. To focus exclusive attention on certain aspects of the social world as seen through the eyes of one or two of the social sciences is to give students a myopic vision of man's social behavior and his institutions. To shape children's conceptions of the social world through exclusive emphasis on the language of the economist, for example, to the exclusion of the language of the sociologist, political scientist, anthropologist, and historian is to determine that they shall interpret human affairs principally in terms which the economist uses to view reality—in terms of supply, demand, scarcity, production, and consumption.

Students must be helped to see the limitations as well as the uses of a single discipline in interpreting events as they actually occur. And for anything approaching a comprehensive view of man's functioning in society, the specialized perspectives of all the social sciences are needed. Curriculum builders in the social studies have the enormously difficult job of providing a place in their programs for all the social sciences, each of which contributes its distinctive perspective on human institutions and human behavior.

It is clear that such a program can be developed only on the basis of collaboration among the various social sciences. Such collaboration does not presuppose a "unified social science" as the basis for planning the elementary and secondary school curriculum. Quite the opposite is the case. For the social disciplines today are characterized by a plurality of methods and conceptual schemes developed by social scientists to deal

---

[3] *Human Society* (New York, The Macmillan Company, 1948), p. 8.

with problems within their individual spheres. Instead of a unity of method or a single universe of discourse, we find a vast confederation of separate areas of study. Modes of thinking and analysis differ from field to field, and even from problem to problem within the same field. In time, a Bacon of the sciences that bear on the social and cultural behavior of man may emerge, but that time is not yet.

At the same time, in spite of increasing specialization and internal differentiation, there are interconnections among the social sciences that curriculum planning for the schools should take into account. For example, the various social sciences borrow rather handily from each other when it comes to both concepts and methods. Historians make use of concepts from all the other social sciences. Political scientists interested in political socialization get their methods from behavioral scientists and seem in many respects more closely related to sociologists and social psychologists than to fellow political scientists. Certain anthropologists have utilized the Freudian view of human development in analyzing patterns of various cultures. Geographers make extensive use of the perspectives of history and concepts developed by all the behavioral sciences.

Furthermore, we find not only interchange of concepts and methods but growing collaboration among specialists. For example, studies of the nature and function of "authority" are now undertaken jointly by political scientists and sociologists, and there have been recent studies conducted by economists in collaboration with anthropologists to determine whether certain economic theories hold for different types of economic systems. The convergence of social scientists upon the same problems has given rise to what Professor Robert Merton calls "interdisciplines," such as social biology, political sociology, and sociological history.

The picture that emerges from this cursory review of the current state of affairs in the social sciences is one of great diversity. Given this mosaic of disciplines and interdisciplines, each characterized by multiple conceptual schemes and methods, the curriculum builder is faced with the problem of developing structures for teaching that relate the social sciences to each other in meaningful ways and avoid undue fragmentation of knowledge.

What has been said about the social sciences applies in principle to the natural sciences, mathematics, and the humanities. The significant point is that there is a need for a broader context for curriculum planning than the separate disciplines, and the broad fields of knowledge furnish a useful framework for this purpose. I am not calling for indiscriminate scrambling of superficial knowledge. Indeed, at this point we would do well to suspend judgment as to when in the school program teaching should be organized around the individual disciplines, and when around the broad groupings of the disciplines. In all likelihood, different patterns of organization will be found to be appropriate for different levels of the school program. Dewey's notion of the "progressive organization of knowledge," long ignored by most of his interpreters, might serve as a guiding hypothesis in planning the sequence of the program through the elementary and secondary school years.

In sum, scholars in the natural sciences, the social sciences, mathematics, and the humanities should now be invited to join in the search for new structures for teaching—structures that respect the integrity of the individual fields and at the same time help these fields find their place in a pattern of studies that provides a substantial measure of coherence and relatedness for the program as a whole.

II. Relationships among Broad Fields of Knowledge

There is not only the question of relationships among disciplines that deal with similar problems or phenomena, but also the question of the relationships among the broad areas of knowledge—the sciences and mathematics on the one hand, and the humanities on the other. The growing separation and lack of effective communication between the arts and sciences have been widely noted and greatly deplored. C. P. Snow's analysis of this situation in terms of the two cultures of the literary intellectuals and the scientists is well known to all of us. That this state of affairs should somehow be remedied is the theme of many earnest discussions. The upshot of the discussion is usually that there is one way out of all this: it is, as Snow suggests, by rethinking our education.

But how shall the school go about bridging the gulf between the literary and aesthetic and the scientific studies? It seems reasonable to inquire first of all if human knowledge in its many dimensions forms a recognized unity within which the fields of inquiry and creativity fall neatly into place. Is there a sense in which all knowledge is one, with the arts and the sciences having a place in a unity of fundamental principles or basic methods of inquiry?

The progressives, taking their cue from Dewey, found for themselves such a unity in the "scientific method" (or the "method of intelligence," as it was frequently labeled) that was assumed to characterize all types of rational, intelligent activity in academic pursuits and in artistic and practical affairs as well. The problem-solving method came to be viewed as the basic ingredient in programs of general education.

But by no means is there agreement among scientists that there is a single all-encompassing set of procedures, even in the natural sciences, as assumed by those who talk about *the* scientific method. There seems to be little warrant for assuming that there is one overarching method sufficiently flexible and inclusive to deal with problems in the various scientific fields, to say nothing of the arts, crafts, and applied areas. Indeed, as we have already noted, the intellectual world today is characterized by a plurality of methods and conceptual schemes developed by the disciplines to deal with problems within their individual spheres. Analysis of the various disciplines reveals a wide range of organizations and intellectual methods associated with them. Instead of a unity of method or a single universe of discourse, we are confronted with a vast confederation of separate areas of study. Modes of analysis differ from field to field, and even from problem to problem within the same field.

The heterogeneous character of the intellectual resources that are a part of the culture is a fact of major significance for the curriculum builder. We would do well frankly to recognize this and make a place in our programs for the variety of logical orders that characterize the fields of knowledge on which we draw in building the curriculum.

But what then of the relationships among the various fields of creativity and inquiry? Is it perhaps possible, in spite of the variety of logical orders characteristic of knowledge in its various branches, to identify the principal kinds of cognitive operations or modes of thinking that characterize man's intellectual activities?

A proposal to facilitate students' insight into relationships among the various fields of knowledge by introducing them to the "principal modes of intellectual activity" comes from Professor Peterson of Oxford University. In making suggestions for the reform of secondary education in Britain, Peterson urges educators to stop thinking of general education in terms of "general knowledge":

"It is not a sign that a man lacks general education if he does not know the date of The Treaty of Utrecht, the latitude of Singapore, the formula for nitro-glycerine or the author of the *Four Quartets*. It does denote a lack of general education if he cares nothing for any of the arts, confuses a moral judgment with an aesthetic judgment, interprets the actions of Asian political leaders in terms of nineteenth-century English parliamentarianism or believes that the existence of God has been scientifically disproved."[4]

Peterson urges therefore that the British secondary schools devise programs of general education not in terms of wide general knowledge, but in terms of development in the main modes of intellectual activity, of which he identifies four: the logical (or the analytic), the empirical, the moral, the aesthetic. These different modes of thought are associated

[4] Oxford University Department of Education, *Arts and Sciences Sides in the Sixth Form* (Abingdon-Berkshire, The Abbey Press, 1960), p. 13.

with different uses of language. For example, the empirical mode has to do with statements about the world based on our experience of it. The analytic mode has to do with statements that do not describe the world of fact, but rather tell us how the meanings of symbols are related to one another logically. (A definition is a special case of analytic sentences.) The moral and the aesthetic modes are concerned with statements of preferences, evaluations, and judgments of the good and the evil, the beautiful and the ugly, the desirable and the undesirable.

Any one discipline gives opportunity for the development of more than one mode of thought, and each mode can be developed through more than one of the disciplines. For example, literature can contribute to the development of both moral and aesthetic judgment. Mathematics and philosophy both contribute to the development of the analytic mode. History has probably the widest range of any discipline, for the historian employs all four modes in constructing his comprehensive interpretation of what happened in the past.

If students are to gain understanding of the similarities and differences among the fields of knowledge, the different modes of mental activity must be made explicit to them:

"They must have time and guidance in which to see that what is a proof in the Mathematics they pursue on Tuesday is not the same kind of thing as a proof in History, which follows on Wednesday; that the truth of George Eliot or Joseph Conrad is not the same thing as the truths of Mendel or Max Planck; and yet that there are similarities as well as differences.[5]

Peterson accordingly suggests that in addition to giving attention to these varying modes of thought in the subject fields, the secondary program include a special course in which these ways of thinking are the object of study. One important aspect of such teaching has to do with ways in which these modes of thought are verified. Verification is particularly significant in that it is the guide to meaning of the various types of thought. For example, empirical statements are verified by tests conducted in terms of experience, whereas moral statements are verified by reference to criteria or principles of judgment. On the other hand, analytic statements depend for their truth on an agreed upon set of rules, and follow logically from accepted definitions.

Thus far I have suggested that in structuring the curriculum with due regard for the relationships among the fields of knowledge we view knowledge from two complementary perspectives. In the first, emphasis is on the conceptual schemes and methods of inquiry associated with the broad fields of knowledge, the natural sciences, the social sciences,

[5] *Ibid.*, p. 18.

mathematics, and the humanities. In the second, attention is focused on modes of thought—the analytic, the empirical, the aesthetic, and the moral—that transcend the boundaries of the individual fields. These two views thus represent mutually reinforcing conceptions of knowledge that serve well as the basis for curriculum planning.

Professor Toulmin has coined two terms that might be helpful in clarifying the relationships between these two views of knowledge. He distinguishes between "participant's language" and "onlooker's language."[6] Participant's language is the language used by members of a professional group or discipline as they carry on their work in their specialized field. Hence we talk today about the language of science, the language of psychology, the language of mathematics, and even the language of education. In the context of our discussion, participant's language has to do with the language systems that are the distinguishing characteristics of the various disciplined areas of study such as the sciences, mathematics, and the humanities.

Now if we want to examine or talk about the language we use in any one of these fields, we must use another level of discourse. We must, in Toulmin's terms, use onlooker's language. For example, it was suggested that students need help in understanding that a proof in mathematics is not the same as a proof in science or that the "truth" of a scientist is not the same as the "truth" of the poet or novelist. To make these comparisons and contrasts we need a language system that enables us to look at these various areas of study from the outside, as it were. The principal modes of thought—the analytic, the empirical, the moral, and the aesthetic—furnish us with language tools that are useful for this purpose. Hence their importance in teaching.

III. Relationships of Knowledge to Human Affairs

That the schools ought to provide students with the means for intelligent action is not a new or controversial idea. When, however, it comes to deciding what to teach and how to teach to accomplish this goal, we find marked differences of opinion.

Is it sufficient in general education, for example, to have students learn how to think like physicists, historians, or economists? I think not. For the economist *as* economist (to mention just one field) is in no position to prescribe courses of action regarding the host of public policy issues we face, and questions of public policy and decision loom large in general education. To be sure, economics does provide us with a body of theory

[6] S. Toulmin, *Philosophy of Science* (London, Hutchinson University Library, 1953), p. 13.

that is essential in examining the probable consequences of alternative economic policies, and a good many of these analytical tools ought to become part of the intellectual equipment of all students. Economists are able to tell us what the probable consequences will be if the supply of money is increased, or if the interest rates are lowered; but they cannot *as* economists tell us whether or not we ought to take either of these two courses of action. Decisions regarding these alternative courses of action involve technical economic analysis *and* weighing of values.

It is therefore clear that both values and economic theory are involved in deciding courses of action in economic affairs, and both must find their place in social studies teaching. Here the different modes of thought come prominently into play. Technical economic analysis involves the empirical mode of thinking (that is, it is concerned with matters of fact and theory), while considering alternative values involves the moral mode (that is, it is concerned with criteria of what is desirable or undesirable). The teacher's job is to help students learn to make these necessary distinctions, so that they recognize when questions of fact and analysis are under consideration and when questions of value are at stake.[7] This would of course hold as well for instruction in fields of study other than economics.

Thus far we have been talking about problems associated with a single field. But problems in the world of human affairs do not come neatly labeled "historical," "economic," or "political." They come as decisions to be made and force us to call upon all we know and make us wish we knew more. It was concern for broad cultural and moral questions that go beyond the boundaries of any one discipline that led the progressives to urge that students have the opportunity to deal with them in all their complexity. They proposed a new curriculum, one centered on the problems of youth and broad social issues and drawing upon the academic disciplines as they become relevant to the problems under study. This idea became the hallmark of progressivism in curriculum building. It gained wide acceptance among educators and found expression in many influential statements of policy and opinion during the 1920's, '30's, and '40's. Attempted applications of this viewpoint were made in courses labeled core, common learnings, and the like.

Difficulties in this approach soon became apparent, not the least of which was the students' lack of first-hand acquaintance with the disciplines that were the source of the concepts and ideas essential to structuring problems under study. Without adequate understanding of

---

[7] See *Economic Education in the Schools,* Report of the National Task Force on Economic Education, 1961.

the various fields of knowledge, students had no way of knowing which fields were relevant to problems of concern to them. Indeed, without knowledge of the organized fields it was difficult for them to ask the kinds of questions about their problems that the various disciplines could help them answer.

Giving students an opportunity to grapple with broad social and cultural problems was basically a promising innovation. But at the same time one is forced to recognize that problem solving on such a broad base cannot be pursued successfully without growing understanding of the fields of knowledge on which the problem solver must draw.

Recognizing then the value in systematic study of the fields of knowledge and the importance of developing competence in dealing with problems and issues that are broader than those of any one field, the question arises of why opportunities for both types of activities should not be included in the program for all students. One might envision a general education program that would include basic instruction in the major fields defined earlier in this paper (the natural sciences, the physical sciences, mathematics, and the humanities), together with a coordinating seminar in which students deal with problems "in the round" and in which special effort is made to show the intimate relationships between the fields of study as concepts from those fields are brought to bear on these problems. Such a seminar would also furnish excellent opportunities to help students become aware of the different modes of thought and various types of language usage involved in dealing with problematic situations and the necessity for making clear distinctions among them.

This is not a new proposal. I am here dusting off an old idea first set forth in the 1956 ASCD Yearbook, *What Shall the High Schools Teach?* In making this suggestion, we were much influenced by Dewey's contention that

> "The aim of education should be to secure a balanced interaction of the two types of mental attitude (the practical and the theoretical), having sufficient regard to the disposition of the individual not to hamper and cripple whatever powers are naturally strong in him. The narrowness of individuals of strong concrete bent needs to be liberalized. Every opportunity that occurs within practical activities for developing curiosity and susceptibility to intellectual problems should be seized. Violence is not done to natural disposition; rather, the latter is broadened. Otherwise, the concrete becomes narrowing and deadening. As regards the smaller number of those who have a taste for abstract, purely intellectual topics, pains should be taken to multiply opportunities and demands for the application of ideas, for

translating symbolic truths into terms of everyday and social life. Every human being has both capabilities, and every individual will be more effective and happier if both powers are developed in easy and close interaction with each other."[8]

Let it be recognized that the difficulties in building a curriculum that takes account of the relationships among the various fields of inquiry and creativity are overwhelming. The greatest difficulty is that the job involves the collaboration of specialists—in the various disciplines, in curriculum development, and in teaching. In such collaborative efforts it would seem that curriculum specialists, concerned as they are with the instructional program as a whole, have a crucial role to play. But in all frankness it must be recognized that they do not play a central crucial role in curriculum revision projects now underway. Whether they will be able to do so in the future is another matter. And I suspect that whether they will indeed make the contribution one might reasonably expect them to make will depend, first of all, on their ability to work effectively with representatives of the various fields of knowledge to identify important relationships among these fields and to fashion programs of instruction that take due account of these relationships and connections; and secondly, on their ability to build curricula that help students see the relevance of the intellectual resources of the culture for their own lives as productive workers, as citizens, and as individuals. For as Professor Bestor, who scarcely qualifies as an advocate of education for life adjustment, has reminded us, "The basic argument of the intellectual disciplines in education is not that they lift a man's spirits above the world, but that they equip his mind to enter the world and perform its tasks."[9]

[8] *How We Think* (Boston, D. C. Heath and Co., 1933), pp. 228–229.
[9] *Educational Wastelands* (Urbana, Ill., University of Illinois Press, 1953), p. 15.

Questions for Discussion

Aristotle shows why he believes that men by their very nature desire to *know*, and claims that the best combination for men is to have knowledge along with experience. He believes teaching is based more on knowledge than experience, for men of mere experience cannot teach. The things that are universal are the most difficult to know and the wise man is one who has universal knowledge. The Theoretical refers to the sciences which provide exact knowledge of first principles and causes. Aristotle points out the differences between acting and making and considers Practical Wisdom as the ability to make judgments and act in social and political affairs, while the Productive is concerned with making and creating things.

Does Aristotle recognize individual differences? How could Aristotle's system be used to classify knowledge and establish a basis of a curriculum? Take a stand by either defending or opposing his position.

Comte arranges the sciences in a hierarchial order. He distinguishes between the abstract or general sciences and the concrete ones. The former are distinguished as those which derive or develop laws, while the latter apply laws to concrete situations. His classification starts with general or simple phenomena and moves to particular or more complex phenomena. Notice how he carries out his classification in relation to his interpretation of the different disciplines. What do you believe to be the strengths and weaknesses of this approach? How would you organize a curriculum using Comte's system? Explain the essential differences between the approaches of Aristotle and Comte.

Schwab notes in his essay that the structure of the disciplines has changed as knowledge has advanced. Even though in recent times there has been an integration of separate bodies of knowledge, some of the distinctions that are presently found among the disciplines may be perennial. By determining the relations of the disciplines, it is possible for us to know how instruction is to be organized. Furthermore, we need to understand the substantive conceptual structure that constitutes each discipline and the logical modes of operation by which new knowledge is gained. Notice, too, that Schwab offers interpretations of Aristotle's and Comte's contributions to contemporary theories of the disciplines.

Bellack examines the claims of the adherents of the structure of knowledge school of thought and compares their contributions to some of those that grew out of the progressive education movement. The latter gave greater attention to the student and to ways in which the teacher could foster learning. There are certain advantages to the broad fields approach that still merit consideration. Bellack believes that we need to seek relationships among the disciplines to avoid anarchy in the curriculum as a whole.

Compare the positions of Schwab and Bellack and indicate the contributions of each essay. What do you believe is today the most vital philosophical problems surrounding knowledge and the curriculum?

CHAPTER SIX

EDUCATIONAL CONCEPTS AND PHILOSOPHICAL ANALYSIS

DURING the 1930's, philosophy began turning away from metaphysical investigations of the nature of reality and being, and began concentrating on small scale, rigorous investigations of the methodology and logical operations of the sciences. Other groups attended to the resolution of philosophical puzzles that arise through the misuse of language. The interest in language and conceptual problems, which resulted in an active movement (commonly referred to as ordinary language analysis) in the United States and Great Britain, is generally attributed to the later works of Ludwig Wittgenstein of Cambridge University.

Philosophers of education have increasingly concerned themselves in recent years with ordinary language and the conceptual *structure* of education. Analytic philosophers have sought to expose ambiguities and illogical uses of educational terms which lead to conceptual confusions, both in theory and in practice. This approach repudiates the dominance of philosophies that endeavored (in the past) to encompass all aspects of education within an overarching systemic framework; instead, those engaged in philosophical analysis now deal with a more limited domain of key conceptual problems. Philosophical analysis traces the misuse of concepts, clarifies their logical operations, and reinterprets the role they play in education.

Philosophical analysis is not just one technique or one type of activity but consists of a number of activities that can be grouped together because they share a family resemblance. Analysts point out that there are a number of ways of operating

274

with language, or that there are a number of language games. Some philosophers have tended to think of all languages as words whose "meanings" consist of the objects or ideas or activities that the words "stand for" or "name." But this is only one language game, a naming game. One learns to play the game by pointing to the thing denoted and pronouncing its name. But just learning the names of things does not teach us how to use them; instead, we learn the meaning of a word by learning its use. There are language games other than naming: reporting events, giving orders, testing an hypothesis, telling a joke, solving a problem, describing an object, and others. To understand how to use a language is to understand how to operate within the rules of various language games.

The richness and the ambiguity of language is both its strength and its shortcoming. For example, our basic educational concepts are *framed* in a variety of ways and may also be *expressed* in an ambiguous or conceptually confused fashion. The search for alleged essences is anathema for analysis. Instead, philosophical analysis seeks to identify the uses of terms in educational discourse and to observe their linguistic movement. It also examines educational assumptions and the criteria and adequacy of arguments. After this primary work of analysis is completed, a logical reconstruction of the conceptual structure is made to remove the original source of perplexity and to render educational discourse more adequate for carrying its conceptual load.

Philosophical analysis has led to a refinement of techniques of inquiry and to a rigorousness in their use. Its proponents believe that theirs is a more fruitful way of approaching philosophy of education and, although one should not expect spectacular results—on a broad scale—within a short period of time, the results of such analyses should not be underestimated. Others believe that building philosophical systems is the activity in which philosophers of education should be engaged. The reader will have the opportunity to judge the merits of philosophical analysis in the essays in this section.

These selections are taken from writings of educators who have become known for their work in philosophical analysis. They have used their analyses to deal with the shortcomings they have found in the conceptual structure of education.

The essay by Newsome (Selection 21) provides a clear and accurate overview of the value of analysis for education, while the other selections in this section deal with specific educational concepts. Newsome shows how analytic philosophers operate with concepts and points up the shortcomings they have found in more traditional approaches to philosophical problems. He then relates how analytic philosophy may contribute to the development of education theory.

Almost no concept has received more of a workout in educational literature than has that of "need" or "needs." It would little matter if the concept did not play a substantive role, but all too frequently educators have used the concept in various ways to establish educational aims, determine curriculum content, and evaluate desirable teacher-pupil relations. In Selection 22 Archambault makes a systematic and scholarly review of the "need" concept, shows its ambiguities, and offers direction for a clearer conceptual structure.

Selection 23 is a careful philosophical analysis of a concept that is of primary importance in education. Komisar and Coombs present two different interpretations of equality in education, explore their educational consequences, and then provide a critique. Proposals are made for a more exact and fruitful use of the concept, along with the educational import of using it in this fashion.

For too many years, educators have concentrated their study of the teaching-learning process on the principles of learning and motivation; rarely has the teaching act itself and what the teacher does been carefully examined. In Selection 24, however, B. Othanel Smith sheds light on a host of problems and explodes a few misconceptions along the way. He shows how teaching is confused with related activities, and he tries to clarify the nature of the teaching act—a central concern of education.

21 / GEORGE L. NEWSOME, JR.

Analytic Philosophy and Theory of Education

For better or worse, analysis, logical and linguistic, is being offered by some of its advocates as a theory of education, or possibly even as a theory of educational theories. What are some of the distinguishing features of analytic philosophy? What are the pitfalls in relating analysis to education? Is analytic philosophy a second order theory of education? How may analytic philosophy contribute to the development of theory in education? Can analytic philosophy adequately meet the demands of a practical discipline such as education? For the purposes of discussing

George L. Newsome, Jr., "Analytic Philosophy and Theory of Education," *Proceedings of the Sixteenth Annual Meeting of the Philosophy of Education Society*, published by the society, June, 1960. Used by permission of Ernest E. Bayles, editor of the *Proceedings*, and George L. Newsome, Jr.

and clarifying these kinds of questions, an analytic approach will be taken in this paper.

Distinguishing Features of Analytic Philosophy

Although analytic philosophy may be termed a "school of thought," it is not a system of philosophy. Indeed, from the analytic point of view, systems of philosophy are repudiated.[1] Within the school of analytic philosophy there are numerous differences of opinion concerning matters philosophical. It seems to make little difference, however, whether one looks to the group stressing informal logic and common language or to the group emphasizing symbolic logic and philosophy of science, philosophical analysts seem to agree on one major function of philosophy: clarification. By and through philosophical analysis (logical and linguistic) what men say (statements, sentences, or propositions) can be clarified and made meaningful or exposed as nonsense.

The statements that men make are, of course, sometimes clear and meaningful, but because of the "open texture" of language, ambiguity, vagueness, and other linguistic difficulties, confusion arises. Furthermore, and probably even of greater concern, because of "improper" philosophical training, common sense notions, or just plain ignorance, emotive and metaphysical statements worm their way into discourse. Lest such emotional expressions and "nonsense" pass for statements of fact or "profound insights," language must be subjected to a thorough and dispassionate scrutiny loosely termed "analysis."

Just how one performs analysis, the particular methods and techniques by which language is analyzed, and the various tests or criteria of meaning are matters of major concern and debate among analytic philosophers. Although analytic philosophers disagree about many aspects of analysis, they do seem to be in general agreement concerning several ways in which analytic philosophy differs from the traditional philosophies of Western culture.

1. Analytic philosophers strongly contend that truths about human experience and the universe cannot be discovered by philosophical means.[2] Matters of empirical fact and truths about the world are discovered or established by science—not by philosophers.

---

[1] Herbert Feigl, "Aims of Education For Our Age of Science: Reflections of a Logical Empiricist" in *Modern Philosophies and Education* (Chicago: The University of Chicago Press, 1955), p. 304; Israel Scheffler (ed.), *Philosophy and Education* (Boston: Allyn and Bacon, Inc., 1958), p. 7; and Richard W. Dettering, "Philosophical Semantics and Education," *Educational Theory*, 7:143–149, July, 1958, p. 146.

[2] Alfred Jules Ayer, *Language, Truth and Logic* (New York: Dover Publications, Inc.), n.d., pp. 71–72; Arthur Pap, *Elements of Analytic Philosophy* (New York: The Macmillan Company, 1949), p. 6 and p. 478; and D. J. O'Connor, *Introduction to The Philosophy of Education* (New York: Philosophical Library, 1957), pp. 5–6.

2. Analytic philosophers seriously question (many completely reject) the idea of logical unity of truth, goodness, and beauty.[3] Many, if not most, analytic philosophers maintain that statements concerning matters of fact and statements of value are radically different kinds of statements which require entirely different means for verification.[4] Some analytic philosophers seriously doubt that statements of value can have any meaning beyond that of personal preference.[5]

3. Analytic philosophers strongly maintain that language does not give us a true picture or copy of reality.[6] Verbal expressions have only such meanings as we give them, and hence do not derive their meanings from objects in the world. We relate words to the world, and the relationship is not a "one-to-one" relationship that makes language exactly correspond to reality.

4. Analytic philosophers prefer to deal with the problems of man one by one and strongly resist the urge to construct broad, general, and speculative theories.[7]

5. Analytic philosophers, since they construct no general and speculative theories, do not consider analytic philosophy to be composed of metaphysical, ethical, or epistemological theories. To them the subject matter or analytic philosophy is thought of as theories for the clarification of language, and such concepts, methods, and presuppositions as might be found in most sciences.[8]

6. Since analytic philosophy is concerned only with clarification of language, most often the language of science or some other discipline, one can philosophize about almost anything, because to philosophize is to analyze language.[9]

Analysis, both logical and linguistic, has always in some form or other characterized philosophy. It was the stock in trade of Socrates, Plato, and

[3] Ayer, *op. cit.*, pp. 102–103; Dettering, *loc. cit.*, p. 147; and Charles L. Stevenson, *Ethics and Language* (New Haven, Conn.: Yale University Press, 1944), p. 173.

[4] Pap, *op. cit.*, pp. 23–26; Henry D. Aiken, "Moral Philosophy and Education," *Harvard Educational Review*, 25: 39–59 (Winter 1955), p. 51; and John Hospers, *An Introduction to Philosophical Analysis* (Englewood Cliffs, N.J.: Prentice-Hall, Inc., 1953), pp. 476–482.

[5] Reference here is made to those who view ethical statements as purely emotive expressions. For example, see Hospers, *op. cit.*, pp. 471–476 for discussion of this view, or Ayer, *op. cit.*, pp. 102–113 for a classic argument by one of the chief exponents of the emotive theory of ethics.

[6] Max Black, "Language and Reality," *Proceedings and Addresses of The American Philosophical Association*, 1958–59 (Yellow Springs, Ohio: The Antioch Press, 1959), pp. 16–17; Ayer, *op. cit.*, p. 42; and O'Connor, *op. cit.*, pp. 39–40.

[7] Scheffler, *op. cit.*, pp. 6–7; and Dettering, *loc. cit.*, pp. 146–147.

[8] Pap, *op. cit.*, p. 1.

[9] *Ibid.*, p. 478, and O'Connor, *op. cit.*, p. 4.

Aristotle.[10] From the time of Socrates to the present, analysis has frequently been employed as a means for ushering in synthesis and speculation, or philosophy in the "grand manner." Whatever analysis reduced, separated, or exposed, *a priori* metaphysics promptly restored, unified and justified as an ultimate reality, a transcendental entity, a state of the mind, or as some kind of unobservable, unknowable reality beyond the corrupting influence of linguistic analysis and the positive verification of science. Furthermore, *a priori* philosophers have, in spite of Ockham's Razor or the Principle of Parsimony, often multiplied entities beyond necessity. By assuming much, *a priori* philosophers sought to prove much, but their proof was no better than their assumptions, and frequently no more than the assumptions.[11] It is against this synthetic and speculative philosophy that analytic philosophers rebel.

Pitfalls in Relating Analysis to Educational Theory

Educators, when confronted with the problem of relating analytic philosophy to education, are likely to find analytic philosophy to be "strange" and different, and the usual ways of relating philosophy to education not very rewarding. Analytic philosophy seems to be lacking in the "systematic niceties," ideological, doctrinaire, and moralistic canons, and the more immediate practical applications to education to which educators seem to be accustomed. Analytic philosophy also confronts the educator with a new and strange terminology, with a "frightening calculus of language," with "distinctions too subtle for the practical minded," and with an alarming restriction upon treasured emotive and metaphysical statements. Moreover, in attempting to relate analytic philosophy to education, educators should be careful not to make one or more of the following mistakes: (1) Attempting to construct an analytic philosophy of education modeled after traditional systems and ideologies,[12] (2) Attempting to derive implications for education from analytic philosophy,[13] and (3) Becoming so fascinated with language games, logic, or philosophy of science that the relation of analysis to education becomes superficial.

The fact that philosophical analysis is analysis of language rather than

---

[10] Pap, *op. cit.*, Preface vii.

[11] Philosophy is not a system for proving by axiomatic methods truth about the universe in a metaphysical fashion. Logic, of course, does contain methods for proving, but such proofs are logical not metaphysical. For further discussion, see O'Connor, *op. cit.*, pp. 29–35.

[12] Scheffler, *op. cit.*, p. 2.

[13] Feigl, *op. cit.*, pp. 304–305.

analysis of feelings, mental states, or concrete situations, indicates that it is a second or third level order of analysis. Consideration of this fact suggests that instead of constructing an analytic philosophy of education or deriving educational implications from analytic philosophy, all one need do is employ analytic methods and techniques in analyzing statements about education.

Analytic Philosophy as Second Order Theory of Education

Education as a practical activity is a process which should not be confused with education as a discipline and body of knowledge. Education as a disciple is related to the process of teaching and learning, but it differs from the process in that it is composed of statements, rules, directives, principles, and the like about various aspects of practice. The discipline of education then is verbal and linguistic; it is knowledge that purports to be in a considerable measure propositional and cognitive in character. Frequently this discipline of education is termed "theory of education" although it might more appropriately be termed "pedagogical knowledge."[14]

The body of pedagogical knowledge contains many statements which do have genuine philosophical connotations. They appear on their face to be propositions which assert something significant about education. For example, such statements as "real and life-like activities produce more learning than assign-study-recite procedures," and "education is the process of self-realization in which the self realizes and develops all of its potentialities," appear to be genuine and significant propositions about education. How may these statements be verified? What kind of evidence would be needed for verification? What cognitive meanings do the propositions have? What matters of fact do they assert? What do such terms as "real," "life-like," "self," and "potentialities" mean? What does it mean to say a self realizes itself? When is a self, self realized? Questions of this sort suggest that neither of the two statements is clear or cognitively meaningful. Suppose a teacher were asked to implement either or both statements, how could one determine empirically the result or consequence? Are these statements metaphysical (necessary and synthetic), purely analytic (tautologies), emotive; or are they commands, questions, or resolves?

It is precisely questions of this sort about statements, as ambiguous and meaningless as those just cited with which analytic philosophy deals. By and through analysis, both logical and linguistic, educational philosophy

---

[14] Paul Komisar, "Pedagogical Knowledge and Teacher Education," *Proceedings of the Fifteenth Annual Meeting of the Philosophy of Education Society* (Lawrence: The University of Kansas Press, 1959), pp. 15–22.

as a second order of analysis can clarify and make meaningful or expose as nonsense many statements about pedagogy. When one carefully explores the meaning, the means of verifying, the semantics, the structure, and the context of such statements, he is playing the role of analytic philosopher. Furthermore, he is dealing with education at the second level of abstraction; namely, the level of clarifying statements of pedagogy.

How May Analytic Philosophy Contribute to the Development of Theory in Education?

Those who deal with pedagogy and philosophy of education frequently feel considerable pressure to provide, if possible, and justify, if necessary, a theory of education.[15] Can criticism and analysis meet the more positive challenge of helping to construct an integrative theory of education? Does not the discipline of education, since it is a hodge podge of facts and theories derived from other disciplines, need a unifying theory? Is not the chief function of philosophy that of constructing generalized theories (philosophies), be they metaphysical or not, as a prerequisite to a critical and analytical approach to theory?[16] Or is it that philosophy only needs to be clear about the more general relations that exist between and among matters of fact; or what one philosopher has termed "synoptic clarity"?

If a synoptic clarity be admitted, then can analytic philosophy clarify statements concerning the more general relations of matters of fact, and can it clarify the more general features of a theory of education? In certain respects analytic philosophy, if it be conceived relative to the task, can meet this demand. Analytic philosophy need not be viewed merely as sentence editing, or as lexicography, or as literary censorship.[17] Analytic philosophy can help to develop a defensible theory of education in the sense that it can help analyze and clarify language, provide models of theory, state criteria for meaning and verification, and in general, help unsnarl the logical and linguistic tangles in pedagogical knowledge.[18]

---

[15] Example of such concern for a "defensible theory" of education are "Symposium: The Aims and Content of Philosophy of Education," *Harvard Educational Review*, Vol. 26 (Spring 1956), and "A Symposium: What Can Philosophy Contribute to Educational Theory," *Harvard Educational Review*, Vol. 28 (Fall 1958).

[16] For example, *see* Harry S. Broudy, *Building a Philosophy of Education* (Englewood Cliffs, N.J.: Prentice-Hall, Inc., 1954), and J. Donald Butler, *Four Philosophies and Their Practice in Education and Religion* (New York: Harper and Brothers, 1957).

[17] Ayer, *op. cit.*, p. 59ff.

[18] Probably with the exception of a few articles and O'Connor's little book, not much seems to have been done along this line.

The degree to which analytic philosophy can actually bring about a unity of knowledge in education similar to that undertaken by some logical empiricists in the unified sciences movement remains to be seen.

Some of the characteristics of pedagogical knowledge present genuine difficulties for analytic philosophers. Many of the so-called "principles and theories" of teaching, learning, and curriculum are merely descriptions of practices, summaries of case studies, matters of opinion, or application of certain concepts such as democracy, socialization, or creative expression to educational practice. Pedagogical knowledge contains very few, if any, general laws under which individual facts can be adequately subsumed and explained. The so-called theories and principles of pedagogy are not only descriptive, but they frequently are directive as well. Descriptions and directives (prescriptions)[19] point to consequences rather than to logical conclusions.[20] Yet, somewhere between description and prescription, dealers in pedagogical knowledge apparently make some kind of logical inference. Such inferences are not deductions because no conclusions follow necessarily from established premises. Similarly, the inference is neither a valid inductive causal inference, nor a statistic inference in terms of probabilities. The only alternative left is that it is a probable inference, in some cases an inference based on reasoning by analogy.[21]

Probable inferences and reasoning by analogy, though weak, are not always false or unproductive. The major problem is to be found in evaluating such arguments and explanations. Though such arguments and explanations can be logically evaluated in part, ultimately one must appeal to some more fundamental explanation such as one finds in the sciences.[22] But, probable inference cannot always be so tested and verified. The prescriptions which come from the inference might be rather significant, in the opinion of many competent judges. The problem-project method of teaching and the core curriculum, for example, are frequently thought to be more productive than more traditional methods of teaching and curricula designs, yet empirical testings have not shown them to be decidedly superior. Educators, however, must make decisions; they must choose methods and curricula designs in terms of the best evidence and logical arguments available.

[19] Technically speaking, directive and prescriptive language is not the same and do not have the same meanings. Directions are, however, frequently put in persuasive form. For example, see Bernard Rabin, "Teachers' Use of Directive Language," *Educational Leadership*, 17:31–34 (October 1959), for various forms in which directive language appears.

[20] P. H. Nowell-Smith, *Ethics* (Penguin Books, Ltd., 1954), p. 149.

[21] See Irving M. Copi, *Introduction to Logic* (New York: The Macmillan Company, 1953), Chapter 11, pp. 311–326.

[22] *Ibid.*, p. 322.

They cannot postpone action until some remote future when scientific inquiry will have confirmed some one particular method or curricula plan. If choice must be made in absence of decisive evidence, then the educator would at least like to know as clearly as possible the probable consequence of his choice. Analytic philosophy can help the educator clarify statements of probable inference and help him clearly and logically state the probable consequences of choosing one course of action over another.

Since pedagogical knowledge is often prescriptive, practical, and not logically precise, one of an analytic persuasion might be tempted to dismiss too quickly pedagogical statements as emotive, cognitively meaningless, unanswerable, or the like. This however, might be a serious mistake based upon an untenable separation of thought from action, language from language function, ends from means, and logical and linguistic clarity from empirical consequences. Many of the significant statements in pedagogical knowledge do not seem to fit into the neat classifications of logic and language.[23] Facts do appear to color values and values do apparently influence choice among facts. Actions have consequences and consequences of actions seem ultimately to relate back to the logic and language of inquiry and deliberation which led to choice.

Pedagogical prescriptions are not all as illogical or emotive as one might suspect. Some prescriptions are much like those of the physician who, for example, might prescribe certain medicines and a diet as a remedy for some particular physical condition. Surely the prescription and its predicted consequences are not emotive or unscientific. Similarly, when the educator prescribes: "to promote interest and facilitate learning, employ life-like activities that meet the felt needs of the learner and come within the learner's range of experience"—he is providing a prescription and predicting consequences of its employment. Such a prescription with its stated consequences is not beyond empirical confirmation. If the kinds of evidence needed for confirmation can be specified, then the statement has meaning and can be clarified.

Many pedagogical statements are not as logically and linguistically "pure" as the foregoing illustration. Some are rather moralistic in character and their consequences, if any, "intangible." For example, if one should prescribe that "students ought always be treated as ends and never as means only," then a moralistic imperative has been introduced, the consequences of which seem to defy empirical confirmation. What is an end? How does one treat a student as an end? What meaning, if any, does the statement have? Similarly, many statements about educational

---

[23] For example, see Gilbert Ryle, *Dilemmas* (Cambridge University Press, 1954), Chapter 8—"Formal and Informal Logic," pp. 111–129.

aims and values and a wide variety of value judgments, when subjected to analysis reduce to statements of preference or emotive expressions of the form "I like such and such and so should you" or "hurrah for X."[24]

Mere preference, as a simple expression of desire or a "I like it," and intellectual preference based upon experience and anticipated consequences of action are quite different.[25] To be sure, some educational moralisms and value preferences are statements of simple preference which have little or no cognitive meaning. An intellectual preference, however, may be discussed in terms of experience, evidence, and probable consequences. Not only may it be intelligently discussed, but statements about it can be clarified.

Analytic philosophers who dismiss intellectual preference (moralistic or valuational) seem to hold to a rather narrow and truncated view of analysis. Such a narrow view might result from a confusion of substantive ethics with analytic ethics.[26] Substantive ethics deals with first-level problems of deliberation and choice. In pedagogical knowledge statements of substantive ethics serve as practical modes of communication, the main function of which is direction and control of conduct, not prediction of empirical fact.[27] Analytic ethics, on the other hand, is a second-level analysis of the language of ethics and hence is concerned largely with problems of logic and meaning.

Can Analytic Philosophy Meet the Demands of a Practical Discipline?

So far, in the short history of modern analytic philosophy its major successes have been in the fields of science and mathematics.[28] It is rather paradoxical, however, that modern natural sciences achieved their preeminence without analytic philosophy, indeed, often in opposition to philosophy. A philosophical analysis of science is somewhat like a chemical analysis of a known solution, neat, easy, and according to the rules. Philosophical analysis of the newer applied and practical disciplines, on the other hand, is more like the chemical analysis of an

---

[24] Many statements in educational discourse are purely statements of personal likes and dislikes. Arthur P. Coladarci and Jacob W. Getzels, *The Use of Theory in Educational Administration* (Stanford University Press, 1955), pp. 10–14, claim educators are afraid to theorize, have an inadequate professional language, and frequently tend to become emotionally identified with their own views.

[25] The distinction which is being made here is John Dewey's distinction between *desire* and *desirability*. See John Dewey, *Democracy and Education* (New York: The Macmillan Company, 1916), p. 279.

[26] Aiken, *loc. cit.*, p. 42.

[27] *Ibid.*, p. 51.

[28] Pap, *op. cit.*, Prefact viii.

unknown solution; very necessary, perhaps, but very difficult and uncertain. In natural sciences and mathematics a rather "firm" language has been developed along with precise methods, techniques, proofs, and verifications. Evidence counts for much more than opinion (even informed opinion), moralisms have been rooted out, and psychological factors reduced to a minimum. Furthermore, the particular things which are studied are frequently material things or abstractions. In either or both cases, statements about such things are much more easily adapted to analytic dichotomies such as synthetic or analytic than are statements about the things studies by the behavioral sciences and practical disciplines.[29]

Some of the particular distinctions, techniques and methodology of analysis, particularly of the logical empiricist kind, though apparently well suited to analysis of scientific language might not be equally appropriate for analysis of the language of pedagogy or social sciences. One might suspect then that the informal logic and common language approach might have more to offer.[30] On the other hand, the languages of education are not common languages, and the logic of educational discourse and argument is a practical logic rather than an informal logic. It may be suggested then that an analytic philosophy of the social sciences and practical disciplines is needed. There seems to be no reason why the logical and linguistic methods of analysis cannot be modified so as to be more applicable to the kind of logical and linguistic problems found in the social sciences and practical disciplines. To this end, educational philosophers of an analytic persuasion might well devote considerable attention.

[29] See Nowell-Smith, op. cit., Chapter 7, pp. 95–104, for explanation of the functions of Practical Discourse and how the Analytic-synthetic dichotomy breaks down.

[30] Reference here is to the John Widsom-Gilbert Ryle school of analysis.

22 / REGINALD D. ARCHAMBAULT

The Concept of Need

Introduction

The influence of John Dewey's educational theory has been broad and far-reaching. His attack upon traditional educational theory led to an entirely new approach to the problems of the field. The broad aspects of this new approach are well known. Perhaps the greatest single revolution in educational theory which Dewey's philosophy instigated was the trend toward a "child-centered" rather than a "society-centered" or "subject-matter-centered" approach to theory. The implications of this broad tendency are multifarious. Given this basic idea of the liberation of the child as a human being with immediately important desires, feelings, and interests, rather than a pliable and passive material to be molded and prepared for a future life, new goals, methods and materials were considered valid which would formerly have been considered wasteful, luxurious and certainly non-essential.

Dewey's experimentalist view of learning and living emphasized the uniqueness of individual experience in the attempt of the individual to adjust to a hostile but pliable environment. Adjustment to prevailing conditions in present experience, and the reconstruction of past experience in order to manipulate, order and control the environment were basic tenets of the Dewey position.

This emphasis on individual desires and needs in relation to the adjustment to a changing environment resulted in a new focus for educational theory. If the process of adjustment was central to the learning process, then the needs of the child were to be considered basic to the educative process. Only by understanding the needs, interests and desires of the child and then using these as a basis for development and growth, could there be a valid and meaningful course of instruction and guidance. The well-known Dewey formula emphasized the importance of first discovering these needs, and then using them to develop future

Reginald D. Archambault, "The Concept of Need and Its Relation to Certain Aspects of Educational Theory," *Harvard Educational Review*, 27, No. 1 (Winter 1957), 38–62. Reprinted by permission of *Harvard Educational Review* and Reginald D. Archambault.

purposes, without "imposing" goals, interests, or attitudes which were logically meaningful to the adult, but meaningless to the growing child who had only his immature perceptions for judging, valuing, and experiencing.

Because of the widespread acceptance of the Deweyan framework of experience as adjustment, new interpretations of traditional concepts began to take form. A new understanding of the relationship between means and ends was one of the most notable and influential. The doctrine of pupil interest was considered to be absolutely basic to any theory of methodology. And the concept of need became increasingly important as an approach to the entire educational scheme.

Dewey had made a clear and concise formulation of his doctrine of interest and effort at the turn of the century. His specific views on this and other major facets of his educational theory were further expanded and clarified in his *Democracy and Education* in 1916. Early ambiguities regarding interest, democratic processes in education, and goals and objectives were further clarified as an admonition to his orthodox but heretical followers in his *Experience and Education* in 1938. But the concept of need received only passing attention from Dewey in these and other writings. He had never made a clear formulation of his views on need, merely referring to it in his more basic writings as an essential construct in his experimentalist schema, as an initiator of the process of constant adjustment and search for equilibrium. The validity of the construct was never questioned by Dewey, nor were the implications of the concept clarified or elaborated. The concept had come into favor, as an essential part of the Dewey *Weltanschauung,* and had achieved an autonomy of its own, sometimes implementing Dewey's basic framework, but often operating as an isolated principle with only peripheral relation to the accepted Deweyan context. The result of this tendency was a widespread use of the concept of need as basic in its own right, with only limited connection with the total Dewey scheme.

The implications of the use of the concept of need as basic to a theory of education are broad and important. The full significance of the concept and its use, however, is largely unknown. While volumes have been written concerning the importance and validity of the doctrine of interest, the Deweyan theory concerning reflective thought, and other basic constructs in the experimentalist system, the concept of need as a basis for educational theory has arisen with a minimum of analysis and criticism.

This paper represents an attempt to examine various facets of the concept of need in the light of its implications for educational theory. Rather than an examination of various lists of needs, the analysis is focussed on the concept of need *per se.* Thus three prime aims emerge from the study: (1) an analysis of the validity of the concept as a hypothetical construct, (2) an evaluation of the concept as a basis for educational policy, and (3) an attempt to distinguish some of the more fundamental ways in which the term can be employed by an examination of its implications and connotations. The study does not pretend to be inclusive, nor to offer a representative sampling. It is an attempt to present the difficulties, shortcomings, and values of a concept which is widely employed but seldom investigated or challenged.

The Ambiguity of the Concept. A major difficulty involved in a discussion of need lies in the ambiguity of the concept. Everyday usage reflects a great variety of different denotations for the term, the distinctions between which are seldom made explicit, and often unrecognized. Thus we hear of the need for food, the need for a cigarette, the need for a telephone, the need for trained doctors, and the need for all pupils to study mathematics. It soon becomes obvious that there are subtle but important differences between these senses of the term as well as definite similarities. Although it is impossible to establish clear and objective distinctions between the various meanings attached to the term, a recognition of the more important differences is essential to an analysis and evaluation of its usage. The necessity of this clarification, and the aura of obscurity which surrounds the concept is often recognized but there are few attempts to bring order out of the chaos, due, perhaps, to the stickiness of the problem. Any attempt at definition must necessarily take into account the connotations as well as the denotations connected with the term, due to the fact that the term necessarily involves, at least in part, a description of inner states of being, whether conscious or unconscious, which are not immediately susceptible to objective measure.

In the light of these difficulties, there will be no attempt here to propose specific definitions of the different senses of the term, but merely to examine and clarify the more basic ways in which the term can be differentiated in accepted usage.

One major way in which the uses of the term can be distinguished is by recognizing the difference between need as a motivational concept and need as functional concept. For example, psychologists have found it necessary to establish a definite distinction between need and drive, on the basis that there are many instances where there are needs without corresponding drives and drives without corresponding needs (35, p. 658). Here "need" designates an organic state of deficiency or excess, and "drive" refers to a source of motivating energy. One example of a simple functional lack might be the existence of the need for a certain vitamin which is essential to the maintenance of a satisfactory state of internal equilibrium or normal bodily function, without a corresponding recognition on the part of the organism that this exists. On the other hand, many psychological studies point to the fact that there is much behavior that does not arise from any known or present need (20, p. 76, p. 294). It would seem, therefore, that a valid means for distinguishing between different notions of the concept would be the difference between needs as motives and needs in the sense of lacks or deficiencies.

In educational literature this distinction is often made by referring to desires or cravings as "felt needs" and contrasting these with the "real," or "genuine" needs of the child, with a usual implication that these felt needs, or immediate interests are to be used merely as a starting point for motivation of student activities, and that the "genuine" needs of the student should be the focal point for the direction of the educative process (33, 6, 26, *passim*).

This distinction, however, has not always been maintained. There have been many early attempts to postulate felt needs as the basis for educational organization, often resulting in dire consequences. Boyd H. Bode states the major difficulties inherent in this notion in that it fails to take into account the fact that many drives or desires are in fact harmful and tend to impede normal adjustment rather than nurturing it. If there is no criterion for ordering affairs than that they satisfy desires, then any attempt to distinguish between good or bad desires or tendencies is irrelevant in the light of the criterion. Such a scheme also fails to take into account the problem of how conflicts between desires are to be reconciled (4, p. 67, ff.).[1]

It seems clear that if the concept of need is to have any value as a determinant of educational policy, it must denote a definite, objective lack of the organism which must be satisfied if the organism is to survive and prosper in a healthy and harmonious manner. In this connection it must be emphasized that a "genuine" need receives its character not from a conscious or unconscious craving on the part of the individual, but from an objective deficiency in the relation of the individual to his environment. It should be noted that a need, when characterized in this way, may often be accompanied by a conscious desire to eliminate the deficiency. This is certainly the case in cases of physiological deficiency where appetites and drives are closely associated with the absence of a

---

[1] There are further and more intricate problems which emerge from the notion of needs as motives. One is the relation between conscious and unconscious motives, of which the work of Freud has made us so aware. There is the danger that fleeting and superficial interests or desires will be taken at face value when these in fact offer no adequate index of the basic motivations which are operative. Another knotty problem is presented by the distinction between immediate interests or desires as contrasted with more objective *purposes* which might be arrived at after careful reflection. Here the individual decides what *poses* which might be arrived at after careful reflection. Here the individual decides what he "really" desires at any given point in the light of the total context of possibilities available to him. These considerations are important, but are beyond the limited scope of this study.

basic satisfier. Pangs of hunger usually accompany the need for food. However, it is quite obvious that this is not universally true. Even in everyday usage, there is a wide recognition of the fact that desires and objective needs are in conflict with one another. The child who craves sweets but needs salt in his diet is a commonplace example. Thus, desire and need are not necessarily in opposition, but should be carefully distinguished. Ideally, desires and objective needs would coincide.

Another broad area of distinction is apparent when educational theorists cite the difference between the needs of the individual and the needs of society. Implicit in this distinction is that individual needs, whether they be conscious or unconscious, merely desires or genuine needs, must be distinguished from the conceptions of optimum conditions postulated by the society. Thus, in most educational schemes which use need as a basic concept, there is an implicit assumption that individual wants and cravings should be nurtured, discovered, or created in the light of the broader needs of society. It should be stressed that "need" in this sense refers to lacks or deficiencies which are essential to the maintenance of a pre-established optimum of equilibrium within a well-defined context of society. Thus we hear of the need of the individual to help maintain natural resources, on the ground that this is his *duty* in relation to his citizenship in the society, and that the maintenance of these resources is essential if the nation is to grow and prosper and maintain an adequate standard of development. Hence the need of the child for self expression and play is said to be tempered and regulated by the broader societal need.

The important point to notice here is that this concept of societal need is clearly qualified by a conditional consideration (*if* the society is to maintain an optimal level of economic efficiency, *then* national resources should be conserved), and that these conditions are in turn dictated by another, more ultimate standard by which adequacy and optimum conditions in a given context can be judged. Exactly what conditions are considered to be optimum is dependent upon basic *values* which are considered by the society to be worthy of commitment.

This qualification is introduced in order to point up the close proximity in many respects between need (in the sense of lack) and value. The criterion which is used to define adequate conditions of adjustment and development is often taken for granted and not recognized specifically in an analysis of need as part of a process of "healthy adjustment to environmental conditions." The failure to make this consideration explicit has led to a great deal of unnecessary confusion on the part of educators with regard to the utility and limitation of the concept of need—an assumption that a need-oriented curriculum, for example, could be free from the subjectivity, idealism, and intangibility of a vague value structure. This is reflected in a widespread tendency on the part of educational theorists to suppose that valid educational practice will result from a "discovery" of the basic needs of youth and the establishment of a program leading to satisfaction of these needs to the maximum extent. The implications of this view will be elaborated in a later section.

The Validity of the Concept of Need

There is a great body of literature intent upon postulating need as a basic construct for determining the goals and directions of the educational enterprise. Numerous lists of "basic needs" are proposed, to be used as criteria for curriculum and aims of education. However, there is very little evidence of an attempt to validate the concept of need itself. The Fifty-second Yearbook of the National Society for the Study of Education is the most recent of a long line of documents attempting to "adapt the secondary-school program to the needs of youth." Camilla M. Low is responsible for an examination of the validity of the concept of need in that volume, but a close examination of the text reveals that this analysis merely accepts the concept as valid, and then attempts to relate it to the educational process in rather vague and uncertain terms (26, p. 22). The result is an attempted clarification of the ways in which the term may be applied without an investigation of the validity of the construct itself. This is indicative of a general tendency to accept the validity of the concept as self-evident and then to seek to interpret it in the light of the problems of an applied field. This is certainly true of other famous and influential studies which use the concept of need as an essentially *a priori* first premise (20, 25, 27, 33). It might be well to examine the more basic arguments in favor of the concept of need as a hypothetical construct and to evaluate the evidence used to sanction the validity of the concept.

Murray's Use of the Need Construct. The work of H. A. Murray and his colleagues on a theory of personality is the most widely used and sophisticated study of the use of need as a basic element in personality structure (24). In his discussion of the use of the concept as a basis for a theory of personality, Murray enumerates no fewer than 23 reasons for postulating the concept as a fundamental construct in a theory of personality.

> "Between what we can directly observe—the stimulus and the resulting action—a need is an invisible link, which may be imagined to have the properties that an understanding of observed phenomena demand. 'Need' is therefore a hypothetical concept." (24, p. 60)

The principal reason for postulating need in Murray's system is primarily a negative one. As he lists the reasons for the validity of the concept we find that there is little positive evidence offered to validate the occurrence of definite universal directional forces for a basis of all behavior. Most often the reason employed for postulating the concept is that some such concept as physical force must be reverted to. "Otherwise it is impossible to construct a dynamical theory without it." The point here is that the entire theory is quite hypothetical, resting on very little direct evidence, and as such, quite vulnerable to the type of attack which Allport (1) and Lee (18) among others, have seen fit to assert. Recognizing the highly hypothetical character of the construct, Murray nevertheless asserts that there are no adequate reasons for hesitating to do what physical scientists have consistently done: conceptualize processes behind appearances. Murray's exposition of the relation between single instances of need occurrence and its relation to broader classes of need is basic to the problem and worthy of quotation:

> "Strictly speaking, a need is the immediate outcome of certain internal and external occurrences. It comes into being, endures for a moment and perishes. It is not a static entity. It is a resultant of forces. One need succeeds another. Though each is unique, observation teaches that there are similarities among them, and on the basis of this, needs may be grouped into classes; each class being, as it were, a single major need. Thus, we may speak of similar things as being different exhibitions of *one need*, just as when we recognize a friend we do not hesitate to call him by name though he is different from the person with whom we conversed yesterday. Between the different appearances of a certain kind of need there may be nothing to suggest it, but everyday experience and experiment show that if proper conditions are provided the need (i.e., another manifestation of the same kind of need) will be activated. Thus, we may loosely use the term 'need' to refer to an organic potentiality or readiness to respond in a certain way under given conditions. In this sense a need is a latent attribute of an organism. More strictly, it is a noun which stands for the fact that a certain trend is apt to recur." (24, p. 61)

In a final enlargement upon his original definition, Murray sums up the basic components of the construct, emphasizing that:

> "A need is a construct (a convenient fiction or hypothetical concept) which stands for a force (the physico-chemical nature of which is unknown) in the brain region, a force which organizes perception, apperception, intellection, conation and action in such a way as to transform in a certain direction an existing, unsatisfying situation." (24, p. 123–124)

It is clear then, that the concept of an inherent force interrelated with certain environmental conditions are the basic factors essential to the manifestation of a latent need state. This scheme is important for the purpose of this analysis for several reasons which will become clear later. To round out the scheme it is necessary to introduce at this point another concept which is integral to Murray's scheme—that of equilibrium.

> "In so far as need is defined as a disequilibrium which stresses toward equilibrium, it falls into the category of finalistic concepts, of which the second law of thermodynamics is typical. The latter has been stated as follows: 'In all processes with which we are acquainted, every known form of energy at a high potential always tends to run down to energy at the lowest potential circumstances will allow.' According to this principle, affairs tend to take a certain course. The need theory calls attention to a similar phenomenon observable in human behavior. A trend is like a tropism, a movement away from or towards some source of stimulation or, again, it is similar to the attraction and repulsion of chemical substances." (24, p. 67)

Murray's schema is presented in some detail because it is the clearest and most sophisticated articulation of the doctrine of needs, the main features of which are incorporated with only slight variation in the motivation theories of many other writers. Most turn directly to Murray for the basis of their analysis and admit an indebtedness to him for his highly detailed construction of the need theory. (14, 25, 32)

Difficulties in Murray's Theory. There are several points in the Murray analysis which are open to further investigation and criticism, especially in light of the use of the concept of need as a basis for educational policy. Allport, in his discussion of the difficulties inherent in any attempt to analyze personality into universal and uniform elements, appraises the work of Murray in this regard.

> "The theory says, in effect, that objects of desire may vary from person to person, but the kinds of desire do not. Men may want different things, but there are only a few reasons why they want them. Two men, for instance, may be animated by a strong need for abasement; one perhaps becomes a sexual masochist, the other a well-disciplined monk. Does it not seem unnecessarily abstract to assume one corresponding need in these contrasting cases? . . . Universalized needs fail to depict with exactness the special foci of organization existing in each individual life. Desire is always integral with its object, and its resulting forms are far more valued than such a limited list of needs would allow. In short, needs are disembodied and de-personalized to a greater degree than is justified in elements that are to serve as radicals of personality." (1, p. 241)

Allport's principal argument with Murray rests on Murray's failure to recognize the importance of individual differences in motivation and the possibility that "a *general* law may be a law that tells how *uniqueness* comes about." (*1*, p. 191). Allport develops the point at great length, emphasizing "the endless variety of goals sought by an endless variety of individuals" (*1*, p. 194).

James L. Mursell, in an attempt to make direct application of Murray's theory of basic needs to a psychology of education, attacks the Allport criticism outlined above by maintaining that:

> "The question is not whether the hypothesis of needs offers here and now a complete, ready-made explanation of everything in human behavior. Most certainly this is by no means the case. The question is whether the hypothesis that behavior is ultimately determined by basic needs is or is not a better principle for explanation and understanding than the hypothesis that all motives are learned from the ground up." (*25*, p. 53)

Mursell further points out that only a concept of universal basic needs is sufficient to provide an explanation of the *limitations* of the variety of human motivation and the evidence of basic similarity in many areas.

It would seem that Mursell's answer falls considerably short of satisfying the difficulties mentioned by Allport. The fact is that Mursell, taking his cue from Murray's own defensive position, emphasizes that the theory of basic needs offers a better explanation for human behavior than a position which states that "all motives are learned from the ground up." However, Allport is not suggesting an either-or choice on the matter. The crux of his argument is that the Murray hypothesis is promising but insufficient, and that its insistence upon universal and uniform personality elements eliminates the possibility of satisfactorily accommodating the rather obvious evidence of variety and variance, not only between cultures, but also within a single society. The Murray theory suffers from the same dangerous tenets long recognized in the older instinct psychology—to blur over existing differences and essentially unexplained phenomena by simply classifying them, thinking that by so doing, the problem was solved.

There would seem to be little reason for accepting whole-heartedly either a complete insistence on uniform elements without recognizing the importance of learning, or a theory which rejects these elements completely. However, Allport's analysis is particularly applicable in the present context because it points up the difficulties and limitations inherent in any attempt to attribute the causes of human behavior to certain basic needs which are rather arbitrarily designated and lacking in sufficient specificity to be meaningfully applicable in a given context.

The criticism is closely related to a second one which emphasizes the differences in cultural norms and their tendency to magnify the great differences in notions of need in various cultures. This point is used as the basis of criticism of the theory of needs by Dorothy Lee (18). Pointing to evidence in the Hopi and Arapesh tribes, Lee concludes that the relationship between cultural norms and values on the one hand and hypothetical needs on the other, necessitates a modification of the theory which emphasizes the negative concept of lack or deficiency rather than a positive concept of *value* as the determinant of trends of behavior. This question is an extremely complex one which will be discussed at length in another section. The Lee article is introduced here merely to emphasize the great variety of differences in various cultures with regard to "basic needs." The Arapesh society is one of abundance where sharing, social activity, and unselfishness create no need for possession or individual self-esteem (at least not in the sense these terms are used in our western culture). Emphasizing that the Kwoma infant, always experiencing abundance and immediate gratification, and essentially undisciplined, experiences no need for love and security, Lee maintains that needs are *creations* of society rather than forces imposed innately and universally on all humans.

This criticism of the concept of needs is closely related to the first in that it postulates, on a culture-wide scale, the importance of learning, and indeed the perception itself of an objective situation, and the corresponding dynamic change in this situation because of a learned change in attitudes. Thus the very perception of the situation itself is altered through learning. Attitudes are developed which do not build up a stoic attitude of suffering through a lack, but rather neglect to postulate the existence of such a lack.

This explanation is closely related, in its basic aspects, to the principle of *functional autonomy* postulated by Allport and based on Woodworth's concept of the transformation of mechanisms into drives.

> "The dynamic psychology purposed here regards adult motives as infinitely varied, and as self-sustaining, *contemporary* systems, growing out of antecedent systems, but functioning independent of them." (35, p. 194)
>
> "In the course of learning, many preparatory mechanisms must be developed in order to lead to the consummation of an original purpose. These mechanisms are the effective cause of activity in each succeeding mechanism, furnishing the drive for each stage following in the series. Originally all these mechanisms were merely instrumental, only links in the long chain of processes involved in the achievement of an *instinctive* purpose; with time and development, with integration and elaboration, many of these mechanisms become activated directly, setting up a state of desire

and tension for activities and objects no longer connected with the original impulse activities and objects that earlier in the game were *means* to an end, now become *ends* in themselves." (*1*, p. 195)

It is important to note that this principle retains the notion of basic, even instinctive needs as *original* sources of motivation, and adds the concept of motivation syndromes which are essentially *learned*. The implications for educational theory inherent in this principle are certainly significant. While the principle recognizes the importance of basic needs as historical originators of motivation, it introduces a new freedom in the concept of the individual. The individual is not faced with a stereotyped list of needs which he must manifest in order to be considered normal. It gives a great deal of stress to *purposive* behavior, while at the same time accounting for motivational force and the importance of environmental conditions in the shaping of personality.

It should be noted that this principle would also account for certain cultural variances in motivation and behavior without sacrificing the validity of the concept of need. Allport himself does not extend the principle to account for cultural differences, but the application seems to be consistent and valid. Allport states:

"At last we can account adequately for socialized and civilized behavior. The principle supplies the correction necessary to the faulty logic of *bellum omnia contra omnes*. Starting life as a completely selfish being, the child would remain entirely wolfish and piggish throughout his days unless genuine transformations of motives took place. Motives being completely alterable, the dogma of Egoism turns out to be a callow and superficial philosophy of behavior, or else a useless redundancy." (*1*, p. 206)

This account would not discount basic similarities among original cultures with regard to initial motivation, but it would underplay the necessity for many specific needs which are often given an aura of universality. The concept of original motive or drive, while remaining genetically prior, loses its power to produce specific behavior, a tendency toward such behavior. All that remain are certain rather unspecifiable adiences which receive their character from a combination of conscious purposes or culturally learned attitudes, in relation to environmental demands and free possibilities. The concept of a specific innate force which must be satisfied due to the inner nature of man is de-emphasized, and the process of adjustment is thrown into a newer light, extending much more freedom to the individual and allowing for much cultural and individual difference due to learning. It opens the way to a freer concept of man as considerably more pliable, but at the same time renders him able to cope with an environment freely, relatively unhampered by passion, desire, or insistent need.

In the light of the above factors, it might be well to question the general tendency to list areas of basic need which are universally binding. Even if it be granted that the physiological needs for food, water and air are universal, the problem remains as to whether the means of acquisition of these essentials do not in effect change for all practical purposes the character of the needs themselves, and whether the concept of need can be considered logically prior to the individual manifestation of the adience toward these satisfactions. The postulation of a wide category of need is at best an oversimplification, even with regard to the physiological needs. In Murray's scheme the general need for food is postulated as essentially prior, and individual instances of need are said to manifest this general tendency. It would seem much more correct to maintain that individual instances are widely recognized and that a general classification is postulated on the basis of a fundamental similarity among the numerous cases. The distinction is an important one, for it emphasizes the individual differences in behavior rather than the similarities, the imposition of which tends to obscure the differences by ruthless rubricizing. One is reminded of the Platonic theory of universals in which the individual instance is merely a participant in the generic form, an organic rather than an organizational system. The scheme at least provides a form of simple categorization, but in the process of classification, violates the essential identity of the individual instance.

Dorothy Lee has compounded the various difficulties inherent in the theory of basic needs and concluded that the use of the concept of need as a basic premise in explaining behavior is false and unjustified. Citing anthropological researches, she concludes that in many cultures (notably the Arapesh and the Hopi), action does not occur in answer to a need or lack, for the lack, due to extreme cultural security, is never manifested. In an economy of abundance, where satisfactions are not withheld, but by mutual agreement lavished on the population, the experience of tension and frustration do not exist. There is one essential point which should be considered as the basis of her position. She writes:

> "If we say that the reason that he has no need for these things (food, security, etc.) is that he does not have them already, we would be begging the question. I believe, rather, that these trends or notions are irrelevant when satisfaction is viewed in terms of positive, present value, and value itself as inherent in a total situation." (18, p. 393)

This notion of the relation of need to value is an important one which will be discussed in a later section. The important point to be made here is that the argument under consideration regarding the validity of the concept of need rests on Lee's assumption that since the individual *experiences* no need for security because he has it already is a question-begging argument. However, the point of the matter is that inherent in the notion of need is the notion that certain experiences or satisfactions are essential if life is to exist and survive. It is doubtful whether the tendency to maintain existence can be considered a value in itself. If so, the Lee theory would hold. This is certainly no place to argue the validity of this notion, but let it suffice to say that the great bulk of definition itself rests upon this *a priori* assumption. The theory of need, presupposing the necessity of continued existence as valid presupposition, holds that certain experiences must be provided in order to maintain the existence of the individual. In its most basic terms, need refers to a necessary dynamic relation of the internal organism of the individual with the external environment, with the definite implication that a stable relation between these factors must be maintained if life is to persist. Whether or not the individual experiences a *conscious* need or lack is completely irrelevant. The *test* of the validity of need rests on the withdrawal of environmental factors which would lead to eventual expiration of the organism. However, this does not in itself make the concept of need a negative one. It is neither negative nor positive in a strict sense. It simply postulates a state of affairs which must be maintained by necessity if the organism is to continue living. It seems difficult to consider the tendency to survive as a value in this sense. Hence the argument for need cannot, when reduced to its lowest terms, be considered a question-begging argument.

Equilibrium.   In an attempt to arrive at an adequate notion of need most writers find it necessary to invoke the concept of equilibrium. The concept is particularly appropriate for educators of the modern school who accept the tenets of John Dewey's theory of learning as problem solving, and the basic principle of life as an ongoing process of adjustment to a shifting environment (*11*, p. 107ff., *12*, p. 46ff.). The development of this concept is usually attributed to Cannon (*7*, p. 24ff.), who postulated the concept of *homeostasis* as the basic principle of human adjustment. It refers to the tendency of the body to automatically maintain a constant, normal level with regard to water content of the blood, salt content, etc. The essence of the concept is that there is an optimum state of balance among these various components which must be maintained if the organism is to survive.

The more perfectly these states are maintained, the healthier will be the functioning of the organism. Dewey adopts the scheme as a principle for describing the healthy process of adjustment to a changing environment, holding that it is the tendency of the individual to maintain a state of equilibrium or balance which motivates all learning activity. Due to the nature of the individual as a creature with essential needs, and his operation in a hostile environment, the inevitable conflicts which arise in the process of need-satisfaction necessitate the phenomenon of learning in order to adjust to the environment, satisfy essential needs, and restore equilibrium. A host of writers employ the concept as a basic premise in a theory of learning as adjustment. Gates gives an elaborate description of the relation of need to equilibrium which may be summarized as follows (*14*, p. 620):

(1) A state of equilibrium achieved through satiation with food
(2) A state of weak tension arising due to a lack of food
(3) An increase of tension due to hunger
(4) The active search for food to eliminate the need
(5) Food is eaten, tension is discharged, and the state of equilibrium is restored.

The principle has great value in attempting a definition of need, for it clarifies the factors which are involved in the meaning of the term: (1) an initial lack in the organism (2) which is in turn dependent upon environmental conditions for satisfaction (3) and the necessity of the individual to interact with the environment in order to satisfy the lack. This schema points up the essential interrelationship of the individual with the environment which is implied by the concept. However, it is important to note that although the *satisfaction* of a need is dependent upon the interaction of individual with his environment, it does not logically follow that the *meaning* of need follows from that interaction. The need for food exists without reference to its mode of satisfaction. Thus in this most basic interpretation of the term, a physiological need is innate and related to the *nature of the organism.* It neither implies nor denies optimal conditions of adjustment in this basic sense, but rather an inherent propensity to require certain satisfactions if life is to be sustained. Such a qualifying proposition could hardly be considered a *value* in the generally accepted sense of an evaluation of alternatives. The only alternative to survival is death and the absence of a live context implies no need for valuation. Thus the basic essential component of the concept of a need is the factor of *necessity.* The need must be supplied if a projected state of affairs is to be fulfilled.

When applied to the physiological state of the body, the concept of equilibrium or balance to maintain *normal* functioning can be readily accepted, then, for it implies the necessity for the maintenance of life itself (the elimination of a lack) and the proper, *normal* functioning of the body as it goes on living (the reduction of a deficiency). Lack of disease, the evident value of longevity—these are considered valid objectives because they are the essentials of the life process itself. However, when the concept is widened to serve as a basis of definition of "higher" needs regarding "self-actualization" or "the need for aesthetic experience" the criterion of equilibrium, or normal function seems inadequate and false.

The difficulty rests with the notion of "normality." Universal agreement exists on the positive value of physiological health, and on the norms which must be maintained in order to attain it. Thus, in relation to physiological health, the notion of normality can be stated in certain, even mathematical terms (as in body temperature, proportion of water in the blood, etc.). But when the concept is used to support the notion of need for "socialization" or "spiritual sensitivity," the limitations of the concept become more apparent. The difficulty rests on the fact there is no universally accepted norm with relation to these needs. An attempt to propose a given level of non-physiological need as normal presupposes that an optimum level of adjustment is clearly known and accepted in advance and that it is known through a process of discovery rather than imposition.

The concept of equilibrium, then, is wholly dependent upon a clear-cut notion of a norm of attainment. Given such a norm, any deviation from it —a lack or deficiency—could validly be called an objective need. But the fact of the matter is, that given the dynamics of a social situation involving such intangible qualities as self-actualization, sufficient awareness, etc., an *objective* norm defies construction. Thus it is true that an objective need can be discovered, but only within a completely defined context in which the normal level of attainment can be clarified. It is the contention of this writer that the definition of these standards of attainment are ultimately dependent upon a standard of judgment which is ethical rather than scientific and that norms which are proposed in a given cultural matrix consist of selections and arrangements of the components of the matrix rather than the discovery of a pre-existent pattern which guarantees maximum growth, health and efficiency.

The fallacy involved in this notion of norms as inherent in the contextual situation itself is similar to that involved in the notion of the "cultural lag."[2] A cultural lag is said to exist when the aesthetic, ethical, or non-scientific patterns of a culture fail to keep pace with scientific and technological advances. But this concept presupposes that the stage at which a culture as a whole should be at any given time can be readily ascertained by examining the components of the culture itself. The

---

[2] This discussion draws heavily upon Carl G. Hempel's treatment of the notion of function in his *Fundamentals of Concept Formation in Empirical Science* (The International Encyclopedia of Unified Science, Volume II, No. 7.) See especially p. 45ff.

principle neglects the simple dynamics of the relation of technological to humanistic aspects of the culture and the utter impossibility of ascertaining in advance the precise level of attainment which is optimum in a given culture at a given time.

This point is emphasized by A. E. Murphy in a chapter of his *The Uses of Reason* (23) in which he discusses the role of the social scientist as a marker of values, and the relation of research and objective data to valuing and ordering that data:

> "But the question that has to be settled is not what these cravings or drives demand but what practical wisdom demands when drives are harmonized and disciplined with reference to a represented good which justifies and lends meaning to their articulate urgency. Again, it may be possible to estimate what our present technological equipment 'demands' for its maximum efficient use, and there are bright young men who write as though the 'demands' of technology stood as unconditional imperatives to which the rest of human life must accommodate itself on such terms as it can make. There are also 'imperatives' of history, of geography, and even of thermodynamics which are invoked to tell us scientifically what men and nations require and what, in consequence, they ought to have and to be. In the context of reasonable social action, however, all these are hypothetical imperatives—they are addressed not to partially embodied abstractions which reflect the limits of professional specialization, but to the men whose business it is to decide how, in the kind of world the sciences described to them, they want to live, and to what end." (23, p. 259)

The confusion between need as an objective state of deficiency and the value implications of the term becomes more apparent as the concept of equilibrium is examined in greater detail. In a psychological (as distinguished from a physiological) context, equilibrium has several discernible characteristics, two of which may be singled out:

(1) The concept of equilibrium as *integration.* In this sense the term refers to an inner state of wholeness of the individual, a "proper" balance among the various facets of the personality, a unity of divergent traits so that they work together harmoniously in order to produce efficient, purposive behavior. In this sense we might consider it *internal* equilibrium, the successful attainment of which can be measured negatively by lack of frustration, and positively by a tendency toward growth, purposive behavior, self-improvement, and other accepted indices of proper adjustment. But even here it might be noted that the possibility of attainment of equilibrium is directly related to the nature of the demands which the society makes upon the individual. These demands are in turn dependent upon the value structure of the society or group to which the

individual considers himself committed. The possibility of an individual achieving a well-integrated personality in the light of the demands of the Puritan theocracy, or in our modern complex society, are considerably less than achieving such a state in a Hopi tribe. Thus we see that the culture not only imposes specific demands of varying nature and intensity, but also that in so doing it regulates the nature of the norm of adjustment itself.

(2) There is a second sense in which the concept of equilibrium is even more directly related to standards of value. This sense might be referred to as *external* equilibrium, where the individual's *perception* of normality and proper adjustment are directly related to cultural norms. In everyday life this is exemplified by the common tendency to "keep up with the Joneses." The individual's perception of his own needs, and hence his attainment of equilibrium, are here dependent upon his success in conforming to culturally accepted values. Thus the person who might qualify as an admirable man in the medieval period would be simply maladjusted in the Renaissance. The current needs for a new automobile, life insurance and electric refrigerators are valid only when invoked as necessities in the process of adjustment to changing norms which are in turn based on a further criterion of the good and the desirable.

Malinowski states:

> "The nutritive specialist can define the optimum of a diet in terms of proteins, carbohydrates, mineral salts and vitamins necessary for the maintenance of the human organism in good health. The optimum, however, must be defined with reference to a given culture. For the optimum is only definable with relation to the amount of labor, muscular and nervous, to the complexity of the tasks, to potential strains and efforts demanded by a given cultural configuration of its numbers." (*19*, pp. 79–80)

Malinowski offers this caution with regard to the most basic of physiological concepts of equilibrium, and it has great relevance to the present analysis of social needs. We must not lose sight of the fact that the relation between societal values and personal standards is reciprocal in the sense that they are mutually interdependent. Thus, culturally imposed values operate not only as an objective determinant of the individual's value structure, but in the process of imposition, affect the very perception of what values should be.

Need and Value. The Committee on Reorganizing Secondary Education of the Progressive Education Association, in a detailed attempt to utilize the concept of need as a basis of reorganization, has been careful to avoid the usual obscurities of similar studies by recognizing the importance of distinguishing between desires, individual needs, and societal values.

> "When lacks are defined as the difference between the present personality and what it would desirably become as a factor in future social experience, they may be seen to lie on a continuum with desires. Desires grow out of past social experience and are formulated in response to confronting social situations, and lacks are always represented in some rudimentary form in what is longed for. . . . Revision of educational practices on the basis of needs must begin with an examination into the current activities, concerns, problems, and frustrations of young people; in these it must see a reciprocal process—the person and his medium forever changing through their interaction. In this process, education must seek evidence as to the motivations of young people, the values of which they are in quest as they go about the business of their living." (33, p. 37)

The authors are to be praised for a concise statement of the variety of important factors which come into play in the process of postulating needs as a basis of organization. However, in essence this proposal maintains that the final basis for direction must grow out of an examination of the existent lacks, which in turn are said to be indicated by "what is longed for." This is a representative example of the attempt to establish a process of scientific investigation as a valid means of ascertaining the goals of the educative process. However, goals are not to be discovered through the investigation of common tendencies, desires or longings. Goals and ends represent a conception of what *ought to be* in the light of what is possible. In this sense an understanding of the nature of the child's motivations, frustrations, and perceptions is certainly necessary if goals are to be projected which are meaningful to the child and attainable in fact. The crucial point, however, is that this knowledge is not *sufficient* for establishing a direction for education. Dewey's attempt to postulate a scientific ethic based on the naturalistic foundation of human motivation was careful to point out the necessity of distinguishing between the merely desired and the desirable, the factual and ethical. In Dewey's scheme the merely factual becomes ethical only when intelligent foresight of objectively perceived consequences was employed as a criterion (12). Yet in the scheme under analysis and in similar attempts to postulate definitive directions for conduct there is the assumption that these have been arrived at in a purely objective manner, and carry no stigma of value judgment.

> "We may grant, of course, that in specific situations, where the end in view may be taken for granted, it is entirely appropriate to speak of needs, since the end or purpose furnishes a point of reference for judging the needs. But to undertake to build an educational program by starting with needs is quite another matter. Unless we assume that there is a predestined end for

human living, and that we know what the end is, there is no justification whatsoever for talking so blithely about needs." (4, p. 69)

Sidney Hook states that:

> "A need in education is any want, absence or lack whose fulfillment is a necessary condition for the achievement of a desirable end." (17, p. 45)

It should be noted that the important component here is the qualifying concept of a "desirable" end. Given a sufficient contextual definition of what the desirable is, then genuine needs can be determined by a process of thorough investigation. However, this is the case of a notion of need-as-lack following from a construction of the valuable, rather than serving as an exclusive base for value itself.

A. H. Maslow has projected a theory of motivation (22) which is postulated on a highly elaborate construction of a concept of basic needs. He suggests that needs arrange themselves in a hierarchy, ranging from the physiological to those which insure the maximum actualization of the potential of the individual. Inherent in the scheme is a notion that higher need levels are recognized and attained only when the lower needs in the hierarchy have been successfully gratified. Thus the hierarchy of needs is placed on five levels: (1) Basic physiological needs, (2) Needs for safety and security, (3) Needs for love, (4) The need for esteem, and (5) The need for self-actualization. The lower needs are stronger and hold priority for gratification, but though the higher needs are weaker, they are nevertheless basic and part of man's inner nature.

> "This chapter will demonstrate that there are real psychological and operational differences between those needs called 'higher' and those called lower. This is done in order to establish that the organism itself dictates hierarchies of values, which the scientific observer reports rather than creates. It is necessary thus to prove the obvious because so many still consider that values can never be more than the arbitrary imposition upon data of the writer's own tastes, prejudices, intuitions, or other unproved or unprovable assumptions." (22, p. 150)

Thus Maslow speaks of an absolute concept of normality which can be postulated on the basis of psychological health.

> "Specifically, my prediction or guess about the future of the normality idea is that some form of theory about generalized, species-wide, psychological health will soon be developed, which will hold for all human beings no matter what their culture and no matter what their time." (22, p. 339)

This standard will be postulated on the basis of an analysis of what *can* be rather than what *ought to be*.

> "What we *can* be = what we ought to be, and is much better
> language than ought to be. Observe that if we are being
> descriptive and empirical, then ought is completely out of place,
> as can be clearly seen if we ask about flowers or animals, what
> they *ought* to be. What sense does it make here (or should)?
> What ought a kitten to become? The answer to this question and
> the spirit in which it is put is the same for human children." (22,
> p. 344)

Thus Maslow contends that there is something resembling a potential,
or entelechy which is part of man's nature, and which provides a concept
of the desirable in that nature in its very existence. This scheme is
parallel with that of Rousseau who, postulating the innate goodness of
the child, claimed that all that was essential for a maximum manifestation
of his potential, was to provide good and proper conditions in which
these qualities could flourish naturally and automatically. This parallel
seems to be admitted by Maslow when he claims that the great failing of
our society has been the failure to recognize the fact that instinctive
needs are not bad, but neutral or good, and that careful attention to the
nurturing of these will yield a clear criterion of the good. (22, p. 135)

> "The important difference between man and all other beings is
> that his needs, his preferences, his instinct remnants are *weak* and
> not strong, equivocal and not unequivocal, that they have room
> for doubt, uncertainty and conflict, that they are all too easily
> overlaid and lost to sight by culture, by learning, by the
> preferences of other people." (22, p. 344)

Here are shades of Rousseau's premise that it is the institutions of the
culture which corrupt the innately good human nature and prevent its
maximum fulfilment. We find shades of this argument in the contention
by many present-day theorists that comic books and television are really
the cause of juvenile delinquency.

Several difficulties become immediately apparent in an analysis of this
scheme. The major one involves the fact that a realization and recognition of what *can* be serves only to widen the area of possible choice from
which preferences and goods must be selected. A common cause of
frustration and anxiety lies in this very recognition of possibilities and the
difficulty of making the most satisfactory choice among them. Several
facets of the Maslow scheme are apparently in conflict. Man is differentiated from lower animals on the basis of his ability to transcend his
lower impulses and to order his activities. This allows him a great range
of freedom for choice which is dependent to a great extent upon his
ability to conceptualize, project himself into the future, and foresee
consequences of his actions. Yet this seems to be in direct conflict with

the notion that there is a built-in guarantee that only those decisions will be made which are in fact most advantageous for the individual. Maslow seems to want to eat his cake and have it too. If freedom is to have any meaning at all it must imply the ability to act in a variety of ways in a given instance, and therefore opens up the possibility of error. The concept of an inherent tendency to act in a way which is inevitable, and a notion of freedom, are incompatible in this sense. Given a situation in which desires conflict, the problem remains as to how the conflict is to be reconciled, and which of the tendencies is to be chosen as the most desirable one.

With regard to the notion of institutions corrupting man, it would seem that this view neglects the fact that institutions are in reality manmade, and reflect tendencies of human nature as well as controlling them. Institutions are the means through which individuals attempt to reconcile and avoid conflicts among desires. As such, they are not essentially evil. They are merely instruments which may be used for evil purposes. This "evil" rests not with the nature of the institution itself, but rather with the values and moves that the institution is used to promote. Thus the ultimate ground on which the good and evil in society rests is in the prevalent mores of society rather than in the instruments which are used to nurture and sustain these values.

When we seek to find the "good conditions" which are necessary for a manifestation of these potentialities in Maslow's scheme we recognize another parallel with Rousseau: "In general these conditions may be summed up under the one head of permissiveness to gratify and express." Thus the innate potential of the individual will flourish and reach fruition providing that a completely free environment is provided. Two considerations are in order here. First, it may be noted that any realistic scheme must take into account the fact that in any societal structure complete freedom is an utter impossibility. The well accepted notion of individual freedom is correctly qualified by the admonition that the individual can be free only insofar as his freedom does not infringe upon the freedom of others. The very nature of a society expresses the notion of freedom within given limits. Complete permissiveness is impossible. Therefore, a further step in the scheme is left unmentioned—the necessity for defining what limitations and restrictions are to be imposed on complete freedom, and what tendencies are to be nurtured in the light of these restrictions. Thus any educational program must concern itself with the trends and desires inherent in the individual which are considered to be worthy of nurture, which will insure the maintenance of personal freedom, and which will impose only those restrictions which will allow for the development of selected goods.

Secondly, it might be advisable to invoke John Dewey's well-known contention that a policy of complete *laissez-faire* might in fact prove detrimental to the child in that by failing to provide the proper materials and directions for growth and adjustment it might produce unnecessary and harmful patterns of adjustment. Even if we grant the dubious assumption that in the course of natural adjustment the higher orders of behavior will evolve automatically, the task of education would still remain to abstract and nurture those tendencies which would be naturally evolved, so that a minimum of frustration and a maximum of efficiency would be attained. For example, the present trend toward "problem-centered" areas of activity is based on the assumption that the *introduction* of conflicts and barriers to the natural scheme of events will result in a spurt in the adjustive process, thus accelerating the evolution of desirable characteristics.

Lists of Basic Needs in Education. There are numerous attempts to set up lists of basic needs as guides to the formulation of educational objectives. Most of these studies accept the concept as valid, and then proceed to relate the general needs of youth to a specific curricular program. (*26, 33, 30, 10,* p. 111ff.)

A. H. Maslow sums up several of the difficulties involved in a cataloguing of needs or drives, maintaining that the lists are determined by the degree of specificity with which they are analyzed:

> "Thus we can speak of a need for gratification or equilibrium; or more specifically of a need to eat; or still more specifically of a need to fill the stomach; or still more specifically of a desire for proteins; or still more specifically of a desire for a particular protein; and so on. Too many listings that we now have available have combined indiscriminately needs at various levels of magnification. With such confusion it is understandable that some lists should contain three or four needs and others contain hundreds of needs. . . . Furthermore, it should be recognized that if we attempt to discuss the fundamental desires they should be clearly understood as sets of desires, as fundamental categories or *collections* of desires. In other words, such an enumeration of fundamental goals would be an abstract classification rather than a cataloguing list." (*22,* p. 70)

The difficulties involved here are indeed severe. In an earlier discussion we noted the limitations inherent in an abstract categorization of needs, emphasizing the tendency toward distortion of specific instances in order to maintain a logically imposed classification. Here it becomes apparent that the tendency to err in the other direction is equally dangerous. On the one hand, an abstract classification obscures individual differences. On the other hand, extreme specificity eradicates the essential unity and similarity among individual instances of need, thus posing the question as to the value of an undertaking which pretends to propose a scheme of needs which has validity and justification.

In the light of our earlier discussion it becomes clear that the value of these various listings is dependent upon their success in defining the basis for choice in determining which needs are to be emphasized, and just how the hierarchy is validated. Granted that certain tendencies must be nurtured in order to fulfill carefully specified conditions, such long lists of needs do not in themselves dictate which needs must be given emphasis and which are to be considered most essential in an educational scheme where economy of time is of utmost importance. Essentialists would certainly agree to the description of the characteristics of the well-educated person given by the Educational Policies Commission (26, pp. 39–123), for the listed characteristics are desirable enough. However, the task set for educational theory is to decide which of these characteristics are to be given emphasis, which are to be developed through extracurricular and out-of-school activities, and which are to be eliminated as specific objectives of classroom instruction in light of the obvious fact that the school cannot do all things well.

Many studies precede their postulation of needs with a set of presuppositions which serve to provide the general conditions under which the needs are to be considered valid. The analysis of basic areas of need by Camilla M. Low reflects this tendency, stating three basic assumptions underlying the study. (1) The validity of the ideological framework of the American Democratic culture. (2) The necessity of furthering democratic ends. (3) The supreme worth of the individual (27, p. 22ff.). Yet in an attempt to modify and clarify the concept of need in this context, it soon becomes apparent that such a broad construction as these three principles embrace is woefully inadequate. If education is to receive its direction from the needs of the individual as a future citizen in an American democracy and all that this objective entails, we are at a loss for defining the precise implications that this concept carries for the everyday necessities of classroom practice. We have no clearcut interpretation of the democratic tradition. About all it implies is the necessity of a free exchange of ideas, an opportunity for the airing of individual differences, the right of the individual to life, liberty and the pursuit of happiness. However, the essence of the democratic condition emphasizes the conflicts among individual needs and the importance that these be freely manifested.

We might ask if the "American creed," or the democratic tradition is not too amorphous and vague a criterion to serve as a guide for educational objectives. An attempt to postulate lists of needs as basic to an individual in our democracy is beset with two major difficulties. (1) A tendency to give lip service to ideals which are in turn open to great varieties of individual interpretation, meaning all things to all men. (2) A specific tendency to define the needs of youth in terms of the current superficial values of a society (26). Inherent in this notion is the danger of education to maintain the *status quo*. A list of needs in McGuffey's time would emphasize the good, homely virtues of honesty, humility and respect for authority for the purpose of perpetuating a value structure favorable to vested interests. If education is to serve the dual function of transmitting cultural values and providing for an evolving, changing value structure, then it is essential to provide an adequate program for doing precisely that, with recommendations for specific objectives to be attained in order to practically realize this goal.

The prime difficulty involved in the use of needs as a basis of organization lies in the relation between the felt needs of the individual, the lacks of the individual, and the values of society which are to be nurtured with respect to the individual as an integral part of his society. In our earlier analysis we have stressed the essential interrelatedness of these factors, and the further necessity of distinguishing them for the purposes of clarity and precision. Even if it be admitted that an optimum level of adjustment in the individual is an intrinsic good, the dynamic factors involved in the relation of the demands which the society makes on the individual must be considered as logically prior in any considera-tion of optimum adjustment. The notion of personal adjustment is in itself no adequate criterion for goal-making, for it is ultimately depend-ent upon *what the individual is to adjust to*. The principle of equilibrium in itself points to an optimum state of balance within the individual in relation to his desires, perceptions, and the demands which the culture makes upon him as an integral part of the social scheme, but the concept in itself provides no source of direction.

The various lists of needs, then, suffer principally in that they utterly fail to provide more than a simple admonition that goals must always be postulated with a full cognizance of the limitations of the existing situation, a constant reminder that ideal ends should not be postulated which are incapable of attainment, or which fail to take into considera-tion the physiological and psychological factors involved in an under-standing of the potentialities and limitations of the learner with reference to his intelligence, his maturation level, and his relations with groups. Yet after we admit the importance of such considerations in exposing the possibilities open to us in the educational enterprise, we are left with the essential problem of what should be chosen as aims and objectives within this realm of possibility. In this sense the doctrine of needs resembles the concept of education as growth—a construct which in essence maintains that nothing should be done to deter the full actualization of the potentialities inherent in the learner with regard to his future adjustment to his environment. Certainly everyone would agree with this proposition. The question remains as to which of the potentialities inherent in the learner are to be nurtured, and in fact *created* in the course of his education.

With the tendency toward specificity of analysis there has been a constantly broadened interpretation of need. Thus we hear of the need for consumer awareness, driver-training, and courses in conversation, in order to meet the needs of youth. Even if these are admitted to be genuine needs in relation to a specifically defined context, the very multiplicity of listings requires an arrangement of these needs into a hierarchy of importance. This arrangement involves choice due to the necessity of the economy of time. Multiple listings of the characteristics of the educated person in a democracy thus stress the importance of certain skills, attitudes and values which should emerge from the educative process. However, in the light of the amount of time the school has to spend with the individual child, a guide toward the relative importance of various qualities must be postulated in order to furnish a realistic and attainable set of objectives for education. Thus the postulation of a hierarchy of basic *values* must serve as the core for educational organization. This certainly need not involve indoctrination with an established set of values. The scheme might rather emphasize the need for a recognition of freedom, of the necessity of ethical choice, of the need for logical reasoning, etc. These might in turn be qualified in order to design the specific ways in which these objectives may be nurtured. However, it must be noted that such a scheme must be preceded by the logical formulation of a rationale for the choice of objectives, the reasons for their relative importance and the basic criteria on which the scheme must rest. Only by so doing can a clear and well-formulated direction be proposed for education.

References

1. Allport, Gordon W. *Personality*. New York: Henry Holt and Co., 1937.
2. Beaumont, Henry and Macomber, Freeman. *Psychological Factors in Education*. New York: McGraw-Hill Book Co., 1949.
3. Bode, Boyd H. "Needs and the Curriculum," *Progressive Education*. Dec. 1940.
4. Bode, Boyd H. *Progressive Education at the Crossroads*. New York: Newson and Co., 1938.
5. Breckenridge, Marian and Vincent, E. Lee. *Child Development*. Philadelphia: W. B. Saunders Co., 1943.
6. Burton, William H. *The Guidance of Learning Activities*. New York: Appleton-Century-Crofts, 1952.
7. Cannon, W. B. *The Wisdom of the Body*. New York: W. W. Norton & Co., 1939.

8. Caswell, Hollis L. and Campbell, Doak S. *Curriculum Development.* New York: The American Book Co., 1935.
9. Childs, John S. *Education and Morals.* New York: Appleton-Century-Crofts, 1950.
10. Cole, Luella. *Psychology of Adolescence.* New York: Rinehart and Co., 1954.
11. Dewey, John. *How We Think.* Boston: D. C. Heath and Co., 1933.
12. Dewey, John. *Theory of Valuation.* Chicago: University of Chicago Press, 1939.
13. Fenton, Norman. *Mental Hygiene and School Practice.* Stanford, Calif.: Stanford University Press, 1943.
14. Gates, A. I., Jersild, A. T. and others. *Educational Psychology.* New York: The Macmillan Co., 1948.
15. Hartmann, George W. *Educational Psychology.* Boston: American Book Co., 1941.
16. Hempel, Carl G. *Fundamentals of Concept Formation in Empirical Science.* Chicago: University of Chicago Press, 1952.
17. Hook, Sidney. *Education for Modern Man.* New York: The Dial Press, 1946.
18. Lee, Dorothy. "Are Basic Needs Ultimate?" *Journal of Abnormal and Social Psychology,* 1948, 43, pp. 391–395.
19. Leonard, J. Paul and Gurich, Alvin C. *An Evaluation of Modern Education.* New York: D. Appleton-Century Co., 1942.
20. Macomber, Freeman. *Teaching in the Modern Secondary School.* New York: McGraw-Hill Co., 1952.
21. Malinowski, Bronislaw. *A Scientific Theory of Culture and Other Essays,* Ed. Huntington Cairns. Chapel Hill, N.C.: University of North Carolina Press, 1944.
22. Maslow, A. H. *Motivation and Personality.* New York: Harper & Brothers, 1954.
23. Murphy, A. E. *The Uses of Reason.* New York: The Macmillan Co., 1943.
24. Murray, Henry A. *Explorations in Personality.* New York: Oxford University Press, 1938.
25. Mursell, James L. *Psychology for Modern Education.* New York: W. W. Norton and Co., 1952.
26. National Education Association: The Educational Policies Commission. *Education for All American Youth.* Washington: National Education Association, 1944.
27. National Society for the Study of Education. *Yearbook LII. Part I: Adapting the Secondary School Program to the Needs of Youth.* University of Chicago Press, 1953.
28. Prescott, Daniel A. *Emotion and the Educative Process.* Washington: American Council on Education, 1938.
29. Scheffler, Israel. "Civilization and Value: A Review," *Harvard Educational Review,* Spring, 1953.
30. Skinner, Charles E., editor. *Educational Psychology.* New York: Prentice-Hall, Inc., 1951.
31. Stratemeyer, Florence B. and others. *Developing a Curriculum for Modern Living.* New York: Bureau of Publications, Teachers College, Columbia University, 1947.

32. Symonds, Percival M. *The Dynamics of Human Adjustment*. New York:
    D. Appleton Century Co., 1946.
33. Thayer, V. T., Zachry, Caroline, and Kotinsky, Ruth. *Reorganizing
    Secondary Education*. New York: D. Appleton-Century Co., 1939.
34. Witherington, H. Carl. *Educational Psychology*. New York: Ginn and
    Co., 1946.
35. Woodworth, Robert and Schlosberg, Harold. *Experimental Psychology*.
    New York: Henry Holt and Co., 1954.

23 / B. PAUL KOMISAR
AND JERROLD R. COOMBS

The Concept of Equality in Education

This essay addresses itself to the perennial and prodigal question:
What is equality in education? Concern with this question is ubiquitous
and, according to some authors, particularly germane at the present
moment in human affairs. Herbert Thelen's plea is as symptomatic of this
concern as any other we might quote:

> The imagination of the civilized world has been captured by the
> concept, pioneered but not perfected in America, of "equal
> educational opportunity for all." What does this mean? Does it
> mean, for example, equal opportunity to learn a particular body of
> knowledge set by the school—regardless of its meaningfulness to
> students having different capabilities and need? Or does it mean
> opportunity to learn whatever each child needs to learn in order to
> profit from his particular capabilities? Does it mean that every
> child in every state should have the same amount of money spent
> on him? Assuming that some teachers are better than others, who
> should get the best ones—the child who learns most readily or the
> one who learns least readily? What about the "culturally deprived"
> child, whose "background" has built-in resistance to learning; or
> the emotionally disturbed child, whose preoccupations keep him
> from listening; or the physiologically precocious or immature child,
> whose biological needs are out of step with the social possibilities
> for those of his age—What does equal opportunity mean here?[1]

B. Paul Komisar and Jerrold R. Coombs, "The Concept of Equality in Education,"
Studies in Philosophy of Education, III, No. 3 (Fall 1964), 223–244. Reprinted by
permission. This essay initiates issues that are discussed further in subsequent
publications of *Studies in Philosophy and Education*.

[1] Herbert A. Thelen, *Education and the Human Quest* (New York: Harper
& Brothers, 1960), pp. 11–12.

It is to this question we address ourselves, though perhaps not in quite the way Thelen poses it. Thelen's concern is with what the equality principle requires of us in different areas of education. We approach the question obliquely, by way of a linguistic analysis of the *term* "equality."

In the course of this paper we advance and try to justify the following claims: There are two concepts of equality—"equal as same" and "equal as fitting" tied usually to two different uses of language—descriptive and ascriptive.[2] The sameness concept has a determinate definition and a singular meaning in all contexts of application. Equality in the fittingness sense has an indeterminate definition; its meaning shifts across contexts and language users.[3] Since the principle of equal opportunity employs the fittingness concept, it is not possible to give it a unique and definite interpretation without prior ethical commitments. Therefore, the equality principle is a second-order principle, derivative with respect to the necessary first-order ethical premises. Nor can the equality principle itself confer distinctiveness on one philosophy of education *vis à vis* any other philosophy. Philosophies with different commitments can, all the same, champion their own version of equal opportunity.[4]

Though these are the only fish we care to fry here, there is much more to the story. "Equality" and the equality principle seem always to have been with us in American education, from the classical liberals through the recent humane welfare theories of education. And even our contemporary austere educational Calvinists do not simply pump for a crash program in excellence. They pause to ask almost plaintively, can we be excellent and equal too? Indeed these contemporary educational philosophers, engaging in what has been called, euphemistically, "The Great Debate" have shown concern for only the narrow question of whether equal educational opportunity requires a common curriculum for all students, or variegated curricula in which students with unique clusters "interests, abilities, and needs" will find a clutch of studies peculiarly congenial to them.

But in addition to the areas enumerated by Thelen, we find other areas

[2] This apt expression, the Fittingness Concept, was suggested to us by Harry S. Broudy. It is more suitable than our original label, the Fairness Concept. We take this opportunity to express our thanks to Broudy and James E. McClellan for their generously offered criticisms and, as custom would have it, absolve them of further responsibility.

[3] I.e., the sameness concept can be defined in the accepted way—more or less in terms of the necessary and sufficient conditions for applying or assessing applications of the term. The fittingness concept is not susceptible to definition in this way. The difference is roughly analogous to the divergence in definitional strategy one would follow with "brown" and "good" as applied to shoes.

[4] If one educational philosophy proclaims support of equal opportunity and another disavows it, to this extent they differ. But this is a trivial difference of sheer avowal or disavowal. Nothing of significance follows from it.

in which equality plays a disputed role. In the legal context, even before the Supreme Court unanimously supported the words "Separate educational facilities are inherently unequal," there were attempts to broaden "equality" to cover "intangible" factors of schooling.

In the area of school finance, the equality principle has been invoked by supporters and opponents of federal aid. But surer indications of its importance here are the dispute over the variables to be included in equalization formulae and the surprising distinction made between equal expenditures and equal educational effort.

The concept of equality, then, stands astride the path of educational thought as does no other term. Indeed, it is one of the few terms employed in nearly all the departments of educational language. Add to this the presence of disputed meanings, and conceptual analysis needs no further temptation or justification. It may be that our analysis is wrongheaded, but it is honor enough to be part of the search for clarity. When arson is the desideratum, they also serve who only blow.

Two Concepts of Equality

A. The Sameness Concept

Let us begin putting meat on these abstract bones by contrasting two speech acts—one descriptive, the other ascriptive. Consider first a common sort of case wherein we say of students that they are of equal height or ability or have read an equal number of books. This we dub the descriptive use of "equal" and put it on a par with reports of hair color and the like.

What is the sense of the term "equal" when it is so employed? In these cases "equal" means "same" as in "same height" or "same IQ." One forewarning is in order, however. As Chappell[5] has recently noted, the term "same" has itself a dual use. We can refer to an object as "the same one we saw yesterday." Here the force of "same" is to identify as *one* thing what might appear on hasty, *prima facie* grounds to be distinct things. This is the *identifying* function of "same." But the term also serves a comparative purpose, in which it is presupposed that there are multiple objects and a comparison is made of them for this or that purpose (though not all purposes), with respect to certain characteristics (though not all characteristics). It is in this latter role that we take "same" as synonymous with "equal." Now our definition:

To say that X and Y are equal with respect to some characteristic C, is to

[5] V. C. Chappell, "Sameness and Change," *Philosophical Review*, LXIX (July, 1960), 351–362.

1. *presuppose* that an appropriate (valid) scale for measuring units of C has been correctly applied to X and Y under standard conditions; and to

2. *presuppose* that the scale applied to X is equivalent or identical to the scale applied to Y; and further to

3. *presuppose* that the units of measurement employed have a degree of fineness suitable to the context; and, then, to

4. *assert* that the resultant scores or measurements in both applications are the same.

We need not tarry here very long. Equality as sameness gives us little trouble. Our main reason for specifying this concept is to contrast it with another sense of equality yet to come. There are those, however, who would make all uses of "equal" cleave to this sameness sense, and the temptation for such a move lies in the sameness concept itself.

Given two speakers sharing the above definition, there need not be *automatic* agreement in recognizing instances of sameness. That is, descriptive claims of equality are not *completely* rulebound. One is given one's head to a limited extent; there is room for individual judgment in even such a hardheaded task as determining whether two characteristics are the same.

The source of this freedom is criterion 3 of the definition. Thus we may say of two students that they fared equally well (or fared the same) in a course of instruction when they received the same letter grade (A or B, etc.), despite discrepancies in their test scores or their dissimilar performance at varying stages in the instruction. But in such a circumstance we could not say that their test scores were necessarily the same. A college admissions officer might want measurements on a finer scale before allowing the two candidates to be "equal in school achievement." A shift to an unexpected level of precision is the stuff of contrived melodrama.

> "Yes, but they are not precisely equal," says Villain to Goodheart, who never imagined we were going to use calipers on cauliflower. So Goodheart loses the bet and coughs up his soul, his deed or daughter (for even tastes of Villains run in different directions). Goodheart's intentions were of the best but the moral is not to let your logic slide."

Consequently, there is a place for context, individual perspective to make a difference. Claims of equality are not *just* reports, not "a mere reading off of the facts." They reflect, to some degree, judgments of the speaker that can vary from case to case and speaker to speaker, depending on purpose, seriousness of concern and kinds of scales available.[6] There is a chink here in the wall of complete determinateness, but next we are considering another concept of equality wherein whole sections of this wall are absent. Our concern is that the critic not confuse a chink with a breach.

B. The Fittingness Concept

Consider a second range of speech acts in which we invoke "equality" as the operative term.

(a) "The teacher gave equal treatment to both sides of the dispute."
(b) "This school offers equal opportunity to all students."
(c) "Both candidates were given an equal chance of admission to college."

1. These assertions differ from those made with the sameness concept in several respects.

First, note that these assertions have the force of judgments rather than reports. They avow that some practice was proper to the subjects at hand: they are expressions of approval (or disapproval in claims of inequality). Since we usually do not make a judgment of propriety or impropriety without cause, it is not surprising to find that these assertions have another function. This second function is most clearly seen in the negative case. A claim of unequal treatment constitutes a rebuke, censure of the perpetrator of it. It carries with it the presumption that the agent was responsible. Of course the responsibility can frequently be disclaimed ("I was made to change his grade"), passed on ("The school-board mandated this") or its existence denied altogether ("Really, this is the only thing we can do"). But even when such disclaimers are justified, when responsibility cannot be assigned or assigned definitely, there remains what one writer has called the "evaluative residue."[7] "All right, the unequal treatment may not have been your fault, but it's a shoddy way to treat the student all the same."

The situation is less simple with respect to a positive claim. For if a claim of inequality (impropriety) is censure, what is the force of a claim of equality (propriety)? Given a suitable contextual plot, the positive claim may exonerate an agent of presumed wrong doing ("No, he did treat the students equally") or it may give official certification to an

---

[6] In connection with this point and the discussion in the preceding paragraph, see Robert Crawshay-Williams, *Methods and Criteria of Reasoning* (London: Routledge and Regan Paul, 1957), Chapter 2, expecially pp. 22–24, in which he discusses the role of context, i.e., purpose, in the interpretation of statements, including assertions of sameness.

[7] V. C. Walsh, "Ascriptions and Appraisals," *Journal of Philosophy*, LV (November 20, 1958), 1062ff; and in *Scarcity and Evil* (Englewood Cliffs, N.J.: Prentice-Hall, Inc., 1961), p. 108.

alleged propriety ("We find there is equal opportunity here" announced by some suitable committee or office).

We found above that this use of "equal" has affinities with evaluation. Nonetheless, a claim of equal treatment is not usually praise.[8] "You presented all viewpoints brilliantly" is commendation. "You gave ten minutes to each position" is descriptive. A claim of equal treatment hangs uneasily between. It is not praise because it is a requirement of the *concept* of teaching that the teacher be fair, impartial, just.[9] It is not description for we are passing on the legitimacy of the teacher's behavior.

2. There are two quick forays to make before the undergrowth thickens. Let us preface the first by stipulating that the approving, legitimizing, censuring, etc., acts be called the ascriptive functions of "equal." The sameness concept usually does not have these functions. The report that students have equal grades or read an equal number of books is not of itself approval or disapproval, censure or exoneration. Of course we may take it as such, if we care to, by suitable additions to the context.

This brings us to another point: we do not need additional information to detect that "This teacher treats students unequally' is obloquy. We want to emphasize that it is the word *equal* which has the ascriptive functions we are discussing. That is, we are considering the ascriptive uses of the term itself, not the presence of the term in an otherwise ascriptive speech act. *Equal* is the operative term making the statement "This student was not given equal treatment" a rebuke. If the operative term were to be replaced, the whole force of the assertion would be altered. It is easy enough to note that "You should have players of equal (same) height" is a prescription. But "equal" does not make it so. It's more discerning to see with Benn and Peters, that:

> In social and political theory, however, 'equality' is more often prescriptive than descriptive. In this sense, 'all men are equal' would imply not that they possess some attribute or attributes in the same degree but that they ought to be treated alike.[10]

That is, the ascriptive functions (and Benn and Peters' prescriptive function as well) are built by convention into the very meaning of the

---

[8] There is always the exception. When a teacher maintains equal treatment at a time and in a place calling for unusual skill, forebearance, etc., then it is praise. It is also unexpected.

[9] We would include it in the "restrictions of manner" made part of the concept of teaching in Israel Scheffler, *The Language of Education* (Springfield, Ill.: Charles C. Thomas, 1960), pp. 57f, 68.

[10] S. I. Benn and R. S. Peters, *Social Principles and the Democratic State* (London: Allen & Unwin, 1959), p. 108.

term "equal." The functions don't simply arise from the syntactical form of the assertion. This is the point that is not grasped by those who analyze the concept of equality: the ascriptive functions *are part of the meaning* and must be accounted for in any definition we give.

So there is no doubt that the sameness concept can enter into ascriptive and prescriptive speech acts. It is likewise clear that the fittingness concept can be used purely descriptively, when its approving, censure, etc. functions have been revoked or neutralized.[11] But in both "You should group students of equal ability" and "He said there is equal opportunity here" the term "equal" is not the operative one regulating the kind of speech act involved.

Our point, put in its most forceful manner, is that the fittingness concept of equality has ascriptive and prescriptive functions built into it. These are not part of the sameness concept. So the differences we have been discussing are truly differences between the concepts themselves. They are not differences between various speech acts in which "equal" is merely present.

3. It is this last point that is the sticky one, and it is surely time to stop dawdling over the ascriptive *functions* of "equal" and get to the main question. Granted that when the term is applied in contexts of the sort being discussed, it will have the force of approval or rebuke, etc. However, what is the *sense* of the term in these contexts? This sense of "equal" is *fittingness*. To say that certain treatment is equal treatment is to be saying that it is fitting to the subjects exposed to it. It is difficult, however, to pin this sense down with a definition; for the criteria of fittingness, unlike those for sameness, shift with the ever-moving sands of context. We will offer a general defining formula to fix the concept in place. But it should be borne in mind that it is the ascriptive functions, not the criteria for application, that are common to all contexts in which the fittingness concept is applied.

Skipping further preliminaries, we offer this definition of the fittingness concept of equality:

(a) The provisions or practices being adjudged equal be in accordance with rightful rules, properly applied.

(b) The rules employed be selected with reference to the appropriate characteristics of the subjects, correctly described.

4. The definition stands in need of further explication. But criticism being more delightful than explanation, we will postpone discussion of

---

[11] E.g., A. H. Halsey, Jean Floud, and C. Arnold Anderson, *Education, Economy, and Society* (New York: The Free Press of Glencoe, Inc., 1961), pp. 209–214.

our own definition in order to give protracted attention to an alternative view of the meaning of the fittingness concept. The view we refer to goes something like this:

> When I say "This teacher gave equal treatment" I may very well be approving the teacher's demeanor and what not, but nonetheless I am approving the treatment (of X and Y) because it is the same treatment (X and Y). So we can say that "equal" has the *sense* of sameness despite differences in *functions* or *use*. On this view there is one concept of equality not two, albeit in some speech acts the single concept has ascriptive and prescriptive appendages. But even with a full complement of barnacles and weeds, a boat is a boat for all that.

We want to oppose this single-meaning view, which we call the sameness thesis. "Equal," we will say, has not only taken on new functions but shifted its sense as well; and it is false to claim that sameness is identical with or essential to equality in the fittingness sense.

(Two points of procedure. Since our main interest in the next section is with the fittingness concept, it seems useless to reiterate the designation. Hence we simply write "equal" when we mean the "fittingness concept of equal." However, those who are already disenchanted with the single meaning view of "equal" are advised to skip the next section and proceed to part III where we return to the problem of definition.)

Critique of the Sameness Thesis

There have been varied attempts in education to make sameness a defining characteristic of equality. Philip Phenix supplies us with one recent and notable example:

> Equal opportunity means the distribution of schooling in such a way that the interests of each are served to the maximum, consistent with the equal claims of others. This general principle is not easy to apply in practice because different interests are not truly comparable and thus no definite meaning can be attached to their equality.
>
> Perhaps equality of educational opportunity in the last analysis means simply that the distribution of education shall be determined through discussion and agreement within the democratic community, where each person has the same right of voice and the same standing before the law.[12]

[12] Philip H. Phenix, *Philosophy of Education* (New York: Henry Holt and Company, 1958), p. 144.

Why should Phenix be concerned whether the students' interests (or even the curricula catering to them) are comparable? Presumably because he assumes that equal opportunity requires sameness. But since the interests cannot even be compared, we are in no position to assert their sameness. So Phenix, in the grip of the sameness thesis looks elsewhere—to the procedures followed in establishing school programs—for the necessary aspect of sameness. And here in the midst of democratic decision processes, he finds the desired identical element, *viz.*, that each person's voice and vote count the same, i.e., as one! This is surely a desperate price to pay for retaining sameness in equality.

Myron Lieberman also champions the thesis, but by more labyrinthian paths:

> At this point, it becomes important to recognize that complete equality of educational opportunity is impossible. Not everyone can have the same teacher or live in the same home environment or travel the same distance to school, to mention just a few things that could be the basis of inequality of educational opportunity. The impossibility of complete equality tells us something about what people do not ordinarily mean when they say that there is equality of educational opportunity. They do not mean that there are no inequalities whatsoever. Rather, they mean that some inequalities can be disregarded in judging whether there is or is not equality of educational opportunity.
>
> Minor inequalities are thus disregarded in common usage. But at what point does an inequality cease to be minor? How much equalization is necessary before we are willing to say that there is equality of educational opportunity?

And farther along:

> . . . equality does not mean that every student receive the same grade, but that every student be graded according to standards which apply to all. When we think of equality before the law, we do not suppose that there can be no equality unless all persons on trial are acquitted or all convicted. . . . The 'equality' involved is not one of outcome but of procedure to determine the outcome.[13]

Lieberman is so insistent in his asseverations concerning the practical limits on the amount of sameness that is possible, that we are apt to overlook the fact that he makes sameness—*some* sameness to be sure—

---

[13] Myron Lieberman, "Equality of Educational Opportunity," *Harvard Educational Review*, XXIX (Summer, 1959). Also reprinted in B. O. Smith and R. H. Ennis (editors), *Language and Concepts in Education* (Chicago: Rand McNally and Company, 1961), pp. 133, 137.

the defining element in equality. Thus the problem (to Lieberman) in equal opportunity is determining *which* conditions must be the same. His prejudice in favor of sameness forces him to overlook the obvious: viz, that it is the presence of dissimilarity which *constitutes* equal opportunity in certain circumstances.

Others are less clearly supporters of the sameness thesis, but their ambiguous definitions are as susceptible of this interpretation as of any other:

> In practice it [equal opportunity] means an equal chance to compete within the framework of goals and the structure of rules established by our particular society. . . .[14]

> Education, we now say, equalizes when it matches equally well the variant needs, wants, and abilities of individuals.[15]

Although the quotations above do not reveal the fact clearly, the sameness thesis may take any one of several forms. We will consider each of these seriatim even though some forms are without supporters at present. However, it is likely that even the most neglected bastion, once under attack, will be found bristling with defenders.

We begin by distinguishing two general ways of construing the sameness thesis. Consider the claim "A and B were given equal treatment." The first approach holds that however sameness enters the picture, it obtains between A and B, the explicit subjects of the utterance. This approach we will dub the *explicit comparison*. The alternative approach is, as you would expect, more covert. It assumes that the intended comparison is "A and B treated equally" is not between A and B as explicitly stated, but between A and other presumed A's; B and other presumed B's. The equal treatment, then, exists between the asserted subjects and their respective, but unmentioned, kinsman. This, naturally, we label the *implicit comparison*. What the implicit comparison does is to interpret the single claim about A and B into two separate utterances, one about A's and the other about B's.

A. Sameness Thesis: Explicit Comparison

This approach itself comes in a variety of forms. These are best exemplified through consideration of the elements found in a context in which we make some claim of equal treatment: There are five such elements.

---

[14] John Gardner, *Excellence* (New York: Harper and Row, 1961), p. 12.

[15] M. H. Willing, et. al., *Schools for Our Democratic Society* (New York: Harper and Brothers, 1951), p. 139.

(a) *Subjects:* implicitly or explicitly involved; not only students but competing hypotheses, theories, recipients of funds or other specifiable characteristics; who are exposed or subjected to some treatment.
(b) *Rule(s)* mandating how the subjects are to be treated, called often the treatment-generating rules.
(c) *Justification:* principles invoked to defend the use of rule(s) on certain subjects in particular circumstances.
(d) *Treatment:* the practices or provisions the subjects are exposed to, or the course of action taken in connection with the subjects.
(e) Finally, the *results*, in some relevant sense, of the treatment given.

1. The identity form. In this form the thesis holds that there is equal treatment of subjects if and only if the treatment (d) is literally similar or identical for each subject. This is the form we sketched earlier as the single-meaning view of equality. It posits only one concept of equality fitting all applications of the term, *viz.,* the sameness concept defined earlier. (Recall that this does not deny that some uses may have ascriptive functions. However, it is the *sense* of the term that remains the same.)

Clearly, in some cases we do require that the treatment of A and B be the same before we say that it is *equal* treatment. But this covers only those cases in which the relevant characteristics of the subjects are the same. Our use of "equal" seems to follow the rule: when there is identity in element (a) the subjects, a judgment of equality requires sameness with regard to element (d) the treatment.

But the sameness thesis can't settle for this limited victory; it aspires to hold for all cases, including those in which subjects differ in relevant traits. Simply as a matter of fact we see that it does not hold. If two students are given the same penalties for the same misdemeanor we say that they have received equal treatment. But we judge it to be inequality of treatment to give the same penalties for dissimilar infractions. Here our use of "equal" follows a second rule to the effect that differences in subjects require differences in treatment in order for the treatments to be judged equal.

At this juncture the sameness thesis might take one of two paths: one is to keep the identity between equal treatment and same treatment, but withdraw from the explicit to the implicit comparison. The other is to drop the identity of "equal" and "same" but retain sameness in some other defining capacity. We will follow up on this latter possibility first.

2. Essential aspect form. In the face of the criticism directed at the identity form, the supporter of the sameness thesis might seek some other omnipresent feature of the context as the ubiquitous element of sameness

in all claims of equality. The likely candidates are the elements listed above.

(a) It might appear plausible to choose the rule(s) (element b) as the necessary element of sameness. Now we can recast our definition of "equality" in this manner.

For treatment of A and B to be equal requires that the treatment of each be mandated by rules which are the same for each.

Now the defining element is not found in the disparity of treatment accorded but in the identity of the rules invoked to determine it.

But this definition will not hold for all uses of "equal." The following counter example, wherein the treatment is admittedly equal, yet not generated by the same rules, is illustrative. Imagine a teacher presenting controversial views of a topic. One side is a long, necessarily detailed inductive argument and the other a deductive, nearly stark defense (Hutchins vs. Dewey on curriculum; Catholic vs. humanist on birth control). Equality of treatment here requires not only that the actual treatment be dissimilar (in time, type of presentation); but, more relevantly, it also demands that the treatment of each alternative position be derived from rules which are *different* for the respective sides. That is, the treatment of each side will be mandated by explanatory regulations fitting to arguments of the type at hand, not by any common set of rules for all sides.

(b) In the quotation from Philip Phenix, he seems to select the justification (element c) as the necessary element of sameness in the definition of equality. However it is not clear which of the two definitions he would favor.

Treatment of subjects is "equal" when the treatment-generating rules are justified *either* (1) on the basis of a principle containing an element of sameness in it (e.g., same number of votes for each man principle); or (2) by reference to one principle which covers the disparate treatment-generating rules in the situation.

Position 1 fails whenever we offer a justifying principle with no mention of sameness within it. Phenix's illustration *happens* to be a justification of type (1), justifying a rule of curriculum on the basis of the one man—one vote principle. But certainly it is not this principle, nor any other mentioning sameness within it, which justifies, say, the use of deductive rules in presenting deductive arguments or the rule that applicants for college admission exceeding a certain standard will be admitted.

So it is not the one man—one vote principle which makes an arrangement *ipso facto* an arrangement of equality. The decision, for example, made by the one man—one vote procedure, to treat *all* arguments by deductive rules, would be a violation of equality! There is a limit to the number of actions for which democracy can be conscripted as warrant.

It is the second (2) position which is the more plausible, but not so much so that another clear instance of usage does not refute it. Consider two boys applying for admission to college (or two school districts for subsidies). One applicant with below average qualifying scores is rejected (cut-off rule); another with the same scores but a religion underrepresented on the campus is admitted (proportionate representation of social groups rule).

Here we find different treatment; different rules and a *different justification for each rule.* For the cut-off rule, there is the usual one about the low probability of success in such cases; in support of the other rule we are regaled with stories of the educational advantages of encountering a "balanced" college environment. Yet here is equality of treatment all the same.

It might be objected that there is more to the justification process in these cases. If the justification is pushed to its limits, the critic avers, then all justifications of presumed equal treatment consist finally in one general principle: *all treatment generating rules be appropriate to the subjects being treated.*

But this simply will not do. To defend the sameness thesis on these grounds is suicide for the thesis. For it is precisely this claim, viz., that equality means fitting, we are defending *against* the sameness thesis. It trivializes the thesis to claim that the equality requires sameness because equal treatment must always be fitting treatment!

So much for the use of the element of justification as the essential aspect of sameness in ordinary claims of equality.

(c) There are probably other elements, increasingly inscrutable, more esoteric, which might be invoked as the desired element of sameness. We will consider but one more. It might be contended that equality requires that the *results* of the treatment be the same in any case of equal treatment.[16]

We need not linger here long. The plausibility of the position arises in a case, for example, wherein a teacher may give different coverage to each side of a controversial topic. When charged with giving unequal treatment, the teacher might report that students were very familiar with one alternative, thus requiring less exposure to it to reach a level of understanding commensurate with their understanding of the other side. But what if this "identity in level of understanding" did not come to pass in a case where two sides to a controversy are given divergent, yet

---

[16] See Gregory Vlastos, "Justice and Equality" in Richard B. Brandt (ed), *Social Justice* (Englewood Cliffs, N.J.: Prentice-Hall, Inc., 1962), pp. 41ff. for a discussion of equality in terms of results of treatment.

proper, presentations? Would this render the presentation unfair? Or what if the "level of understanding" (or development or achievement, etc.) is not detectable, are we then unable to judge the fairness of the teaching? Surely not. We would judge such cases by the rules for correctness that apply to the presentation itself, regardless of outcome, known or unknown. This fact is even clearer in a case of college admissions. Equal opportunity here does not require that all candidates be admitted (same result) but that all be handled appropriately (fitting procedure).

In summary, then, we conclude that for every element that is posited as providing the sameness in a claim of equality, we can find legitimate cases where that element is not the same yet the case is a genuine and legitimate application of the expression "equal treatment."

B. Sameness Thesis: Implicit Comparison

In the face of objections raised thus far, the defender of the sameness thesis might claim that the thesis has failed because we are seeking the comparison in the wrong place. In utterances of the form "A and B, were given equal treatment," the intended contrast is not between A and B, but between A and other A's; B and other B's. When so interpreted "equal treatment" will mean "same treatment" (the identity form), albeit not sameness between A and B.

But if this position is correct, then it must follow that every demand *for* equal treatment must be a demand for identical treatment. Consider, however, such a demand in these different contexts.

Here we can retain the sameness thesis in its pure identity form. For, as shown, "equal" has the sense of "same." But this later virtue marks the fall of the sameness thesis. We need only show that *not* all demands for equal treatment are intended as demands for same treatment. This is easily done, for to interpret all such demands as claims for identity is to miss the point of the assertion in many cases and to trivialize the concept of equality.

Consider the following contexts in which demands for equal treatment can arise from different intentions.

(a) A person is correctly grouped, i.e., admitted to be an instance of X, but from oversight or intention is not actually treated as an X. For example, a community is admittedly one of a certain tax classification, but fails to receive the state funds earmarked for communities with that classification.

(b) A subject is treated as others with whom he is grouped but claims to have been wrongly grouped. E.g., a candidate for college admissions is classified as *low* in entrance examination results and rejected along with others in the group but argues that his relation to an alumnus has been overlooked. He should be *low-alumnus*.

(c) A subject is admittedly grouped properly but claims that this treatment is unfair to the entire group. The examples here are profuse. All students who would have once been rejected for further education now demanding it are illustrative.[17]

Case (a) marks the apex in the career of the sameness thesis. The request here, clearly, is to be treated the same as other members of a given group. Identity seems to hold for case (b) as well. But proponents will have to admit the fit is looser. For there are two ways of construing the claim made in (b): (1) as a demand to be treated the *same as* others of like characteristics or (2) as a demand to be treated with respect to one's *proper* characteristics. It seems to be a matter of choice as to which is the relevant description of the situation.

But the (c) type situation is a pickle from a different barrel. The issue here is *not* one of identical treatment, for that condition has already been fulfilled. The issue here is whether the treatment is the rightful, i.e., fitting way to treat the group. This shift from (b) to (c) marks the last extremity of the sameness thesis. For what has just been demonstrated is that even when the subjects and treatment are the same, it still makes sense to ask whether the treatment is equal, i.e., fitting. If "equal" literally *meant* "same," such a claim would be redundant, absurd.

Now certainly sameness is involved even in the (c) case, but only in the secondary sense that once rightful treatment is established, it should apply to all members of the group. But the sameness thesis celebrates this secondary characteristic into an intellectual way of life. To the supporter of sameness, for example, the Negro demand is to be treated the same as the white, not a demand to smash down improper differentiating characteristics. But the misconception is revealed when we realize that evidence of superior intellectual characteristics in the colored race would justify, in the name of *equality*, a demand for education superior to that given to whites.

And this reveals a deep truth about ordinary use of "equal." When we judge A and B to have fared equally, part of what we are saying is that each was managed according to his kind. But more importantly we are claiming that this is the proper kind, and that it is *right* to treat subjects of this kind in this way. This is the moral element involved in type (c) cases (which will be discussed in the next section).

---

[17] These types of challenges are freely adapted from Isaiah Berlin, "Equality," *Aristotelian Society Proceedings*, LVI, 1955–56, 307f.

Both Lieberman, explicitly, and Phenix, by implication, want to include type (c) cases into the class of claims of equality. The reason is apparent. To restrict the concept of equality to (a) and (b) cases is to trivialize the concept. The term would only operate, then, in cases of simple error and apparent corruption. As such the concept would be a fraud, considering the weight it is asked to carry in social and political philosophy, as well as philosophy of education. The trick is to retain the significant scope for the concept while holding fast to the sameness thesis. But when the former is done, the latter is already a dead thesis. The way to keep the horse from escaping the barn is never to bring him in.

Summary

So much for the attempt to wed equality to egalitarianism by reportive, not persuasive, definition. Generally we have tried to show that to interpret "equal" as "same" (*in any way*) is to distort the meaning of the term in some ordinary contexts. On the other hand, to interpret "equal" as "fitting" retains the ordinary sense of the term in all contexts. We do not deny, of course, that same treatment may constitute equal treatment *in some contexts*, as a special case of fitting treatment. Or to put the matter differently: we are contending that "equal" is *defined* as "fitting" and that same treatment may on occasion be equal treatment *as a matter of fact, not definition.*

Why be concerned with this issue—so concerned that we follow the sameness thesis through its tedious convolutions? The reason is that a definition in terms of sameness offers the last best hope for a determinate, single interpretation for such a ubiquitous educational ideal as equal educational opportunity for all. To this topic we now turn.

III. The Fittingness Concept and the Equality Principle

Having assayed and rejected varied attempts to define equality in terms of sameness, we turn now to an explication of our own definition. Earlier we cited the following rules as constituting a definition of "equality" in its fittingness sense:

a. The provisions or practices being adjudged equal be in accordance with rightful rules, properly applied.
b. The rules be employed with reference to appropriate character- istics of the subjects, correctly described.

A. Indeterminacy

Ponder now the state of our system. If equality were defined in terms of sameness, then there would be at least one constant criterion for the application of the term in each and every context. But the upshot of our discussion in the previous section was negative with respect to this hope. The definition offered here in place of sameness is indeterminate. It is indeterminate with respect to the content of the rules to be followed and the characteristics of the subjects that are relevant.

Furthermore, the definition stands in constant danger of redundancy on the score that relevancy of subject characteristics and propriety of rules are functions of one another. That is, whether a candidate's religion is relevant in college admissions is dependent on the presence or absence of a rule about treatment of candidates with respect to this characteristic. And whether we have such rules is dependent on the importance we attribute to the characteristic.

B. Primacy of Ethical Judgment

This indeterminacy in the definition of the fittingness concept is apparently analogous to that encountered in connection with the sameness concept. With regard to the sameness concept, the selection of a suitable scale for gainsaying measures of things to be compared is a matter of *practical* judgment. In applying the fittingness concept, however, one is choosing the morally right rules to adhere to in a given case. This is a *moral* judgment.

It is commonly recognized that assent to equality is a moral act. What we here assert is that the decision as to what *constitutes* equality in concrete cases is likewise a moral decision and a logically necessary one. Allegiance to the equality principle as such is an empty gesture. The principle is a secondary one, depending on logically prior moral commitments to make it meaningful. For example, it is meaningless to support the idea that school subsidies should be distributed to communities on an equal basis. It is not until a commitment is made as to what constitutes rightful allocation that assent to the equality principle becomes significant. Therefore no philosophy of education is identified or made controversial by its belief in educational equality. What is distinctive about an educational philosophy is the particular way it interprets this belief, the judgments and commitments it makes along the way. For to round out this topic on a note of redundancy, the definition of equality does not dictate our educational preferences. Rather it is the case that our educational preferences constitute *our* meaning for equality.

C. Essentially Contested

Thus it is that the specific criteria or rules by which we determine a treatment to be equal are not part of the definition of the concept. As illustration, consider the distribution of state funds to local districts on an "equal" basis. A rule (read "formula") which allocates funds on the basis of local tax *effort* is no more or less "true equality" than rules which dispense moneys to compensate for deficiencies in local tax resources or which give the same amount to each local district or which reward districts manifesting greatest educational improvements; or any combination of these. Any of these can be defended as the right, and hence fitting, way to distribute subsidies. The same holds true for, say, the allocation of teaching talent to students of differential ability. The best teachers might be allocated to the most able students; to the least able, or assigned on some compromise basis. There is nothing in the linguistic conventions which render any one rule as the "real" or "true" meaning of "equal treatment."

We would borrow from Gallie at this point and speak of "equality" in its fittingness sense as an essentially contested concept, i.e., as one of the "concepts the proper use of which inevitably involves endless disputes about their proper uses on the part of their users."[18]

This does not apply, however, to the ascriptive functions of the concept depicted earlier. These functions (approving, assigning responsibility, etc.) are invariant from one context to another, and from one language user to another. However, what particular criteria a person will use will depend on that to which his moral commitments will allow him, justifiably, to apply these functions.

D. Consequences of the Sameness Thesis

Thus it should be clear why a definition of the fittingness concept in terms of sameness is to be so vehemently rejected. For if the concept is so defined *and made to retain its ascriptive force,* the result is the thoroughgoing egalitarianism, so well depicted by Berlin:

> In its simplest form the ideal of complete social equality embodies the wish that everything and everybody should be as similar as possible to everything and everybody else. . . . I doubt whether anyone has ever seriously desired to bring such a society into being, or even supposed such a society to be capable of being created. Nevertheless, it seems to me that demands for human equality which have been expressed both by philosophers and by men of action who have advocated or attempted to reform society, can best be represented as modifications of this absolute and absurd ideal. In this ideal egalitarian society, inequality—and this must ultimately mean dissimilarity—would be reduced to a minimum.[19]

[18] W. B. Gallie, "Essentially Contested Concepts," *Aristotelian Society Proceedings,* LVI (1955–56), 169. Our borrowing of this designation does not adhere to the strict requirements for the employment of this term as set down therein.

[19] Berlin, *op. cit.,* 311f.

Even to hold to a less strict form of the sameness thesis is still to give priority to uniformity over variety.

So as a *reportive* definition of the fittingness concept, the sameness thesis is not only factually incorrect; it is also morally wrong. The results are no less severe if the sameness thesis is offered as a stipulated definition. For if the ascriptive force of the term is retained, then the "stipulated definition" becomes an ethical recommendation. If the ascriptive functions are dropped, then the stipulation is pointless. We would still need a term to perform the ascriptive services of the fittingness concept.

E. Other Misconceptions

1. Even those who realize that "equality" cannot be defined in terms of sameness fall into the error of supposing that it still has a determinate definition. This is probably the source of the crude circularity in the definitions by Willing, *et. al.* and Gardner, cited earlier, and in the following definition:

> ". . . equality does not mean identity. . . . Let me suggest again that equality in our sense involves an *equal right* of every child . . . to achieve excellence, to excel. This is what equality means. . . ."[20]

It is quite conceivable for someone to adopt "right to achieve excellence" or "right to compete" or "right to express judgment" as criteria for determining equality of treatment in appropriate contexts. Of course, it is understood that these are not *definitions* of the term, since different and even contrary criteria might also be justified. What is fostered here is the illusion that "equality" has a determinate sense which modifies in some way the criterion of application. But "equal right to achieve" means no more than "right to achieve." One's equality with others, then, consists in the right one shares with others to achieve. It consists in no more than this, because there is nothing beyond having the right. Adding "equal" to the right is a redundancy.

---

[20] Peter H. Odegard, "Education and American Values," in *Foundations for Excellence*, Fifteenth Yearbook of the American Association of Colleges for Teacher Education, *Proceedings of the 1962 Annual Meeting* (Washington, D.C., 1962), p. 39. Italics added.

Dewey appears to have gone down this path also: "Belief in equality is an element of the democratic credo. It is not, however, belief in equality of natural endowments. Those who proclaimed the idea of equality did not suppose they were enunciating a psychological doctrine, but a legal and political one. All individuals are entitled to equality of treatment by law and in its administration. Each one is affected equally in quality if not in quantity by the institutions under which he lives and has an *Equal Right to Express* his judgment, although the weight of his judgment may not be equal in amount when it enters into the pooled result to that of others. In short, each one is *Equally an Individual* and entitled to *Equal Opportunity of Development of His Own Capacities* . . ." John Dewey, *Problems of Men* (New York: Philosophical Library, 1946), p. 60. Italics added.

To sum up. Being given equal opportunity does not consist in being given a *special* right, viz., an *equal* right; it consists in being *given* the right. The point in saying that this right is a criterion of equality (what equality means) is that it is morally justified to employ this as a criterion to apply in appropriate contexts.

2. Still another definition of the fittingness concept misconstrues the moral element in the concept and suppresses its essential contestability.

> . . . The expression 'equality of educational opportunity,' as it is used, refers . . . to the environmental circumstances that influence the growth and development of the individual. No reference to equal intellectual capacity or to any other native endowments is intended. The intended reference is the *chance* to get an education, *of whatever amount and kind one's* endowments make possible. It is the chance that is to be equalized.[21]

The illusion is created here that the criteria specifying what is equal treatment in some context are simply "read off" from the facts of the environment and student's characteristics. (As, for example, equal right can be "read off," merely from the facts.) But a student's endowments make different kinds of education possible. Which should we give the student a chance to get? And which of his endowments do we judge to be appropriate to encourage? The authors state that fair play is the sense of "equal opportunity," but they ignore the fact that this is a moral notion. What is equal treatment is a matter of moral choice, not factual reporting, and this yields contesting, not uniform views.

24 / B. OTHANEL SMITH

On the Anatomy of Teaching

The procedures and techniques of teaching, like those of any art, are not to be worked out by reference to ready-made ideas. Rather they are to be devised in terms of the materials and conditions at hand, and by

B. Othanel Smith, "On the Anatomy of Teaching," *The Journal of Teacher Education*, VII (December 1956), 339–346. Reprinted by permission. (This article is adapted from the James William Norman Lecture, delivered at the University of Florida, Gainesville, on July 2, 1956.)

[21] William O. Stanley, B. Othanel Smith, Kenneth D. Benne, and Archibald W. Anderson, *Social Foundations of Education* (New York: The Dryden Press, Inc., 1956), p. 228. Some italics added.

reference to discoveries about these circumstances and what they require for the achievement of intended effects. Knowledge of what teaching is in fact is prerequisite to its systematic improvement.

We shall, therefore, attempt to give an analysis of teaching as it is. We shall begin with the most general conception, namely, that teaching consists of a succession of acts by an individual whose purpose is either to show other persons how to do something or to inform them that something is the case. The word "teaching" thus defined is used to refer to what the teacher does rather than to the behavior of the student or to what happens to him as a result of instruction. It makes no sense to say that if the student has not learned, the teacher has not taught. For learning is not stipulated as a characteristic of teaching.

It should therefore be remembered throughout this discussion that we have chosen to separate learning from teaching. We do not even use the hyphenated expression teaching-learning. For if it is intended to signify that learning is supposed to result from teaching, it is superfluous. Were the expression used to indicate that where there is learning, there is teaching, such is obviously not the case. Or if the double-barrelled expression is used to mean that teaching always results in intended learning, again such is not the case. Finally, if it is used to indicate that teaching is not teaching unless it does result in learning, the usage is arbitrary. Connecting learning and teaching verbally in this hyphenated expression serves to increase the complexity of the concept of teaching without compensating gains. So we have decided to treat teaching as teaching and learning as learning.

What Teaching Is

Before turning to the acts constituting teaching, we shall point out certain things which are not strictly a part of teaching but which are so closely related to it as often to be mistaken for it. These are method, skill, style, and control. By method is generally meant a particular order imposed upon teaching activities. It is a construction of how teaching ought to be done. We speak of the project method, lecture method, question-answer method, and unit method. Of course, to follow any of these methods is to teach. But teaching is more than a method. And the tendency to equate the two of them has led to more than one pedagogical dogma.

When we speak of a teacher's skill we are referring to how well he performs the acts of teaching. It is sometimes said that the proficiency of a teacher is to be decided by the achievement of his students. But this way of thinking about the teacher's skillfulness is a choice among alternatives and is in no sense necessary. It is no less defensible to say that a teacher is proficient if his instruction satisfies criteria derived from pedagogical research and practical experience. In this event, the teacher might be very proficient and still some students learn little or nothing from his instruction. In the same way a physician may be very skilled and yet some of his patients may not recover. As the doctors say, the operation was a success but the patient died. Or a lawyer may display unusual skill in defending a client but still lose the case. No practitioner can rightly be held responsible for the outcome of his practice beyond adherence to the knowledge and techniques of his profession.

By style of teaching we mean the characteristic demeanor in which the teaching acts are performed. For example, a teacher may operate in a sympathetic frame of mind, or he may be aggressive toward both the students and the ideas with which he deals. A teacher may be habitually dramatic, or he may show little or no feeling at all as he teaches. Unlike skill, teaching style is personal and somewhat unique for each individual. The failure to distinguish between style of teaching and teaching itself, is one of the primary sources of the mistaken notion that teachers are born and not made.

The custodial and disciplinary duties of the teacher are frequently confused with teaching. Of course, a measure of order in the classroom is a necessary condition for instruction. But the maintenance of order is not itself instruction. In college and university classrooms the custodial and disciplinary functions of the teacher are negligible, and the distinction between these functions and instruction stands out clearly. In the public schools, however, these duties take so much of the teacher's time and energy that the line between teaching and discipline becomes blurred in his mind. At any rate, the job of housekeeping is one thing and teaching is quite another thing.

However, telling what something is not, does not tell us what it is. So let us turn to a positive description of the teaching process. If we go to the classroom, we shall see what it is that the teacher does. We shall see that what he does follows an order of events which are not of his own making, but which occur because of the very nature of the enterprise going on there. As the teacher faces a classroom group, what do we see him do? First of all he induces the students to give attention to himself. By virtue of his position, he is necessarily the central figure in the classroom, and no amount of ingratiation or sharing in activities on his part can hide the fact. While the day's disasters need not be read upon his morning face, it is still true that the first significant act of the teacher is to focus the attention of his students upon himself. When this has been accomplished, he then directs their attention to what is to be learned. He may do this in a number of ways—by telling the students what to do, by engaging them in planning what to do, or by other means. The teacher then directs the students in those activities which are designed to bring about the desired learning. Such activities may include listening to the teacher, watching him do something, trying to solve problems, practicing exercises, and so on.

These acts of the teacher are, of course, gross performances. And we shall miss the subtle, but significant aspects of his work, if we do not look at the things which the teacher does when he executes them. Throughout his performance the teacher is observing the students, diagnosing their feelings and interests, and following as best he can the progress of their understanding. He also talks, for he is called upon to explain, interpret and give directions, and these duties can be performed in no other way. Then, too, he uses all sorts of pedagogical and social sanctions to approve and disapprove, to reward and to punish, to persuade and to restrain the students at every turn in the day's work.

Signs and Symbols in Teaching

An analysis of these elusive aspects of teaching will take us to the heart of the teaching process. Let us see what the teacher does when he is doing these things. We see him use all sorts of signs and symbols as he diagnoses the state of the students' feelings, interests, and under-standings, and likewise as he explains, interprets, and persuades. Now, the teacher cannot know the feelings and interests of his students by observation alone; for feelings and interests are not accessible to the senses. The only way he can know them is by inference. Neither a smile nor a frown is a feeling. Nor is anger a sharply spoken reply. These are external manifestations of inner states and processes. Like one who must find out the contents of a sealed box by inference from its external features, the teacher can know the inner facts about his students only by inference from visible signs. From a student's facial expression, he infers that the student does or does not want to do something. The tone of the student's voice and the expression in his eyes tell the teacher whether or not the student is angry, happy, or apprehensive. And the light in his mind shows up in the light on his face.

The fact that the deeper reactions and feelings of the student are hidden and that they are present to the teacher only by implication has been little noticed. Yet it may well be that the success of the teacher depends in large measure upon his accurate perception and under-standing of such natural signs as posture, tone of voice, and facial expression. From practical experience it would seem that there is wide variation among teachers with respect to sensitivity to these cues. Some teachers of outstanding intellectual ability appear to be insensitive to what is going on around them, oblivious to the inner life of the student if not to the classroom itself until something happens to jolt them to their senses. Then it is often too late to redeem their status as teachers. Others seem to see all sorts of cues, but, knowing not what they mean, become rattled by them and thus lose control of the teaching process. Still other teachers appear to be keenly aware of every change in these natural signs and to understand their significance. They, therefore, direct their moment-to-moment behavior as teachers in terms of information coming to them by implication from the multiplicity of natural signs around them. If we could but find out how to read these natural signs accurately and how to teach prospective teachers to do so, their proficiency in the art of teaching might be better secured.

The teacher learns about his students not only from natural signs but also from their use of language. What the student says is of significance to the teacher partly because it supplies him with data by which to understand the student. Just as facial expressions and other natural signs convey by implication the feelings and thoughts of the student, so do linguistic expressions reveal the inner life to him who is able to interpret them. Suppose a student says, in response to the question of how the streams of New England differ from those of the coastal plains "I ain't sure. But is it that the rivers run slow in New England and fast in the coastal plains? Well, maybe I'm wrong. I don't know." Now what do these words tell the teacher? It all depends upon how he is tuned in and how versatile he is in changing wave lengths. These data indicate a number of things. They tell the teacher that the student is deficient in linguistic usage, hesitant in answering the question, and deficient in geographic knowledge. Other linguistic expressions of the student may indicate that he is emotionally upset, reasons fallaciously, and does not know how to explicate words.

In general, then, the symbolic expressions of the student tell us: (1) his emotional state, (2) the grammatical and linguistic errors he makes, (3) whether or not he understands something, (4) the values he holds, (5) the logical errors he makes, and (6) his factual errors. Language as a source of information about the student has, of course, been used since teaching first began. But the conceptualization of its functions should enable us to make better use of language as an instrument of instruction. For the teacher can mold his behavior intelligently to the extent that he is aware of the conditions which affect the outcome of his acts. Hence the teacher, at his best, is sensitive to this total spectrum of things which the student's linguistic expressions tell him.

Teaching as a Linguistic Process

The teacher not only interprets signs and symbols coming to him from the students, but he also expresses himself to his students by signs and symbols as he instructs. In fact, teaching cannot occur without the use of language. Teaching is, above all, a linguistic activity. The teacher makes assignments, gives directions, explains events and statements, interprets words and other expressions, proves propositions, justifies decisions and actions, makes promises, praises and blames students. He cannot teach without doing these things. And he cannot do any of them without using language. Can an assignment be made without language? Can anything be explained or an action justified without saying something? Can a proposition be proved or an expression interpreted without using language? To raise such questions is to indicate the way in which language is inextricably involved in the processes both of learning and of teaching. It is to show that language is at the very heart of teaching.

Let us look at some of the ways in which the teacher uses language. In the first place, he uses language to teach students how to do something. In teaching a student how to typewrite, for example, the teacher may show the student how to do it by performing the activity himself. But this will not be sufficient. The student must himself perform the activity, and he must be directed in the performance of it. So, the teacher will tell him from time to time what to do. But it is not intended that the student remember the sentences spoken by the teacher. The teacher will tell him to try so and so, don't do so and so, or you are making this movement and you should be doing thus and so. The purpose of the discourse is immediate. Its use beyond the moment may be insignificant. For once the student learns to typewrite, what the teacher told him drops out of the picture.

This sort of telling is to be found in nearly all teaching. And it is more complex than we might suppose. It entails a triple relationship in which the elements are the teacher, the student, and a third something, for example, a map, a piece of apparatus, a book, an act of either the student or the teacher. Suppose a teacher is instructing a science class by means of a demonstration. As the demonstration proceeds, the student must observe what is done and what happens. At the same time he must listen to the teacher tell what is being done, why it is being done, and so on. The student is thus in a double role of observer and listener. The teacher, too, is involved in the same way. He must pay attention to what he is doing and at the same time talk about what he is doing. But he must do even more. He must also pay attention to the entire class and choose words and ideas appropriate to the capacities of the students. This three-way intellectual performance is seldom found outside of a teaching situation. It is not an easy one to learn, and many elements of the situation escape the eye of the novice. Even the experienced teacher is seldom well enough aware of his performance to tell the beginner what to do and how to do it.

There is a second and even more significant use of language in teaching. In this instance the teacher tries to increase the student's fund of knowledge. In order to do this he explains, he defines, he justifies, he offers proof, and so on. And, as we have already said, to do these the teacher must use language. But it is a use of language which differs from that employed in the direction of an activity which a student is learning to perform. It is a discourse that expresses ideas which are to be retained, and which can be retained only as they are embodied in linguistic symbols. The teacher who explains Boyle's law by showing its logical relation to the molecular theory of matter does not do so on the assumption that what he says will be forgotten. Nor does a teacher who explains an event in human history by reference to a general proposition about the behavior of human beings intend that the students forget what he says. Of course, the teacher does not intend that the student remember the exact words or the particular sentences. But the teacher does expect the student to be able to express the ideas in his own words and to show in other verbal ways that he grasps what the teacher has said.

Since the discourse of the teacher embodies ideas to be learned, it is designed to convey ideas in accurate and succinct statements. In this sense, it is studied discourse. Unlike informal talk, its order is shaped by the nature of the task. Ideas are expressed in a sequence calculated to make them easily understood. Even the teacher's demeanor and tone of voice are affected by the nature of the task. Children recognize this fact, and when they play "school," the one who has the role of teacher adopts the voice and studied manner of the teacher.

Thus the significance of the role of language in teaching is clearly evident when we stop to think about it. Yet the plain fact is that all we know about language in this regard is a kind of unanalyzed common sense distilled from practice. It could be that when we have analyzed the language of teaching and investigated the effects of its various formulations, the art of teaching will show marked advancement.

The Logic of Teaching

Teaching involves logic as well as language. This is the case because reasoned discourse leads to conclusions. It begins somewhere and ends somewhere. And logic, in its deductive sense, is a way of clarifying our linguistic expressions and of ordering sentences in such a way that we can decide upon the truth of our conclusions.

Just as we have neglected the role of language in teaching, so have we disregarded logic. This neglect of logic has resulted partly from our erroneous notion that the research which dislodged faculty psychology and its theory of formal discipline also discredited the study of logic, and partly from our erroneous ideas of what logic was supposed to do for us. The overthrow of formal discipline had no bearing upon the uses of logic when properly perceived. Logic does not purport to tell us how we do in fact think. It has nothing to do with the pondering processes, whatever they are, by which ideas occur to us and by which we reach conclusions. The principles of logic describe neither thinking nor thought. Nor do they tell us how our thinking ought to proceed. They are not norms to which the thinking process should conform. Rather logic is useful to us when we scan our thinking to tell whether or not the conclusions we have reached follow necessarily from our premises, or, as in inductive thinking, to decide the probable truth of our conclusions.

Seen in this light, logic plays an important role in the process of teaching. For one thing, a statement becomes clear to us either when its key words are adequately defined or when it is fixed in the chain of sentences to which it is logically linked, or when both of these obtain. Now, teaching in its didactic sense embraces both of these performances. For, as we have already said, such teaching includes the activities of defining, explaining, justifying, proving, and the like. And these without exception are logical operations.

The fact that these activities are logical activities is seldom recognized. We have failed to recognize their logical nature because of our tendency in education to psychologize everything. In pedagogical discussion we use two sets of concepts, both of which we believe to be psychological, when in fact only one set is so. One of these sets consists of such concepts as inferring, perceiving, conceiving, generalizing, thinking, and judging. We use these in talking about psychological processes. And we are correct in doing so. Of course, there is a legitimate question as to whether there are internal processes corresponding to these names, but that question is one which we leave to the psychologists. The other set of concepts are identified by such terms as define, interpret, explain, justify, and prove. These are logical rather than psychological. They are operations which we perform with words and sentences and which we cannot perform without words and sentences. And these operations are found in the domain of logic.

For purposes of illustration we shall consider definition and explanation. It hardly need be said that a great deal of school learning consists of definitions. Our books and discussions are filled with definitions. Now in logic we are told that there are different ways of defining words. To define a word is to tell how it is to be used. We can define the word "seed" by saying that "a seed is that part of a flowering plant that holds the embryo and associated structures." What we have done is to tell the class of things to which a seed belongs, by saying that it belongs to the class of things called "parts of a flowering plant." Then we have told how a seed differs from other members of the class of things to which it belongs such as leaves, roots, and stem. Wherever the expression "part of a flowering plant which holds the embryo and associated structures" appears in our discussion we can substitute the word "seed" without changing the meaning. This is what we do when we define a word. Thus a definition represents a decision; for it lays down the rules for the use of a word. Since they are decisions, definitions are neither true nor false.

The amount of time used inefficiently in the classroom because the teacher does not know how to deal with questions involving definitions is greater, I fear, than we like to think. Classroom discussion is often snarled up by disagreements about the meaning of words, as though words somehow had meanings in the same way that dogs have fleas. Many fruitless discussions might be avoided were the teacher capable of handling definitions through a knowledge of logic and its operations.

Similarly, the logic of explanation is appropriate when the teacher is called upon to explain either statements or events, or to evaluate explanations given by students. Suppose the teacher is called upon to explain the fact that in the early morning the wind blows from the land toward the sea. What must he do? The answer is that he must try to find the premises from which the factual conclusion—the wind blows from the land toward the sea in the early morning—can be drawn. Now any number of premises may be chosen, depending upon the teacher's knowledge. But if he is trained in physics, he will reason from the general law that heated bodies expand and thus become lighter per unit of volume. It is not necessary here to follow the logical steps the teacher must take to get from the general law to the particular event to be explained. But he will go on to show that the air over the ocean becomes warmer at night than the air over the land, and that the cold, heavier air over the land then displaces the ocean air which is warmer and lighter. An explanation thus consists in showing that the fact to be explained can be taken as an instance of the general law which has been used as the explanatory principle.

Failure to understand what an explanation is leads to all sorts of entanglements in the classroom. Sometimes the discussion centers in the question of whether or not an explanation is a true one. To answer the question it is necessary that the truth of the premises be tested. But unfortunately the teacher often lacks the knowledge of logic necessary to test the truth of statements used as premises. Then, too, teachers sometimes mistake the mere recounting of events for explanation. A student is asked to tell why the French Revolution happened. So he relates events leading up to the revolution as an explanation of why the revolution occurred. Now, the mere recounting of events is not an explanation in the logical sense, for there is no general principle from which to derive the event to be explained. Sometimes, however, a student, or even a teacher, uses a general principle without making it explicit. Consequently it is subjected neither to critical appraisal nor to the test of fact. Partly for this reason, instruction in history often lacks rigor and thus fails to engage the higher mental processes of students.

Conclusion

It has been our purpose in this discussion to describe teaching, teaching as it is in fact. We have not sought to set forth any new theory of how teaching ought to be done. Rather we have analyzed teaching into some of its essential elements because it is our belief that he who would improve an art must first understand it. And the understanding of any art begins not with loose abstractions, but with systematic and painstaking analysis of that art.

It has been a common practice to think of teaching almost exclusively in psychological terms. This practice has too long kept us from facing the realities, the hard plain facts of teaching. I have tried to speak in terms of the facts of teaching—of what it is that we actually do when we teach. Our analysis has, perforce, been all too brief. Hence it has presented merely the bold contours and the grosser elements of the general process of instruction. Many details remain to be laid out. And since the present analysis represents an early exploration, it is to be expected that under further study and further elaboration, the present general outline will undergo changes.

Nevertheless, I believe that any candid view of teaching will throw into sharp relief most features of the teaching process that I have described. If we look frankly at teaching, I believe that we shall become aware at least of the truly linguistic and symbolic nature of the teaching process, and that the fundamental role of logical operations in teaching will become abundantly clear. If this be the case, we shall be dealing with problems that we have not recognized heretofore. And yet, it may be that through the solution of these problems the art of teaching will make its most rewarding advancement.

Questions for Discussion

NEWSOME shows that analytic philosophy is diverse, does not seek some higher truth (as do most philosophies), and does not attempt to build systems. He shows the types of theoretical and conceptual problems in education that may prove amenable to philosophical analysis —problems related to meaning and verification, models for theory, analysis of terminology, the logical operations of educational discourse, and others. On the basis of Newsome's article, examine the other three selections in this section as the tools of philosophical analysis used in their inquiries, and evaluate the success of their ventures.

The concept of need has been widely used but infrequently examined; it has served as a focal concept in a number of educational theories. Archambault examines the uses of the term, the basis for the term as a guide in educational policy, and the validity of the concept as a hypothetical construct. In what way does this investigation bring out the misconceptions surrounding the concept? Examine and evaluate several basic texts in education relative to the use and implications they draw from the concept of need.

Equality, another vital educational concept, is examined by Komisar and Coombs in terms of 'equal as same' and 'equal as fitting' as they relate to descriptive and ascriptive uses of language. What are the authors doing when they employ a linguistic analysis of the concept? What differences in educational practice can be traced to the use of one interpretation rather than another? Examine the educational literature relative to the use and implications drawn from the equality concept. Study several contemporary issues in education and show how a philosophical analysis of equality may provide a clearer sense of direction for educational policy.

Smith shows that a number of things, such as method, skill, style, and control, are confused with teaching. He discusses natural and overt signs of students as well as the linguistic aspects of teaching and explains their importance. Because of our tendency to psychologize in education, we tend to overlook the need for an analysis of the role that logic plays in teaching. In what ways do you believe teaching and instruction could be improved if careful attention were given to the interpretation of teaching which is provided in this essay?

PART THREE /

THE PHILOSOPHIC QUEST

CHAPTER SEVEN

PHILOSOPHY OF EDUCATION

PHILOSOPHY began in ancient Greece before the time of Socrates and relied on the best reasoning the human mind could devise to explain the world and the nature of man. It posed an alternative to other approaches, such as myths, superstition, tradition, mysticism, and dogma, which have persisted as modes of dealing with life during man's short stay on this planet. Since philosophy antedates the discoveries of modern science, some philosophers sought knowledge and understanding of physical phenomena in the world around them as well as knowledge about the nature of man and the good life; these investigations have resulted in important contributions to mathematics and sciences.

The philosophic quest, generated by a sense of profound wonder concerning human life—its expressions and manifestations—attempts to sort, sift, and analyze phenomena and then to reorganize them into a logically consistent, embracing framework. This process enables the philosopher to see life in broader perspective and with greater depth and meaning; it makes possible the organization and systematization of human experience. The philosopher traditionally has raised perennial questions concerning man and the cosmos such as "What is mind and what is matter?" "Is the universe purposive, or does it seem to have purpose only because of our imaginations?" "Can man ever have definite knowledge?" "How do we determine what is good and bad?" "What is beauty and how can it be recognized?"

These are just a few of the philosophical questions that have puzzled men for centuries. However, with the advent of modern science and the division of knowledge into numerous disciplines, some have come to see the role of philosophy as limited to those remaining areas where science does not investigate or have special competencies in gaining knowledge. Philosophers who accept this point of view contend that some philosophical problems have been formulated in such a manner that no evidence could be adduced for either their support or refutation, and thus, such statements are philosophically meaningless unless they can be reformulated. With advancements in philosophy and with the need to conduct precise and penetrating analyses of the type previously mentioned, philosophy (as is the case with other disciplines) has become more specialized. There are still philosophers who attempt to formulate major systems of thought, but there also has been a growth in the number of specialists who operate with great precision on problems of a more limited range.

Major works in the philosophy of education begin with the writings of Plato. But (as in the case of philosophy itself) philosophy of education is undergoing re-examination to clarify its role in the study of education. Its task was originally conceived to be the study and construction of large systems of thought drawn primarily from philosophy, with the later addition of relevant findings from psychology and the social sciences. The objective was to draw out their implications and relate them to education. This approach has been questioned as investigations in the philosophy of education have turned more to philosophical analyses of educational issues and decision-making, to studies of values in education, and to inquiries into the logical operations of the theoretical and conceptual structure of education.

Philosophers of education frequently utilize findings of empirical studies but usually do not conduct such investigations. Before one can make proposals or espouse certain values as to the direction that education *ought* to take, one must first know—through empirical studies of present conditions—what *is* actually possible and feasible to recommend. Philosophy of education is concerned with value dimensions of issues, such as religion and education, academic freedom, loyalty and censorship, desegregation, professional ethics, and others. Also it investigates the aims of education and problems surrounding what knowledge is of greatest worth. Studies dealing with conceptual problems, such as the meaning of equality of educational opportunity, the nature of freedom in education, and analyses of such key conceptual terms as 'needs' and 'mastery,' fall within the framework of philosophy of education. Analysis of the criteria and methodological procedures of theory construction constitute another area of inquiry. Combined with all of these is the study and development of philosophical systems and their implications for education.

The ability of the student to think philosophically on educational issues and problems is considerably influenced by his understanding of the uses of philosophy of education and by his ability to broaden his philosophical perspective and sharpen his tools of analysis. Several different interpretations of philosophy of education are represented in the selections in this section. It will be necessary to evalute the arguments presented and attempt to determine the relation that philosophy of education has with philosophy, educational theory, educational policy and practice.

Mortimer J. Adler, widely recognized for his ideas on liberal education and his role in the Great Books program, offers in Selection 25 an interpretation of philosophy of education from the perspective of classical humanism. The essay, which sharply contrasts with other selections in this section, discusses the meaning of education and the nature of philosophical inquiry.

A carefully reasoned essay, which explicates education as a process and a discipline, is found in Selection 26. William K. Frankena, a leading figure in contemporary moral philosophy, shows the relation of philosophy to philosophy of education and that of the empirical or 'scientific' aspects of education to philosophy of education. Finally, the dimensions of philosophy of education are illuminated.

John Dewey (Selection 27) presents the thesis that "if we are willing to conceive education as the process of forming fundamental dispositions, intellectual and emotional, toward nature and fellow men, philosophy may even be defined *as the general theory of education.*" Thus education is the laboratory in which philosophical distinctions become concrete and are tested. Dewey's essay is already considered a landmark in the field and, at the time it was written, marked a sharp break with previous interpretations.

Elizabeth Steiner Maccia (Selection 28), who has done extensive work in educational theory construction, challenges the preceding statement by Dewey; namely, she attempts to show that philosophy is not the general theory of education and that acceptance of this view leads to certain misconceptions. Her conception is that the language of education falls into four categories or "realms of meaning"—scientific, humanistic, technological, and epistemological. Their functions are clarified in relation to analytic and synthetic phases of philosophy of education.

25 / MORTIMER J. ADLER

The Problems

I am here concerned to indicate the questions about education which are for the philosopher to answer, and to distinguish them from those which are beyond the sphere of his special competence. This is important to do because the existing literature which is called "philosophy of education" reveals the lack of such distinction: Problems which are not philosophical are treated as if they were, and men who are not philosophers try to solve philosophical problems. In either case, confusions of subject matter result and critical standards, standards of competence, become obscured. Everyone today would be shocked if a theoretical chemist did not know the difference between a problem for chemical research and the problem of running a drug store, or if a practicing pharmacist did not realize that he had to have the special competence of a theoretical chemist before he tried to solve the latter's research problems. In the field of the natural sciences we do acknowledge the significance of distinctions in subject matter and types of problems; we do recognize the requirements of technical competence for distinct intellectual tasks. It is unfortunate that, in our time, philosophy is not similarly respected either by the general public or by the "scholars." And this is particularly true in such fields as the philosophy of law or the philosophy of education in which the subject matter is constituted by a set of problems which can be solved only in the light of prior philosophical knowledge. Not all legal problems are philosophical; nor is technical competence in law sufficient for answering all questions about law, for some of them are truly philosophical. The same can be said for the problems of education: Only those which can be answered in terms of prior philosophical knowledge are philosophical; and the possession of such knowledge is indispensable to solving them. Technical competence as an educator, or practical experience in the work of education, is not enough.

Mortimer J. Adler, "In Defense of the Philosophy of Education," 41st Yearbook of *National Society for Study of Education,* Part I (Chicago: University of Chicago Press, 1942), pp. 205–231. Reprinted by permission.

1. Theoretical and Practical Problems Distinguished

The first step to be taken in defining the limited sphere of the philosophy of education rests upon the distinction between theoretical and practical problems. A theoretical question is one which asks about the nature of things, about what is the case in any realm of existence or phenomena. A practical question is one which asks about what should be done, about what men should do in any realm of action or production. This distinction is currently made in other ways: We speak of questions of fact or questions of value, we speak of descriptive and explanatory formulations vs. normative. The answers to theoretical questions describe or explain the facts; the answers to practical questions set up the norms or define the values which determine what men should do, for they are the standards whereby we discriminate between a better or worse choice in any case in which we face alternatives, and every practical problem is ultimately constituted by alternatives between which we are free to choose. If there were no alternatives between which we could freely choose, we would have no practical problems. The denial that men have free will—in this precise sense, that they can make genuine choices between alternatives—completely destroys the sphere of the practical as a domain of genuine problems worth thinking about.

The ultimate problems of education, like those of law and medicine, are practical. They are questions about what should be done to educate a man—one's self or another. This does not mean, of course, that purely theoretical questions cannot be asked about education. The history of education, for example, is strictly theoretical knowledge about education, for it answers countless questions about what *has been done* by men in their effort to solve the practical problems of education. It describes the institutions and practices of education in different cultures, at different times, under different conditions. Similarly, the history of the philosophy of education is theoretical, because it answers questions about the general policies men have formulated for setting up educational institutions and directing educational practices. But the policies themselves, precisely because they are policies, are not theoretical, but practical, and the general principles on which they are founded constitute the philosophy of education as a set of answers to the most general practical questions which can be asked about what is to be done educationally.

It may be objected that there are still other *theoretical* questions about education than those which can be answered by an historian, whether of contemporary or past practices. The correlation of certain educational procedures with their educational effects can be measured; all sorts of measurements can be made of what goes on in the schools, educationally or administratively. But clearly the knowledge thus gained by empirical researches, metrical or otherwise, is *scientific,* not philosophical. We must grant, at once, that if there is a genuine *science* of education, it is a theoretical, and not a practical, science, for all of its problems are exactly like the problems of any of the other natural or social sciences. This is an extremely important point; for if the ultimate problems of education are practical, it follows necessarily that such problems can never be solved in terms of scientific knowledge alone, though science may be of secondary or minor utility in helping to solve them. Educational practices are guided by general policies, and these policies in turn can be intelligently formulated only in terms of basic practical principles. Scientific knowledge, whether it be specifically the science of education or any of the other natural or social sciences, can never by itself direct educational practices or determine the formulation of educational policies for the simple reason that such knowledge is purely theoretical. *It is descriptive or explanatory; it is not normative.* Anyone who understands the method of science, the methodology common to all the investigative sciences, natural or social, knows that by such method no questions of value can be answered, no norms determined. (The methods of testing establish norms or standards only in the sense of averages, or the modes of *normal* distribution. This is theoretic knowledge, which can be *interpreted* practically, but the interpretation is not accomplished by scientific research or method.) Thus we begin to see, not only the distinct sphere of the philosophy of education, as answering questions unanswerable by science, but also the need for a philosophy of education—for without it there could be no certain determination of the basic practical principles underlying the policies which direct actual day-to-day educational practices.

But it may still be objected that it has not yet been shown that philosophy can be practical knowledge, or that the philosophy of education does answer distinctively practical questions. That philosophy includes both theoretical and practical knowledge, whereas science is exclusively theoretical, can be shown, briefly, by the fact that the theory of the good, and the definition of the good of anything, is philosophical. We know that the nature of the good in general, or of the types and order of goods, are matters incapable of being investigated by scientific method. We know, furthermore, that every practical problem involves the good, for every choice is between a better and a worse object, or course of action, or policy. Hence, we are faced with this dilemma: *Either* there is no knowledge, but only opinion, about what the good is in general, or what is a good life or a good society, in which case, of course, there is no practical philosophy; *or* there is such knowledge, as distinguished from opinion, and this is practical philosophy, its two major branches being ethics (concerned with the good life) and politics (concerned with the good society). If we take the latter alternative, we shall be able to define the philosophy of education as answering certain practical questions subordinate to those of ethics and politics. If we take the former alternative, then there is no knowledge at all which answers practical questions, and educational policies are at best guesses or opinions without any foundation in demonstrably true principles; in which case, a book on the philosophy of education is not worth writing or reading.

One objection remains, namely, that the philosophy of education may be both theoretical and practical. That it is practical follows from the existence of ethics and politics as branches of practical philosophy, and the recognition that philosophical questions about what should be done educationally are subordinate to questions about the conduct of life or the constitution of society. It may be said, however, that there are some theoretical questions about education which the philosopher answers, as, for example, *what education is,* and *what causes are operative in the process of education.* There is some truth in this point, but its full significance requires analysis. Education itself, as something which goes on in the world, can be viewed either theoretically or practically. Viewed theoretically, education may be regarded as a process taking place in the course of human development. Viewed practically, we see that this process is not *purely natural* for it seldom, if ever, takes place without one man purposely employing skills and other means to help another man become educated. The production of an educated man is no more natural than the production of any other work of art, a shoe or a statue, if by a *purely natural* process we mean one in which the exercise of human art is not one of the efficient causes. Now, of course, the definition of education as the process whereby one man helps himself or another to form good habits is itself a piece of theoretical knowledge; and so is the proposition that the arts of teaching or learning are indispensable as efficient causes in this process. But these two items of theoretical knowledge about education—both philosophical truths—show us at once that education is fundamentally a practical affair, because it is not purely natural, because it is an artistic enterprise.

2. Definition of Education

I shall subsequently defend the definition of education I have just given as the only true definition which can be given. Let me restate it, now more precisely than before: Education is the process by which those powers (abilities, capacities) of men that are susceptible to habituation are perfected by *good* habits, through *means artistically contrived,* and employed by any man to help another or himself achieve the *end* in view (i.e., good habits). I say that this definition can be proved to be true, and that the full statement of the proof will answer many fundamental questions in the philosophy of education. But that is a matter reserved for subsequent discussion. Here I am concerned only to use the definition in order to formulate the problems of educational philosophy. It may be thought that I am thus involved in circular reasoning, for am I not saying that we shall first use this definition to determine the problems, and then, after proving it, we shall find that it helps us solve these very problems? Yes, but it should also be obvious that no one can define the problems of educational philosophy without first defining education itself, and that if only one true definition be possible, and that one be proved true, no vicious circularity is involved in the process. This will become apparent to the reader as he observes the use to which the definition is put.

a. **Practical Aspects of Education.** In the first place, let me call attention to the fact that the definition, as its italicized words indicate, makes the problems of education practical, in three ways. (1) They are concerned with the good, for education aims to form not any sort of habits but only good habits, traditionally analyzed as the virtues. (2) They are artistic problems, problems of how to use means for producing certain desirable effects as ends. (3) They are ethical problems in so far as they require us to consider the virtues and to understand their role as means in achieving the ultimate end of life, happiness; and they are political problems in so far as they require us to consider the responsibility, not simply of one man to another, but of the community to its members, with regard to helping them become educated.

When, in these three ways, I say that the problems of education are practical, I am talking about the problems which any man faces when he undertakes to educate himself or another, or to say what the community should do to educate its members. I am not talking about the problems of the science of education, or the history of education (both of which are purely theoretical—concerned with knowing what has happened or how it is happening now). I am talking about the problems of education itself, concerned ultimately, not with knowing, but with actions to be taken. If such actions are to be intelligently directed, there must be knowledge of the ends to be sought and the means to be used. The range of practical problems in the field of education, therefore, includes questions about the ultimate ends of the whole process and about the means in general. These, as we shall see, are the basic problems of the philosophy of education, and in solving them it is *practical* because it directs action. In fact, the answers to these questions, constituting the philosophy of education, are the only practical *knowledge* in the field of education, for no other practical judgments which educators can make have the certitude of knowledge.

b. Education as a Coöperative Enterprise. In the second place, let me comment on the fact that the definition makes the process of education an artistic enterprise. I shall assume that everyone understands what it means to say that shoemaking or house-building, the writing of poetry and the painting of pictures, are artistic enterprises. Shoes and houses, poetry and pictures, do not happen naturally. They are things made by man, in the production of which definite skills or techniques are at work, and this is the fundamental meaning of *art*, the skill or technique which a man has for making things. An artistic enterprise is, therefore, a process in which human art is an indispensable efficient cause for the production of a certain effect—the product being aimed at.

It is necessary to go further, however, and see precisely what sort of artistic enterprise education is. All human arts are not the same. We are all acquainted with the familiar division of the arts into fine and useful (according as the product is something enjoyed or used), and into free and servile (according as the product is an immaterial thing, such as a poem or a piece of music, or a transformation of matter, such as a shoe or a house, or even a statue). But, for our purposes, the only important distinction is that between the operative and the coöperative arts. The operative arts are those by which something is produced that would not happen in the course of nature without human intervention. These arts are completely productive in the sense that they are an indispensable cause of their products, whether the product be a shoe or a statue or a poem. In contrast, the coöperative arts are not completely productive, for they *only assist* nature in the achievement of the product at which they aim. Thus, for example, the arts of agriculture and medicine are coöperative: Without human intervention, the earth produces its vegetation, and the living body possesses health and sustains itself against the forces of disease. Neither the farmer nor the physician is *absolutely* needed. But the arts of agriculture and medicine, coöperating with natural causes, make the desired result more likely and achieve it in ways and under circumstances which more regularly satisfy human needs. The physician's technique is a skilful way of coöperating with natural causes to sustain health and cure or prevent disease. When we understand this distinction between operative and coöperative art, we see at once that the various arts of the educational enterprise—among which, of course, the arts of teaching and learning are preëminent—are clearly coöperative, and not, as shoe-making or picture-painting, completely productive. Take the case of knowledge, which is one of the virtues, or good habits, at which education aims. The human mind naturally tends to learn, to acquire knowledge, just as the earth naturally tends to support vegetation. The arts of learning and teaching merely assist in the cultivation of a mind by coöperating with its natural processes of knowing, just as agricultural techniques assist nature in the production of vegetables. What is here seen to be true of knowledge as a good habit is equally true of every other good habit which men can form, for in every case men possess natural capacities which tend naturally toward certain developments, and the arts of education, the arts of human cultivation, merely coöperate with nature to achieve the desired result—a good habit rather than a bad one.

Implications of Coöperative Basis of Educational Procedures. In the third place, we must consider several consequences which follow from the conception of the educational arts as coöperative. One is the relation between education as an artistic enterprise and education as an ethical and political affair. In both cases, the problems of education are practical, but the ethical and political problems of educational philosophy concern the end to be achieved, either by a single man in his own life or by a community with regard to its members, whereas the artistic, or *technical,* problems of educational philosophy concern the means in general to be used, their variety and order.

A further consequence is the relation between education as the process in which a man *helps himself* to form good habits and education as the process in which one man is helped *by another* or *by the community* in which he lives. It may be asked whether, if the educational arts are coöperative, education must not always be the latter sort of process, that in which a man is helped by others. Can a man educate himself? Certainly, it must be true that a man is able to learn, to form every sort of good habit, without the aid of others, for if this is not the case, then the educational arts are not coöperative but completely productive. But when a man learns in this way, the process may be entirely natural or it may be facilitated by certain skills or techniques of learning by which he coöperates with his own natural tendencies toward habit formation. Only in the latter case should we speak of the man as educating himself, for in the former the learning is entirely natural, and where no art intervenes, we cannot properly speak of education. But certainly self-education, thus conceived, is either nonexistent or very rare. Man is a social animal. Most of the habits formed in childhood are formed under tutelage or direction of some kind. The very skills of learning, by which a mature man may educate himself, are usually habits which others help him form in his youth. We can conclude, therefore, that probably no man has ever completely educated himself—not that it is impossible, but that it is unlikely in the normal social development of human life. It would appear that self-education usually follows education-by-another, for two reasons: (1) In infancy and childhood, habit formation is usually under the direction of adults; and (2) the skills of learning, indispensable to self-education as an artistic enterprise, are themselves usually products of education-by-another. The only sort of learning which is excepted from this discussion is the type I have called purely natural, and as such, it is not education at all—neither self-education nor education-by-another. It is highly doubtful whether there is much learning of this sort. It would have to occur in early life, since once some art of learning is possessed, a man no longer learns naturally; yet, as we have seen, in early life most learning is education-by-another.

3. Major Divisions of Education

These considerations lead us, finally, to the major divisions of the educational process as defined.

a. Self-Education and Education-by-Another. The first division has already been mentioned, self-education and education-by-another, but it is necessary to clarify this distinction by making three further points. (1) All learning is of two sorts: It is either learning by discovery, without the aid of others in respect of the matters being learned, or learning by instruction, with the aid of others in respect of the matters being learned. Now, as we have seen, learning by discovery may, in turn, either be natural learning, totally without the benefit of art, or it may be self-education, in which some art is employed coöperatively by a man to facilitate the natural process. Learning by instruction is always education-by-another. Here it is important to observe that teaching is an art always used by one man with respect to another. No one teaches himself, even when he educates himself by using some art in his learning, for he who teaches must possess actually whatever the person being taught possesses only potentially and hence is able to learn. This being so, a man cannot teach himself, for then he would already have to possess actually what he is about to learn, which is impossible. Moreover, in every case in which one man is taught by another, the primary activity of learning is on the part of the man who it taught. *Otherwise, teaching would not be a coöperative art.* Thus, we also see that learning by instruction should be conceived as *aided discovery.* (2) Not every way in which one man causes learning in another is teaching. I shall use the word "stimulation" for every way, other than teaching, in which one man is the cause of learning in another. Here it is important to observe that what I have said about teaching does not hold for stimulation. A man need not actually possess the knowledge or other habits which he succeeds in stimulating another to acquire. Hence, although a man cannot teach himself, he can, in a sense, stimulate himself to learn. We now face the very difficult problem of whether to classify learning-by-stimulation as education-by-another or as self-education. If we consider stimulation, in all its forms and varieties, as one of the educational arts, along with teaching, then learning-by-stimulation, as well as learning-by-instruction, is education-by-another. But if the stimulation one man gives another is not artistically contrived, and if it is not intended as an aid to that other's learning, then, it seems to me, we should regard the stimulation as an accidental cause and classify the resultant learning as learning by discovery, whether that be a purely natural process or one of self-education. Education-by-another (i.e., learning under instruction or stimulation) must always be a process artistically planned and intentionally executed by that other. In the absence of educational artistry and intention on the part of others, all learning is by discovery. I trust it is not necessary to explain that the other need not be a man living and present; it may be a man, either dead or absent, who operates causally through books or other media of communication or influence. (3) Learning by discovery, especially self-education, may be joined with learning by instruction or stimulation (education by another) in every phase of the educational process. Neither excludes the other; on the contrary, both are usually involved in every field of learning, although at different stages or in different kinds of learning one or the other may predominate. There is only one further qualification here: It is impossible for a man to learn *the same thing* both by discovery and by instruction, for with respect to an *identical* item to be learned, discovery and instruction necessarily exclude each other as *proximate* efficient causes (although each may, *in any case*, function as auxiliary to the other). But this is not true of stimulation (in contrast to instruction), for with respect to a given item one man may stimulate another to learn by discovery. In fact, stimulation is only effective educationally if it is completed by the work of discovery on the part of the individual stimulated. Hence we see that when education-by-another is by instruction, self-education is either excluded entirely or subordinated as an auxiliary, but when it is by stimulation, self-education dominates the process.

b. Types of Habits Established by Education. The second division is in terms of the types of habits which are the proximate ends of the process. The basic division of habits is into intellectual and moral, according as they are habits of knowing and thinking, on the one hand, or habits of desiring and acting, on the other. Thus, intellectual and moral education are divided, the one aiming at the intellectual, the other at the moral, virtues. But intellectual education can be further subdivided, according as the habits aimed at are habits of knowledge or of art. A habit of knowledge is a habit of knowing *that*, whereas a habit of art is a habit of knowing *how*. Because every art is an intellectual virtue, every sort of artistic education is intellectual. There are as many subdivisions of artistic education as there are types of art, but principally there are three: (1) physical education, which cultivates the most basic arts, the arts of using one's own body well as an instrument; (2) vocational education, which cultivates all the useful arts, whether simply productive or coöperative; and (3) liberal education, which cultivates a special sort of useful art, the liberal arts, the arts of learning itself, the arts of thinking well, of using language well, and so forth. It is difficult to classify that part of education which aims at the habit of any one of the fine arts: Certainly, it is intellectual education, but whether it is vocational or liberal is almost impossible to decide, except in particular cases when all the relevant circumstances are known. If we now call *speculative* that part of intellectual education which aims at habits of knowledge (either practical or theoretic knowledge), in contrast to *artistic* education, we can see at once that speculative education is usually auxiliary to artistic education, in so far as it is necessary to know *that* in order to know *how*. This is obviously the case in most of the learned professions, such as law or medicine, preparation for which must combine the speculative and the vocational types of intellectual education. We can also see the artistic education, of one sort at least, is almost indispensable to speculative education, for some degree of competence in the liberal arts is prerequisite to speculative education at every stage; though not to the same degree, liberal education is also auxiliary to vocational education. Finally, we can at least see, though we cannot here discuss, the problem of the relation of moral to intellectual education, a relationship which may be expressed in terms of the dependence of intellectual education of any sort on the possession of moral virtues, and the dependence of moral education upon the possession of intellectual virtues, especially speculative habits of knowledge and the habit of the liberal arts.

   c. Individual Differences in Relation to Education. The third division is in terms of various attributes of the person being educated. In the first place, it should be noted that we are here considering only human education, not the training of brute animals. That men and animals are radically distinct in essence, differing absolutely in kind, not relatively in degree, is a proposition I shall discuss later; it is of paramount importance to the philosophy of education. Strictly speaking, brutes can be trained or conditioned, but they cannot be educated, for education, whether by one's self or by another, is always a work of reason, and brutes are irrational. In the second place, the human person, as the subject of education, may be normal or abnormal, and the abnormality may be either in excess or deficiency of the median quantities with respect to intelligence and other temperamental characteristics. There are also variations in the external and accidental circumstances of the person to be educated: his sex, his economic status, his social background, etc.

But most important of all is the division in terms of age. The subjects of education are either immature persons (whether infants, children, or adolescents) or they are mature (adults). Education is the business of a whole human life; it is not exclusively the occupation of the young. It begins with birth and ends with death. When we fully understand all the conditions of infantile and adolescent education, on the one hand, and adult education, on the other, we must realize that adult education is the most important of all the temporal phases of education; the education of youth is at best a beginning, and it can only be at its best when it pretends to be nothing else but preparatory for adult education. While it is true that the immature, precisely because their immaturity consists in deficiencies of habit and experience, *need* education more than adults, it is also true that the mature, precisely because their maturity is constituted by ampler experience and by stable habits, can *profit* by education more genuinely than children. No philosophy of education which restricts itself to the education of the young can be adequate; worse than that, it will be distorted and misleading because the ends of education can only be defined in terms of an educated man; they cannot be properly defined in terms of a child merely in the process of becoming a man.

d. Institutional or Noninstitutional Education.   The fourth and last division turns on whether education-by-another is institutional or noninstitutional. Institutional education may be of two sorts; either by institutions which are primarily created for educational purposes, such as schools, colleges, universities, and adult education institutes of various types; or by institutions which serve purposes other than education, such as the home or the church. This does not mean that the home and the church are not genuinely educational institutions, but only that they are not exclusively such; whereas, in contrast, what I shall call educational institutions (schools, colleges, etc.) have no other function than to educate. That is the sole end which their existence, personnel, and administration serve. This holds true even in the case of universities which claim to be devoted to research and the advancement of knowledge, as well as to teaching, for the advancement of knowledge is meaningless except as increasing the scope and substance of what men can learn. By thus distinguishing exclusively educational institutions from all others involved in education, we are enabled to distinguish the professional educator, whether teacher or administrator, from all other persons, such as parents or writers, who may also be engaged in the work of educating others.

Educational institutions can be divided in many ways, of which I note these four: (1) according as they are privately endowed and operated, or maintained by state subsidies and politically controlled; (2) according to the character of the subjects being educated, i.e., whether normal or abnormal, immature or mature; (3) according to the primary educational aim of the institution, whether moral or intellectual, and if intellectual whether speculative or artistic, and if artistic, whether liberal or vocational, and so forth; and (4) in the sphere of intellectual education, according to the level of the institution with respect to the age of the persons being educated and the proportionate gradation in the substance of what is being taught, i.e., whether elementary, intermediate, or advanced. So much for the types of institutional education. Education-by-another which is noninstitutional may take a variety of forms, but they are difficult to classify exhaustively. Suffice it to mention the cultural agencies which the community is able to provide its members: books and libraries, radio programs and lectures, periodical literature, various types of vocational apprenticeship, and last, but not least, the law as promulgated, administered, and enforced. In addition, of course, there are such incidental operative causes as friends, or any individual who is helpful to another educationally.

4. The Scope of Educational Philosophy

These four divisions of the educational process enable us to indicate the full scope of the philosophy of education.

In the first place, educational philosophy cannot be restricted to the consideration of education-by-another. The ends of education, which are the ultimate principles of educational philosophy, must be conceived in such a way that they hold equally for self-education and education-by-another.

In the second place, in considering education-by-another, the philosopher must not confine himself to institutional education, and certainly not to those peculiar institutions which are exclusively educational; and if this be so, how much more is it true that educational philosophy is neither principally nor exclusively concerned with the work of the elementary or even the secondary schools. All educational institutions, from the lowest school to the university, are only one way in which the means of education are organized and become effectively operative. The philosopher of education is concerned with the means in general, and not with any mode of the means, except in relation to other modes. I wish to emphasize this point because so much of what currently offers itself as educational philosophy not only is not philosophical in method, but also is not properly philosophical in the scope of its subject matter, for it consists largely in a discussion of the extremely limited aims of and the means peculiar to educational institutions, especially the public school system at the elementary and secondary levels. It addresses itself only to professional educators; it is even written in a peculiar technical language, which is called "pedaguese" and is almost totally unintelligible to anyone who has not "done time" in a school of education.

The most important phase of the educational process is that which can and should take place in adult life, when a mature individual is responsible for carrying on his own education, whether that be, in mode of causality, self-education, or education-by-another. Certainly adult education-by-another is noninstitutional for the most part. Hence the philosophy of education, properly conceived in scope, must address itself to any intelligent adult who, first of all, is responsible for accomplishing the completion of his own education since it can never be completed in youth or in educational institutions of any sort; who, secondly, as a parent or an elder, may be directly or indirectly responsible for the education of youth; and who, as a citizen, shares responsibility for the educational policies of his community, for the establishment and admin- istration of its educational institutions. Concerned with the ends of education and with the means in general (and their relationships), the philosophy of education has nothing to say to professional educators over and above what is addressed to any intelligent adult.

There are, of course, many problems which belong peculiarly to professional educators. These problems appear at various levels and in various types; but none of these problems is philosophical, as I shall subsequently make clear. That so much current discussion is of these peculiar professional problems is due not only to the fact that the method and character of philosophical knowledge is unknown or disregarded, but also to the fact that, in America today, we are blinded by a romantic adoration of the child. We thus come to suppose that the most important problems of education concern the rearing of children, and we exagger- ate the importance of the educational institutions which deal with children. But clearly the beginning of anything is not as important as the end, and the beginning can only be well thought about in terms of the end. The end of education is the educated man; in a sense, therefore, the whole process of education is one of overcoming the deficiencies of immaturity. Our interest in children should be in them as potential adults. In this light, the educational institutions which deal with children and youth should, at every stage, be working to help the young cease to be immature and become adults. The significance of this point will be recognized only by those who realize how much of contemporary schooling is devoted, by explicit policy, to preserving all the undisciplined waywardness, all the inchoate habits, of childhood.

In the third place, the philosopher of education can discriminate among educational institutions according to the level of their preparatory operations, although he must always consider the education of youth as merely preparatory to adult education, and all education-by-another, whether or not institutional, as preparatory to self-education. The work of some of these institutions must be regarded as preparatory to the work of others; and the work of some can be regarded as terminal, so far as institutional education goes. Excluding, for the moment, the institutional care of subnormal persons, and considering only intellectual, not moral, education, we can see the reason for a tripartite division of educational institutions into schools (elementary and secondary), colleges, and universities. The first of these divisions is preparatory to further institutional education; the second is both preparatory and terminal; the third is terminal. To understand this, it must be remembered that no educational institution completes the process of education. University education is terminal only institutionally. By doing the fundamental work of liberal education (the formation of habits of liberal art), the college is preparatory to the speculative and vocational education of the graduate and professional divisions of the university; but it is also institutionally terminal, in so far as a person who is trained in the liberal arts *needs* no more institutional education to undertake the noninstitutional completion of his own education. And the schools, disregarding any difference between elementary and secondary institutions, are preparatory for liberal education. I am aware that there are many problems here, largely raised by the fact that there are many individuals who, for one accidental reason or another, receive institutional education only on the first level, and perhaps not even all of that. There are other problems concerning the determination of the age periods for these different levels of institutional education, concerning the relation of vocational education to liberal education at various age levels, and of both to speculative education, but they are not capable of philosophical resolution and, therefore, the philosopher should refrain from discussing them. I shall comment on this point presently.

In the fourth place, because he knows the distinction between the moral and the intellectual virtues, particularly with respect to the aetiology of these types of habit, the philosopher knows that educational institutions cannot be primarily responsible for moral education. Institutionally, the primary responsibility for moral education lies in the home and the church and in the law-making and law-enforcing functions of the political community. Noninstitutionally, moral education depends upon the ministrations of elders, other than parents, and of friends. So far as educational institutions go, moral education is accomplished by them secondarily and only in so far as (1) they are communities which, as such, can, by rule-making and rule-enforcement, regulate the conduct of their members; (2) the professional educators who compose the personnel of such institutions are elders who can advise and direct conduct, or otherwise stimulate the growth of moral habits; (3) strictly intellectual education (especially liberal and speculative), which is the primary work of educational institutions as places of teaching, is auxiliary to the formation of moral virtues.

There are here two further questions for the philosopher to consider: One concerns the relation, in general, between moral and intellectual education, not only as to division of responsibility for each, but also as to their functional or causal interdependence; the other concerns the whole matter of religious education which is, of course, both moral and speculative, but in both respects rests upon supernatural knowledge, the ultimate source of which is Divine Revelation. The philosopher of education cannot, of course, make any essential determinations with regard to the ends or means of religious education; but he must certainly ask whether the education of a man can be completed, morally or intellectually, without religious education. In so far as he knows, by strictly philosophical knowledge, that God exists and that man is divinely created with an immortal destiny, he knows, negatively, that the whole of natural (as opposed to supernaturally founded) education is fundamentally inadequate for the perfection of man. He knows *negatively* that the highest type of natural knowledge, metaphysics, is inadequate with respect to the very questions the metaphysician is able to answer *in part,* namely, the nature of God and the nature of man; he knows, at least, that another kind of knowledge is *possible,* supernatural knowledge possessed through the gift of faith, and that in this supernatural knowledge lies the possibility of more complete answers to these ultimate questions; hence, in knowing that wisdom is the highest of the speculative virtues, he also knows that natural wisdom, which is the highest end of intellectual education, is not, by itself, a complete or sufficient end for anyone who aims at the perfection of the human intellect. Again, negatively, he knows that the natural moral virtues may not be sufficient for the conduct of life, in so far as he can entertain the possibility that, without the grace of God, human weakness makes the attainment of even the natural moral virtues unlikely. These items of negative knowledge enable the philosopher to discuss the relation of secular to religious education only in the most general terms. He cannot solve any of the difficult practical problems which confront a secularized society, such as ours, in which church and state are separated, and in which there is a variety of religions, each of which should claim to be the only true one, or at least operates, in fact, as if that were the case. But at least he recognizes that an educational philosophy can be *adequate practically* only if it is subalternated to moral theology.

5. Ends and Means in Education

In the fifth place, and finally, the several divisions of the educational process which it has been necessary to make (according to the type of agent operative—one's self or another; according to the type of habit aimed at; according to the character of the subject to be educated; according to the type of agent other than one's self which is causally operative—the various sorts of institutional and noninstitutional agencies), enable the philosopher of education to formulate basic questions about the variety of the means in general, their relation and order to one another. So far as his effort is to determine the ultimate ends of education, which are the ultimate principles of educational philosophy, the philsopher need pay no attention to these major divisions of the educational process. The *ultimate* ends of education are the same for all men at all times and everywhere. They are absolute and universal principles. This can be proved. If it could not be proved, there would be no philosophy of education at all, for philosophy does not exist unless it is absolute and universal knowledge—*absolute* in the sense that it is not relative to the contingent circumstances of time and place; *universal* in the sense that it is concerned with essentials and abstracts from every sort of merely accidental variation. Similarly, it must be said that educational means *in general* are the same for all men at all times and everywhere. If the *ultimate* ends of education are its first principles, the means *in general* are its secondary principles, and the scope of the philosophy of education goes no further than this—*to know these first and secondary principles in an absolute and universal manner*. To aim at knowing less than this, or to regard this as unknowable, is to deny that there is any philosophy of education; to aim at knowing more than this, without realizing that one ceases to function as a philosopher in so doing, is to confuse the philosophy of education with other subject matters and methods, or to confuse one's self by trying to solve, philosophically, problems which cannot be philosophically solved.

As I have already indicated, there are several types of problems about the means *in general:* (1) the enumeration of what they are and the definition of each; (2) their functional relationships; (3) their order to one another in various modes of coördination and subordination. With respect to the last two sorts of problems, the various divisions of the educational process become significant in two ways. On the one hand, the division of education into moral and intellectual (and intellectual into speculative and artistic, and artistic into liberal and vocational) defines different parts of the total process by reference to one or another type of good habit (or virtue) as the exclusive end of that part; and this enables us to consider the type of means which can be best employed for achieving that type of end. On the other hand, the division of education according to the type of agent causally operative (whether one's self or another, and if another, whether that agency be institutionalized or not, and if institutionalized, what sort of institution) gives us a classification of means in terms of aetiological considerations, and this enables us to determine how the means should be related to one another in any part of education or in the process as a whole—for they either exclude one another or they can be coöperative in various modes of coördination and subordination. Thus, for example, we know that, in intellectual education, the means in general are the exercise of one's own powers and the coöperative activity of others helping one in the exercise of his own powers. This reveals, at once, the most fundamental truth concerning the means in general—that there is never any learning without the exercise of one's own powers, for the second of the two fundamental means named above is always a coöperative agency and not a completely productive one. The second type of fundamental means is, therefore, always subordinate to the first, whereas the first can be independent of the second. The second can, moreover, be further subdivided according as the activity of the other agent is mediated (by the recorded word) or direct (as in personal confrontation); whether mediated or direct, the coöperative activity may take the form of teaching, in the strict sense, or the form of stimulation (which includes every other sort of guidance).

Analysis, which I shall not state here, is able to show that these means are differently related in moral and in intellectual education. In moral education, coöperative activity which is both direct and stimulative is better than that which is mediated and doctrinal, whereas in intellectual education, teaching is always better than stimulation, and it can be equally effective as mediated or as direct activity. Moreover, self-education is much more indispensable in moral education than in intellectual education. When the difference between artistic and speculative education in the intellectual sphere is considered, analysis also shows that the ordering of the means in artistic education is, in part, like their ordering in moral education. The sharp distinction, with respect to the ordering of means, is, therefore, between the extremes of moral and speculative (intellectual) education, with artistic (intellectual) education occupying a middle ground and resembling each extreme in part.

Since my present aim is not to expound the philosophy of education, but to define its subject matter by a precise delimitation of its scope of problems, much that I have so far said must be taken as it is intended— illustratively, for the purpose at hand. Were I expounding the philosophy of education, all of these points (and others not indicated) would require much more precision of analysis as well as adequate demonstration. In the next section of this essay, I shall try to suggest the analytic and demonstrative mode of exposition, but I shall not be able actually to do more than suggest what it is like—and even then only for the ends, and not for the means—because precision of analysis and adequacy in demonstration is impossible within the confines of this volume. In this section, two steps remain to complete the definition of subject matter. Of these, the first task is to state the criteria for distinguishing those practical problems about education which are philosophical from those which are not; and the second task is to distinguish between the ethical and political dimensions of the basic problems.

6. Principle, Policy, and Practice

I have already implicitly indicated the criteria for distinguishing the problems of educational philosophy from all other problems relevant to education. In the first place, they are essentially practical, whereas the problems of educational science and history are essentially theoretic. But not all practical problems about education are philosophical. So, in the second place, we distinguish between those which are capable of being solved *absolutely* and *universally,* in the sense already suggested, and those which can be solved only *relatively* and *contingently.* Since solutions of the latter type are practical judgments having, at best, the status of probable opinions, and since practical philosophy, like theoretic, must consist of knowledge and not opinions, however probable, the only practical problems about education which are philosophical are those which can be solved by practical judgments which have the status of knowledge. These problems have already been identified. They concern the ultimate ends (what the processes and activities of education *should* always and everywhere aim at) and the means in general (what activities or devices are available for attaining each of the recognized aims, how these devices are related, and in what order they are to be used—or, in general, what means *should* be employed).

So much is already clear. It is necessary, however, to understand these problems by contrast to other practical problems which are definitely not philosophical. In every field of practical activity, in law and medicine just as in education, there are three distinct levels of practical thinking and problem solving. They are ordered according to the degree of their proximity to or remoteness from action itself, and according to the kind of practical judgment which can be made at each of these degrees. The practical problem which is proximate to action itself is always a question about what to do *in this case here and now.* The type of practical judgment which answers questions of this sort is *singular:* It applies only to the case at hand. The immediate object of such a judgment is a particular action to be performed under these unique circumstances. When it is verbally expressed, though it often is not so expressed, it takes the form of a *decision*. On the second level, in the direction of greater remoteness from action, is the practical problem of what to do, not in this particular case, but in a whole class of cases, constituted by a set of contingent circumstances considered in general. The type of practical judgment which solves problems of this sort is *general:* It applies to more than a single case; it applies to a type of case, or a class of cases all of which conform to a certain pattern of generalized contingencies. Particular actions now become the remote object of such general practical judgments, which, when verbally expressed, as they frequently are, take the form of *rules*, statements of general *policy*. On the third level, most remote from action, is the practical problem of what to do *in any and every case*. Such problems completely abstract from every contingent circumstance, whether uniquely singular or generalized for a class of cases. They regard only the *essential* factors in the practical situation, disregarding accidental variations in the human agent and disregarding the contingent circumstances which are accidental variations in the conditions of his action. The type of practical judgment which solves problems of this sort is *universal:* It applies to every case. When verbally expressed, such judgments take the form of statements of *principle*, the principles being practical in the same sense that rules and decisions are, for they are all judgments directive of action, either proximately or from afar.

For brevity of reference, let me name these three levels, in the order indicated, as the levels of *practice*, of *policy*, and of *principle*. The whole analysis can be briefly summarized as follows:

Level	*Problems About*	*Type of Judgment*
Practice	This case	Singular: Decision
Policy	This class of cases	General: Rule
Principle	Every case	Universal: Statement of principle

Now with respect to everything practical, we must distinguish the order of execution from the order of intention or thinking. Thus, in practical thinking we must begin with the ends first, with the ultimate ends, and then, in successive steps, determine the means in general, then particularizations of these means, and finally we must decide on the singular means here and now to be employed. In the order of execution, however, action starts always with the choice of these singular means here and now and only through many stages do we attain the ultimate ends which were first determined in the order of intention. Hence when we say that the ends (and the means in general) are the first (and second) principles in the practical order, we mean they are first (and second) in the order of practical thinking, not in the order of execution or action itself. This shows us two ways of viewing the three levels we have distinguished. From the point of view of thinking, the level of principles is first, and the levels of policy and practice are second and third, because until principles are determined, policy cannot be formed by general rules, nor can singular decisions be made intelligently in the light of general policy. From the point of execution, the level of practice is first in the sense that the immediate action is the first thing attained after a decision to act has been made. It is the first step taken, the proximate means. By taking many such steps we gradually achieve more generalized results, which reflect the successful execution of a policy, and finally we may attain to the complete result, the full realization of the ultimate ends, and this reflects the successful execution of our principles.

At every stage of execution, of course, the means may be regarded as the proximate ends of action, but the true ends, the ends which are not means in any sense, are reached only in the final stage of execution. The ultimate ends are always potentially present in the means, for the means are the ends in the process of being realized. Thus, the ultimate ends are potentially involved in the general means (on the level of principles); and, in turn, the universal means, or the means in general, are potentially involved in the particularized means (on the level of policy); and these, in turn, are potentially involved in the singular means (on the level of practice). Thus, we see how, in the order of thinking, we pass progressively from the universal determinations of ends and means to particularized and singular determinations of means, in order to decide how to act in this case for the sake of achieving our ultimate ends, however remote; whereas, in the order of execution, we pass from the least complete realization of the ultimate end (in the singular means in which it is most potential) through various stages in which it is more and more completely actualized.

These considerations being understood, it will now be clear that the philosophy of education treats only of problems which are on the highest, or universal, level in the order of practical thinking about education. Problems of policy and problems of practice cannot be philosophically solved, for on both of these levels the problems are constituted by accidental factors and contingent circumstances. That is why, strictly speaking, the practical judgments which solve such problems are only more or less probable opinions, not knowledge, for it is never possible to be certain that an exhaustive enumeration of accidents or contingencies has been made. But the philosophy of education, which is practical knowledge, must abstract from every accident and contingency, and hence it considers human education only in terms of what is essential to human nature, and the essential conditions and causes of human development or habit formation. To say that problems of policy and practice cannot be philosophically solved does not mean that the philosophy of education, which solves problems of principle, is not practical. If by practical thinking we understand thinking directive of action, either from afar or proximately, then educational philosophy is practical thinking about educational problems, for it is indispensable to an intelligent formulation of educational policies and to an intelligent application of these policies in actual practice. Unless we know the principles which underlie them, our policies can be no better than rules of thumb or merely empirical, trial-and-error procedures; and unless our decisions concretize policies, which are particularizations of principles, they are entirely unenlightened and arbitrary.

It must also be clear that even a perfectly formulated philosophy of education would not by itself suffice for the direction of education, for it must always be supplemented by practical judgments on the levels of policy and practice. In the light of the principles, rules must be intelligently formulated and decisions intelligently made in order that the practical knowledge which the philosophy of education can offer may have its effects in guiding action. Although the philosopher of education cannot solve these problems which arise from the consideration of contingent circumstances, generalized or singular, the educator must do what he can to solve them by forming the best opinions he can in the light of all the available evidence. It is here that the experience of the educational practitioner becomes useful; for it is not by philosophical analysis, but in the light of ample practical experience that one is able to make sound judgments in matters of policy. Here, too, all the theoretical knowledge about education which is afforded by the science and the history of education becomes useful to the practitioner who, using it judiciously in the light of his own experience, particularizes philosophical principles into rules of policy for this or that kind of case. (It should be noted that the science and the history of education remain essentially theoretic knowledge even when used by the practitioner in the making of practical judgments on the level of policy. Furthermore, it is doubtful whether such purely theoretic knowledge would be practically useful to him except in the light of his own experience as a practitioner.) On the lowest level of practical thinking, in the making of a decision in this particular case, it is primarily practical experience and the practitioner's careful inspection of the detailed circumstances of the case in hand which help him to make a sound practical judgment.

All of this can be summarized by saying that the philosopher of education moves on the same level as the philosopher of law or the political philosopher: He formulates the principles of education, but he determines no policies and makes no decisions. The legislator and the statesman formulate rules of law and governmental policies, and in doing so they must consider the *kind* of society they are regulating, in so far as it differs from other societies in a variety of general accidents or contingencies. In doing this they are aided by their own practical experience and by social science and history, as well, of course, as by legal and political philosophy. Whoever, in any community, assumes the task of formulating its educational policies, considering not man and society in their essential natures, but these men and this society in their contingent types, functions as do the legislator and the statesman, not as the philosopher. Finally, there is the judge, who applies rules of law to particular cases, and the official who executes governmental policies by deciding on this or that singular course of action. These men must be primarily men of experience, though of course they should be informed or directed by policy and principle. Here the analogy is with every man who is obligated to make educational decisions, whether concerning his own education or the education of another entrusted to his charge.

This analogy helps us to see one further point about the philosophy of education. In political philosophy, two questions must be distinguished. The first asks, "What is the best form of government, absolutely speaking?" Here one tries to determine the political ideal, and in doing so must abstract from every variable or contingent circumstance and consider only the essence of man and of human society. The second asks, "What is the best form of government, relatively speaking?" That is, what form of government is best for men and societies typified by these contingent circumstances or other specified situations? Now it is obvious that the best form of government, absolutely, may not be best relative to this type of society. If the typical circumstances are inferior, the best form of government relatively will be an inferior form, absolutely speaking. Hence we see that the best form of government absolutely is that form which is best relative to a society typified by the best circumstances. The political philosopher must solve these two problems in the order named. His first task is always to define the political ideal; only after that is done can he determine the various approximations to it, each of which may be best relative to some typical set of inferior conditions.

There are, however, two important qualifications concerning his solution of the second problem. In the first place, he can never be sure that he knows every grade of approximation or every set of contingent circumstances to which an approximation of the best must be relatively adapted; hence, his solution of the second problem is on the borderline between philosophical knowledge of principles and the sort of highly probable opinion with which practical men form policies. In the second place, the solution of the problem of what is best relative to a certain contingent type of society must never be confused with the statesman's judgment concerning the type of this particular society and the best governmental policy proportionate thereto; for the political philosopher, in so far as he deals with contingencies at all, moves only in the realm of possibilities, whereas the statesman is always concerned with the actual case even when he considers it as a case of a certain type, in order to see it in the light of a philosophical consideration of possible types.

The educational parallel is perfect. The philosopher of education is primarily concerned with the educational *ideal*, with answering the question: "What is the best education *absolutely*, that is, for any man according to his essence?" This is the problem he solves by defining the ultimate ends and the means in general, as the absolute and universal principles of education. But the philosopher of education must also consider a second problem, the one concerning various approximations of the ideal, answering the question: "What is the best education relative to this type of man or relative to this type of society, the types of men and society differing accidentally from one another according to a variety of general contingencies?" As in the case of political philosophy, this second problem, unlike the first, cannot be perfectly solved, because whenever one deals with accidents and contingencies, the enumeration of the relevant factors is always imperfect, and the resultant classification of possible types is both insecure and somewhat arbitrary. Strictly speaking, the realm of the accidental and the contingent is the domain of potential infinity, both with respect to addition and division. Hence this second problem is on the borderline between philosophical knowledge and the sort of highly probable opinions which constitute the educational practitioner's judgment when he forms a policy for this or that type of situation. Nevertheless, it is important not to confuse the educational philosopher's consideration of approximations to the ideal, relative to an analyzed variety of possible conditions, with the practitioner's judgment concerning what is the best policy relative to this type of man or society. The importance of the borderline problem, considered in one way by the philosopher and in another way by the practitioner, is that it mediates between the ideal and the real, by applying the ideal to what *can* be actual (the variety of contingent possibilities), on the one hand, and by viewing the real as an actualization of one type of possibility, on the other.

7. Ethical and Political Problems of Education

The problems of the educational philosopher have now been sharply distinguished from the problems of the educator (whether on the level of policy or of practice). They have also been divided in two ways. The basic division is in terms of the two questions: "What is the best education absolutely?" and "What is the best relatively?" The other division is subordinate because, with respect to both the ideal and the variety of possible approximations thereto, consideration must first be given to the problems of the ends (or first principles) and of the means in general (or secondary principles). Only one further division remains to be made. The problems of educational philosophy can be viewed in either the ethical or the political dimension. Thus, in the ethical dimension we are concerned with what is the best education for man, according to the essence of human nature, and what is the best education for men of different accidental types. In the political dimension we are concerned with what are the educational obligations of society to its members; and here we must consider, first, the ideal society and, then, the variety of possible approximations thereto; and in each case we must consider the educational obligations of a society to its members, first, according to their essential, or common, humanity and, second, according to types of accidental or individual differences.

Two things become obvious at once. (1) In the light of the basic political truth that the political community, and all its institutions, is not the end of human activity, but a means toward the happiness or well-being of its members, we see that the political problems of education are concerned with the means, and then only with their organization or disposition. The ends of education are always properly determined by the nature of man, taken essentially or in accidental varieties, and never by political considerations. Whenever political considerations influence the determination of the ends of education, we know that they are being improperly determined and that we are dealing with some form of political corruption. (2) Since the ends are the first principles and the means are secondary principles, the problems of educational philosophy are primarily ethical and only secondarily political. Furthermore, the ethical dimension is not limited to a consideration of the ends but also treats of the means without regard to their social organization; the political dimension is limited to a consideration of the means and only from the point of view of their social organization.

It is clear, therefore, that all the basic problems of educational philosophy must first be solved in their ethical dimension before political questions concerning the obligations of a state to its members can be treated. Certain qualifications must, of course, be added to this conclusion. On the one hand, it must be remembered that political justice, the virtue of a good citizen, is one of the virtues included in the scope of moral education; hence, there is a sense in which, considering the education of the individual man essentially, we must regard him as a political agent and so refer a part of his education to the service of the political community as an end; but, in so doing, we must always remember that service of the state is only an intermediate end. He who serves the common welfare ultimately works for his own welfare. He does not serve the state, deified as an end in itself. On the other hand, it must be said that when we consider the political obligations of a community to its members, we must determine them by reference to the ultimate ends of education. This is not inconsistent with the conclusion reached above, for the ultimate ends having been ethically determined, the political problem can be solved by reference to them, but the solution itself deals with the social organization of the means. . . .

26 / WILLIAM K. FRANKENA

Toward a Philosophy of the Philosophy of Education

With many others I share a feeling of concern about what is offered to our future teachers in some quarters as the philosophy of education. The remedy for this situation is, of course, not to write papers like this on the aims and content of the philosophy of education, but to encourage people to teach the philosophy of education who are better trained in philosophy than teachers of this subject usually are. It may be, however, that by way of doing the former, one can accomplish something in the latter direction. This paper is written in that hope.[1]

Something must be said first about philosophy. Looking back over its history, it appears that philosophy has done three sorts of things. It has

William K. Frankena, "Toward a Philosophy of the Philosophy of Education," *Harvard Educational Review*, 26, No. 2 (Spring 1956), 94–98. Reprinted by permission of *Harvard Educational Review* and William K. Frankena.

[1] In writing it I am partly indebted and partly reacting to (among others):

H. S. Broudy, "How Philosophical Can Philosophy of Education Be?," *Journal of Philosophy* LII (Oct. 27, 1955), 612–622.

K. Price, "Is a Philosophy of Education Necessary?," *Journal of Philosophy* LII (Oct. 27, 1955), 622–633.

C. L. Stevenson, "The Scientist's Role and the Aims of Education," *Harvard Educational Review* XXIV (Fall, 1954), 231–238.

H. D. Aiken, "Moral Philosophy and Education," *Harvard Educational Review* XXV (Winter, 1955), 39–59.

sought to work out a conception of the universe as a whole in all of its aspects, and of man's place in it. In this endeavor it has been synthetic, making use of the results of the various sciences of the day and adding to them the fruits of the aesthetic, moral, and religious experience of mankind, in order to see life steadily and see it whole. It has also been speculative, venturing more or less questionable hypotheses in order to fill out the picture or to find a meaning where none was obvious.

Besides seeking such "world-hypotheses," as S. C. Pepper has called them, philosophers have sought to afford some wisdom in the conduct of human affairs. That is, they have tried to provide, not only a picture of the world we live in, but a guide to action, whether individual or social, by discovering and formulating goals, norms, or standards to serve as pillars of cloud by day and pillars of fire by night.

In their twofold pursuit of the real and the ideal, philosophers have often been engaged in a less exciting but still essential kind of enquiry—analysis or criticism. This includes a critical evaluation of the assumptions and methods used by philosophers, as well as by scientists and common sense people, and a careful attempt to define such terms as "real," "true," "good," "right," "cause," "matter," "substance," and "time," which play so important a part in both ordinary and systematic thinking. Here, whatever his ultimate goal may be, the proximate goal of the philosopher is simply conceptual clarity and methodological understanding.

Let us call these three philosophical activities, respectively, speculative, normative, and analytical philosophy. Then it may be claimed that they constitute three branches or *parts* of any full-fledged philosophy—that any "compleat philosopher" must do all three of them, as Plato, Aristotle, and Spinoza did. On the other hand, they may be regarded as three distinct *kinds* of philosophizing, so that philosophers must choose between them. This view of them is often held today. Thus Dewey and his followers argue that philosophy should eschew speculation and become a normative enquiry—a "search for the ends and values that give direction to our collective human activities." Other philosophers, following Russell and Wittgenstein, contend that philosophy should be neither speculative nor normative, but should devote itself entirely to logic and analysis. The most doctrinaire of them are the logical positivists, but other analytical philosophers take more generous points of view, and analytical philosophy should not be identified with positivism, as it frequently is by unsympathetic writers.

The point I wish to make here is that on the three-parts theory of the nature of philosophy as a whole, the philosophy of education will have three parts, one speculative, one normative, and one analytical; while on the three-kinds theory philosophers of education must choose between being speculative, being normative, and being analytical in their approach to their subject, as contemporary philosophers in general have been doing. My own disposition is to hold to the three-parts theory for both philosophy in general and philosophy of education in particular, but I cannot try to argue this now, and shall content myself with saying simply that I should like to see either of two states of affairs prevail, (a) one in which each philosopher of education is engaged in all three kinds of enquiry, or (b) one in which some philosophers of education are engaged in one kind of enquiry, some in another, and some in the third. In either case the three sorts of philosophizing would all be going on with respect to education, and this is the chief desideratum.[2]

We must now take a look at education, in order to see how philosophy may come to bear upon it. At once a distinction must be made between education as a process and education as an academic discipline. In the former sense, education is the process by which society makes of its members what it is desirable that they should become (not merely what it desires them to become), either in general or in so far as this may be carried on by what are called "schools." In the second sense, education is the discipline which studies this process in one way or another, its findings being reported and passed on in professional courses in schools of education.

By the philosophy of education one might, then, mean either the philosophy of the process of educating or the philosophy of the discipline of education. To help us to see how it should be conceived, let us examine the discipline more closely. It consists or might be thought to consist of three parts. First, there is the factual "science" of education. This is especially concerned to gather facts, particular and general, about the process of educating. It may be descriptive or experimental, describing or experimenting with methods of instruction, observing the consequences, etc. To this extent it will make its own contributions to scientific knowledge. But it will also collect from history, psychology, and other fields, any further facts which may be relevant to the business of educating human beings.

Next, there is the normative part of education. This makes recommendations, instructional or administrative, with respect to the process of educating. It proposes ends, goals, or norms for this process which teachers and administrators are to promote, and it advocates the means by which these ends are to be achieved. It also seeks to justify its recommendations about ends and means, so far as this is possible, by reference to such facts as may be discovered or collected by the science

---

[2] They are, of course, going on after a fashion already; the desideratum, it seems to me, is that they should all be going on in *professional courses* on the philosophy of education.

of education and to such moral principles as it may itself borrow from ethics in general.

Finally, the discipline of education has or might have an analytical part. This would be concerned partly with analyzing the concepts of the factual science of education, for example, "intelligence" or "growth," and with evaluating the assumptions and methods of this science. But it would also be interested in the normative part of education, analyzing its concepts, for example, "good," "justice," etc., and scrutinizing the methods by which it seeks to justify its recommendations.

The connection of philosophy with each of these parts of the discipline of education is now readily apparent. Consider the factual science of education. For the most part, this will be scientific, not philosophical in character, and will belong among the social sciences. But one of the fields from which it may borrow facts or hypotheses is speculative philosophy (including for the moment theology). For example, it may borrow from philosophy the naturalistic-humanistic view of life and the world, as so much of our recent educational philosophy does; or, like traditional theories of education, it may adopt the beliefs in a superior reality, a spectator theory of knowledge, and an immortal destiny, which Dewey has so long decried. To the extent to which it depends on or applies such doctrines, a "science" of education will not be really scientific, it will be philosophical; in fact, it will be an adjunct of speculative philosophy, whether it is aware of this or not (in saying this, I do not mean to bury such educational philosophy, nor even to dispraise it).

There is another possible connection between education and speculative philosophy. One might derive from a study of the process of education some hypothesis about the nature of the world, for example, the idealistic thesis that the history of the universe is the self-education of Mind. Here, however, the goal of enquiry is not insight into education but insight into the nature of the universe, and hence such thinking cannot properly be called philosophy of education, even though thinking of the reverse sort may be.

As for the normative part of education—this seems to me to contain the heart of the philosophy of education. All of it may with some propriety be called philosophy, since it consists of judgments about what should or should not be done in the process of education, together with the reasons for these judgments; indeed, it is really nothing but a branch of normative philosophy as a whole. However, some hesitate to include recommendations about the means to be used by the schools under philosophy, and would prefer to regard the science of education as consisting of two parts, as political science does, viz., a factual part and a part which makes recommendations about means. But, in any case, theories about the ends of the process of education are properly called normative philosophy.

It should be pointed out that the recommendations made by the philosopher of education, whether they concern means or ends, will normally be based partly on normative premises taken from ethics (and so from philosophy, though, of course a given philosopher of education may work out his own ethics in his capacity as a philosopher, and need not borrow from anyone *else*), and partly on factual premises derived from common sense, science, or philosophy. For example, any recommendation he may make about the treatment of religion in the schools will depend in part on his views about the aims of education, which will rest on his moral and social philosophy in general, and in part on his views about the validity of religious beliefs and the importance of religious literacy.

The analytical part of education as a discipline belongs entirely to philosophy—analytical philosophy. In so far as it is concerned to study the methods of educational science it is just a part of the philosophy of science in general, and there is no point in speaking of it as philosophy of education, unless the science of education has features which are peculiar to it. The analysis of the concepts and methods of the normative part of education, again, is to a considerable extent just a part of ethical theory; it is not as such philosophy of education, although philosophers of education should be at home in it. However, there is left as a proper part of the philosophy of education the analysis of concepts which are peculiarly central to either the scientific or the normative parts of education, for example, "growth," "learning," "independence," "intellectual freedom," etc.

I want particularly to stress the importance of doing such analytical work as a part of educational theory. Even if the object is the guidance of the educational process, and not just clear and distinct understanding, the analysis of crucial concepts is still essential—thought and action alike require us to be clear-headed in our use of crucial terms in the field of education as well as elsewhere. As H. D. Aiken has put it, ". . . the task of clarifying such golden words as 'liberty,' 'justice,' 'democracy,' 'person,' and 'love' is . . . essential to the well-being of any people whose way of life is expressed in terms of them. For if they are unclear or confused or inconsistent, then the way of life is so also."[3] If this is so, then it is imperative both that philosophers of education master the methods and results of contemporary analytical philosophy, and that analytically trained philosophers enter the field of education theory.

[3] *Op. cit.*, p. 57. Broudy and Price also emphasize the importance of analysis, *op. cit.*

This review of philosophy and education, first separately and then in relation to one another, has enabled us to distinguish at least the outlines of (1) a speculative philosophy of education which looks for hypotheses about man and the world which may be relevant to education as a process, (2) a normative philosophy of education which discerns the goals to be achieved and the principles to be followed in the education of human beings, and perhaps also makes recommendations about the means to be adopted, and (3) an analytical philosophy of education which seeks to clarify crucial concepts. Of these the first and second can now be seen to belong to the philosophy of the process of education and the third to the philosophy of the discipline of education.

On the three-parts theory of philosophy, each philosopher of education should engage in all three sorts of enquiry. On the three-kinds view, one philosopher of education will choose the first, another the second, and still another the third, or perhaps all of them will choose to do one of them and avoid the others. As I have indicated, I hope that all philosophers of education will take part in all three sorts of enquiry, or, if not, that some will choose one and some another.

In any event, it will be clear from what has been said that the educational philosopher need not and should not work in isolation. Just as the educational scientist borrows from and contributes to other sciences, so the educational philosopher borrows from and contributes to speculative, normative, and analytical philosophy in general, besides drawing upon the work of the educational scientist. Even if he limits himself to analysis, he will still make use of the findings of analytical thinkers in ethics and political theory, and may reward them with analyses of his own.

27 / JOHN DEWEY

Philosophy of Education

. . . Our further task is to extract and make explicit the idea of philosophy implicit in these considerations. We have already virtually described, though not defined, philosophy in terms of the problems with

John Dewey, "Philosophy of Education," in *Democracy in Education* (New York: The Macmillan Company, 1916), pp. 378–387. Copyright renewed in 1944 by John Dewey. Reprinted with permission of The Macmillan Company.

which it deals; and we have pointed out that these problems originate in
the conflicts and difficulties of social life. The problems are such things as
the relations of mind and matter; body and soul; humanity and physical
nature; the individual and the social; theory—or knowing, and practice—
or doing. The philosophical systems which formulate these problems
record the main lineaments and difficulties of contemporary social
practice. They bring to explicit consciousness what men have come to
think, in virtue of the quality of their current experience, about nature,
themselves, and the reality they conceive to include or to govern both.

As we might expect, then, philosophy has generally been defined in
ways which imply a certain totality, generality, and ultimateness of both
subject matter and method. With respect to subject matter, philosophy is
an attempt to *comprehend*—that is, to gather together the varied details
of the world and of life into a single inclusive whole, which shall either
be a unity, or, as in the dualistic systems, shall reduce the plural details to
a small number of ultimate principles. On the side of the attitude of the
philosopher and of those who accept his conclusions, there is the
endeavor to attain as unified, consistent, and complete an outlook upon
experience as is possible. This aspect is expressed in the word "philosophy"—love of wisdom. Whenever philosophy has been taken seriously, it
has always been assumed that it signified achieving a wisdom which
would influence the conduct of life. Witness the fact that almost all
ancient schools of philosophy were also organized ways of living, those
who accepted their tenets being committed to certain distinctive modes
of conduct; witness the intimate connection of philosophy with the
theology of the Roman church in the Middle Ages, its frequent
association with religious interests, and, at national crises, its association
with political struggles.

This direct and intimate connection of philosophy with an outlook
upon life obviously differentiates philosophy from science. Particular
facts and laws of science evidently influence conduct. They suggest
things to do and not do, and provide means of execution. When science
denotes not simply a report of the particular facts discovered about the
world but a *general attitude* toward it—as distinct from special things to
do—it merges into philosophy. For an underlying disposition represents
an attitude not to this and that thing nor even to the aggregate of known
things, but to the considerations which govern conduct.

Hence philosophy cannot be defined simply from the side of subject
matter. For this reason, the definition of such conceptions as generality,
totality, and ultimateness is most readily reached from the side of the
disposition toward the world which they connote. In any literal and
quantitative sense, these terms do not apply to the subject matter of
knowledge, for completeness and finality are out of the question. The

very nature of experience as an ongoing, changing process forbids. In a less rigid sense, they apply to *science* rather than to philosophy. For obviously it is to mathematics, physics, chemistry, biology, anthropology, history, etc. that we must go, not to philosophy, to find out the facts of the world. It is for the sciences to say what generalizations are tenable about the world and what they specifically are. But when we ask what *sort* of permanent disposition of action toward the world the scientific disclosures exact of us we are raising a philosophic question.

From this point of view, "totality" does not mean the hopeless task of a quantitative summation. It means rather *consistency* of mode of response in reference to the plurality of events which occur. Consistency does not mean literal identity; for since the same thing does not happen twice, an exact repetition of a reaction involves some maladjustment. Totality means continuity—the carrying on of a former habit of action with the readaptation necessary to keep it alive and growing. Instead of signifying a ready-made complete scheme of action, it means keeping the balance in a multitude of diverse actions, so that each borrows and gives significance to every other. Any person who is open-minded and sensitive to new perceptions, and who has concentration and responsibility in connecting them has, in so far, a philosophic disposition. One of the popular senses of philosophy is calm and endurance in the face of difficulty and loss; it is even supposed to be a power to bear pain without complaint. This meaning is a tribute to the influence of the Stoic philosophy rather than an attribute of philosophy in general. But in so far as it suggests that the wholeness characteristic of philosophy is a power to learn, or to extract meaning, from even the unpleasant vicissitudes of experience and to embody what is learned in an ability to go on learning, it is justified in any scheme. An analogous interpretation applies to the generality and ultimateness of philosophy. Taken literally, they are absurd pretensions; they indicate insanity. Finality does not mean, however, that experience is ended and exhausted, but means the disposition to penetrate to deeper levels of meaning—to go below the surface and find out the connections of any event or object, and to keep at it. In like manner the philosophic attitude is general in the sense that it is averse to taking anything as isolated; it tries to place an act in its context—which constitutes its significance.

It is of assistance to connect philosophy with thinking in its distinction from knowledge. Knowledge, grounded knowledge, is science; it represents objects which have been settled, ordered, disposed of rationally. Thinking, on the other hand, is prospective in reference. It is occasioned by an *un*settlement and it aims at overcoming a disturbance. Philosophy is thinking what the known demands of us—what responsive attitude it exacts. It is an idea of what is possible, not a record of accomplished fact.

Hence it is hypothetical, like all thinking. It presents an assignment of something to be done—something to be tried. Its value lies not in furnishing solutions (which can be achieved only in action) but in defining difficulties and suggesting methods for dealing with them. Philosophy might almost be described as thinking which has become conscious of itself—which has generalized its place, function, and value in experience.

More specifically, the demand for a "total" attitude arises because there is the need of integration in action of the conflicting various interests in life. Where interests are so superficial that they glide readily into one another, or where they are not sufficiently organized to come into conflict with one another, the need for philosophy is not perceptible. But when the scientific interest conflicts with, say, the religious, or the economic with the scientific or æsthetic, or when the conservative concern for order is at odds with the progressive interest in freedom, or when institutionalism clashes with individuality, there is a stimulus to discover some more comprehensive point of view from which the divergencies may be brought together, and consistency or continuity of experience recovered. Often these clashes may be settled by an individual for himself; the area of the struggle of aims is limited and a person works out his own rough accommodations. Such homespun philosophies are genuine and often adequate. But they do not result in systems of philosophy. These arise when the discrepant claims of different ideals of conduct affect the community as a whole, and the need for readjustment is general.

These traits explain some things which are often brought as objections against philosophies, such as the part played in them by individual speculation, and their controversial diversity, as well as the fact that philosophy seems to be repeatedly occupied with much the same questions differently stated. Without doubt, all these things characterize historic philosophies more or less. But they are not objections to philosophy so much as they are to human nature, and even to the world in which human nature is set. If there are genuine uncertainties in life, philosophies must reflect that uncertainty. If there are different diagnoses of the cause of a difficulty, and different proposals for dealing with it; if, that is, the conflict of interests is more or less embodied in different sets of persons, there must be divergent competing philosophies. With respect to what has happened, sufficient evidence is all that is needed to bring agreement and certainty. The thing itself is sure. But with reference to what it is wise to do in a complicated situation, discussion is inevitable precisely because the thing itself is still indeterminate. One would not expect a ruling class living at ease to have the same philosophy of life as those who were having a hard struggle for existence. If the possessing and the dispossessed had the same fundamental disposition toward the world, it would argue either insincerity or lack of seriousness. A community devoted to industrial pursuits, active in business and commerce, is not likely to see the needs and possibilities of life in the same way as a country with high æsthetic culture and little enterprise in turning the energies of nature to mechanical account. A social group with a fairly continuous history will respond mentally to a crisis in a very different way from one which has felt the shock of abrupt breaks. Even if the same data were present, they would be evaluated differently. But the different sorts of experience attending different types of life prevent just the same data from presenting themselves, as well as lead to a different scheme of values. As for the similarity of problems, this is often more a matter of appearance than of fact, due to old discussions being translated into the terms of contemporary perplexities. But in certain fundamental respects the same predicaments of life recur from time to time with only such changes as are due to change of social context, including the growth of the sciences.

The fact that philosophic problems arise because of widespread and widely felt difficulties in social practice is disguised because philosophers become a specialized class which uses a technical language, unlike the vocabulary in which the direct difficulties are stated. But where a system becomes influential, its connection with a conflict of interests calling for some program of social adjustment may always be discovered. At this point, the intimate connection between philosophy and education appears. In fact, education offers a vantage ground from which to penetrate to the human, as distinct from the technical, significance of philosophic discussions. The student of philosophy "in itself" is always in danger of taking it as so much nimble or severe intellectual exercise—as something said by philosophers and concerning them alone. But when philosophic issues are approached from the side of the kind of mental disposition to which they correspond, or the differences in educational practice they make when acted upon, the life-situations which they formulate can never be far from view. If a theory makes no difference in educational endeavor, it must be artificial. The educational point of view enables one to envisage the philosophic problems where they arise and thrive, where they are at home, and where acceptance or rejection makes a difference in practice.

If we are willing to conceive education as the process of forming fundamental dispositions, intellectual and emotional, toward nature and fellow men, philosophy may even be defined *as the general theory of education.* Unless a philosophy is to remain symbolic—or verbal—or a sentimental indulgence for a few, or else mere arbitrary dogma, its auditing of past experience and its program of values must take effect in conduct. Public agitation, propaganda, legislative and administrative action are effective in producing the change of disposition which a philosophy indicates as desirable, but only in the degree in which they are educative—that is to say, in the degree in which they modify mental and moral attitudes. And at the best, such methods are compromised by the fact they are used with those whose habits are already largely set, while education of youth has a fairer and freer field of operation. On the other side, the business of schooling tends to become a routine empirical affair unless its aims and methods are animated by such a broad and sympathetic survey of its place in contemporary life as it is the business of philosophy to provide.

Positive science always implies *practically* the ends which the community is concerned to achieve. Isolated from such ends, it is matter of indifference whether its disclosures are used to cure disease or to spread it; to increase the means of sustenance of life or to manufacture war material to wipe life out. If society is interested in one of these things rather than another, science shows the way of attainment. Philosophy thus has a double task: that of criticizing existing aims with respect to the existing state of science, pointing out values which have become obsolete with the command of new resources, showing what values are merely sentimental because there are no means for their realization; and also that of interpreting the results of specialized science in their bearing on future social endeavor. It is impossible that it should have any success in these tasks without educational equivalents as to what to do and what not to do. For philosophic theory has no Aladdin's lamp to summon into immediate existence the values which it intellectually constructs. In the mechanical arts, the sciences become methods of managing things so as to utilize their energies for recognized aims. By the educative arts philosophy may generate methods of utilizing the energies of human beings in accord with serious and thoughtful conceptions of life. Education is the laboratory in which philosophic distinctions become concrete and are tested.

It is suggestive that European philosophy originated (among the Athenians) under the direct pressure of educational questions. The earlier history of philosophy, developed by the Greeks in Asia Minor and Italy, so far as its range of topics is concerned, is mainly a chapter in the history of science rather than of philosophy as that word is understood today. It had nature for its subject, and speculated as to how things are made and changed. Later the traveling teachers, known as the Sophists, began to apply the results and the methods of the natural philosophers to human conduct.

When the Sophists, the first body of professional educators in Europe, instructed the youth in virtue, the political arts, and the management of city and household, philosophy began to deal with the relation of the individual to the universal, to some comprehensive class, or to some group; the relation of man and nature, of tradition and reflection, of knowledge and action. Can virtue, approved excellence in any line, be learned, they asked? What is learning? It has to do with knowledge. What, then, is knowledge? How is it achieved? Through the senses, or by apprenticeship in some form of doing, or by reason that has undergone a preliminary logical discipline? Since learning is *coming* to know, it involves a passage from ignorance to wisdom, from privation to fullness, from defect to perfection, from non-being to being, in the Greek way of putting it. How is such a transition possible? Is change, becoming, development really possible and if so, how? And supposing such questions answered, what is the relation of instruction, of knowledge, to virtue?

This last question led to opening the problem of the relation of reason to action, of theory to practice, since virtue clearly dwelt in action. Was not knowing, the activity of reason, the noblest attribute of man? And consequently was not purely intellectual activity itself the highest of all excellences, compared with which the virtues of neighborliness and the citizen's life were secondary? Or, on the other hand, was the vaunted intellectual knowledge more than empty and vain pretense, demoralizing to character and destructive of the social ties that bound men together in their community life? Was not the only true, because the only moral, life gained through obedient habituation to the customary practices of the community? And was not the new education an enemy to good citizenship, because it set up a rival standard to the established traditions of the community?

In the course of two or three generations such questions were cut loose from their original practical bearing upon education and were discussed on their own account; that is, as matters of philosophy as an independent branch of inquiry. But the fact that the stream of European philosophical thought arose as a theory of educational procedure remains an eloquent witness to the intimate connection of philosophy and education. "Philosophy of education" is not an external application of ready-made ideas to a system of practice having a radically different origin and purpose: it is only an explicit formulation of the problems of the formation of right mental and moral habitudes in respect to the difficulties of contemporary social life. The most penetrating definition of philosophy which can be given is, then, that it is the theory of education in its most general phases.

The reconstruction of philosophy, of education, and of social ideals and methods thus go hand in hand. If there is especial need of educational reconstruction at the present time, if this need makes urgent a reconsideration of the basic ideas of traditional philosophic systems, it is because of the thoroughgoing change in social life accompanying the advance of science, the industrial revolution, and the development of democracy. Such practical changes cannot take place without demanding an educational reformation to meet them, and without leading men to ask what ideas and ideals are implicit in these social changes, and what revisions they require of the ideas and ideals which are inherited from older and unlike cultures. . . .

28 / ELIZABETH STEINER MACCIA

The Separation of Philosophy
from Theory of Education

I. The Problem Stated

> If we are willing to conceive education as the process of forming fundamental dispositions, intellectual and emotional, toward nature and fellow men, philosophy may even be defined *as the general theory of education*.[1]

We may be willing to conceive education as Dewey did, yet we may be unwilling to define "philosophy" as the theory of such a process. We might decide to define "philosophy" in such a way that a separation of philosophy from theory of education results. Furthermore, we might not agree with Champlin and Villemain that

> To maintain this separation is to block the creative exploitation of Dewey's thought and, at the same time, to ignore and violate his vision of the subject matter and purposes of philosophic reflection.[2]

Rather we might aver that such a separation alone frees us to be creative in the use of Dewey's thought and clarifies a blurred vision of the subject

Elizabeth Steiner Maccia, "The Separation of Philosophy from Theory of Education," *Studies in Philosophy and Education,* II, No. 2 (Spring 1962), 158–169. Reprinted by permission of the editors and the author. The views expressed in this selection have been modified by the author in her later writings.

[1] John Dewey, *Democracy and Education* (New York: Macmillan Co., 1916), p. 383.

[2] Francis T. Villemain and Nathaniel L. Champlin, "Frontiers for an Experimentalist Philosophy of Education," *The Antioch Review,* XIX (Fall, 1959), 346.

matter and purposes of philosophic reflection. All of this, however, is not arbitrary—neither the conception, the definition, nor the agreement of disagreement. There is a decision process—the analysis of man's knowing.

II. The Analysis of Man's Knowing

Man's knowing is set forth in his languages, his ways of communicating. "Language" is not restricted to a body of words and ways of combining them which are used to communicate. It is extended to include any means which is used to communicate. Consequently, we may speak of the language of the visual arts—a body of lines and colors and ways of combining them used to communicate, and of the language of doing—a body of actions and ways of combining them used to communicate, e.g. the language of building. These two means other than words— lines and colors, and actions—are not intended to be exhaustive of all other means. They were cited to indicate what I have in mind when I extend the term, "language," in this way. It is also important to note that "used to communicate" is crucial to the characterization of language. "Communicate" comes from the Latin *communis,* meaning common. A language, therefore, to be a language must be means held in common. It must be objective in the sense of intersubjective. Some person's private means, unless shared by another, does not constitute a language. No communication is possible where there is no commonality, no community of users.

Language that sets forth knowledge in a precise way is precise language. As Wittgenstein tells us (and as we well know), language is not always precise.

> Our language can be seen as an ancient city: a maze of little streets and squares, of old and new houses with additions from various periods; and this surrounded by a multitude of new boroughs with straight regular streets and uniform houses.[3]

This analogy points up that all of language (the city) consists of what we might call "ordinary language" (the hub of the city) and "special languages" (the suburbs). The special languages have precision (there is a self-consciousness about their construction), and thus present knowledge in a precise way. Ordinary language has contained in it knowledge in an imprecise form, what we might term "common sense knowledge." To illustrate, consider that ordinary language speaks of

---

[3] Ludwig Wittgenstein, *Philosophical Investigations* (New York: Macmillan Co., 1953), p. 8.

what happens when confined air expands with temperature—tire walls that are weak blow; but the special language we call "Physics" speaks of this with an equation we know as Charles' law, $^\mathrm{v}t = {}^\mathrm{v}o(+\alpha\rho^\mathrm{t})$, and such a statement is precise.

Whether we take a close look at ordinary or special language, we find that it attempts to set forth knowledge. What we mean by "knowledge" is meanings or bringings together or interrelations that are true. Bringings together constitute theory. Statements interrelate terms, and theory is an interrelation of one statement to another. The result is a bringing together of all the terms. Stated more precisely, a theory is a system of statements because they were so related that from one or more statements (the postulates) we can draw out by means of transformation rules other statements (the theorems). Since a statement consists of terms that are related; before we set forth our postulates, we must set forth a group of primitive or undefined terms. Then, following syntactical rules, we can relate these terms to form statements or postulates. Other terms may be introduced provided they are defined by means of the primitive terms. The postulates should be consistent, i.e. contradictory theorems cannot be drawn out of them, or else our total interrelation breaks down. The postulates should be independent, i.e., one should not be deducible from the other, or else we are confusing levels of generality —the non-independent postulate is actually a theorem. Finally, the postulates should be fruitful, i.e. should allow us to draw out as many statements as needed to encompass the realm in which meaning is sought. Now it is patent that all language does not set forth theory in such a rigorous way. Yet levels of generality can be found in all language, and in the special languages care is taken to structure theory. It is also clear that some language, particularly ordinary language, contains non-knowledge. There are contradictions or breaks in the total interrelation and parts of the total interrelation do not apply to the realm in which meaning is sought. But there is an attempt in all languages to remove contradictions and to obtain application. In the special languages this attempt reaches greater proportions.

Meaning may be sought in four realms: about what is, about what ought to be, about implementing the ought through the is, and about meaning itself. Language, then, falls into four categories: scientific, humanistic, technological, and epistemological. We do not characterize ordinary language as scientific or humanistic or technological or epistemological due to its lack of precision, even though it is concerned with setting forth knowledge in all four realms. Special languages are constructed just because ordinary language fails in precision. It is to the special languages that the terms apply.

Scientific language contains statements about the is, in the sense that the statements relate either directly or indirectly to observational data. The observational data can be of three main types, because they can relate to either non-living entities or non-human living entities or human entities. On these grounds, we can distinguish the physical sciences, the biological sciences, and the homological sciences.[4] If we are concerned with the is of the teaching-learning process, then our concern is with the aspects of the homological sciences that relate to this. This concern usually is termed "Psychology of Education" and "Sociology of Education."

Humanistic language contains statements of oughts. Such statements are value statements. Value statements contain, either implicitly or explicitly, directives for action. For example, "Lying is wrong" is a value statement within the language of ethics which directs us not to speak, write, etc. that which is not true. On the other hand, scientific statements do not direct us to act in a certain way; they only tell us that if we do certain things, certain things will follow. Scientific statements contain, either implicitly or explicitly, consequents in action, not directives for action. An example which will point up the difference between value and non-value statements and which will also clarify a confusion as to the value neutrality of the homological sciences is "Men hold that they ought not to lie." This statement tells us that if we observe men's actions we shall find them holding that one ought not to lie. It does not direct us not to lie. Of necessity, the homological sciences will contain statements about values, for valuing is one form of man's behaving. To include such statements does not make them non-scientific. Statements about values are not statements of values.

Statements of oughts are said to constitute humanistic language, because the word, *humanité*, recalls to us our manness. It reminds us to consider what is central to the condition of being human. The human condition is one in which we are decision-makers—one in which we decide upon a way of living (what we ought to do or our valuing). The evolution of culture may be a matter of regress as well as progress. Decisions count. It can, therefore, be seen why, in the fifteenth century, studies concerned with human culture should have become known as *les humanités*.

If we are concerned with the oughts of the teaching-learning process, then our concern is with the aspects of the humanities that relate to this.

---

[4] I prefer to use the term, "homological," rather than "social" or "psychological" or "behavioral." "Social" has the difficulty of ruling out the psychological which emphasizes the individual. "Psychological" has the difficulty of ruling out the social, and the added difficulty of emphasizing mind as an entity over and above the body ("psychological" comes in part from the Greek, *psychikos*, meaning soul or spiritual component). "Behavioral" has the difficulty of bringing in concerns relating to animal behavior which properly belong in biology. "Homological" formed in part from the Latin, *homo*, indicates the true concern which is man.

That is to say, we are concerned with the aspects of philosophy, of history, and of literature and the other arts that relate to the oughts of behavior to be brought about through the teaching-learning process—the kind of human beings our institutions of education ought to produce. This concern is termed "Philosophy of Education" and "History of Education."[5] Unfortunately, we have no term for literature and the other arts as they relate to education. The lack of a term indicates a deeper lack, a lack of serious consideration.

Philosophy as a part of the humanities is the synthetic phase of philosophy. "Synthesis" comes from the Greek and means to place in order or to put together. Philosophy which deals with puttings together or meanings in the realm of the ought, thus, is synthetic. Philosophy of education which deals with puttings together or meanings in the realm of the oughts of the teaching-learning process is the synthetic phase of philosophy of education.

Technological language contains statements about how to implement the ought through the is. It is both applied sciences and applied humanities, for the knowledge of one area is applied to the other area. "Technology" comes in part from *technicus* meaning craft or way of doing.

Usually "technology" is limited to ways of doing that utilize the knowledge of the physical sciences. For example, the manufacture of automobiles is considered to be a technology—knowledge of ways of doing, constructing, automobiles. Such knowledge depends upon the physical sciences—mechanics, thermodynamics, etc. Instead of the term, "technology," "engineering" is often used. We have our choice of automotive technology or automotive engineering.[6] The above analysis shows that the term, "technology," should be extended to include all crafts based upon science. That this extension is taking place is indicated by the use of the terms, "human engineering." These are technics based upon the homological sciences—psychology, sociology, etc. Education qualifies as such a technology, for it consists of ways of doing which utilize the scientific knowledge of human teaching-learning events. Education is a part of human engineering.

Technology involves more than science. It involves value judgments or statements of oughts. We must decide what we want to do before we

---

[5] History of education has a scientific as well as a humanistic dimension. The scientific dimension places it partly in the homological sciences.

[6] In the past, "technology" indicated more an application of common sense knowledge, while 'engineering' indicated more an application of scientific knowledge. In our modern day, when we no longer rely as heavily upon common sense knowledge due to the greater development of special languages (sciences), the distinction between the terms no longer holds.

develop ways of doing. There are many things that our knowledge of events allows us to do. We must select, therefore, one rather than another to do; we must value one or favor one over the other. This thing to do becomes the ought we will implement through science. Science is applied to do something. The construction of a hydrogen bomb is a part of technology. We want to protect ourselves through potential destructive power; so we utilize the knowledge of nuclear physics and other knowledge of science to work out ways of implementing the want or value, and the hydrogen bomb results. We want to preserve life; so we utilize the knowledge of biology to work out ways of implementing this value, and medicine results. We want to maximize profit; so we utilize the knowledge of economics to work out ways of implementing this value, and business as a discipline results. We want to produce changes in behavior (learning) that lead to socialization; so we utilize the knowledge of psychology and sociology to implement this value, and education as a discipline results. Notice that it is possible to question the value being implemented. Questioning of the want to protect ourselves through hydrogen bombs is the source of the controversy between Teller and Oppenheimer. Euthanasia is a questioning of the want implemented in medicine. Socialism is a questioning of the want implemented in business. The current controversy about education has one centering in the questioning of the want of socialization. These are not questions for science. Science deals with what we want and not with what we ought to want. These are questions for the synthetic phase of philosophy and the other humanities.

Epistemological language contains statements about language. What is being set forth in such metalanguage is knowledge of knowledge. Metalanguage constitutes analytic philosophy. "Analysis" comes from the Greek and means to unloose or to take apart. Analysis, then, is a taking apart of language or knowledge and setting forth its structure. Analysts of ordinary language analyze common sense knowledge, while analysts of special languages analyze sciences or humanities or technologies. Philosophers of ordinary language, and philosophers of science (philosophers of physics, philosophers of biology, etc.) or philosophers of humanities (philosophers of synthetic philosophy, philosophers of literature, etc.) or philosophers of technologies (philosophers of medicine, philosophers of education, etc.) emerge. All of these analytic philosophers are doing the epistemological task. An epistemologist differs from other analytic philosophers in that he is a generalist who is mainly concerned with language in general and not with any given language.

Knowledge of the scientific knowledge that enters education, of humanistic knowledge that enters education, and of the technology which is education comprise the analytic concerns of the philosopher of education. Stated differently, philosophy of psychology of education, philosophy of sociology of education, philosophy of synthetic philosophy of education, philosophy of history of education, philosophy of literature and other arts of education, and philosophy of education (metalanguage of the technology which is education) make up the analytic phase of philosophy of education.

III. The Separation of Philosophy from Theory of Education

The above analysis of man's knowing has established a basis for separating philosophy of education from theory of education. Education is ways or methods of carrying on the teaching-learning process. Education, then, is a technology or methodology, where "methodology" is taken in its broadest sense. Theory is interrelations or a system of meanings, and so theory of education would be interrelations or a system of meanings about ways or methods of carrying on the teaching-learning process. If the theory is true, it would be the technology of education. It is clear that the theorist of education is the methodologist of education. His constructing of theory depends upon the sciences relating to the teaching-learning process (psychology of education and sociology of education) and upon the humanities relating to the teaching-learning process (synthetic philosophy of education, history of education, and literature and other arts of education). The methodologist or theorist of education must build up means-ends or actions-consequents interrelations concerning changes in behavior (learning) brought about through other behavior (teaching). The sciences of education give him knowledge about teaching-learning behavior. The humanities of education give him knowledge about the oughts of teaching-learning behavior. He, as an educational theorist, must set up relationships between knowledge of teaching-learning behavior (means) and knowledge of oughts of teaching-learning behavior (ends).

The process of being educated is sometimes taken to be as broad as life itself, since human living is behaving and is characterized as a behaving that changes as one lives. Consequently, there is a sense in which education is the technology that encompasses all human engineering, and the sources of education encompass all of the homological sciences and all of the humanities. This cannot be denied, but there is a merit to sorting out a formal process of educating (educating undertaken in institutions specially set up for that purpose) and labeling the technology concerned with this, "education." The broader sense of the process drives the roots of education deeper into all the disciplines concerned with man, and makes artificial our separations of psychology of education from the remainder of psychology, of sociology of education from the remainder of sociology, of synthetic philosophy of education from the remainder of synthetic philosophy, of history of education from the remainder of history, and of literature and the other arts of education from the remainder of the arts. This indeed is an insight of Dewey and others worth preserving and noting, but we should not let it blur all distinctions.

One other point must be made in relation to the sources of the technology of education. We have limited the sources to the sciences of education and the humanities of education (we honored also the intimate connection of these sources with the remainder of the homological sciences and the humanities). Analytic philosophy is a source of concepts for the homological sciences, and so indirectly a source of the technology of education. Man's behavior consists largely of grammatical movements. He is a maker and user of language. If the homological scientist is to deal adequately with the is of man—his behavior, then he must utilize concepts arrived at through a consideration of language in general and through a consideration of specific languages. What I have in mind is this. The science educator in developing methods is prone to utilize psychology of education and sociology of education in such a way that there is an ignoring of the aspect of teaching-learning behavior that deals with the structure of the language of science. He is not entirely to blame, for this aspect has yet to be fully appreciated by the psychologist and sociologist of education. There is, however, increasing awareness.

While theory of education is a technological theory, philosophy of education is a theory of values of education, a theory of theory of education, a theory of theory of the sciences of education, and a theory of theory of the humanities of education. Philosophy of education as a theory of values of education is synthetic. There is a creation of values to be considered for implementation through our sciences of education. It is one source of the humanistic dimension from which education, the technology, is constructed, from which methods of educating are constructed. Philosophy of education as theory of theory is analytic. It functions in laying bare the structure of our technological language which is education, and thus gives us power in further construction. It functions in laying bare the structure of our scientific languages of education which are psychology of education and sociology of education, and thus gives us power in their further construction. It functions in laying bare the structure of our humanistic languages of education which are synthetic philosophy of education, history of education, and literature and other arts of education, and thus gives us power in their further construction. Also, as indicated above, these analytic or epistemological considerations lead to concepts regarding language or knowledge which are necessary in psychology of education and sociology of education, which are necessary to understand man's teaching-learning behavior.

IV. The Sources of the Confusion

The confusion between philosophy of education and theory of education arises from a failure to sort out the humanistic dimension from the scientific dimension. Once these two dimensions are sorted out, it becomes clear that education which embraces both dimensions can not be the same as synthetic philosophy of education which is concerned only with the humanistic dimension. Another source of confusion is the failure to recognize the analytic or metatheoretical dimension as well as the synthetic or theoretical dimension. Once these two dimensions are sorted out, it becomes clear that education which is theory or synthesis can not be the same as metatheory or analysis or analytic philosophy.

V. The Significance of the Separation

If philosophy of education is taken to be theory of education and theory of education is viewed rightly as methodology, ways of carrying out the teaching-learning process, then inquiry or further development of knowledge stops. Pragmatism is dead. Truth no longer is a consequent. Truth is an absolute, an antecedent. The creative exploitation of Dewey's thought is blocked. Theory of education involves an implementation of values. There is no development of science other than that needed to implement the values selected. Science dies. Consider man's awareness of the death of science due to excessive emphasis on wanting to do certain things (value commitment), as evidenced in his push for basic rather than applied science, in his push for no value commitments to hem in the scientific endeavor. Also there is no development of values other than those accepted for implementation. The humanities die. Dogmatism, absolutism, in the realm of values results. The objectives of education are known once and for all.

This is an error I shall term "METHODOLOGISM." Education is cut off from the sciences and from the humanities. The values are given and only the science necessary to implement the values is required. The only inquiry necessary is inquiry into methods. The only endeavors necessary in education are methodological. There is no need for foundational endeavors, for the values are known and no science other than that required to implement the given values is wanted. Education faculties become autonomous. They are cut off from all knowledge. The liberal arts criticism rightly would batter the door down, provided the criticism is not loaded with prejudice that leads to their ignoring the door. But more, methodologists within education faculties become autonomous. There is no need for philosophy of education, history of education, literature and other arts of education, psychology of education, and sociology of education. Methodology covers all.

If philosophy of education is taken to be theory of education and theory of education is viewed erroneously as scientific theory, then inquiry into values of education or development of value theory of education stops. Also there is a loss of a true technological base which depends in part on value theory. Of course, wants must be implemented, but wants are made ises. One can not ask the question, "Ought I want what I want?" A man simply wants what he wants (even a Hitler), and so wants are brought under the scientific inquiry. Values are constructed, or better selected, by counting noses.

This is an error I shall term "SCIENTIFICISM," where "experiment" is taken in its scientific context. Education has been cut off from its humanistic source. Now psychology of education and sociology of education are glorified. Philosophy of education courses become psychology of education and sociology of education courses.

If philosophy of education is taken to be theory of education and theory of education is viewed erroneously as value theory, then development of scientific theory of education stops. Also there is a loss of a true technological base which depends in part on scientific theory. Of course, some kind of knowledge about what is must be utilized to implement the values; but, since scientific knowledge is ruled out, there is a reliance on common sense knowledge. We hear education being spoken of as an art.

This is an error I shall call "ANTI-SCIENTIFICISM." Education has been cut off from its scientific source. Now synthetic philosophy of education, history of education, and literature and other arts of education are worshiped.

All the above erroneous positions also include a denial of the analytic role of philosophy of education. Philosophy of education is equated only to theory. Analysis of theory or metatheory is inquiry into modes of theory construction. To deny this is to cut off the possibility of power in the realm of theory construction. This is an error I shall call "ANTI-ANALYTICISM."

One final error can be noted which does not necessarily arise from equating theory of education and philosophy of education. Philosophy of education may be rightly viewed as metatheory or as analysis, but wrongly viewed as including no more. The synthetic phase of philosophy of education is denied. This is an error I shall term "ANALYTICISM."

If philosophy of education is rightly taken as value theory construction and metatheory, and theory of education is rightly taken to be technological in nature, then knowledge grows. Education is related to all of knowledge yet issues in practice. The graven images of METHODOLOGISM, SCIENTIFICISM, ANTI-SCIENTIFICISM, ANTI-ANALYTICISM, and ANALYTICISM are shattered.

Questions for Discussion

ADLER examines educational questions which can be treated philosophically in contrast to those which must be treated in a different fashion. He defines education and claims that he can prove the definition by advancing evidence for its support. Can definitions be proved? Several functions of philosophy of education are delineated in the discussion and the discipline is compared to political philosophy and the philosophy of law. Adler holds that philosophy of education is concerned with the ultimate questions of education, even though the philosopher cannot ignore the contingencies that arise in particular times and societies.

Frankena holds that there are three forms of philosophical activity: speculative, normative, and analytical. Education can be distinguished in terms of a process and in terms of an academic discipline. The dimensions of inquiry within the speculative, normative, and analytical domains of philosophy of education are developed in the essay. Contrast the interpretation of philosophy of education advanced by Frankena with that proposed by Adler.

Dewey warns that unless philosophy is to become a sentimental indulgence for a few, it must take effect in conduct. It is healthy when philosophical issues are approached in terms of the difference they make in educational practice when acted upon. So that if we think of education "as the process of forming fundamental dispositions to nature and fellow men, philosophy may even be defined *as the general theory of education.*"

This definition has captured the attention of thousands of philosophers and educators. Why do you think it has received such widespread attention? Analyze its significance within the context of the complete essay.

Maccia does not accept Dewey's definition. Instead, she distinguishes theory of education from philosophy of education. Education focuses on the ways of conducting the teaching-learning process, and theory consists of an interrelationship of a system of meanings; therefore theory is a system of meanings concerned with ways of carrying on the teaching-learning process. Thus, theory of education is technological because it enables us to implement previously established values. Philosophy of education has a synthetic and an analytic phase. The synthetic phase concerns educational values, while the analytic phase propounds theory about the theories of education. We call theories about theories the metatheoretical dimension.